Publication

This yearbook is published by the Flemish-Netherlands Foundation 'Stichting Ons Erfdeel', with the support of the Dutch Ministry of Health, Welfare and Cultural Affairs (Rijswijk) and the Flemish Ministry of Culture (Brussels). The Foundation 'Stichting Ons Erfdeel' also publishes the Dutch-language periodical *Ons Erfdeel* and the French-language periodical *Septentrion, revue de culture néerlandaise,* the bilingual yearbook *De Franse Nederlanden – Les Pays-Bas Français* and a series of booklets in different languages covering various aspects of the culture of the Low Countries.

The Board of Directors of 'Stichting Ons Erfdeel'

Address of the Editorial Board and the Administration

'Stichting Ons Erfdeel', Murissonstraat 260,
8931 Rekkem, Flanders, Belgium
tel. +32 (0) 56 41 12 01
fax +32 (0) 56 41 47 07

THE LOW COUNTRIES

ARTS AND SOCIETY IN FLANDERS

AND THE NETHERLANDS

A YEARBOOK

1993-94

Published by the

Flemish-Netherlands Foundation 'Stichting Ons Erfdeel'

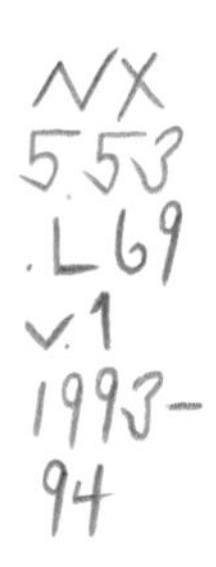
NX
553
.L69
v.1
1993-
94

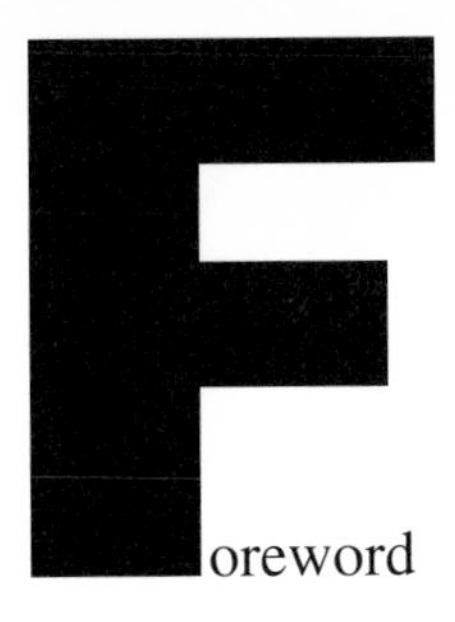

Foreword

'The triumph of culture is to overpower nationality'

Ralph Waldo Emerson

With this new yearbook, *The Low Countries,* the editors and publisher aim to present to the English-speaking world the culture and society of the Dutch-speaking area which embraces both the Kingdom of the Netherlands and also Flanders, the northern part of the Kingdom of Belgium.

The articles in this yearbook, by British and American, Dutch and Flemish contributors, survey the living, contemporary culture of the Low Countries as well as their cultural heritage.

In its words and pictures *The Low Countries* provides information about literature and the arts, but also about broad social and historical developments in Flanders and the Netherlands.

The culture of Flanders and the Netherlands is not an isolated phenomenon; its development over the centuries has been one of continuous interaction with the outside world. In consequence the yearbook also pays due attention to the centuries-old continuing cultural interplay between the Low Countries and the world beyond their borders.

In a world which is growing ever smaller and becoming more and more interdependent, international, even supranational in character, we regard Ralph Waldo Emerson's statement as a call for independent cultures to look beyond their national frontiers.

By drawing attention to the diversity, vitality and international dimension of the culture of Flanders and the Netherlands, *The Low Countries* hopes to contribute to a lively dialogue between differing cultures.

Jozef Deleu
Chief Editor / Managing Director
Flemish-Netherlands Foundation 'Stichting Ons Erfdeel'

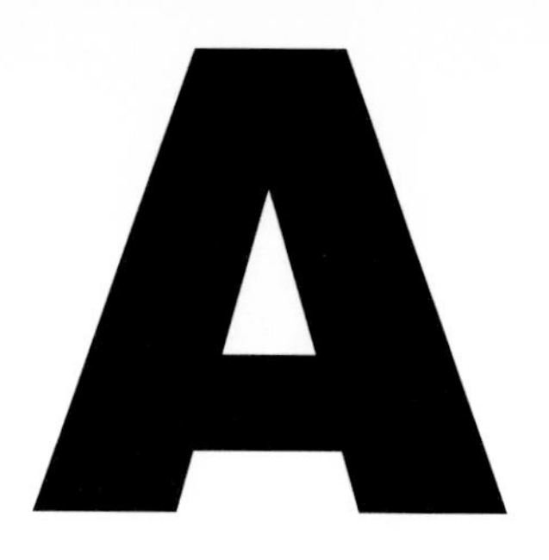

Paradise for Modern Architecture

Recent Architecture in Rotterdam

Rotterdam has played a leading role in the field of architecture since the twenties. It is the city in which can be found the housing complex in Spangen designed by J.J.P. Oud, the Van Nelle coffee factory by Brinkman and Van der Vlugt, the *Bergpolder* flats, the Wholesalers' Building by Van Tijen and Maaskant, the *Lijnbaan* shopping centre by Van den Broek and Bakema and such textbook examples of modern housing estates as *Pendrecht* and *Alexanderpolder*. It is not easy to explain why modern architecture has been able to develop like this in the Netherlands' second city. For the post war period one might argue that the destruction brought about by the German bombing of May 1940 opened the way to an extensive reconstruction of the city. However, it has to be borne in mind that the rebuilding of many other Dutch towns and cities was much less modern in character. Furthermore, this can hardly account for the disproportionately large number of examples of modern architecture in the period up to 1940.

Rotterdam has retained its role as the leading city in the field of architecture to the present day. In recent years, projects of every kind have been carried out which are among the most unusual in the country. In this respect it is remarkable that Rotterdam calls on the services of big names from abroad to a lesser extent than cities such as The Hague, Amsterdam, Groningen and Maastricht. Rotterdam tends to give opportunities to young architects.

Rotterdam may seem, therefore, to be a paradise for modern architecture, but at the same time this unique modern heritage is frequently treated in a quite lamentable way. Countless modern buildings have disappeared as a result of demolition or been spoiled by tasteless renovation. Oud's work in Rotterdam has been decimated, Van Ravesteyn's masterpiece, the *Blijdorp* Zoo, is being left to crumble, Van Tijen's *Zuidwijk* estate and the traditionalist-modern *Vreewijk* estate by Granpré Molière have both lost their original character after renovations carried out in the name of so-called housing improvement. This catalogue could easily be expanded into an enormous list, for there is certainly little sympathy with post-war modern architecture.

If we consider only the most recent architecture in Rotterdam, however, it must be concluded that, as throughout this century, once again remarkable developments are under way. One of the most notable recent projects is the

High rise blocks on the Weena: at the centre the cylindrical housing complex by H. Klunder (1990). On the foreground the Hilton Hotel by H.A. Maaskant (1964) (Photo by Michiel Ibelings).

high rise street which has gone up on the Weena. For years the Weena was a bare open space with nothing but the buildings put up in the fifties and sixties: the Wholesalers' Building, the modern-baroque Central Station by Sybold van Ravesteyn, the concrete station post office by the Kraayvangers and the chic modern Hilton Hotel by Maaskant. Otherwise there was little on the Weena except one or two kiosks and a deer-park left over from the C'70 cultural event of 1970. It was only in the eighties that this unique *tabula rasa* in the heart of the city was cleared for the construction of a group of, by Dutch standards, unusually tall buildings.

Whilst the scale of the high rise buildings on the Weena and their grouping may be exceptional, their architectural appearance sadly falls short of the urban development potential of this ensemble on the only high rise boulevard in the country. None of the buildings meets the requirements of the famous definition of the skyscraper which the American architect Louis Sullivan gave in 1896: 'It should be tall, in every inch tall.' The tower blocks on the Weena are indeed large, but nowhere is this size expressed in an imposing and compelling way. This is most of all the case with the tallest of the group, the double tower of the Nationale Nederlanden Insurance Co.,

The Weena with two designs by Jan Hoogstad: the Unilever head office (1992) and a housing complex (1991). In the background the station post office by E.H. and H.M. Kraaijvanger (1959) (Photo by Michiel Ibelings).

designed by Abe Bonnema, which, with its shimmering glass façades, already looked dated at the moment of its completion in early 1992.

Among the office buildings on the Weena stand the two tallest housing complexes in the Netherlands, designed by Henk Klunder and Jan Hoogstad respectively. While these tower blocks do compare favourably from an architectural point of view with those around them, they are principally interesting as a phenomenon. They are of a piece with the urban development ideology of the 'compact city' which was all the rage in the early eighties. This concept of the 'compact city' is based on a high density combination of various urban functions. The idea behind it is that this would provide the basis for a lively city. The building of more expensive accommodation is supposed to provide the richer sections of society with apartments to suit their taste and the presence of these people with means will then stimulate the cultural life of the city. Despite the uncertain nature of these hypotheses - and despite the relatively restricted scope of the whole project - the area around the Weena has clearly become more lively, partly because in several places at street level shops, cafés and sandwich bars have opened. However, the effect of this is only felt at lunch time and on Saturdays. If you

Office for Metropolitan Architecture, *Kunsthal* (1992), in the *Museumpark*, both designed by OMA. On the left the Museum of Natural History, which will be renovated by *Mecanoo* (Photo by Michiel Ibelings).

Mecanoo, café-restaurant *De Boompjes* (1989) (Photo by Michiel Ibelings).

visit the Weena after 6 pm on an ordinary weekday it looks the same as any other part of the city: it is dead. It is not surprising that the Weena with its mix of functions has led to no fundamental change in this. The deserted state in the evening of an earlier experiment in mixed functions, the nearby *Lijnbaan* built in the fifties, underlines the fact that Rotterdammers are not really the sort for a night life on the streets.

Nevertheless evening and night life in Rotterdam have made enormous strides over the last few years, partly because café life has received such a strong architectural stimulus. This category of buildings demonstrates a remarkable development in Rotterdam architecture, a development which began with the opening of the *Café Lux* and the reconstruction of the exterior of the *Café De Unie,* originally designed by J.J.P. Oud in 1924, with a completely new interior by the Opera office.

Since then several places notable for their decor and furnishing have opened throughout the city, such as *Zochers* which is housed in a nineteenth-century pavilion in the park beneath the *Euromast.* This café-restaurant has been done up in 'dilapidated prefab' style. The very spacious *Café Loos* has a more traditional layout but is notable for its splendid size. *Café Dudok,* which is located in old office space within a building designed by W.M. Dudok, takes pride of place for size. This café with an interior by architects Dijkman & Kossman is notable for the absence of glamour and of inconvenient design, which has found its way only into the toilets, where the taps on the hand basins have been replaced by beer pumps. Architecturally, the high point of Rotterdam café design is the café-restaurant *De Boompjes* by the architect group *Mecanoo.* Beneath an undulating roof is a building largely of glass with an extremely pleasant ambience, which takes maximum advantage of the magnificent view of the busy waterway of the river Maas. This marvellous glass pavilion forms part of the reconstruction of the Maas

Frits van Dongen, housing complex in the *Afrikaanderbuurt* (1989) (Photo by Michiel Ibelings).

DKV, Housing Project Veerseheuvel (1991) (Photo by Michiel Ibelings).

Boulevard following the plans of Kees Christiaanse. Its aim is to give the Boulevard, which serves primarily as an urban artery, an alternative existence as a route for runners and walkers by introducing cafés, seating and recreation areas. In the evenings runners can run along the quay, where a line of lights has been sunk into the paving to mark the route – that is if there are no cars parked on them.

De Boompjes is one of the many projects carried out by *Mecanoo* in Rotterdam in recent years. The office was set up in 1983 by a group of young architects from Delft in order to take part in the competition for young people's housing on the *Kruisplein.* They won the competition and so laid the foundations for a career that has remained extremely successful to date. After concentrating on social housing in urban renewal projects in the early years, *Mecanoo* now receives commissions in all areas, from the extension to a luxury hotel to the building of a large new project. Two of the partners have also built their own detached home in Kralingen.

This recent work by *Mecanoo* is free of the sometimes blatant references which characterised their early designs. Their close association with the modern tradition remains but no longer leads to literal borrowings, paraphrases or homages. Instead there is a relaxed way of designing which, however, increasingly inclines to a formal and material extravagance, which can already be seen in *De Boompjes* but is even more marked in the interior of the tower block built as an extension to the Park Hotel.

As well as opportunities for social life in cafés and restaurants, the cultural life proper of Rotterdam has also expanded. The *Museumpark* continues to be developed. In an area where previously there was only the Boymans-van Beuningen Museum, October 1992 saw the opening of the *Kunsthal* (Exhibition Hall), a building designed by Rem Koolhaas's (1944-) Office for Metropolitan Architecture. The *Kunsthal* is Koolhaas's largest Dutch building to date and an even greater proof of his powers than his other designs. The building, which from the outside appears to be no more than a simple box, houses a snail-like structure of exhibition spaces arranged around a sloping inner street. This sloping walkway spans the difference in height between the dike against which the *Kunsthal* is constructed and the *Museumpark,* designed by Koolhaas and the French landscape architect Yves Brunier. The longitudinal axis of the *Museumpark* which begins at the *Kunsthal* extends to the new building of the Netherlands Architecture Institute, the work of Jo Coenen, Koolhaas's most important contemporary in the Netherlands. The Institute opens in the autumn of 1993. The *Museumpark* is then able to function fully as the cultural heart of the city, on a par with the *Museumufer* created in Frankfurt in the eighties.

Housing is an important area of work for architects active in Rotterdam. Several young architects' offices have made their name with this type of commission. For example, Frits van Dongen created one of his first independent projects in the *Afrikaanderbuurt* in South Rotterdam: a curving block of flats on pillars which has an ingenious entry system via lifts, galleries and interior stairways. This is moreover a remarkable project in terms of housing typology, traditionally a strong point with Dutch architects. The same is true of the work of the *DKV* office, named from the initial letters of the surnames of the three partners, Dolf Dobbelaar, Herman de Kovel and Paul de Vroom. They built some excellent, well thought out projects in urban renewal areas and recently in the new suburb of Veerseheuvel, where they were also responsible for the town plan. Just as with Frits van Dongen and *Mecanoo,* the relationship with classical modern architecture can be seen in the idiom used by *DKV*; it is a source of inspiration from which they draw freely.

This undogmatic association with the modern tradition is not only typical of the current young generation of designers but also, sadly, of the way in which architecture is treated in Rotterdam. On the one hand this means that Rotterdam's municipal council is not afraid to choose radical new approaches. One fruit of this is that the city is to be enriched with a spectacular single suspension bridge over the Maas designed by the young Amsterdam architect Ben van Berkel. On the other hand its modern heritage is regularly treated without consideration. If that heritage were supported with the same enthusiasm as the bridge then the title 'a paradise for modern architecture' would be justified in all respects.

HANS IBELINGS
Translated by Lesley Gilbert.

Claus the Chameleon

A prophet is never honoured in his own country. Hugo Claus has always had a love-hate relationship with his fellow countrymen, and has left the country of his birth on several occasions – only to return each time. With his characteristic mythomania, he has explained this apparent instability as being due to traumas in his youth, such as his birth by Caesarian section in the Sint-Jans Hospital in Bruges on 5 April 1929, and his early separation from his mother, when at the age of 18 months he was placed in the care of nuns at a boarding school, only being allowed home again when he reached the age of 11.

Whatever the truth of these explanations, Claus' life, like that of his parents, has to date been a succession of moves from one place to another. Following an undistinguished secondary school career, during which he acquired the rudiments of Greek and Latin, he left the parental home for good in 1946. His attempts to make a living included working as a house-painter and employment as a seasonal labourer in Northern France. In Paris

Queen Beatrix of the Netherlands and Hugo Claus at the presentation of the Prize for Dutch Literature (1986) (Photo by Marc Cels).

he met the surrealist playwright Antonin Artaud, whom he regarded for a long time as a spiritual father. While staying in Ostend he made the acquaintance of Elly Overzier, the daughter of a Dutch shipowner. Together they moved to Paris where Claus, then beginning as a painter and writer, came into contact with the international CoBrA movement, while Elly appeared in French films. This led them to become involved in the Italian film world. In 1955 he returned to Ghent and married Elly. Ten years later he moved to the countryside of East Flanders, which he left in 1970 to move house yet again, this time to the metropolis of Amsterdam. There he began a relationship with the Dutch actress Kitty Courbois, whom he later abandoned in favour of the film actress Sylvia ('Emanuelle') Kristel. With this new companion at his side he wandered through various countries before settling in Paris once again. Following his break with Sylvia Kristel he returned to live in Ghent once more. Today, with a new companion at his side, he divides his time between a penthouse in the centre of Antwerp and a country home in Cavaillon, in southern France. But for how long?

The all-round artist

Just as confusing as his restless wanderings and amorous escapades are Claus' explorations in the world of art. He was 18 years old when his first poetry collection, *Short Series* (Kleine reeks) appeared. A few years later his novella *The Duck Hunt* (De Metsiers, 1950) won a quadrennial prize for the best unpublished novel. The experimental poetry collection *Poems from Oostakker* (De Oostakkerse gedichten, 1955) firmly established his reputation as the 'child prodigy of Flemish literature'. In the same year his play *A Bride in the Morning* (Een Bruid in de morgen, 1960) enjoyed a succesful première in Rotterdam.

These events were just the beginning of an uninterrupted flow of poetry collections, stories, novellas, novels, plays, translations, adaptations, radio plays, television dramas, scenarios and even opera libretti. Claus sometimes jokingly claims that his example is Lope de Vega, the Spanish playwright reputed to have written more than 2,000 plays. The wonder of this enormous production is that, while sometimes rushed, it has seldom led to repetitive-

The Lion of Flanders (directed by Hugo Claus, 1984).

ness. The author does not adhere to any single formula, not even when critics and public are clamouring for it.

Pushed to the background somewhat by his literary activities is his work as a painter and drawer, work whose diversity virtually matches that of his efforts as a writer and storyteller. His unwillingness to develop anything akin to a 'personal style' has led more than once to him destroying the majority of works from a particular period, so that his 'special exhibitions' sometimes give the impression of being 'group exhibitions'. His striking eclecticism is also evidenced by the diversity of his cover designs for his own books.

Several times Claus has directed his own plays and driven actors to amazing performances. Although he has a whole series of film scenarios to his name, film-makers and film committees have given him too few opportunities of working as a film director. His debut *The Enemies* (De vijanden,

1967) can be counted a success, given the modest financial resources with which the film was created. Alongside the failure of *The Lion of Flanders* (De leeuw van Vlaanderen, 1984), the films *Friday* (Vrijdag, 1980) and *The Sacrament* (Het Sacrament, 1989) stand out for their sheer professionalism. In a more favourable economic climate, Claus would without doubt have been capable of using his feeling for film to create an original cinematographic oeuvre.

The polymorphic poet

If the title 'poet laureate' existed in Flanders, Claus would have been awarded it long ago. Even his opponents admit that he is the most gifted and versatile poet of his generation.

The first verses produced by Claus are examples of a fairly traditional confessional lyric. International contacts later pointed him in the direction of modernism. French surrealism became the model for his experimental,

---

I'd like to sing you a song in this landscape of anger,
Livia, that would penetrate you, reach you through your nine openings,

Blonde and elastic, fierce and hard.

It would be an orchard song, a canto of the plains,
A one-man choir of infamy,
As though my vocal chords discorded rose from me and called you,
As though
In this landscape abasing me, in this location impairing me
(Where I fourfooted wander) we appeared singular no longer
And locked our voices,
Spring to new shoots,
Come to me, the one who is elusive, unapproachable,
Don't think me strange as the earth,
Don't run from me (lame humans)
Meet me, feel me,
Crease, break, break,

We are the werewind, the rain of days,
Tell me clouds,
Flow open wordless, become water.

(Ah, this light is cold and weighs its horned hands
On our faltering, folding faces)

I'd like to sing you an orchard song, Livia
But the night comes to its end and fills
My plains ever closer closed – I can reach you
Only unfulfilled
For the throat of the male deer chokes at dawn.

From *Poems from Oostakker* (De Oostakkerse gedichten, 1955)
Translated by Paul Brown and Peter Nijmeijer.

---

associative style, a style which he shared with the Dutch Experimentalist poets, such as Lucebert, Jan Elburg and Paul Rodenko. In *Poems from Oostakker* he combined his intuitive wordplay with an intellectual 'quotation poetry' following the example of T.S. Eliot and Ezra Pound. The result reminds one of the poetry of Dylan Thomas and Ted Hughes.

The title of this collection refers to the place of pilgrimage dedicated to the Virgin Mary at Oostakker near Ghent. The Holy Virgin is used by the poet as a symbol for the unapproachable mother figure, who is worshipped and feared by father and son. This family theme is embodied in the anthropological mythology of James Frazer's *The Golden Bough* (1890); Claus interprets the relationship between the earth-mother and the god of nature in a Freudian sense as an incestuous love, which is reborn in the passion between woman and lover. Reason, order and lawfulness give way to the almost animal regression and aggression of sexuality.

Following this outburst of emotionalism the collection *A Painted Horseman* (Een geverfde ruiter, 1961) was more rational, more desperate and more critical. Poems making use of personae and more narrative pieces broadened the range of themes. Claus' first volume of collected verse, published in 1965, concluded with the long poem 'The Sign of the Hamster' *('Het teken van de hamster')*. In this summation of his youth the criticism of society and religion is also a self-criticism: is the poet not formed by a reactionary past just as much as are his fellow countrymen? From this time on, his attention focused on a broader existential and social set of problems.

In *Lord Wild Boar* (Heer Everzwijn, 1970), man is portrayed as a creature laboriously seeking a balance between nature and culture. The title is highly suggestive: man is both the 'lord' of creation and a 'wild boar', a lowly beast. The collection *Hearsay* (Van horen zeggen, 1970) offers undiluted criticism of Flemish provincialism and ends with a description of a socialist Utopia. Both collections have a place in the second volume of collected verse (1979), which is just as heterogeneous as the first, containing among other things five-line billets-doux, objectifying personae and caricatures of Christianity.

In putting together his next collection, the anarchist Claus abandoned the ordered arrangement of poems and created instead a chaotic *Almanac* (Almanak, 1982) containing 366 'doggerel verses', whose playfulness was not appreciated by the critics. The collection *Alibi,* which appeared in 1985, revealed a poet who, though now older, was still not reconciled to life.

Intertextuality, playing with the work of predecessors, is a constant feature in his oeuvre. A nice example of this can be found in the collection *Sonnets* (Sonnetten, 1986) which, though it consists entirely of transformed Shakespearean sonnets, can be read as a series of contemporary declarations of love.

Claus never ceases to amaze. The minute we think we have catalogued – and thus neutralised – him, he produces a new experiment: the modernist begins rhyming, the moralist produces banal nonsense verses, the lyricist turns into a rhetorician. The only constant is the chameleon-like inconstancy.

The polyvalent prose-writer

It is only rarely that good poets are also good prose-writers. Claus is an exception to this rule, as he is an exception in everything. Who else has written novellas and stories at the age of 20 which still stand up today? Who else has published in the course of a single year two novels – *Wonderment* (De verwondering, 1962) and *About Deedee* (Omtrent Deedee, 1963) – both of which have become classics? Who else is capable of writing books as diverse as the novelette *The Year of the Lobster* (Het jaar van de Kreeft, 1972) and the mannerist novel *Shame* (Schaamte, 1972)?

Like Claus the poet, Claus the prose-writer has also evolved in his writing from a thematic content based around his own youth, through problems of relationships, to social criticism. His best work interweaves these three components. The problems of adolescence dominate the novella *The Duck Hunt* and the story collection *The Black Emperor* (De zwarte keizer, 1958), in which the immature main character is pitted against the all-powerful mother figure and the absent father figure. The relationship between man and woman is dealt with in *Dog Days* (De hondsdagen, 1952) and *The Cool Lover* (De koele minnaar, 1956), but is clouded by a failure to come to terms with the traumas of youth. A mother-son bond drives the main character of *Dog Days* into the arms of a young girl (three years before Nabokov's *Lolita*), and inhibits the main character of *The Cool Lover* (the Italian setting of which is reminiscent of Moravia).

Claus reached a high point with the novel *Wonderment*. Once again the main character is a man who is unable to build a satisfactory relationship because of his close ties with his mother. The story is constructed as a quest for the father, who is presented as a symbol of adult love. But this fascist leader who is to serve as an example proves to be just as much a victim of the mother as the main character, so that the latter is left with no alternative but a flight into madness. As in *Poems from Oostakker*, these personal problems have a Frazerian and Freudian loading. *Wonderment* seeks to show how the fascination for authoritarian fascism in rural Flanders is cemented in family structures.

A similar social analysis is undertaken in the novel *About Deedee*, in which a young homosexual man is destroyed in a hypocritical petty bourgeois environment. The only intellectual, the priest Deedee, proves unable to break through the facade of respectability and show genuine understanding and sympathy. The skilful switching of narrative perspectives in this book portrays the situation from the point of view of all the characters. The diagnosis is left to the reader himself, but cannot be a very favourable one.

The Sorrow of Belgium (Het verdriet van België, 1983) is Claus' magnum opus, a book on which he worked, albeit with some interruptions, for ten years. All the characters and motifs of his world, which, by analogy with Graham Greene's 'Greeneland' we could perhaps call 'Clausitania', are brought together here in a grandiose synthesis. The book is in the first place a *Bildungsroman* which traces the spiritual development of the young Louis Seynaeve between 1939 and 1948. In a bewildering interplay of fact and fiction, Claus recounts the story of his own youth and his first steps towards becoming a writer. At the same time it is a picaresque novel, in which the boy who began as a victim of the lies and treachery of adults himself becomes a cheat and a liar. The novel is a psychoanalysis in which the neurotic tendencies of the main character are explained as being due to an Oedipus complex with which he has not yet come to terms: the young Louis remains firmly attached to his mother and fails to find a positive model in

Dust-jacket of *The Sorrow of Belgium* (translation first published in 1990).

his father. The author expands this psychological analysis into a sociological and political critique by showing how psychological infantility of this type opens the way to a petty bourgeois ideology with fascistic tendencies (which manifest themselves in nationalism, racism and anti-socialism). He does not express his social criticism directly, through commentary or by setting out arguments, but indirectly, by quoting cliches from the mouth of the common man. A more brutal exposé of the spiritual poverty of both Flemish society and its intellectuals has seldom been presented. Little wonder that the novel was received much more warmly in the Netherlands than in Flanders itself: no one likes to be confronted with such an unembellished self-portrait.

It is not given to every writer to be able to present his personal problems in such a way that they throw light on the society of which he is a part. In novels such as *Wonderment* and *The Sorrow of Belgium* Claus has achieved this with brilliant success, thus demonstrating how polyvalent are the effects of his prose.

The diversiform dramatist

As a playwright, Claus is virtually without rivals in Flanders and the Netherlands. The four national prizes he has won for his stagework could even be seen as an under-appreciation of his talent, so great is the extent and diversity of his dramatic production. Comedy is the field for which he has the least aptitude, a deficiency for which he compensates by turning virtually all his plays into tragicomedies.

Blind Man (Blindeman), a play written by Claus for the Ghent Theatre Company (*NTG*) and performed in 1985 (Photo by Luc Monsaert).

Claus began as an experimental playwright following in the footsteps of Artaud. Later, too, he was to allow himself to be influenced by foreign examples, authors such as Anouilh, Tennessee Williams, Büchner, Strindberg and Beckett. Among writers whose plays he has reworked are Seneca, Tourneur, Fernando da Rojas, Ben Jonson, Euripides, Aristophanes and Shakespeare. Particularly remarkable are the antique pieces, which through translation, adaptation and reinterpretation have been turned into modern plays. In these endeavours he has made his own the device employed by Ezra Pound, a writer whom he greatly admires: 'Make it new'.

As in the other genres which he practises, Claus strives to achieve a diversity of approach: he is an experimentalist in *The Witnesses* (De getuigen, 1952), a neoromantic in *A Bride in the Morning,* a satirist in *Life and Works of Leopold II* (Het leven en de werken van Leopold II, 1970), a naturalist in *Friday* (Vrijdag, 1969), and a writer of slapstick in *Serenade* (1984). His dramatic work is remarkable for the shifts in tone which take place within a single play, always giving his work a slightly surrealist effect. A good example of this is *Jessica* (1977), which begins as a modern realistic drama and ends in a nightmare atmosphere. These continual shifts in style were not always appreciated by audiences: only his most traditional works such as *Sugar* (Suiker, 1958) and *Friday* have achieved unqualified success, while more innovative work such as *Look, Mummy, no hands!* (Mama, kijk, zonder handen!, 1959) were given a much cooler reception.

In spite of all this diversity, something resembling a basic structure can be found in the majority of Claus' dramatic works. His plays usually divide into two parts: a first part in which the unsustainability of a particular situation is described, and a second part in which, in spite of a number of unexpected twists, the basic problem ultimately remains largely unchanged, so that the play ends at more or less the same point at which it started. The only thing which has been gained, apparently, is a certain insight into a hopeless situation.

The liberal artist

However perilous it may be to attempt to pin down an artist as protean as Claus to a single basic attitude, it is perhaps possible to trace his incessant experimenting and his continual shifts in form of expression back to a fundamental sense of a lack of freedom. Time and time again the artist makes it clear that he is stuck fast, a prisoner of his own past, hemmed in by the traumas of his youth, constrained by social compulsions, moral convention and religious dogma. In the face of this paralysing slavery the only thing he has to offer is his creativity. The realm of liberty which he has vainly sought in sexual profligacy or in the permanent revolution of a Utopian socialism proves to be a figment, if not of thought then of dreams, which can exist only in the continually changing products of the imagination. Variety is the motto of this chameleon, whose art is one long ode to freedom.

PAUL CLAES
Translated by Julian Ross.

List of translations

The Duck Hunt (Tr. George Libaire). New York, 1955. Re-issued as *Sister of Earth,* London, 1966.
A Bride in the Morning, New York, 1960.
Karel Appel, Painter, Amsterdam, 1962.
The Erotic Eye (Tr. Morton Seif). Amsterdam, 1964.
'The Lieutenant' (Tr. J.S. Holmes & Hans van Marle). *Delta,* VI, 1964, 4, pp. 63-72.
'The Black Emperor' (Tr. J.S. Holmes & Hans van Marle). *Delta,* XIII, 1970, 1, pp. 59-65. Reprinted in *Modern Stories from Holland and Flanders* (ed. Egbert Krispyn). New York, 1973, pp. 8-13.
Friday (Tr. Hugo Claus & Christopher Logue). London, 1972.
Two-Brush Painting (Tr. Hugo Claus & Christopher Logue). Paris, 1980.
'In a Harbour' (Tr. Jane Fenoulhet, Theo Hermans, Paul Vincent a.o.). *Dutch Crossing,* 14, July 1981, pp. 36-48.
Back Home and *The Life and Works of Leopold II* (Tr. David Willinger & Luk Truyts). In: *An Anthology of Contemporary Belgian Plays 1970-82* (ed. David Willinger). Troy (NY), 1984.
The Sign of the Hamster (Tr. Paul Claes, Christine D'haen, Theo Hermans and Yann Lovelock). Leuven, 1986.
Selected Poems 1953-73 (Tr. Theo Hermans & Peter Nijmeijer). Isle of Skye, 1986.
The Sorrow of Belgium (Tr. Arnold Pomerans). New York / London, 1990; Harmondsworth, 1991.
Four Works for the Theatre. (Tr. David Willinger, Luk Truyts and Luc Deneulin). New York, 1990.

The Threat of Rapid Language Death

A Recently Acknowledged Global Problem

It is an indisputable fact that the existing linguistic variety is rapidly being eroded in virtually every part of the world. Many languages, now known to only a few people or spoken only by small groups of older people, are on the verge of disappearing, and there are a great many other languages which are very likely to undergo the same fate at some point in the future.

The present state of our knowledge makes it difficult to indicate with any precision just how many languages are currently still spoken, or at least were spoken until very recently. There are still a number of blank areas on the human language map, although the work of people such as the Voegelins (1977), Grimes (1988) and Krauss (1992) has gradually led to the conclusion that the number of languages still spoken will prove to lie somewhere between 6,000 and 6,500.

The dying out of languages is not a new phenomenon. We know of several languages which existed in the past but which are no longer spoken today, such as Hittite, Iberian, Sumerian and Etruscan, and languages such as these are by no means exceptions. Language death is a continuous process which is as old as history itself. What is happening now, however, is a dramatic acceleration of this dying-out process, due to a whole gamut of far-reaching political and social changes, which have taken place primarily in the twentieth century and which have left no culture untouched.

Michael Krauss, head of the Alaska Native Language Center in Fairbanks, recently (1992) attempted to produce an accurate quantitative picture of the current situation in the various continents of the world. The greatest linguistic variety is to be found in Asia and the Pacific, with 3,000 languages, and in Africa (1,900 languages). In Europe and the Middle East 275 languages have been recorded, compared with 900 in the Americas. Approximately 5,000 languages are concentrated in 22 countries. Of these, 9 have more than 200 different languages each: Papua New Guinea, Indonesia, Nigeria, India, Cameroon, Australia, Mexico, Zaire and Brazil. The remaining 13 countries (the Philippines, the former USSR, the United States, Malaysia, China, the Sudan, Tanzania, Ethiopia, Chad, the New Hebrides, the Central African Republic, Burma and Nepal) each contain between 160 and 200 languages.

As regards the prospects for their continued existence, we can divide these languages roughly into three categories. Those languages which are no longer learned by children as their mother tongue, and which are consequently not being transferred from the older to the younger generations, would appear to be irretrievably lost. According to Krauss, of the 20 indigenous languages in Alaska, for example, only two are still learned by children. Similarly, in the whole of North America, i.e. Canada and the United States together, only 38 of the total of 187 languages are still being learned. The situation in Australia is even more striking. Of the 250 indigenous languages, 90% are no longer learned by children.

At the opposite end of the scale from this category of doomed languages are the languages whose position Krauss regards as 'safe' (at least for the moment). These are languages which are not only learned by children as their mother tongue, but also spoken by large numbers of speakers (at least 100,000), and which are the official language of a nation or a particular country, often receiving support from the government as a result. Krauss estimates the number of languages in this category at 600.

Between these two categories is a third group of languages which, while they are still learned by children as their mother tongue, are used by less than 100,000 speakers in countries where they are in competition with other languages – languages which are sometimes clearly dominant and which are seen by young people as a more attractive alternative than the original language. These are languages which exist in bilingual or multilingual communities, and for which Krauss employs the qualification 'endangered'.

In summary, we can join Krauss in assuming that, 'the coming century will see either the death or the doom of 90% of mankind's languages'. (Krauss 1992, p. 7).

II

It is surprising that the science of linguistics has for so long remained indifferent to this rapid language death, which undermines its own empirical basis to such a great extent. This passive attitude becomes even more surprising when it is compared with the biological sciences, which have for so long offered powerful resistance to the extinction or threatened extinction of plant and animal species as a result of human actions. There are many national and international organisations actively pressing governments for legislation and for all kinds of protective measures, and attempting – often with success – to arouse public opinion and make people sensitive to the threats facing Nature. It is enough to point to Greenpeace and the United Nations International Union for the Conservation of Nature. Linguists campaigning for the survival of languages, by contrast, are very scarce, and organisations which pursue such aims are virtually unknown.

It is not possible to explore the possible causes of this discrepancy in any detail here. A prime cause undoubtedly lies in the way linguistics has developed. Since around 1930 this discipline has been increasingly characterised by a strong orientation towards acquiring an understanding of the system which is thought to form the basis of the actual language use of the members of a language community. Since the middle of the century the emphasis has been on study of the universal principles which govern every language system. Put another way, linguistics in the twentieth century has devoted more attention to the individual, psychological language aspect than to the social aspect, i.e. language use in all its variety, and to the functioning of languages in societies in general.

Apart from the desirability of language preservation in every specific case, it is essential for the science of linguistics that languages threatened with extinction are described. This is true not only for historical / comparative linguistics and language typology, but also for general linguistics, which is dominated by the tension between the fundamental similarity between all languages on the one hand, and their uniqueness on the other. The fact that this is beginning to get through to many of those working in linguistics must be attributed to the fact that, since around 1970, an increasing number of linguists have begun to take a broader, more sociolinguistic view of language.

III It was in 1970 that the Norwegian-American linguist Einar Haugen, at a symposium organised by the Wenner Gren Foundation at Burg Wartenstein near Vienna entitled *Towards the Description of the Languages of the World,* presented a paper entitled 'On the Ecology of Languages', which – as I can testify from personal experience – made a deep impression on those present. This paper (Haugen 1972) expounded the view that linguists should not limit themselves to grammatical analyses of individual languages, but must set themselves a broader aim. Among other things, they should in Haugen's view be devoting attention to the entirety of languages which are spoken in a given *area.* According to Haugen, a number of ecological questions need to be answered with respect to every language. The most important of these questions are as follows:

1 Who are the people who use the language? This, says Haugen, is a question of linguistic demography, which can be answered by studies of the region, social class and religion, and possibly other relevant factors.
2 Is the language used in all domains or is its use limited to particular domains (e.g. only within the family circle, or only in relation to certain activities or subjects)? This question must be answered through sociolinguistic research.
3 What other languages are in use in the area concerned, in competition with the language in question? This is a question relating to the degree of bilingualism or multilingualism.
4 What internal variations are there within the language? This is a question which can be answered by the discipline of dialectology.
5 What written traditions are there, and to what extent is the written form of the language standardised?
6 Does the language receive support from public authorities or from organisations, or is there a policy of *laissez faire* or of deliberate neglect?
7 What is the attitude of the language-users to their own language in terms of *status* and *intimacy*; in this context, Haugen considers *status* as indicating the link with power and influence in the social group concerned, while he sees *intimacy* as the degree of attachment of the language in terms of solidarity, shared values, friendship, love – in short, the contacts which are established through living in a family or group (Haugen 1972, p. 329).

A gradual awareness is evolving that in order to develop a good language policy and, in particular, in order to determine whether attempts to sustain a given language are worthwhile, it is essential that answers be found to the above questions, particularly questions 3 to 7.

IV Interest in language ecology has grown rapidly. I shall restrict myself here to mentioning a few of the most important publications.

In 1979 a symposium was organised in Brussels by the Research Centre for Multilingualism, on *Language Contact and Language Conflict,* in which many prominent linguists, including Haugen and Fishman, took part. The proceedings of this symposium were published in 1980 in a special issue of the *Zeitschrift für Dialektologie und Linguistik,* and were followed in 1984 by a collection of 16 articles in the same journal which were intended, as stated by the editors Enninger and Haynes in their foreword, to examine more closely the vitality of the concept 'language ecology' and to assess the applicability of an ecological approach in various fields of study. According to general opinion, the most important publication in the broad field of language ecology is the monograph by Nancy Dorian (1981), in which she reports an extremely careful study of the process of decline of a Gaelic dialect still spoken in Scotland. Her study was preceded and followed by a long series of articles, which appeared in well-known journals between 1970 and 1990. For bibliographical details see her collection *Investigating Obsolescence* published in 1989. Her work has made an important contribution to the increased awareness among linguists of the seriousness of the problem of language decline.

At the 14th International Conference of Linguists, held in 1987 in Berlin, 60 linguists approached the CIPL *(Comité International Permanent de Linguistes),* the international organisation which has organised these conferences since 1928, with a request that it should help to increase people's awareness of the rapid disappearance of languages (at an estimated rate of 12 per year), and to make the dying out of languages a central theme of the next conference. Shortly after the Berlin conference, CIPL began to make the necessary preparations, not only for a discussion of the problems of language death at the 1992 conference, but also for obtaining financial and moral support via UNESCO. It quickly became clear that the first requirement was to obtain a reliable picture of the current situation in the various continents.

Twelve linguists, each familiar with the situation in a particular area, were found willing to compile surveys. The result was a book, *Endangered Languages* (1991), which was intended to serve as a basis for the discussions at the 1992 conference in Quebec. The collection of articles in this book was also intended to give UNESCO and other national and international organisations with an interest in this problem some idea of the seriousness of the situation. *Endangered languages* was published under the auspices of the CIPSH (*Conseil International de la Philosophie et des Sciences Humaines* – International Council for Philosophy and Human Sciences) as a separate issue of the UNESCO journal *Diogène,* in which four of the articles from *Endangered Languages* appeared in French translation.

The high level of interest in the problem of language loss at UNESCO, and particularly at the CIPSH, was already apparent from the monograph *Arctic*

Languages, the result of a decision taken by UNESCO as early as 1974 to commission studies into the Arctic cultures. Further, in February 1992 the CIPSH, under the expert leadership of Professor Stephen Wurm, who has experience of language decline in various parts of the world, organised a gathering of a number of those directly involved, at which the CIPL was naturally also represented. At this meeting there was a wide-ranging exchange of ideas on the various aspects of the problem. A very important announcement was also made at this meeting to the effect that, thanks to generous financial support from Japan, a 'Clearing House' and 'Data Bank' will shortly be established in Tokyo. Here, all information relating to threatened languages will be collected, updated, and made available to interested parties. Finally, the report to UNESCO included a list of five urgent research projects. One of these, which has since got under way, relates to two rapidly disappearing languages in Papua New Guinea.

Just how much the interest in language decline has grown in recent years is illustrated by the number of recent symposia and conferences: for example in January 1990 in Bad Hamburg on *Language Death in East Africa,* or in September 1992 in Harare in the context of a CIPSH meeting on the language situation in Africa. In January 1991 the Linguistic Society of America organised a symposium on *Endangered Languages and their Preservation,* a report of which can be found in the journal *Language* (68.1; 1992). In addition, the new Academia Europaea has announced that the subject of language death will be on the agenda at its meeting in Uppsala in 1993.

V Although many people tend to see the dying out of languages as a phenomenon far removed from them, the question is now also being raised in the Netherlands as to whether the anticipated unification of Europe poses a threat to the continued existence of the Dutch language.

Clearly, no-one can guarantee that Dutch will remain in existence for ever. A new war involving the use of nuclear weapons, large-scale deportations or sharp rises in the sea level, could all bring an end to this language community, or at least substantially weaken it. Even if we rule out such drastic events, however, we still cannot say that the continued existence of the Dutch language is assured for all time; enough cases are known in which rapid changes have occurred. One example is Breton, which not so long ago had a million speakers and which is now the mother tongue of only a small number of children.

The most important facts from which reassurance can be derived, at least for the time being, are the following:

1 Dutch is learned by children on a large scale as their first language, and there are no indications at the moment that this is likely to change.
2 Dutch is a language with more than 20 million speakers (15 million in the Netherlands and between 5 and 6 million in Belgium).
3 Dutch is the official language of two member states of the European Community (the Netherlands and Belgium), is taught on a large scale at various levels, and is used daily by the media as its language of communication.
4 There is a written Dutch language with an extensive, living literature.

Standing against the above arguments are the following points:

1 Increasingly, languages other than Dutch are being spoken in the Netherlands, such as Moroccan Arabic and Turkish; by contrast, the Frisian language (spoken in the Dutch province of Friesland) appears to be holding its own.
2 English is replacing Dutch at a rapidly increasing rate in scientific publications written by Dutch native-speakers.
3 Bilingualism is increasing to a limited extent. In the Netherlands this is mainly due to a simultaneous command of English and Dutch. In Belgium the dominance of Dutch as a second language is increasing in Wallonia (the French-speaking area of Belgium). In Flanders (the Dutch-speaking part of Belgium), by contrast, knowledge of French as a second language is declining. Both in international industrial relationships and in scientific contacts, knowledge at least of English and / or French and German has become indispensable.
4 The adoption of English words and phrases is increasing rapidly.
5 The Netherlands is surrounded by three large, socioculturally important communities in which different languages are spoken and in which there is virtually no knowledge of Dutch.
6 There appears to be little evidence in the Netherlands of any nationalistic feeling of attachment by the population to the Dutch language. As speakers of a language which is not generally known elsewhere, people quickly switch from Dutch to English, French or German in foreign contacts, however inadequate their command of these languages.
7 Although cutbacks in the teaching of the three so-called major modern languages have led to a reduction in the knowledge of these languages, a considerable number of Dutch-speakers still come into contact with one or more modern languages in various ways (holidays, television, etc.).

If we attempt to weigh these two sets of factors which may be important for the future of the Dutch language against each other, we cannot fail to reach the conclusion, like De Swaan (1990), that Dutch is one of the 10% of languages which Krauss has designated with the term ‘safe’. Furthermore, no evidence can be detected of ‘language shift’, which in a bilingual community is normally the first stage in the decline of one language in favour of a second language which is becoming dominant (Dressler 1981). Of course, the (slowly) progressing European integration and increasing tourism (to limit ourselves to just these two developments here) will lead to an increase in the level of bilingualism. Equally clearly, the Dutch language 100 years from now will not be identical to the Dutch language spoken and written today. However, both developments can only be seen as positive. Increasing bilingualism is necessary for our economy and sciences, and language change through productivity and creativity are essential characteristics of language use which enable a language to follow social changes and to meet new communicative needs.

However, these statements are by no means intended to imply that things can simply be left to themselves. As we know, languages whose position appears assured can in the course of time end up in the category of endangered languages; as stated earlier, a great deal depends on the attitude of the speakers to their language. If it has been decided that Dutch must continue to function as the mother tongue of the Low Countries into the distant future in all domains of language use, then an active language policy is indispensable. Some aspects of such a policy are the following: permanent support for Dutch-language magazines and books which inform monolingual Dutch-speakers about developments in science, art and culture, is essential. The same applies to translations. In addition, greater attention than at present will have to be given to the publication of Dutch literary works and to the study of Dutch language and literature. In particular, a much greater role will have to be accorded in both secondary and university education to acquiring a command of written Dutch.

On the other hand, it will also be essential to equip advanced students during their university training to express themselves adequately in English or, for certain subjects, in French or German, both verbally and in writing, so that they are able to take part in the international debate in those subject areas.

If the Netherlands wishes to remain a Dutch-speaking country, while at the same time benefiting from its situation surrounded by language communities where three major world languages are spoken, there will have to be a willingness to invest more time and money than at present in the teaching of Dutch and of the three major modern languages. We have to realise that language is an extremely important factor for the Netherlands, both internally and for our vital contacts with an international environment which will, in a sense, increasingly become a domestic environment for the Dutch.

E.M. UHLENBECK
Translated by Julian Ross.

REFERENCES

CLAIRIS, CHRISTOS, 'Le processus de disparition des langues', *La Linguistique*, 27.2, 1991, pp. 3-13.

COLLIS, DIRMID R.F., *Arctic Languages: An Awakening,* Paris, 1990. *Diogène; Revue trimestrielle,* 153, Paris, 1991.

DORIAN, NANCY C., *Language Death. The Life Cycle of a Scottish Gaelic Dialect,* Philadelphia, 1981.

DORIAN, NANCY C. (ed.), *Investigating Obsolescence, Studies in Language Contraction and Death,* Cambridge, 1989.

DRESSLER, WOLFGANG U., 'Language Shift and Language Death, a Protean Challenge for the Linguist', *Folia Linguistica,* 15, 1981, pp. 1-28.

ENNINGER, WERNER AND HAYNES, LILITH M., 'Studies in Language Ecology', *Zeitschrift für Dialektologie und Linguistik,* Heft 45, 1984.

GRIMES, BARBARA F. (ed.), *Ethnologue: Languages of the World,* Dallas, 1988.

HALE, K., KRAUSS, M. a.o., 'Endangered Languages', *Language,* 68, 1992, pp. 1-42.

HAUGEN, EINAR, 'The Ecology of Language', in: Anwar S. Dil (ed.), *The Ecology of Language, Essays by Einar Haugen,* Stamford, 1972.

NELDE, PETER HANS (ed.), Sprachkontakt und Sprachkonflikt. *Zeitschrift für Dialektologie und Linguistik,* Heft 32, 1980.

ROBINS, R.H. AND UHLENBECK, E.M., (eds.), *Endangered Languages,* Oxford, 1991.

SWAAN, ABRAHAM DE, 'Het Nederlands in het Europese talenstelsel' ('Dutch within the European language system'), *De Gids,* 153, 1990, pp. 431-440.

VOEGELIN, C.F. AND F.M., *Classification and Index of the World's Languages,* New York, 1977.

Seven

Woman Poets from the Low Countries

Miriam Van hee

Miriam Van hee (1952-) made her debut with the collection *The Frugal Meal* (Het karige maal, 1978). This title, with those of her subsequent collections, marked out the boundaries of her poetic world: *Inner Rooms and other Poems* (Binnenkamers en andere gedichten, 1980), *Snowed In* (Ingesneeuwd, 1984), *Winterhard* (1988) and *Travelling Money* (Reisgeld, 1992). Time and again she is concerned with the contrast between immobility and isolation on the one hand and the desire for activity and movement on the other. And with the dream of making the two of them coincide. The dream, therefore, of security without petrification and adventure without loss of self. All other motifs in her work derive from this Utopian longing: loneliness, melancholy, doubt, farewells, waiting, memory, travel, looking and wandering.

The only attainable compromise, the special places where the First Person of this poetry resides, are waiting rooms and tram shelters: protected spaces, but without warmth; promises of journeys, but with no end to the waiting for them. Or the same thing in reverse: the image of the traveller, looking from behind the window of the moving train at the ever-changing environment, everywhere at home but never for long.

In the collection *Travelling Money* this nostalgia for the impossible mainly concerns love, the relationship with mother and children. Here too, the dream of perfect happiness is not proof against reality. And Miriam Van hee's use of language is as reserved and nuanced as the sensory universe of her poetry: sober and direct, but at the same time blurring and suggestive.

Miriam Van hee (1952-) (Photo by Michiel Hendryckx).

le tréport

wait, he says
do not leave yet
I never saw you
with this harbour behind
these gulls about your head

so we stayed
without reason
on the beach
the gulls searching
a departed ship
it is time
which goes somewhere
bearing our lives

sensing it we offered
brief resistance
for it grew colder
we sought food and
shelter for the night
as gulls,
for tomorrow is another day
even if no one knows for sure

From *Travelling Money* (Reisgeld, 1992).
Translated by Greta Kilburn.

Elma van Haren

Elma van Haren (1954-) (Photo by Herman van den Boom).

With *The Journey towards Welcome* (De reis naar het welkom geheten, 1988) and *The Wobbling* (De Wankel, 1989), a quite new and surprising voice was heard in Dutch poetry: that of Elma van Haren (1954-). Her poems were striking because of their loose versification and their whimsical typography, as though arbitrary impressions and fragments are tied together at random. And in a certain sense this is true. Van Haren's poems originate in a boundless amazement at reality, at all that exists, happens and imposes itself chaotically on any who walk around without blinkers or prejudice. All these arbitrary elements may appear in the poem, where they become entangled with memories and associations. They are put into words, which then generate their own associations.

Eventually a bizarre world is created, in which trivial anecdotes attain the glow of the miraculous, lighting up and dimming again. Almost surrealistic, it remains utterly recognisable and is coloured with relativisation and self-irony. It was obvious that her third book of poetry *Looking Sidelong* (Het schuinvallend oog, 1991) would take the form of a poetic diary. At the same time the form of the poems evolves in the direction of poetic prose. In this way she can allow the stream of her ideas and images to flow unhindered and circumvent the danger of too much obscurity, which had imperilled her previous collections. It may be true that many of these texts come dangerously close to impressionistic babbling, but they are a perfect expression of her desire to describe 'that which drifts formlessly pleasurable in the head'.

The Wobbling

1

Compared to a house
common ground is small
but once engaged
blood and tears
follow.

A body has so many crevices,
for which the world
stamps and paws.

I want to measure the distance
in stone's throws, but
let me lie low,
till the wobbling stops.

I possess an extension cord, giving
me three metres more.
In my ear I wear a copper steering wheel.
When I meet someone, I am able now
– without standing still –
to greet and say farewell.

2

Some people purse their lips.
An edge of ice
against dark water.

Their glass eyes are wilful,
their chill is overwhelming.

They say, it is timidity, but this
coolness this chill,
which blows against you through
the long brick corridor.

Sometimes I'm able
– when meeting someone –
to stand unmoved.
Ichneumon, motionless in the air.
Imperceptibly my wings whir
up and down
like a Fury.

From *The Wobbling* (De Wankel, 1989).

Translated by Greta Kilburn.

Anneke Brassinga

Anneke Brassinga (1948-) (Photo by Peter Yvon de Vries).

Ever since she published her first collection *Aurora* in 1987, literary critics have spoken of the work of Anneke Brassinga (1948-) in such terms as 'versatility', 'contradictions', 'arbitrariness'. It is indeed difficult to provide a single consistent characterisation of this small, but varied oeuvre. Even in that first collection, simple observations appeared next to exuberant and baroque turns; clear and precise imagery conflicted with archaic and intricate constructions. In a similar way, she switches from objective descriptions to lyrical effusions.

In her later collections, *Country Estate* (Landgoed, 1989) and *Thule* (1991) the meaning and background of this fortuitous arbitrariness become clearer. Its origin is to be found in an extreme love affair with language, which prevents her from choosing between registers or tonalities. 'I was born / from words' she writes in her first collection, and *Country Estate* contains among other things the section 'Words', with long poems which do nothing else but caress and fondle a word in such a way that it yields up all its meanings and associations.

At the same time it becomes clear how the arbitrariness of her poetry relates to a fundamental thematic contrast between desire for the clarity of the 'estate', 'where one can rest / in water and water-crowfoot' and for the fascinating world of restless, confusing emotions. It is no coincidence that the collection *Thule* has two contrasting sections, with titles, significant in this respect, such as 'Frozen Sea' *(IJszee),* and 'Grass' *(Gras).*

The Obscure

Words, well-known, kept in custody,
grate like gravel between the teeth.
They sound and pronounce: nothing
sheds light in the dark dungeon,
we do not see things from above.
A Tyrolean, yodelling, makes more
sense. But will feet of epic
ivory, roving the lily fields of
Elysium, startle up a voice
simply raising itself? I would be
and hear that voice, polishing
no poems as burning-lenses
for your grief, nor as stones
for bread of wisdom – but quiet
as a pond until at dusk the duck,
taking off, trips a farewell poem
on the water, without a thought.

From *Country Estate* (Landgoed, 1989).
Translated by Greta Kilburn and Anneke Brassinga.

Anna Enquist (1945-) (Photo by Klaas Koppe).

Soldiers' Songs (Soldatenliederen, 1991) by Anna Enquist (1945-) was almost unanimously praised by critics as the best collection by a new poet of the year. It is the work of a mature woman, mother of two grown children, intelligent, trained both in psychoanalysis and in music. This background is explicitly involved in the way in which the poet gives form to her view on life. These are rather reflective poems about the tension between the soothing ordinariness of life, which sometimes even displays idyllic features, and all the fear, rebellion and despair seething underneath.

This is why the poems are 'soldiers' songs', with so much military imagery, but also so much music, which is to give form and structure to all the chaotic turmoil of war. This is why the whole collection is so tightly controlled, from its structure to its use of language. One could say that Anna Enquist approaches her work like the psychiatrist who speaks in the poem 'The Consultation Room': 'I control as dike-warden / of reality the polder: / the strength of banks, whether the sluice works.' Her poems are such sluices, between the comfortably familiar and the terrible.

This is also true of her second collection, *Hunting Scenes. Poems* (Jachtscènes. Gedichten, 1992). These poems are hunting scenes because they show how man tries to gain control over all that assails and threatens him, to catch it in a net of rationality and ordered language. But man, no less than the hunter, is prey to fears, pain, passion and death.

The Gardens of Wanrode

Late in the afternoon we reached the estate
of Wanrode, danced the tango through the long
chestnut avenue, played the game of all, all,
four times. By evening the roses began
to smell like water, but stronger, stronger, oh.

From the balcony thundered Brahm's Requiem,
a hundredfold: that all flesh was grass. This
surprised us, body that we were. There was
a misunderstanding on the register, that here
two houses stood, actually you saw their contours
twilighting ever fiercer through the lawn. If you looked.

Alarmed I went railing loudly at the dancing
master, who with merely a handspan of days, suddenly
stood mouthful of teeth. Step after step I left
the gardens, where it was more than autumn. Leaves
lay on the ground, sound accelerated over land.

From *Hunting Scenes. Poems* (Jachtscènes. Gedichten, 1992).
Translated by Greta Kilburn.

Christine D'haen

Christine D'haen (1923-)
(Photo by Bart Blomme).

Christine D'haen (1923-), who won the three-yearly Prize for Dutch Literature in 1992, is without doubt the most striking woman poet of the past half century. In 1958 she made her debut with poems which seemed to be totally in line with the pre-war neo-classical tradition of poetry: fixed in form and deeply rooted in the ideas of Christianity and antiquity. From her later work, especially since the 1970s, it had become increasingly clear that she belongs rather to a baroque, mannerist tradition which is directed less towards harmony and balance than towards luxurious beauty of form, and draws on an enormous and varied background of literature and art.

Onyx (1983), in particular, established the idea of a poetry trying through language to come to grips with a world which goes far beyond individual

O Caro Lactea

Rose is a rose is a rose is a rose, deathless and fragile,
enfolding sultriness and coolth, lip to eyelid, light
around interwoven dimness, scent-filled creases, borders
of rolled-up fleshy lining; pierced by sunlight
it is roses with which I pair, folding each petal,
but in pairing find stigma and pollen, only a phytic sex.

This edible tissue, tangible entrails, but lacking
the bloodwarm intestines in the belly, and lacking the bitter
death-sweat that erupts from the veins and the bones, the red
bubbling and curdling blood that one day for good
in the sharp shock of death tears from us self and all
strangling us who once laughed, chokes laughter in rattle.

Backwards, backwards he stares, advancing, bent
under the old man, feet copper-plated with leaves
the autumnal hero
between the flaming and the rising city,
still helmeted and plumed, but more hesitant because
he has yet to give birth to Rome, with Troy already lost.

Rose is a rose, rose is a rose is a rose, rose is a rose is a rose is a rose

On their backs, under so many roses, Rilke and Redouté lie
with no complaint.

O caro lactea: oh milky flesh, quotation from Bernardus Morlanensis.

Rose is a rose etc.: quotation from Gertrude Stein, 'Sacred Emily'.

Phytic: tó phutón: plant.

The autumnal hero: reference to Aeneas, who escaped from Troy to found Rome.

Rilke: wrote poetry about roses.

Redouté: painted roses.

From *Today I Close a Ring* (Ick sluit van daegh een ring, 1975).
Translated by Tanis Guest.

experience. Everyday occurrences such as cooking and cleaning, as well as more drastic experiences such as love, birth and death, are situated in a historical and mythical perspective. In this way she shows the whole of reality to be interwoven with language and symbolism. Her most recent work, *Mirages* (1989), goes one step further in this respect in that she now links the trivial and the cosmic, the fortuitous and the whole of creation.

But even more fascinating than the subject matter, is the extreme way in which she controls language. Elliptical fragments and unbridled sentences, archaic turns and scientific formulations, unrestrained sound-associations and refined structures conspire to produce poems, which in the full sense of the word can be called 'art works of language'.

Eva Gerlach

Eva Gerlach (1948-)
(Photo by Bert Nienhuis).

Eva Gerlach (1948-) made her debut in 1979 with *No more Sorrow* (Verder geen leed). This title, combined with the poems, which often referred to fear, oppression, loss and death, suggested that she would become part of the trend of ironically-detached poetry which was very dominant in the Netherlands during the 1970s.

In her later work, however, she resolutely breaks with irony, in order to place greater emphasis on the formal control of intrusive emotions.

Most of her poems are concerned with memories connected with childhood, mother, father, houses and landscapes. She often starts with an anecdotal situation, a careful observation. But such an image is no more than a point of departure for all sorts of shifts and associations, which bring about a total alienation. This alienation is further enhanced by the lack of any context: it is not clear where and when something takes place, who the actors are, where exactly the tangible fears and threats originate from. In brief, her poems are akin to dreams and have also the obsessional power and suggestiveness of dreams. On the other hand, the effect of Gerlach's poetry is due, to a great extent, to the tight form through which she controls the irrational world, and the laconic and imploring tone with which she resists chaos, patheticism and sentiment.

No, don't

The one in the sandpit says
whenever I think of you your name
and she touches me and lays
down spade and bucket and pretends
to call me against wind and rain.

I call back, not you
for in the dark cupboard
where I keep you locked
you would not hear me
however I should call and call
against fear and distance
but all I want
now death hurriedly turns
and diminishes you.
Body, hurt him again.
Flesh of his, clasp his bones.
Seed do not lie still in him.
Hair on his head that
thinks of me, do not get lost.

From *The Power of Paralysis* (De kracht van verlamming, 1988).
Translated by Greta Kilburn.

Marieke Jonkman

Marieke Jonkman made her debut in 1991 with *Daughters of Darkness* (Dochters van het Donker, 1991). A surprising and mysterious debut, in which a murky world, characterised by disease and violence, vice, fear, masochism and suicide, is evoked in a disillusioning manner. It almost seemed to be a display window for all human lapses. This is in itself a risky point of departure for writing poetry, as sensation and patheticism are not far removed. Marieke Jonkman was able to circumvent these traps by employing a tight form and an almost emotionless, measured language, but also because the situations and characters referred to are very concrete, though at the same time difficult to define precisely. Information is withheld, we read fragments of dramas, and the background can only be guessed at.

With *Pleiades* (Plejaden, 1992) she continues along her chosen path. The title refers to the star sign of the same name, which according to ancient mythology originated when Zeus placed the seven daughters of Atlas as stars in the sky to protect them against their assailant, the beautiful, wild hunter Orion. Marieke Jonkman uses this mythological framework as background to her subject matter and as pattern for the structure of the book. One of the Pleiades, pursued by one of the manifestations of Orion, is central to each of the seven series. Together they express the fate of a woman's life: dead children, a handicap, the loss of a partner, male sexual aggression and her own unsatisfied desire, but also the tyranny of fashion and diet. The one, meagre way of making the reality of humiliation and frustration bearable is through the poems, 'my daughters of darkness'.

HUGO BREMS
Translated by Greta Kilburn.

Link to Orion

So you had sacrificed me on the picnic table
I offered no resistance,
the wood felt damp when we were through.

I stood again and smoothed my feathers. And now?
Where is the house that you can offer me?

I touched you as I should and acted satisfied.
Who brought me in darkness to the place of sacrifice,
carried the fire and lay down to be slaughtered?

Darkness threatens and your reproach: you never even crowed.
Lust which wrings the peacock's neck.

From *Pleiades* (Plejaden, 1992).
Translated by Greta Kilburn.

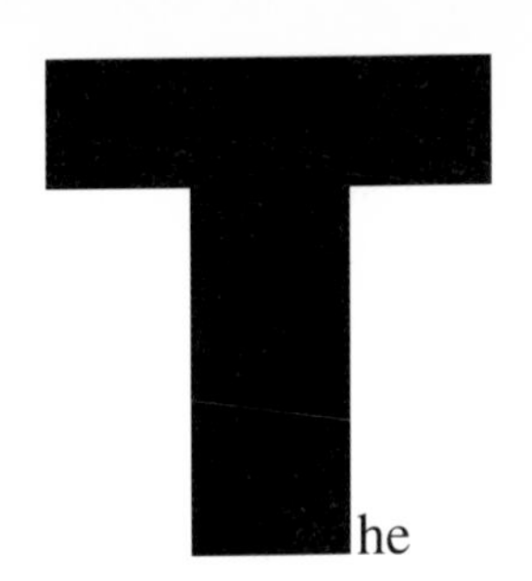

The Art of Give and Take

Musical Relations between England and Flanders from the 15th to the 17th Centuries

The 15th century

John Dunstable, Guillaume Dufay and the *'frisque concordance'*

In the early 1440s Martin le Franc wrote a lengthy poem about love, which he called *Le Champion des Dames* and dedicated to Philip the Good, Duke of Burgundy. This work contained the following well-known passage about music on the continent at that time.

Car ilz ont nouvelle pratique
De faire frisque concordance ...
Et ons prins de la contenance
Angloise et ensuivy Dunstable
Pourquoy merveilleuse plaisance
Rend leur chant joyeulx et notable.

('They have a new method of composing, full of fresh harmonies and melodiousness ... They have adopted the English way of writing, imitating Dunstable. Their joyful noble song is greatly pleasing.')

By *'ilz'* the poet means Guillaume Dufay and Gilles Binchois, the two best known composers of polyphonic music around the middle of the 15th century. Both came from the Southern Netherlands, which at that time was ruled by the Burgundians, enemies of the French Royal House and, therefore, supporters of the British conquerors during the Hundred Years' War. By a clever marriage policy and a series of military successes the dukes of Burgundy were able to extend their territories and their power still further until it was finally checked in 1477, when Charles the Bold died in the battle of Nancy during one of his vain attempts to link the Southern Netherlands with his home territory of Burgundy, with the intention of creating a buffer state between France and Germany.

The Dukes of Burgundy, with Philip the Good in the van, led an ostentatious and somewhat eccentric life style (famous for their pointed shoes and the pointed hats of the women) in which the arts and above all music played

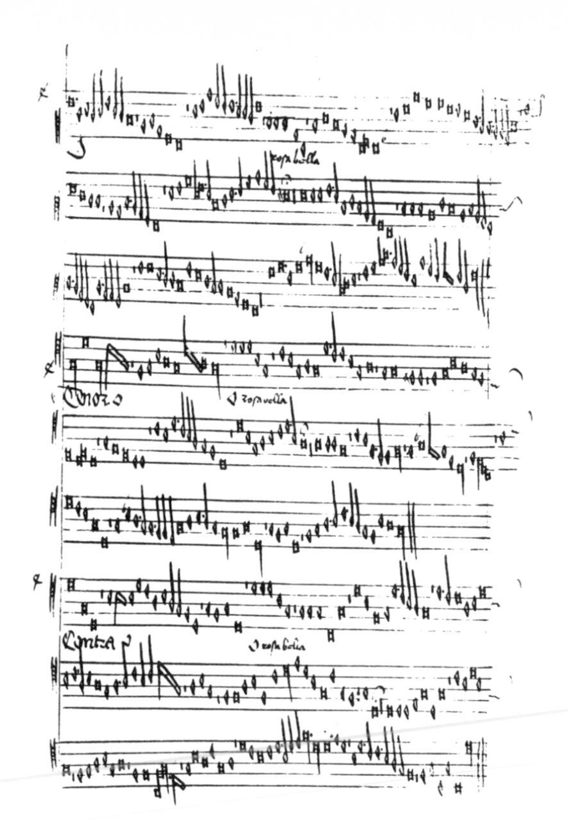

O rosa bella, a secular song attributed to John Dunstable and preserved in a continental manuscript (Trienter Codex 89, fal. 119v.).

a central part. Favourable circumstances, that is to say the Burgundians' high regard for the arts on the one hand and the presence in their beloved Southern Netherlands of exceptional talents on the other, meant that from 1430 on composers in those areas which cover what is now Belgium, the north of France (as far as Arras) and much of the Netherlands very soon became famous throughout Europe. They maintained their hegemony over Western European music for almost a hundred and fifty years.

Yet this 'Flemish polyphony', as this high point of Renaissance music is often called, would never have reached maturity but for its intensive contacts with English music, which had become known on the continent as a result of the Hundred Years' War. This music from England sounded very different from what the Flemings had been accustomed to. In contrast to the angular melodic lines, the austere mathematical constructions and the hard dissonances of continental, and particularly of French music, this strange insular repertory overflowed with spontaneous melody and with a homogeneous chordal sound they had not encountered before – in the words of Martin le Franc with a *'nouvelle pratique de faire frisque concordance'*. This English influence put new life into continental polyphony. One of the pioneers of this surprising new world of sound was John Dunstable, the greatest English composer of the first half of the 15th century, who is said to have spent some time in France in the retinue of the Duke of Bedford, commander of the English troops. His compositions and those of a number of his English contemporaries, among them Lionel Power, were copied in many local manuscripts. The Burgundians also employed English musicians, such as Robert Morton, composer of a number of popular French songs.

Quite the best known secular genre at the Burgundian court was the *chanson.* It was so characteristic that the 15th-century *chanson* repertory has been called 'the Burgundian *chanson*' by modern scholars. The structure may be typically French (the so-called *'formes fixes'* – *rondeau, ballade* and *virelai*) but the style of composition points unmistakably to England. Lyrical, melodic lines are brought together in a three-part texture which excels through its distinctive combination of melody and harmony. Dufay and Binchois were the uncontested masters of this form. So far as religious music is concerned, Dufay completed a process which the Englishman Lionel Power had begun – namely the development of the polyphonic mass into a monumental cycle in which the five parts of the Mass Ordinary

Opening of the anonymous *Missa Caput,* based on a Gregorian melody from the *Sarum use.* The manuscript of c.1470, the so-called 'Lucca Gradual', is from Bruges (Lucca, Archivio di Stato, Bibl. Manoscritti 238, fol. 17v.).

(*Kyrie, Gloria, Credo, Sanctus* and *Agnus Dei*) are welded into a musical whole by the use of one and the same borrowed melody in all the sections. This so-called *'cantus firmus'* mass, based on a pre-existing chant, stood at the summit of the hierarchy of genres. It became the touchstone by which the composer could display his skill, taking a melody either from secular music or from plainsong and weaving new independent lines around it to make a lasting work of art of the highest quality. The borrowed melody was sometimes drawn from English chant. One of the best known melodies is the antiphon *Venit ad Petrum* of which the extensive melisma on the last word *'caput'* served as the *cantus firmus* for a number of continental masses. This chant is from the liturgical repertoire which was unique to Salisbury Cathedral (the so-called *Sarum use*). Three similar *Missae Caput* are known: one is anonymous (it was previously ascribed to Dufay), a second is by Johannes Ockeghem, the best-known Flemish polyphonist of the 'second generation' and the third is by Jacob Obrecht, a contemporary of the brilliant *princeps musicae* Josquin Desprez, the leading representative of the 'third generation'.

However, during the time of Johannes Ockeghem, who served the kings of France for forty years, the English influence on continental music diminished greatly. As a result of unfavourable political circumstances during the Wars of the Roses (1459-1485), English composers worked in an isolation which was not broken until the Tudors came to the throne. Around 1475 the Flemish music theorist Johannes Tinctoris reproached the English for their conservatism and for the failure of their music to evolve. Tinctoris did praise Dunstable, but the latter was of an earlier generation.

The 16th century

Henry VIII, Philip van Wilder and continental music

The restoration of musical contacts between England and the continent at the beginning of the 16th century led to a lively exchange of musicians, repertory and instruments. This was particularly marked during the reign of Henry VIII, who was himself a competent composer. His compositions from the first decade of his reign (1509-1519) include his well known 'smash hit' *Pastime with good companye* which is to be found in *Henry VIII's Manuscript* (London Brit. Lib. Add 31922). It consisted of a court repertory with many popular songs which as yet gave no hint of the King's subsequent preference for more Flemish sounding music.

Later on, however, Henry VIII did incline his ear towards Flanders. In 1516 he recruited Benedictus de Opitiis, organist at Antwerp Cathedral, as court organist. Little further was heard of him, but another Fleming, Philip van Wilder, made a more lasting impression. A lute player at the court from 1525 on, he was a man of many talents and an outstanding composer. Thanks to the high quality of his *chansons* the French repertory was both known and well-loved in England. Van Wilder was a typical exponent of the Flemish contrapuntal style typical of the 'fourth' or 'post-Josquin generation'. As well as being a lute player and composer he was in charge of the musicians of the King's Privy Chamber and the extensive collection of musical instruments. By the time he died he had made a detailed catalogue of the splendid collection, which still survives. When Van Wilder died an anonymous poet honoured him with the following lines:

The stringe is broke, the lute is dispossest,
The hand is colde, the bodye in the grounde.
The lowring lute lamenteth now therfore
Philips her frende that can touche her no more.

The King was also interested in the very latest developments. About 1520, the Italian madrigal became known in Medici circles in Florence. This new secular genre enjoyed an unprecedented popularity and later influenced English music profoundly. The first eminent madrigal composers were *Fiammenghi* (Flemings who were employed at the Italian courts) amongst whom was Jacob Arcadelt, whose madrigals immediately became especially popular. Even before these works appeared in print Henry VIII received a manuscript of madrigals – a gift of the city of Florence in 1529.

All these were signs reflecting the way in which England was gradually adopting the innovations in continental music. New forms emerged and a new style of writing was developed, particularly by Josquin Desprez, who added profound emotion to an unsurpassed command of imitative counterpoint. This emotion was expressed above all in his psalm motets, religious compositions based on texts from the psalms, those moving poems which gave voice to the personal relationship between the faithful and God. A manuscript copied between 1517 and 1520, perhaps a present to Henry VIII (London B. Lib. Roy. II. E. xi) with compositions by, among others, Benedictus de Opitiis and the Englishman Richard Sampson – a diplomat in Antwerp and Tournai who later became successively Bishop of Lichfield and Coventry – also contained two psalm motets, a form which was already in vogue on the continent but had not yet reached England.

Orlandus Lassus and Philippus de Monte in England: an interlude from the 1550s

By chance Orlandus Lassus and Philippus de Monte, the two leading figures of the 'fifth generation' of Flemish polyphonists, both visited England as young ambitious composers during the short Catholic revival in Mary Tudor's reign. Although they left no immediate musical traces, these visits do seem to have been, as it were, symbolic of the decisive influence their work was to have later; Lassus' above all on religious music, mainly the motet, De Monte's on the Italian madrigal. After spending 12 years in Italy, Lassus travelled to England in 1554 in the company of Giulio Cesare Brancaccio, an Italian nobleman. The reasons for his journey have never been properly explained. It has even been suggested that Brancaccio had been commissioned to murder the Queen ...! Two years later Lassus' first volume of motets appeared in Antwerp. It was dedicated to Antoine Perrenot de Granvelle, Bishop of Arras and Chief Minister of Charles V and Philip II. In 1554 Granvelle, together with the English Cardinal Reginald Pole, had played a leading role in arranging the marriage of King Philip of

The motet *Quomodo cantabimus,* composed in 1584 by William Byrd for Philippus de Monte (British Library, Add. 23624).

Spain to Mary Tudor. Orlandus Lassus must have met Pole, probably in Antwerp, for his volume of motets of 1556 contains a motet in homage to the English cardinal *(Te spectant Reginalde).* Pole died on 17 November 1558 – exactly the same day as Mary Tudor.

When Philip II travelled to England, the Fleming Philippus de Monte was in his retinue, as is apparent from a letter from the envoy of Duke Albrecht of Bavaria in Brussels, recommending De Monte as Kapellmeister. Lassus must finally have established himself at the Bavarian court in Munich, while De Monte became Kapellmeister of the Emperor in Prague and Vienna. During his visit to England De Monte met Thomas Byrd, father of the 13-year-old William Byrd, later to become the most important Catholic composer during the reign of Elizabeth. A musical correspondence between De Monte and William Byrd from the 1580s survives, which shows how the stylistic tendencies of English and continental music were parallel. A manuscript in the British Library (Add. 23624) contains the motet for 8 voices *Super flumina Babylonis* by Philippus de Monte. It has a note on it 'Sent by him to Mr Wm Bird, 1583' and there is also another motet for 8 voices *Quomodo cantabimus* by Byrd on which is noted 'Made by Mr Wm Bird to send to Mr Phillip de Monte, 1584'. These motets constitute a moving document, in which both composers voice their sorrow at the divisions brought about by the religious conflicts. The text of both motets comes from the well-known psalm in which the Israelites express their sorrow at their imprisonment in Babylon, seen by De Monte and Byrd as a symbol of the Reformation in England. Both compositions are convincing examples of the increasing intensification of emotion in religious music, an essential demand made on vocal music, which Byrd expressed so strikingly when he spoke of music 'framed to the life of the words'.

The 'Elizabethan madrigal': 'Musica Transalpina' and Pierre Phalèse

The impact of an international figure such as De Monte was, however, the result of more than this one-off exchange with William Byrd. His secular compositions, together with the madrigals of a number of Flemish and Italian contemporaries, served as models for the English madrigal, which enjoyed a brief but particularly intense efflorescence at the end of the 16th century. In 1588 the initiative of the publisher Nicholas Yonge led to the appearance in London of an anthology of secular music entitled *Musica Transalpina.* The remainder of the title was 'Madrigales brought to speake English'. This collection of 'music from across the Alps' intended for 'private delight' consists of Italian madrigals, of which the music was unchanged but the text translated into English. The Flemish polyphonists represented included not only the big three, De Monte, Lassus and the outstanding Giaches de Wert, but also lesser celebrities such as Noe Faignient and Cornelis Verdonck. Between 1588 and 1598 five anthologies of Elizabethan madrigals appeared, containing altogether more than 150 compositions. The second collection, of 1590, entitled *Italian Madrigals Englished* was compiled (and translated) by Thomas Watson – and it is no coincidence that he was a poet who cultivated the Italian sonnet. The flourishing of the English madrigal was, after all, closely linked to Edmund Spenser and Sir Philip Sydney's stimulation of the writing of English-language poetry. Given that Italian poetic genres were being imitated, it is evident that the texts of the Italian madrigal would also serve as models, including the outstanding texts of Petrarch. The English had a marked preference for the madrigals of Alfonso Ferrabosco the Elder, who worked at the court of Elizabeth, and for that incomparable madrigalist from Rome, Luca Marenzio.

The sources for madrigals were not just Italian, however. They were also to be found in Antwerp where the internationally renowned music publisher Pierre Phalèse was active. Between 1583 and 1591 he published four important volumes of Italian madrigals with the attractive titles of *Musica Divina* (1583), *Harmonia Celeste* (1583), *Symphonia Angelica* (1585) and *Melodia Olympica* (1591). The English drew on these works in particular. The last of these volumes was compiled by Peter Philips, who had only recently fled from England and who was later to achieve fame in the Southern Netherlands as a composer and organist. We shall meet him again later.

The sweeping success of these translations of Italian madrigals inspired a whole range of British composers to write new compositions in their own language. The greatest was without doubt Thomas Morley, who had provided translations for the last two of the five anthologies. The style of the English madrigal was linked to the earlier conservative trends in the Italian madrigal; the wide ranging experiments with chromaticism and the exuberant textual expressions were alien to them for the most part. The most characteristic feature was the preference for the lighter type, the 'canzonet' or

MELODIA OLYMPICA

DI DIVERSI ECCELLEN-
TISSIMI MVSICI A IIII. V. VI. ET VIII.
VOCI, NVOVAMENTE RACCOLTA
DA PIETRO PHILLIPPI INGLESE,
ET DATA IN LVCE.

*Nella quale si contengono i più Eccellenti Madrigali
che hoggidi si cantino.*

CANTO.

IN ANVERSA.
Appresso Pietro Phalesio & Giouanni Bellero.

1591.

Title page of the anthology of madrigals *Melodia Olympica,* compiled by Peter Philips and published by Pierre Phalèse in Antwerp in 1591.

'ballet', compelling songs in a dance rhythm imitating the highly successful Italian *balletti* of Giovanni Gastoldi, which appeared in Venice in 1591 and were reprinted 5 years later in Antwerp by Phalèse.

Sacred music for the household: William Damon, Orlandus Lassus and William Byrd

Unlike Germany, the Reformation in England was not led by a dominant figure like Luther, who took a passionate interest in music – not just in simple songs which could be sung by ordinary people, but also in the 'more scholarly' polyphony – with Latin as well as German texts. Splendid music arranged for several voices was already being composed for the Anglican liturgy (services and anthems), though the church did not inspire these great achievements. What interested the Church in liturgical music was the intelligibility of the (English) text. The primary task of the composer was to ensure 'that the sentence may be understood and perceived'.

Much music was played in private homes – where arrangements of the psalms were especially popular. Though such music was composed by English composers for obvious reasons, a Fleming did also make a noteworthy contribution to this repertoire.

In 1563 John Day published in London the first complete polyphonic version of the English psalter *(The whole psalmes in foure partes),* simple settings for four voices of melodies, which showed the influence of the well-known continental Calvinist (or Geneva) psalter. The publisher called upon several composers. Subsequent editions of psalm harmonisations, among them that of Thomas East (between 1592 and 1611), also included anthologies with works from various composers.

The first psalter after Day's edition of 1563 was not in fact an anthology but was composed in its entirety by William Damon, a Fleming who became

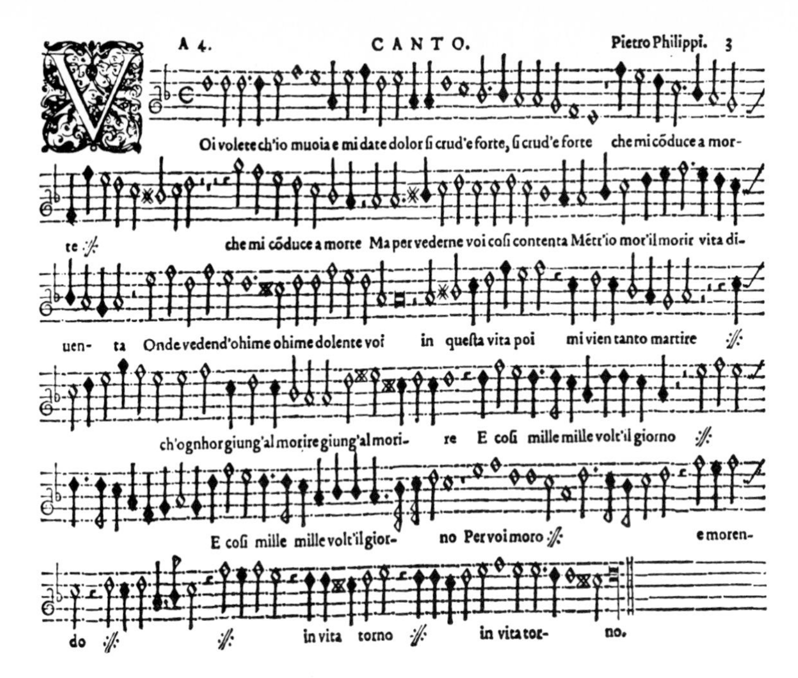

Madrigal *Voi volete* by Peter Philips ('Pietro Philippi') from *Melodia Olympica.*

a naturalized English subject and a 'gentleman of the Chapel Royal'. In 1579 his own four-voice version of the English psalm melodies appeared 'for the use of the godly Christians for recreatying them selves, in stede of fond and unseemely Ballades' as the moralising title page tells us. The edition was published without the composer's agreement. Damon was, therefore, thoroughly irritated that his simple works for private use were being subjected to such publicity. Shortly afterwards he began to rework the melodies in an elaborate manner for more 'learned ears'. The outcome of this was two volumes of more elaborate contrapuntal versions, one with the melody in the tenor (in *The former Booke of the Musicke by M. William Damon*) and one with the melody in the treble (in *The second Booke* ...). They appeared posthumously in 1591. Damon's work stands up well in comparison with the various English editions.

The name of Orlandus Lassus comes up in circles of exiled Protestants. As is well known, the rise and the spread of the Counter-Reformation in the Netherlands led thousands of supporters of the new religion into exile in England. Amongst these there were also Calvinists, for whom John Day published the Uytenhove psalter in Dutch for a single voice in 1561. The French Calvinists, better known as the Huguenots, also sought safety in England. One of them was Thomas Vautrollier who acted as the London agent for the Antwerp publisher Christopher Plantin. In 1570 he compiled a French edition entitled *Recueil de Mellange d'Orlande de Lassus.* Vautrolliers's *chansonnier* can be compared to the editions of Simon Goulart de Senlis, who published the secular (sometimes very worldly and even bawdy!) French *chansons* of Lassus disguised as contrafacta in Geneva, that sanctuary for Calvinists. The music was not changed but the texts were replaced by more suitable poetry. The Huguenot publications are further evidence of how influential the music of Lassus was throughout Europe; no-one, not even the most fervent puritan, could escape its expressive power. Vautrollier also made use of Lassus' well known *'chanson spirituelle' Susanne un jour* – a particularly popular rhyming version of the Old Testament story about the chaste Susanna – which subsequently appeared as *Susanna fair* in the *Musica Transalpina.*

It was only natural that Lassus should be best known in England as an outstanding composer of the freely expressive Latin motet, although this genre did not, of course, enjoy the same circulation as it did on the continent. The most talented composer of Latin motets was undoubtedly William Byrd, a Catholic. As we have already noted, he exchanged motets with Philippus De Monte. His *Cantiones sacrae* (1575, 1589 and 1591) were primarily intended for private performance, since there was no place for them in the Anglican Church. So far as the expressive richness of his motets is concerned, Byrd followed in the footsteps of Lassus. His masterful art found its expression in the unprecedented diversity of emotion, in which, like Lassus, each nuance of the text was translated into a musical equivalent. He reached an absolute high point in the two volume *Gradualia* of 1605 and 1607, polyphonic settings of liturgical texts for Catholic services, in which he achieved the same intensity as Lassus in his late works.

The 17th century

Catholic exiles in Flanders: Peter Philips and John Bull in Brussels and Antwerp

Although William Byrd felt that he was *'in terra aliena',* 'on foreign territory' in England – I quote from the 'psalm from exile' which he sent to De Monte – he never really left his own country. Other Catholics did, however. For some of the best composers Flanders became their new and final home. Their presence on the continent at a time when the Flemish had lost their musical superiority over the rest of Europe, contributed to a considerable extent to the continuity of the religious vocal repertory and above all to the spread of the highly developed English keyboard music in the Low Countries.

Both Peter Philips and John Bull were employed for a time as organists at the court of the archdukes Albert and Isabella, who introduced a certain political stability after the turbulent period of the revolt against Spain. Bull fled from England in 1613 and became organist at Antwerp Cathedral, after a few years service in Brussels. He died in 1628, the same year as Peter Philips, who had gone into exile in Antwerp in 1590. Philips was best known as a composer of Latin motets, Bull on the other hand is one of the most representative figures of English keyboard music. Philips' work was published by Phalèse in Antwerp from 1612 onwards. Since he added the *basso continuo* in later compositions, some of which are for solo voice, Philips must be seen as a transitional figure between the Renaissance and the baroque. But he remained first and foremost a grand master of 'Flemish counterpoint' and the art of the expressive motet in the style of Lassus and Byrd.

The harpsichord, or as it is better known, the virginal, was extremely popular in England. English virginal players pioneered an instrumental music which developed to meet the demands of the instrument's potential and as a result owed less to vocal music. The number of genres was particu-

Opening of a series of variations on the carol *Een Kindeken is ons geboren* (Unto Us a Child is Born), by John Bull.

larly rich and diverse. As well as 'freely' improvised pieces like the prelude and contrapuntal compositions such as the fantasia, the repertoire contained large numbers of variations and dances (particularly the pavan and galliard). It would be difficult to exaggerate the influence which this English virginal music had on the further development of 17th-century keyboard forms. The Amsterdam organist Jan Pietersz. Sweelinck was one of the first to adopt the English 'manner' of writing. It goes without saying that Bull's stay in the Low Countries encouraged the further spread of English keyboard music. In Brussels, for example, he was a major influence on his Flemish fellow organist Pieter Cornet. Bull's exceptional adaptability is shown by the way he could use continental elements. Thus he wrote a series of variations on the Flemish carol *Een Kindeken is ons geboren* (Unto Us a Child is Born). The exchange of ideas was mutual, but the impulse for keyboard music of a very high level came from England.

Conclusion: two pillars and an arch

The musical relationship between England and Flanders from the 15th to the beginning of the 17th century can be graphically portrayed as a monumental arch linking two massive pillars. The first pillar represents the early 15th-century *'frisque concordance'* of Dunstable and his contemporaries, which formed the foundation for the new art of the Flemish polyphonists from Guillaume Dufay to Orlandus Lassus. The second pillar symbolises English keyboard music from about 1600, which blossomed in the Low Countries in a period when vocal polyphony had exhausted itself and new and different influences were badly needed. The great arch symbolises the high point of polyphony between the years c.1440 and c.1600 during which the *Fiammenghi* influenced not just Italy and Germany but also England, albeit less continuously and less systematically. It was a matter of give and take, ranging from general trends to purely personal contributions, in a period riven by political, religious and social unrest. It is apparent that such unrest has never yet prevented contacts between cultures. The relations between England and Flanders in these two centuries are an outstanding example of this.

IGNACE BOSSUYT
Translated by Michael Shaw.

FURTHER READING

The most exhaustive study of music in the 15th and 16th centuries remains G. Reese's standard work *Music in the Renaissance,* London, 1959 (2). There quite recently appeared the first part of a splendid study of English music: CALDWELL, J., *The Oxford History of English Music.* Vol I. *From the Beginnings to c.1715,* Oxford, 1991.
See also:
KERMAN, J., *The Elizabethan Madrigal,* New York, 1962.
LE HURAY, P., *Music and the Reformation in England 1549-1660,* London and Cambridge, 1978 (2).
STEVENS, J., *Music and Poetry in the Early Tudor Court,* London and Cambridge, 1978 (2).

For a similar overview of 'Flemish polyphony' we suggest the lengthy introduction to ELDERS, W., *Componisten van de Lage Landen,* Utrecht / Antwerp, 1985. In 1991 Oxford published an English translation of this under the title *Composers of the Low Countries.*

An outstanding 'case study' in which the relationship of one town's repertory with England is discussed is R. Strohm's monograph *Music in Late Medieval Bruges,* Oxford, 1990 (2).

The 20 volumes of the musical encyclopedia *The New Grove Dictionary of Music and Musicians* (ed. S. Sadie), London, 1980 are indispensable.

The Dutch Documentary

Social Conscience, Humanism and a Taste for Experiment

While Dutch feature films have never attracted great interest in other countries, documentaries have always enjoyed a high reputation at home and abroad. Only three Dutch film-makers have ever been included in an English-language film guide, and two of them are documentarists. The latest edition of *Halliwell's Filmgoer's Companion* says: 'Holland has produced two major documentarists: Joris Ivens and Bert Haanstra. Fiction films have not been the country's forte'. The burden of this crisp judgement is clear: despite the establishment of a national Production Fund in 1956, a film academy in 1958, a Dutch *Nouvelle Vague* in the sixties, generations of new Dutch film-makers and a steady production of between five and fifteen features a year, in the eyes of other countries not much has changed in the Dutch film industry since the fifties.

This was the period when Dutch documentaries enjoyed huge national and international success. The lyrical work of Herman van der Horst, Charles Huguenot van der Linden, John Fernhout and, above all, Bert Haanstra won prizes at many festivals and became known as the Dutch Documentary School. Its distinctive features were solid craftsmanship, a poetic view of nature and society, a certain nostalgia for past glories and a kindly, in some cases slightly chauvinistic, vision of the national character.

Foreign film critics were not slow to point to similarities with seventeenth-century Dutch painting. They recognised Rembrandt in the use of light, Jan Steen in the scenes of family life, Vermeer in the interiors and innumerable landscape painters in the vast cloudy skies.

The members of the Dutch Documentary School were not, however, indebted solely to their predecessors in painting. The true pioneers of the Dutch documentary came from those involved in the Netherlands Film Association (*Nederlandse Filmliga*) which was founded in 1927 by the intelligentsia of Amsterdam in reaction to the 'circus entertainment' offered by ordinary cinemas. It was a proponent of film as art and practised its belief in 'pure, autonomous film' in screenings for members only.

One of the members was Joris Ivens (1898-1989), and as the son of the owner of a camera shop he had the necessary technical knowledge. He was to be the first film-maker to emerge from the ranks of the Film Association.

Joris Ivens and Marceline Loridan, *A Story of Wind* (Une histoire de vent, 1989).

Bert Haanstra, *Beastly* (Bij de beesten af, 1972).

Together with a fellow member, Mannus Franken, he made his first film, *The Bridge* (De Brug, 1928), and, after this highly successful debut, *Rain* (Regen) and *Breakers* (Branding, 1929) – subjective impressions with a strong poetic element which made him a model for contemporaries such as Jan Hin and Gerard Rutten. While Ivens was fascinated by the abstract patterns and rhythms created by the camera and the editing, Franken's preference was for a human presence. Thanks to his knowledge of the French avant-garde, he added a hint of sophistication to Ivens's style. But their ways parted and, after making several commissioned films and documentaries about the Zuiderzee works and building in the Netherlands, Ivens shifted his attention to other countries. There his concern with social issues became apparent in deeply felt documentaries such as *Borinage* (1934) – on the appalling conditions in which Belgian miners lived – and *Spanish Earth* (Spaanse Aarde, 1937) – on the Spanish Civil War – and a number of films shot in Russia. 'My camera is embarrassed when it sees this misery', wrote Ivens during the making of *Borinage*.

His social concerns led him to adopt communist views which were completely unacceptable to the Dutch government. After the government-commissioned film *Indonesia Calling* (1946) – in which Ivens openly sided with the nationalists fighting for independence – he fell from grace and had his passport taken from him. The Netherlands' greatest pioneer turned his back on his native country, became a world citizen and went on making films into old age. His last, partly autobiographical documentary *A Story of Wind* (Une histoire de vent, 1989) was shot in China and has the poetic qualities of his earliest work. It was completed with the help of a financial contribution from the Dutch government, who officially rehabilitated him in 1985.

Ivens's departure gave the young, self-made film-maker Bert Haanstra (1916-) a chance to establish his reputation. In the fifties and sixties Haanstra became what Ivens had been in the twenties and thirties: the doyen of Dutch documentarists. In contrast to Ivens, who put his talent at the ser-

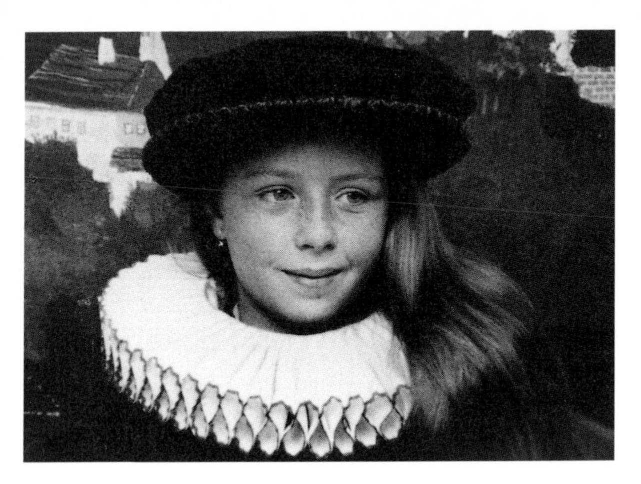

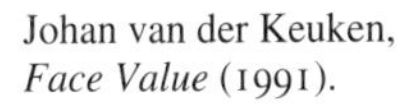

Johan van der Keuken, *Face Value* (1991).

Saskia Vredeveld, *Heartbreak Country* (Hartseerland, 1991).

vice of his political ideals and aimed to make the world a better place through social indictments with artistic merit, Haanstra concentrated on observing and recording society as he saw it in all its tragicomic aspects. A humanist and humorist, he portrayed the Netherlands and the Dutch in films shot with a hidden camera, such as *Everyone* (Alleman, 1963), *Zoo* (1962) and *Beastly* (Bij de beesten af, 1972). These are gently ironic observations of human behaviour which depend primarily on sophisticated timing and montage. In the fifties he was already known as a master of montage techniques through films like *Mirror of Holland* (Spiegel over Holland, 1950), *Phanta Rei* (1951) and *Rembrandt, Painter of Man* (Rembrandt, schilder van de mens, 1957). A simple commission developed into a fantasy about the making of glass objects called *Glass* (Glas, 1958). A classic of Dutch documentary cinema, it won the Oscar for best documentary and the Silver Bear at the Berlin Film Festival.

Perhaps it was the guileless innocence of the years of reconstruction after the war which the next generation reacted against in the late sixties. They lost their innocence in sexual and social revolutions and firmly rejected older masters such as Haanstra, accusing them of tired visual rhymes, uncommitted observation and bourgeois attitudes. The epic of the Dutch battle against the sea was to be replaced by the epic of the sexually emancipated, politically aware citizen; the beauty of landscape and fishing village by the beauty of great cities in social upheaval; lyrical craftsmanship by the authenticity of free cinema. The Dutch Documentary School was dismissed as passé; efforts were concentrated on building up a Dutch feature film industry, the first model being the *Nouvelle Vague.* Later, unfortunately, attempts were made to conquer an international market with commercial stories. In the eighties the lack of success and the problems of securing financial backing for features led many young film-makers to turn again to documentaries. The great forerunner of this new generation was the internationally recognised documentarist Johan van der Keuken (1938-), who

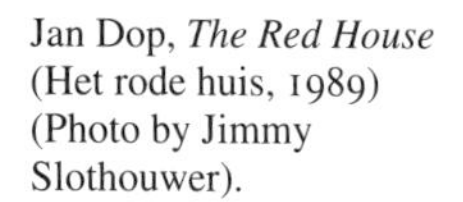
Jan Dop, *The Red House* (Het rode huis, 1989) (Photo by Jimmy Slothouwer).

Hans Keller, *Stories about the Colours of Europe* (Verhalen over de kleuren van Europa, 1992) (Photo by Geertje Lammers).

attracted attention in the sixties with tautly composed, 'jazzy' films on the spirit of the times and had great success in the eighties and nineties with long, personal and socially aware films such as *I love dollars* (1986), *The Eye above the Well* (Het oog boven de put, 1988) and *Face Value* (1991). His subjective photographic vision, his playing with the frame and camera angles, his selection of people and objects and his editing choices are all highly intriguing. Throughout his work Van der Keuken is explicitly present as a third party. Between the images and the audience stands a brave film-maker with an inquiring spirit who is not afraid to experiment, who defies the limits and limitations of the medium and who continually questions the role and effect of the image or the sequence of images. In his subjective vision and artistic insights he shows himself to be a worthy successor to Ivens and in his humanity to Bert Haanstra.

With Johan van der Keuken at its head, an entirely new generation is currently establishing an entirely new documentary tradition whose chief characteristic is that it has no specific characteristics. The term 'documentary' covers everything from reportage-type television films to highly personal artistic impressions and thoroughly researched historical essays enlivened with fiction and archive material. The genre is increasingly popular with film-makers because of the free form, the opportunities for experiment and the relatively cheap, accessible method of production. Looking back on the work of a year, it is striking to see how young Dutch documentarists, showing a social concern worthy of Joris Ivens, have travelled the world to draw attention to injustice. *Heartbreak Country* (Hartseerland, 1991) by Saskia Vredeveld presents a shocking picture of the far-right AWB movement in South Africa, while *The Red House* (Het rode huis, 1989) by Jan Dop is an indictment of the conditions in Indian reservations. On the other hand, there is the cultural and philosophical work of the experienced film-maker Hans Keller, whose *Stories about the Colours of Europe* (Verhalen over de kleuren van Europa, 1992) and *The Invention of America*

(De uitvinding van Amerika, 1992) are beautifully structured, evocative impressions of societies living on a fault line.

Closer in spirit to Haanstra are the portraits of typically Dutch communities in documentaries such as Froukje Bos's *Torch song* (Levenslied, 1992) or the work of the awardwinning duo Maarten Schmidt and Thomas Doebele. Their films are often made for television, so techniques tend to be used in a more traditional way.

For the last five years Amsterdam has been the venue for the *International Documentary Festival,* and it is noticeable that in other countries too the genre has achieved both a high standard and an innovatory approach to film. The fact that more and more cinemas, if at first hesitantly, are deciding to include documentaries in their programme will hopefully encourage young film-makers to continue to test and if necessary go beyond the limits of the genre. In this way small countries will have a chance to make their mark in film despite the commercial productions of such unbeatable rivals as the United States.

GERDIN LINTHORST
Translated by John Rudge.

he Low Countries Do Smell of Manure, Don't They?

Environmental Problems, Environmental Awareness and Environmental Policy in the Netherlands and Flanders

Introduction

During the summer and autumn of 1992 a remarkable debate developed in the pages of the usually serious Dutch economic journal *Economisch-Statistische Berichten* (Economic-Statistical Reports). Briefly summarised, the question at issue was whether and how it was possible to measure damage to the environment in any one country, and which (European) country would then win the dubious award for being the most polluted and the worst polluter. In keeping with the traditions of economics, it had to be possible to quantify the environmental 'performance', preferably in a single figure; on the basis of this the various countries could then be arranged in order of environmental pollution.

The debate was sparked by a 1991 publication by the OECD (Organisation for Economic Cooperation and Development)[1], in which a preliminary set of environmental indicators was presented, including the score attained by various countries for environmental pollution and the quality of their environment. On the basis of this publication, two Dutch economists concluded that the Netherlands was the 'mucky pup' of Western Europe[2] – a highly embarrassing and painful conclusion for a country which likes to pride itself on being extremely progressive on environmental issues. Even more remarkable, if that were possible, was the conclusion by the two economists that the Dutch performance was worse than that of Belgium, a country which in Dutch eyes has a very poor record on the environment. Greenpeace actually labels Belgium the 'dirty little child of Europe' (Britain, incidentally, is referred to as the 'dirty old man of Europe'). The figures collected by the OECD, however, named the Netherlands as the most polluted and most polluting country.

More than anything, it was the conclusion that the Netherlands scored so badly – even worse than Belgium, a country regarded with such disdain on environmental issues – which provoked a great deal of debate. During this debate, it soon became evident that this result clearly depended to a large extent on the way in which environmental pollution is measured. Thus the poor score achieved by the Netherlands was due among other things to high energy and water consumption, high emissions of 'greenhouse gases' and large quantities of domestic waste, all measured per capita. In fact, Belgium's energy consumption is even higher, but the country achieved a rather better score on some other variables. But it was precisely this numerical duel between the two countries which made it clear that the question of which was the most polluted depended principally on the criteria adopted. Energy consumption figures led to a different conclusion from figures illustrating the quantity of artificial fertiliser used; and figures on the quantity of waste led to a different conclusion from data on the quality of the surface water.

The purpose of this paper is not to declare, retrospectively, a final winner of this environmental duel, but to sketch an outline of the most important environmental problems facing the Low Countries and the way in which the Netherlands and Flanders deal with these problems. It will become apparent from the first point discussed below that the environmental problems of the Netherlands and Flanders are very similar, although each country also faces a number of specific problems of its own. Attention is then focused briefly on the level of environmental awareness in the two countries, and on the way in which that awareness has been given social and political form. Finally, the paper looks at the environmental policies which have been developed in the Low Countries. There are significant differences between the Netherlands and Flanders on the last two points; however, these do not so much relate to differing environmental problems, but rather reflect social, political and cultural differences between the two countries.

The environmental problems of the Low Countries

As stated earlier, environmental problems in the Netherlands and Flanders are generally very similar. This is hardly surprising, since the social and economic characteristics of the two countries responsible for these environmental problems are also very alike. Both are densely populated, highly industrialised and extremely prosperous countries. Very many of their environmental problems are connected with these three basic characteristics, the combined effects of which include extremely intensive use of energy, space and land. A significant proportion of the figures in the OECD report relate to this fact, as a few examples will make clear.

Flanders and the Netherlands are among Europe's most densely populated regions, with between 400 and 450 inhabitants per square kilometre. By comparison, the corresponding figure for Britain is approximately 240 and for France approximately 100. Obviously, this extremely high population density is enough in itself to put pressure on the environment through the sheer space required. Combined with a high level of prosperity and a multiplicity of social demands and needs, however, the result is enormous pressure on both space and energy. As an example, the car ownership statistics for Belgium (37 cars per 100 inhabitants) and the Netherlands (36 per 100) in themselves differ little from those for Britain (38 per 100) or France (41 per 100). In combination with the high population density, however, they lead to an exceptionally high degree of spatial fragmentation simply because of the infrastructure which those cars require. This demand for road

Westland greenhouse horticulture in the Netherlands (Photo by Michiel Wijnbergh).

infrastructure is also reinforced by the fact that both Flanders and the Netherlands are countries with an important distribution and export function. Both play a crucial role in the extremely strong development of freight transport on Europe's road networks. In both countries, this export role forms an important basis for the high level of prosperity, but also impacts on the environment. The same applies to the important petrochemical industry in both countries, particularly in the vicinity of their seaports Antwerp and Rotterdam. This economic activity, too, is at the same time a source of prosperity and of environmental damage. Both countries have in this way assured themselves of supplies of reasonably cheap energy, but they have of course also contributed to excessive energy consumption, with its accompanying effect on the environment.

This combination of high population density, industrial development and a high level of prosperity means that only a small amount of land is left for agricultural use. With such a small area available, intensive use of this land is virtually inevitable, particularly when agricultural production is so strongly geared to export. This has contributed to the large-scale shift in both countries towards 'land-independent' forms of agriculture, such as intensive stock farming and – particularly in the Netherlands – the highly energy-intensive greenhouse horticulture. In both the Netherlands and Flanders, however, this intensive agricultural activity brings with it a large number of environmental problems, such as soil and groundwater pollution through excessive use of pesticides, the emission of acidifying substances and, as a consequence of intensive stock farming, an enormous surplus of manure. Many of the environmental problems in the Netherlands and Flanders are a direct result of this intensive agriculture, particularly of intensive stock farming. It is this latter activity, too, which provides large tracts of the Netherlands and Flanders with the characteristic aroma which leads many foreign visitors to remark, shortly after arrival, 'The Low Countries do smell of manure, don't they?'

In short, then, environmental problems in the Netherlands and Flanders are, given their similar demographic and economic situation, very comparable. This applies in the first place to the large-scale, global problems such as the greenhouse effect, the depletion of the ozone layer, the exhaustion of natural resources, etc., to which both countries contribute to a similar extent.

In the second place, it applies to other internationally familiar problems, such as acidification and pollution with hazardous substances. Thirdly, the problems at national level in the Netherlands and Flanders are also highly comparable; widespread pollution of the environment due to emissions by agriculture, industry and domestic households; the production of large quantities of waste; damage to the natural environment from this extensive pollution; damage to the landscape through fragmentation (e.g. road-building), etc. Apart from the OECD figures, comparison of several recent 'state of the environment' reports also leads to the conclusion that the two countries do not differ greatly in terms of their environmental problems.[3]

And yet there is one striking difference which is particularly significant for the disparity in environmental awareness between the two countries. The location of the Netherlands in the delta of three great rivers – Rhine, Maas and Scheldt – with the constant threat and repeated disasters resulting from that location, means that concern for water management has a special place in the collective consciousness of the Dutch; accordingly, the Netherlands has a long tradition of water management policies. As a result, according to Simon Schama in his book *Patriots and Liberators*[4], the country's dependence on and battle with the water has been a constant factor in Dutch social and political history. Traditionally, the main concern was the quantity of water: drainage, flood prevention, etc. When in the 1960s the rapidly deteriorating quality of the water also posed a threat to the Netherlands, this new policy domain was immediately given a high priority and added to the traditional tasks of water management. The long tradition clearly played a part in this, alongside the dependence on surface water for supplies of drinking water. So far, in Belgium – some say, wrongly, only in Wallonia – surface water is not seen as posing any threat, in terms of either quantity or quality. In general, Belgium has always been much less susceptible to flooding and is much less dependent on surface water for its drinking water supplies. As a result, surface water in Belgium tends to be regarded more as something which is simply 'there'; it flows on by, and where it ends up is outside the average individual's sphere of interest. Among other things, then, it is a handy dumping-ground. In comparison with the Netherlands, the Belgian / Flemish surface water is in a totally deplorable condition. There is no doubt that this difference is connected with the difference in the collective consciousness of the two countries, i.e. the presence or absence of a feeling of 'surface water as a collective interest'. But such a connection cannot be expressed in irrefutable figures, let alone in a single figure representing the environmental quality of a particular country.

(Collection Stichting Leefmilieu, Antwerp).

Environmental awareness in the Low Countries

Tackling environmental problems by means of an environment policy assumes that society and politicians are conscious of these problems, that there is a degree of environmental awareness. This must then lead to environmental problems being recognised and placed on both the social and – above all – the political agenda. In the same way that it is impossible to summarise the degree of environmental pollution in a single figure, environmental awareness cannot be determined in a simple fashion. Obviously, opinion surveys give an indication of the problems which engage public opinion and of the level of importance attached to these problems. But opinions are often subject to the vagaries of fashion and are fleeting, dependent on the day's news. Nonetheless, opinion poll statistics are used as a measure of environmental awareness. The figures available show a fairly high level of environmental awareness among both the Dutch and the Flemish populations, an awareness which has been present since the early 1970s and been subject to the same ups and downs as in other countries.[5]

Environmental awareness is less fleeting when it is organised, when it has acquired a definite shape in the form of environmental pressure groups, associations and organisations. Since the early 1970s, both the Netherlands and Flanders have seen the creation of a wide range of local, regional and national organisations concerned with matters such as conservation of nature and the landscape, environmental pollution, etc. On this point, too, both countries are therefore highly comparable.

And yet the form taken by this environmental awareness in the two countries also displays a number of very striking differences between them. The core of this difference lies in two related points: the position of the environmentalists and the political priority accorded to environmental problems. In the Netherlands the environmental movement has for a very long time – since the 1970s – been acknowledged as a legitimate discussion partner of the government. For example, the officials of the Directorate-General for the Environment, which was founded in 1972, were quick to avail themselves (repeatedly) of the benefit of the views and expertise of the environmental movement, partly as a means of strengthening their own policy. The consequence was that the Dutch environmental lobby was included in all manner of consultative committees and advisory boards. This in turn led to a strategy which was increasingly based on advice, lobbying and negotiation. Whether this proves to be the most adequate strategy in the long term remains to be seen. The environmental movement in Belgium, on the other hand, has really only gained recognition in recent years. The reason for this important difference has less to do with the environmental movement itself than with the differences in political culture between the two countries and the consequent widely differing degree to which environmental awareness has found its way onto the political agenda in the two countries. The much more open political culture in the Netherlands enabled environmental awareness among the population to reach the political agenda as early as the late 1960s and early 1970s. Political parties such as the progressive-liberal *D'66* and the progressive-Catholic *PPR*, which together with several other small left-wing parties now form the political grouping *Groen Links* (Green Left), literally took environmental awareness into parliament and government. Both the environmental problem and the environmental movement were therefore rapidly 'acknowledged'. In Belgium, apart from the rise of regional parties and the regionalisation of the traditional political parties, no comparable political innovation took place in the 1960s or 1970s. Moreover, such a development would have been blocked by the tensions, which began in the 1960s and have constantly recurred to this day, between Flemings, Wallons and the inhabitants of Brussels – the so-called *communautaire* ('inter-community') problems. These tensions and difficulties led to an endless process of state reforms, one after the other, which completely occupied the political agenda. Partly as a result of this, (a section of) the Belgian environmental movement both in Flanders and Wallonia felt more or less compelled to found its own environmentalist parties. It was above all the electoral breakthrough of the Flemish *Agalev* party and the Walloon *Ecolo* party in the 1980s which led to an increasing environmental awareness in the political arena in general. At the same time, the process of state reform progressed to such an extent that at least some clarity emerged regarding the division of power.

The river Scheldt near Uitbergen in Flanders (Photo by Paul van den Abeele).

Environment policy in the Low Countries

Space is too limited here to give anything like an exhaustive summary of the environment policies of the Netherlands and Flanders. What follows is therefore no more than a sketch of a few characteristic main points, correspondences and differences. The content, organisation and style of the environment policies are discussed below. The most important difference between the two countries is perhaps to be found in the style and quality of the policy preparation.

In view of their similar environmental problems, it is not surprising that the themes of environment policy in both countries are largely the same. In any case, the identification and development of environment policy themes is increasingly being determined at an international level, and is here being shaped, among other things, by European environment policy. In the same way, the basic principles, objectives and norms of environment policy are also more and more frequently being developed in a European context. Certainly as regards global or international environmental problems, therefore, Dutch and Belgian policy is developing along very similar lines. But there are also striking parallels in the development of policy relating to problems at national level: a high level of attention to the problem of waste, with neither country succeeding in bringing either the volume or the diversity of this waste under control; many fine objectives and a good deal of lip-service paid in the area of prevention and recycling, while in both countries implementation is hampered by technical and – particularly – economic and political objections. There are also striking similarities in the policies relating to the many environmental problems caused by agriculture; the governments of both countries are attempting on the basis of the environment policy to place certain restrictions on intensive agriculture. These concern both pollution, for example through the use of herbicides and pesticides, and acidification and eutrophication, due mainly to the excessive quantity of manure produced. In both countries, however, this policy is constrained by the joint efforts of agricultural organisations and agricultural policy, the main arguments being the need for economic development and the importance of the agricultural sector to exports. The parallels on this issue are so great that virtually identical debates are conducted in both the Netherlands and Flanders on this issue, though sometimes with a time lag of a year or two. In fact the same also applies to the environmental impact of traffic and transport, and to many other areas of environment policy. One striking difference, namely the differing importance attached to the policy on water quality, and the resultant widely differing quality of the surface water, was discussed earlier.

The differences in environment policy between the two countries relate in the first place to the organisation of those policies. These differences result primarily from the differing political structures and division of political authority in the two countries. Thus the provinces and municipalities of the Netherlands have many more environment-related tasks than their Flemish counterparts, because the Netherlands, as a traditionally decentralised unitary state, has in general devolved much more power to local government. The much more centralist tradition in Belgium has certainly not disappeared as a result of the state reforms. In the area of environment policy, the Regions (Flanders, Wallonia and Brussels) have now taken over the central role previously filled by the former unitary state. Differences of this nature, therefore, while not typical of environment policies, are obviously relevant for the effectiveness of those policies. In particular, coordination of the environment policies of different authorities on the one hand, and cooperation between local authorities and social pressure groups on the other, are important factors here. It is precisely on this point that the Netherlands – though this again is something which cannot be encapsulated in a single figure – appears to score rather better.

The background to this better score can, however, be defined: anyone who compares the documents setting out the environment policy in the two countries cannot fail to detect a difference in quality. In the Netherlands, in keeping with the political and administrative style and culture of that country, it was decided right from the very beginning to adopt an approach to environment policy which was well-planned, carefully prepared and supported by many arguments. Dutch environment policy is set out in the finest detail in an ever-growing number of plans, memoranda and other policy documents, in which the underlying principles, objectives, strategies and instruments of the environment policy are laid down, one after the other, in a highly systematic way that could almost have been taken straight from the manual of policy development. This systematic preparation goes hand in hand with the development of a highly specific jargon and analytical framework for describing environmental problems, as well as a highly specific approach to determining policy strategies, objectives, etc. This typical Dutch approach has since spread to other countries, as is apparent for example from *The New Politics of Pollution,* a book by Albert Weale recently published in Great Britain[6]. Dutch environment policy, as set down on paper, has thus become an export product in its own right.

This Dutch approach, as embodied for example in the most recent central policy document, the *National Environment Policy Plan,* has of course found its way into Flanders. In particular, the recent *Flemish Environment Policy Plan and Nature Development Plan* was largely inspired by policy developments in the Netherlands. And yet there is an unmistakeable difference in policy in the two countries[7]. At first sight this appears to be mainly a difference of phase: for the reasons outlined earlier, Flanders tends to lag behind the Netherlands in the development of environment policy. However, apart from this difference of phase, and possibly more important, there may also be a cultural difference at work here. In contrast to the careful preparation of policies in the Netherlands, the administrative tradition in Belgium and Flanders is characterised much more by *ad hoc* policies and a great talent for improvisation. A symptomatic example of this approach is the extremely patchy and fragmented way in which numerical data on the 'state of the environment' are made available in Flanders. In the Netherlands, the National Institute of Public Health and Environmental Protection *(RIVM; Rijksinstituut voor Volksgezondheid en Milieuhygiëne)* is well on the way to becoming an environmental planning office, and thus a central data collection point. At the moment, a similar set-up in Flanders is unthinkable.

It is clear from the above that Dutch policy preparation, particularly in terms of the technical aspects of policy-making, is without doubt superior to that in Flanders. However, this need not necessarily mean that the quality of the environment policy itself or, more important, the quality of the environment are also better. What is important here, after all, is not policy design but policy and, above all, policy performance. And on this point, too, the two countries face almost identical problems: actual implementation of the environment policy, whether prepared in a highly systematic or a more improvisational way, is and continues to be *the* problem area. There is nothing to indicate that the Netherlands deserves a significantly higher score than Flanders on this point. And this is understandable: however great the degree of environmental awareness, an effective environment policy necessitates tackling deeply ingrained habits, firmly established economic activities, and underlying social structures. And that, in the Low Countries as elsewhere, with a well-prepared or a less well-prepared policy, remains an extremely difficult task.

PIETER LEROY
Translated by Julian Ross.

NOTES

1. OECD, *Environmental Indicators: A Preliminary Set,* Paris, 1991.
2. VAN DER LAAN, R. and NENTJES, A., 'Het Nederlandse milieu in Europees perspectief' (The Dutch Environment in a European Perspective), *Economisch-Statistische Berichten,* 24 June, 1992.
3. For the Netherlands see the reports *Zorgen voor morgen* (Concerns for Tomorrow) and *Nationale Milieuverkenning 2* (National Environment Survey 2), published in 1988 and 1991, respectively, by the National Institute of Public Health and Environmental Protection *(RIVM).* For Flanders there is the *MINA-Plan 2000* and the *Milieubeleidsplan en Natuurontwikkelingsplan voor Vlaanderen* (Environment Policy Plan and Nature Development Plan for Flanders), published in 1989 and 1990, respectively, by the Flemish Ministry of the Environment.
4. SCHAMA, SIMON, *Patriots and Liberators: Revolution in the Netherlands 1780-1813,* London, 1977.
5. LEROY, P., and DE GEEST, A., *Milieubeweging en milieubeleid* (The Environmental Movement and Environmental Policy), Antwerp / Utrecht, 1985.
6. WEALE, ALBERT, *The New Politics of Pollution,* Manchester, 1992.
7. LEROY, P., 'Milieubeleid en planning in Nederland en Vlaanderen: omnis comparatio claudicat?' (Environment Policy and Planning in the Netherlands and Flanders: omnis comparatio claudicat?), *Ons Erfdeel,* XXXII, 1989, 5, pp. 665-674.

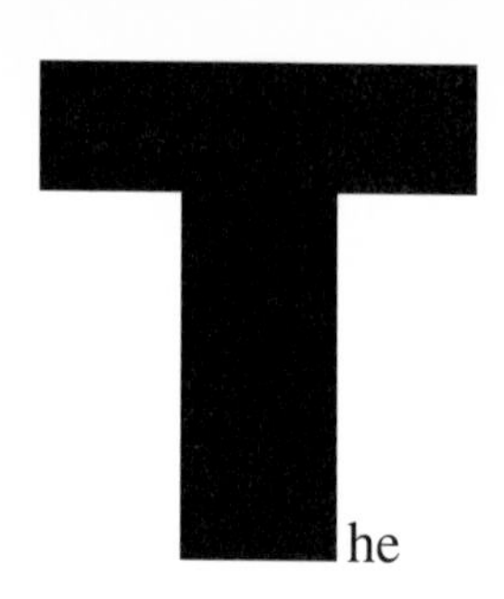

The Painter and his Surroundings

The Work of Roger Raveel

The painting *Double Portrait of Arnolfini and his Wife,* the masterpiece by the Flemish primitive Jan van Eyck (1390/1400-1441) in the National Gallery in London, contains in the background a mirror which reflects not only the space within the room and the two protagonists, but also several other silhouettes from outside the painting. It is as though Van Eyck wanted to use this as a way of involving all the space in front of the painting.

Centuries later we see mirrors appearing in the work of another Flemish artist, Roger Raveel (1921-). This time they are not painted mirrors but real ones, literally breaking through the flat surface and the illusion of the painting. It is no coincidence that Raveel is a great admirer of Van Eyck's merciless eye, the spatial structure of his paintings and the depth of his illuminating coloration. Raveel's contemporary painting is rooted in a tradition which begins with the Flemish Primitives.

Roger Raveel was born in Machelen-aan-de-Leie in 1921. During his childhood years he was often sick, so he frequently had to stay at home and could not attend school regularly. His special gift for drawing led him to decide quite early to become an artist. He first saw works by Flemish expressionists at the age of 13 in a doctor's waiting room in Ghent, and also in the gallery *Ars* where he paid a quick visit after visiting a doctor with his mother. This gave him a shock. At that time he was a student at the academy of Deinze, where his work had to conform to academic criteria. However, at home he began to paint in a rather expressionistic way.

From 1941 to 1945 he studied at the Royal Academy of Fine Arts in Ghent. After this period of study he stubbornly remained in the village where he was born. It was in Machelen that he was closest to himself, both literally and figuratively. He wanted to create a headstrong and self-willed artistic language, free of any aesthetic or academic prejudice. In an interview Raveel recounted: 'I observed a man in front of a wall. The man's torso made a very tangible shape, and so did the wall, because of the interplay of its lines – it was a concrete wall. I therefore went for the extreme contrasts, and drew the wall using lines. I painted the man's torso from pale to dark, including the necessary curves, but the face was far less noticeable as a fea-

Roger Raveel, *The Yellow Man.* 1952. Canvas, 105 x 75 cm. Collection of the artist (Photo by Heirman Graphics).

Roger Raveel, *Stooping Man and Cat.* 1952. Hardboard, 122 x 90 cm. Private collection, Marke (Photo by Heirman Graphics).

ture than the rest, in fact least of all. This may have been partly because the man's cap threw a shadow over his face. In any case, the face was far less noticeable as a concrete object. I wanted to go to the extreme, so I had to use stipples. That was still not enough, because the stipples were still too concrete, they looked too much like hair for instance, they had to be larger. I made them larger and larger and finally they were rectangles painted in complementary colours. So geometrical elements and elementary colours were necessary to arrive at the correct relationship and avoid isolating the painting as an object.'

The Impressionists already knew that the distinctive features of things disappear in shadow or in excessively bright light. For them however this loss of identity did not create a tension between the object and its surroundings. For the Impressionists, the distinctive features of objects were subordinated to the coloristic atmosphere of the painting. Raveel worked in a very different way. Wherever shadows or excessively bright light obscured the features of a perceived object, plant or person, he sensed an abstraction and translated it into a geometric element, an empty space or a colour which was out of context in the painting. In this way his work developed a spatial effect which transcended the confines of the painting. In a painting from 1952 such as *The Yellow Man* we can see how an empty white space between two black lines runs from the top to the bottom edge of the canvas. The empty

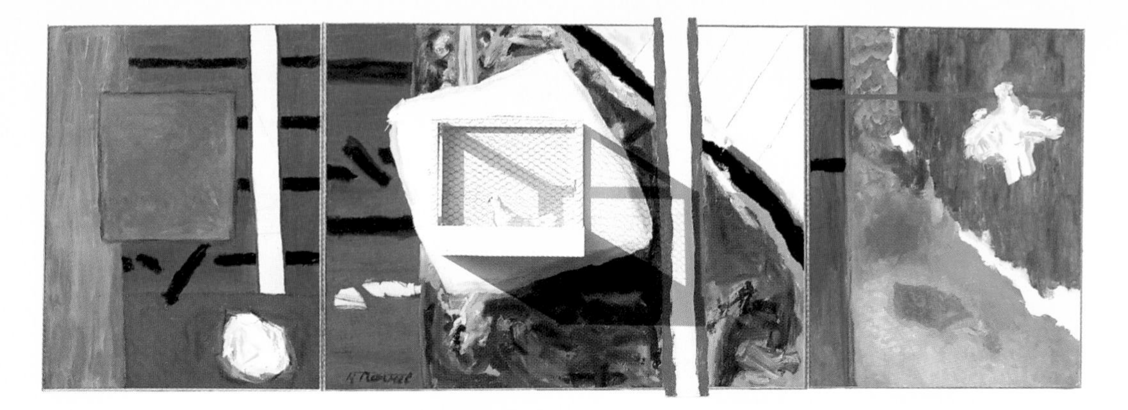

Roger Raveel, *Poultry-house with Live Pigeon.* 1962-63. Canvas, 150 x 440 cm. Private collection, Lovendegem (Photo by Heirman Graphics).

Roger Raveel, *Illusion Group.* 1965-67. Wood + mixed media, three objects (180 x 70 x 70 cm.) + (176 x 126 x 40 cm.) + (180 x 70 x 70 cm.). Museum voor Hedendaagse Kunst, Ghent (Photo by Heirman Graphics).

Roger Raveel, *The Creation of Woman.* 1990. Canvas, 61 x 50 cm. Private collection, Ghent (Photo by Heirman Graphics).

white space not only affects the space within the painting, but it also detaches itself from the representation to create a link with the edges and hence with its surroundings.

It is therefore not surprising that from 1961 Raveel did sometimes integrate mirrors into his work in places where he would previously have left white spaces. These took control of the environment in an unambiguous way. However not only the environment is involved in the paintings, but time as well. Sometimes he painted a prominent mark on the edge of the mirror, thereby creating a connection between mirror and painting and hence having an immediate pictorial effect on the reality reflected in the mirror. Raveel initiated a very explicit dialogue between art and reality.

However to assert that his work moves out into its surroundings only by means of the mirrors, would be to narrow his view of things. In fact the entire structure of the painting contributes to this, including the strongly coloured planes which can get out of hand, the abstract lines which cut off corners or edges of the composition, the geometric shapes.

Raveel not only wanted paintings to touch their surroundings, he also wanted them to be touched by reality and by their surroundings. He did not wait for Johns and Rauschenberg to use real objects before he began to do so in his paintings. In *Self-portrait with Cigarette* (1952) a slanting piece of aluminium frame is fixed across the canvas. This functions as an interfering element, and it is used consciously. If one makes an effort and ignores it, other interferences come into view, for example the slanted intersection, the pronounced black edging of the collar or the white spots formed by the cigarette or the small pot.

In the beginning of the 1950s, people didn't know what to do with Raveel's very obstinate and contrary view of things. At about that time the anti-aestheticism of CoBrA (a group of painters from *Co*penhagen, *Br*ussels and *A*msterdam), abstract expressionism, matière art and the *Ecole de Paris* were all in their heyday. One only has to look at works from 1952 such as *The Yellow Man, Supine Man* or *Stooping Man and Cat* to realise Raveel's very specific place in the art scene at the time. While the abstract expressionists were laying the emphasis on the lyrical touch and physical painting, Raveel chose an economical, rather thin coat of paint and seemed not to be afraid of constructivist elements. While the CoBrA painters were seeking refuge in authenticity and the spontaneity of children's drawings, graffiti and shapes which have come about naturally or by chance, Raveel was again departing from visible reality. He found the material for his paintings and drawings in his contemporary environment. Instead of masses of paint and emotionally painted abstract works, we see Raveel's paintings from this period depicting trivial objects and situations which have not yet been poeticised, such as a concrete wall, a bicycle cart, a pole or an anonymous vacant-looking man in a garden.

It was above all the way Raveel depicted these things which had such a bewildering and innovative effect: figurative elements were given an abstract or concrete meaning, reality juxtaposed with absence of reality, local colour set against colour as space. From 1960 he pushed these oppositions still further, thanks to the lessons learned from an abstract period (1956-60) which, paradoxical as it may sound, left him with a touch borrowed from nature.

The power of his art lies in the exceptionally varied way in which he attempts to give shape to the complexity of life. It is not possible to stick a straightforward label on his view of things. He cannot be catalogued. The variety and richness of his art come from his striving to juxtapose order and chaos, clarity and confusion in the most intrusive possible way. His work testifies to an elusive artistic freedom.

ROLAND JOORIS
Translated by Steve Judd.

Postmodernism

in the Literature of the Low Countries

The Dutch language area, like the rest of Europe, did not see the term postmodernism come into use until the early 1980s. The interest generated by this new 'concept of criticism' soon gave rise to a welter of publications, all more or less inspired by Jean-Francois Lyotard's philosophical essay, *The Postmodern Condition* (La condition postmoderne, 1979). The term itself may be relatively new, but the phenomenon it denotes is not: 'postmodern literature' is used retrospectively to include all the new writing – mainly prose – which emerged after the Second World War.

In the United States the term was already current in the 1960s, alongside others such as 'the new fiction' and 'sur-fiction'. But in Europe there were originally a variety of other definitions of the 'new' post-war prose. Umberto Eco, for example, introduced the term 'open' for literary works which are somehow in motion, producing a famous example himself in *The Name of the Rose.* Roland Barthes, like Eco no stranger to semiotics, worked with the concepts 'writerly text' and 'plural text', which he contrasted with the 'traditional' 'readerly text'. The open, plural or polyinterpretable text actively involves its readers so that they interpret creatively – they write – whereas the traditional text merely requires uncomplicated, passive consumption.

It is remarkable that the study of literature in the Low Countries also employed similar concepts to distinguish the new postwar literature from the traditional prewar literature. The innovative poetry of the 1950s was called 'experimental' poetry. Descriptions like 'experimental', 'innovative' and 'breaking new ground' were applied to the prose which developed in parallel with this new poetry. Other terms such as 'meta-literature', 'neo-avant-garde' are also found, together with the term 'other prose' (the title of an anthology compiled in 1978 by Sybren Polet), which is an effective, though slightly simplistic way of indicating a break with tradition.

The earlier terms 'open work' and 'polyinterpretable text' clearly show that postmodernist literary work was approached by critics from a semiotic point of view. The postmodernist novel is a literary form which is theoretically underpinned by semiotics, and according to which meaning is not embedded in the sign (i.e. the actual literary work), but is conferred by the creative activity of the reader, listener, looker, critic. The reader of the postmodernist text is actively involved in giving rise to its meaning. More than this even: meaning is in fact produced by the reader and not by the text. The reader is even called an 'accomplice'.

Another of the earlier terms, metafiction, stresses one of the most striking features of the postmodernist text – that of its *selfconsciousness* or *selfreflexivity:* the 'new' postwar novel is a self-preoccupied form of expression which comments on itself and, corresponding entirely to the (postmodern) philosophy of doubt, is given to self-relativity and self-irony. 'Undermining' is the word which deconstructionism, under the influence of Derrida and Foucault, uses to describe this. Reflections on the novel and on writing are built into the novel itself, breaking open and calling into question the very conventions of the form. Similar 'breaks' with convention can also be found in the modernist novel, but not until the postmodernist novel is the underlying doubt as to the adequacy of the narrative medium (and of language in general) foregrounded as an obsessive theme of self-doubt and self-irony with no way out.

The postmodernist novel has proved itself astonishingly resourceful at creating opportunities for this self-relativization and for the expression of uncertainty. In the Low Countries, the work of the Flemish writer Louis Paul Boon (1912-1979) provides an early example of such a radical renewal of form, first in 1947 with *My Little War* (Mijn kleine oorlog) and more importantly in the 1950's with the masterly diptych *Chapel Road* (De Kapellekensbaan, 1953), and its sequel *Summer at Ter-Muren* (Zomer te Ter-Muren, 1956). An advantage of using a term like postmodernism is that it can highlight how some products of a small national literature and of a minority language like Dutch can be situated unproblematically in an international context and even be seen to gain in significance as a result. In this way, it is possible to draw attention to Boon's unique position.

In his comparatist study *Text to Reader* (1983), Theo D'Haen shows that the kaleidoscopic form of Boon's work, his use of fragmentation and collage, is not an isolated phenomenon in the Western tradition. Boon employs techniques which he has borrowed from American (John Dos Passos) and French (Louis-Ferdinand Céline) examples and which are also comparable with the postmodernist experiments with form carried out by John Fowles (*The French Lieutenant's Woman,* 1969), John Barth (*Letters,* 1979) and Julio Cortázar (*Libro de Manuel,* 1973). However, this comparative study also demonstrates that Boon's work anticipates these experiments by many years and furthermore that Boon is one of the few writers who combine technical renewal with a politically and socially committed view of society.

There are other writers of Boon's generation; among them W.F. Hermans (1921-), whose achievements could also be given greater prominence in an international context if the developments and concepts of postmodernism were to be used to shed light on his work – not so much on the form this time, as on the central theme, the fundamental unfathomability of human beings. The same could also be said of Harry Mulisch (1927-). Unfortunately, the term postmodernism is still not usually used retrospectively in studies of authors with a long-established reputation. The only recent example is E. van Alphen's dissertation *So to Read* (Bij wijze van lezen, 1988), in which he discusses the novels of Willem Brakman (1922-)

Louis Paul Boon (1912-1979).

as postmodernist texts. Apart from this there are a few more or less systematic presentations of postmodernist authors writing in Dutch, but these surveys or analyses deal exclusively with authors and works from the Netherlands, leaving innovative work from the Dutch-speaking part of Belgium completely out of the picture. This is very hard to justify, particularly from an international perspective. The picture of postmodernist writing in Dutch-language literature is an extremely one-sided one if one loses sight of the facts that it was in Flanders that the phenomenon of avant-garde prose produced the more radical and consistent experimentation, and that Flanders embraced the new trend first. The fact that Flanders was more open to the influence of the French *nouveau roman* is of course not unconnected with this.

In the early 1960s there was something of an explosion of postmodernist experimentation with form in the literature of the Low Countries. The best known and most influential of the new writers were Sybren Polet (1924-) in Holland and Hugo Claus (1929-) and Ivo Michiels (1923-) in Flanders. In the Netherlands, the real breakthrough came with Harry Mulisch and Cees Nooteboom (1933-), followed by Jacq Firmin Vogelaar (1944-), Gerrit Krol (1934-) and Willem Brakman.

Sybren Polet (1924-).

It is quite possible, although no-one has yet done so, to see Sybren Polet as the postmodernist *par excellence*. He expounded his views on literature in a theoretical work entitled *Literature as Reality. But which one?* (Literatuur als werkelijkheid. Maar welke?, 1972), in which he examines the frontiers between literature and reality and the nature of literary reality. For him, literature is primarily a 'mental adventure', a mobile game with words in which there are no fixed rules. Literary reality is a mental experiment; it is only one possible projection of reality, one of many possible 'ontologies'. The characters in literature are merely 'open' models which are to be filled in and changed as one pleases. In Polet's early work, for example, there is a recurring template character called Lokien, an outline character who constantly takes on new forms, like a kind of 'Mr X' with a changing identity. Polet himself called them variable, transformational figures. In the novel *Breakwater* (Breekwater, 1961) Lokien, starting out on a career as a writer, meets Mr Godgiven whom he transforms into the central character of a novel and whose movements he notes down precisely, day by day. However, at the end of the 'first new week of creation' the narrator interrupts his story with the announcement that he is going to change the name of Mr Godgiven: Godgiven is 'a name which is full of connotations and evokes memories of a previous life'. He insists that his main character really exists 'after 10 pages of written life', but also thinks that as long as someone exists, the name under which he exists is of little significance and: 'Mr Godgiven and literature are different in this respect.' Godgiven's new name is Breakwater; he has the same occupation and the same body.

Such intrusions by the narrator, also known as 'frame-breaking', are a typical device in postmodernist fiction. Fowles's *The French Lieutenant's Woman* provides a well-known example, where the narrator inserts a long digression on the fact that the story he is telling is his own invention: it is 'all imagination'. Not only does this break through the convention of realism in the novel, but the authority of the central, omniscient narrator is also undermined. This breaking through the boundaries between literature and reality and the undermining of central authority, together with the problematization of the difference between high and trivial literature and between the genres themselves, are at the same time, literary expressions of the general tendency to democratization in the 1960s and 70s.

A year after Polet's *Breakwater, Wonderment* (De Verwondering) by Hugo Claus appeared. It is an extremely complex novel, full of literary and cultural references. Claus himself called it an allegory and worked into it emphatic references to Dante's *Divine Comedy,* Carroll's *Alice in Wonderland,* Eichendorff's *From the Life of a Good-for-nothing* (Aus dem Leben eines Taugenichts), Robbe-Grillet's *Last Year at Marienbad* (L'année dernière à Marienbad) and many others. Meanwhile, semiotics introduced the term *intertextuality* for this typically postmodernist procedure of references and reworkings. There is, however, much more to Claus' novel than the 'mannerist contemplation of the cultural tradition', as it was described by one critic. The story itself, that of a mentally ill teacher, is told in four narrative layers and gives the impression, through its ironic and relativistic multiplication of narrative viewpoints, that there is no fixed perspective and that there can be no solution in the quest for the truth of the novel. In this novel, Claus, like so many other postmodernist authors, has in his own way demonstrated the lack of a unified vision. The postmodern attitude to life which underlies this novel is dominated by the assumption that the truth does not exist, that the world is a figment of our minds and that everything is pure imagination.

In the 1970s a new group of authors centred around the literary journal *De Revisor,* which was set up in 1974, were using typically postmodern forms and themes. Their writing has been characterized as 'academic prose' because they place so much emphasis on the structural, technical, formal aspects of writing and appear to have at their disposal all the postmodernist tricks of narrative syntax. The main prose writers of the group – Dirk Ayelt Kooiman (1946-), Frans Kellendonk (1951-1990), Nicolaas Matsier (1945-), Doeschka Meijsing (1947-) and Patrizio Canaponi, the latter a pseudonym of A.F.Th. van der Heijden (1951-), who has come to the fore recently with his series of novels *Toothless Time* (De tandeloze tijd) – also fit easily into the postmodern tradition as far as the content of their writing is concerned. Using complex linking of motifs, mirroring and doubling, they develop doubt, insecurity and uncertainty into themes. In the work of Leon de

Ivo Michiels (1923-) (Photo by Paul van den Abeele).

Louis Ferron (1942-) (Photo by Jan van der Weerd).

Winter (1954-), an author who does not belong to the *Revisor* group, but who certainly has affinities with it, the attempt to get a grasp on reality always ends in disillusionment, and the story, the narrative, is seen as a tentative reconstruction of a past which remains constantly uncertain.

A much more drastic 'solution' is that of the removal of the constraints imposed by time proposed by Louis Ferron (1942-) in his novels. Ferron writes what is known in the subject literature as 'historiographic metafiction'. In his texts, which usually evoke a phase of German or Austrian history, an amalgam of various fictional realities and historical realities is produced and the line between imagination and reality, between narrative and history, is completely erased. The novel *Turkish Vespers* (Turkenvespers, 1977), for example, is situated in the Vienna of the turn of the century, but in the main character Kaspar Hauser's world of experience, other historical points in time are also experienced as real: both the Turkish siege of Vienna at the end of the seventeenth century and the totalitarianism of the Third Reich spill over into the main story in one 'anachronistic collage'. 'If there is no such thing as a history which is fixed and certain', the writer said in an interview, 'then I reserve the right to "falsify" historical reality in my own way in my novels.' Not only has Ferron mixed together various historical realities in this novel: it has also been shown that he entered into a literary dialogue with Robert Musil's *The Man without Qualities* (Der Mann ohne Eigenschaften).

There is one more facet of the postmodernist world view which has left interesting traces in the literature of the Low Countries, in particular of Flanders. As a consequence of the view that literature only presents us with 'ontologies', i.e. theoretically possible descriptions of (parts of) the universe, possible worlds without any pretence that they are the world (for we cannot know the world anyway), some authors have increasingly come to emphasize the non-referential, linguistic aspect of the novel. For them the novel is an autonomous world, a world in words, an abstract opus which refers only to itself and which emphatically presents itself as a complete alternative to the world.

Experiments with this form of 'absolute' or 'abstract' prose are found mainly in the French *nouveau roman* (Alain Robbe-Grillet, Michel Butor, Nathalie Sarraute, Claude Simon). It is with this tradition that Ivo Michiels, Willy Roggeman (1934-) and Claude van de Berge (1945-) have become associated. Michiels's 'alpha cycle' has undoubtedly been responsible for pushing back the frontiers in the history of prose writing in the Low Countries. In the successive parts of the cycle – *Book Alpha* (Het Boek Alfa, 1963), *Orchis Militaris* (1968), *Exit* (1971), *Dixi(t)* (1979) and the volume *Samuel, o Samuel* (1973), intended as a tribute to Samuel Beckett, which interrupted the series, the experiment was pursued relentlessly to its conclusion.

Although *Book Alpha* was originally seen by the critics as a chaotic, uninterrupted stream of consciousness, it is now clear that the fragments of the book can be read as parts of an 'open' or plural text, a construction based on snatches of 'now-moments' which are simultaneously present, constructed around an uncertain initial situation. There is no logical temporal or causal coherence, no starting or ending point, nor a rounded or fleshed out character. In 1983 Michiels published the first part of a new ten-volume series under the overall title of *Journal brut.* The five volumes which have appeared so far build on the achievements of the alpha cycle, to which they often refer back literally through quotation. Here the text has become, in accordance with the postmodernist and deconstructionist principle, self-perpetuating 'productivity'. The *Journal brut* series is indeed one of the most impressive projects produced by postmodernism in the literature of the Low Countries.

ANNE MARIE MUSSCHOOT
Translated by Jane Fenoulhet.

REFERENCES

FOKKEMA, D.W. & BERTENS, HANS (ed.), *Approaching Postmodernism,* Amsterdam / Philadelphia, 1986.

BERTENS, HANS & D'HAEN, THEO, *Het postmodernisme in de literatuur* (Postmodernism in Literature), Amsterdam, 1988.

MERTENS, ANTHONY, 'Postmodern Elements in Postwar Dutch Fiction', in: *Postmodern Fiction in Europe and the Americas* (ed. Theo D'Haen & Hans Bertens), Amsterdam / Antwerp, 1988.

IBSCH, ELRUD, 'Postmoderne (on)mogelijkheden in de Nederlandstalige literatuur' ('Postmodern (Im)possibilities in Dutch-language Literature'), in: *De achtervolging voortgezet* (The Pursuit Continued), (ed. W.T.G. Breekveldt a.o.) Amsterdam, 1989.

MUSSCHOOT, ANNE MARIE, 'The Challenge of Postmodernism', *Dutch Crossing,* 41, Summer 1990, pp. 3-15.

LIST OF TRANSLATIONS

LOUIS PAUL BOON:
Chapel Road (Tr. Adrienne Dixon). New York, 1972.
Minuet (Tr. Adrienne Dixon). New York, 1979.

HUGO CLAUS:
The Sorrow of Belgium (Tr. Arnold Pomerans). New York / London, 1990; Harmondsworth, 1991.

W.F. HERMANS:
The Dark Room of Damocles (Tr. Roy Edwards). London, 1962.
'W.F. Hermans: An English Sampler' (Tr. Paul Vincent). *Dutch Crossing, 16,* March 1982, pp. 19-53.

DIRK AYELT KOOIMAN:
A Lamb to the Slaughter (Tr. Adrienne Dixon). New York, 1986.

GERRIT KROL:
'In the Service of Shell Oil' (Tr. Elizabeth Daverman). *Dimension,* 1978, pp. 94-105.
'A Stranger in Hogezand-Sappemeer' (Tr. Greta Kilburn). *Contemporary Literature in Translation,* 32, 1981, pp. 42-45.

IVO MICHIELS:
Book Alpha and Orchis Militaris (Tr. Adrienne Dixon). Boston (Mass.), 1979.

HARRY MULISCH:
The Assault (Tr. Claire Nicolas White). London / New York 1985; Harmondsworth, 1986.

CEES NOOTEBOOM:
In the Dutch Mountains (Tr. Adrienne Dixon). London / Baton Rouge, 1987.

LEON DE WINTER:
The Day before Yesterday (Tr. Scott Rollins). New York, 1985.

'I do not know how I shall turn out, ...'

The Development of the Work of Mondrian, from Naturalism to Victory Boogie-Woogie

Photographs of the last studio used by Piet Mondrian (1872-1944) show a large lozenge-shaped canvas standing in the corner. This painting is entitled *Victory Boogie-Woogie,* and is built up of planes of colour which dance across the surface of the painting. Mondrian worked on the painting until a few days before his death on 1 February 1944. It shows some similarities with *Broadway Boogie-Woogie,* which was completed in 1943.

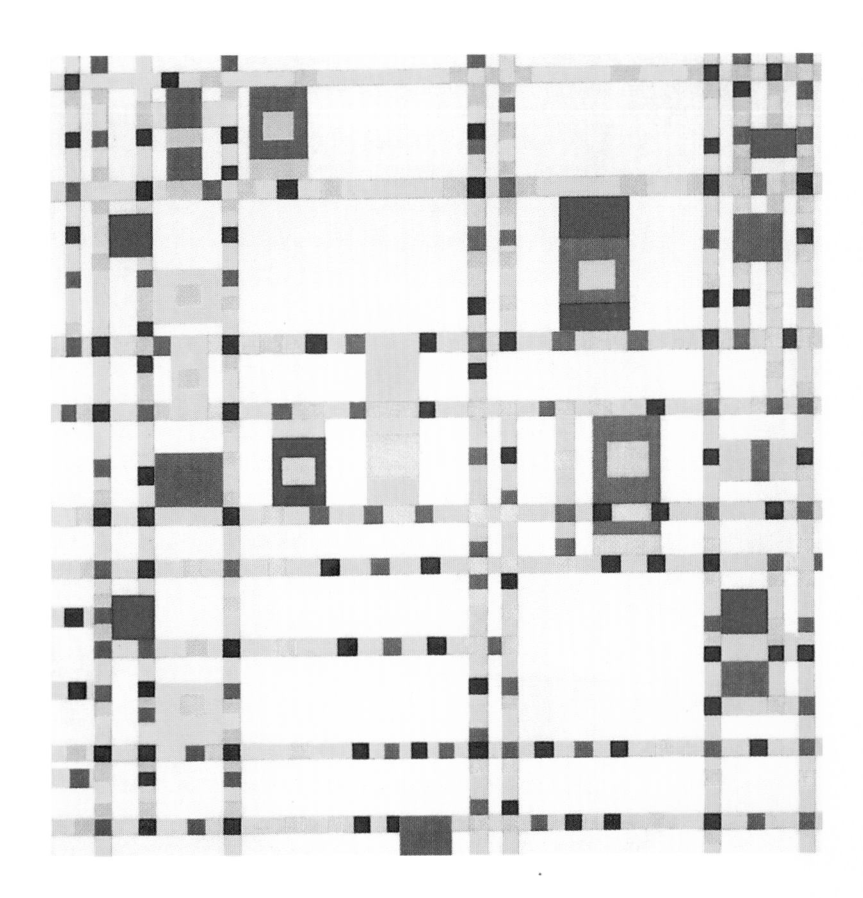

Piet Mondrian, *Broadway Boogie-Woogie*. 1942-43. Canvas, 127 x 127 cm. The Museum of Modern Art, New York.

Broadway Boogie-Woogie is composed of horizontal and vertical lines, with red, blue, yellow and grey blocks of various sizes arranged along them. The horizontal and vertical lines are distributed over the picture in an irregular pattern. The lines are closer together at the left and right edges of the painting, and here and there the rectangular areas between the lines are painted in the same colours as the rest of the painting. Due to the succession of blocks of strongly contrasting colour, the eye does not come to rest at any point, but jumps along the lines across the painting. This evokes a feeling of rhythm and speed. Mondrian was living in New York when he worked on *Broadway Boogie-Woogie,* having fled from Europe as war threatened in 1940. He had already left Paris in 1938, after living in the city since 1919, but stayed in London for another two years before moving to New York.

The New York period saw the beginning of a new phase in Mondrian's work. Since 1919 he had been composing his paintings with horizontal and vertical lines and red, yellow and / or blue colour planes. However during the New York period the black lines gave way to coloured ones, and in *Victory Boogie-Woogie* and *Broadway Boogie-Woogie,* as described above, the lines were made up of coloured blocks placed side by side. The titles of both paintings refer to the Boogie-Woogie music which Mondrian – who was a great Jazz enthusiast – was hearing in New York clubs and on gramophone records. The fast, pulsating rhythm of this music bears some similarities to the rapid succession of coloured blocks in the *Boogie-Woogie* paintings.

In 1943 Mondrian mentioned the analogy between his work and Boogie-Woogie music in a letter to the American art historian James Johnson Sweeney: 'True Boogie-Woogie I conceive as homogeneous in intention with mine in painting: destruction of melody which is the equivalent of destruction of natural appearance, and the construction through the continuous opposition of pure means-dynamic rhythm.
I think the destructive element is too much neglected in art.'

At first sight this is quite a cryptic comment, with Mondrian saying that the destructive element plays an important part in his work. As his oeuvre developed, the part played by the destructive principle became clear.

This artist, who was born in 1872 in a small provincial town in the Netherlands, came from beginnings which were far from spectacular. Pieter Cornelis Mondrian trained as an art teacher, and in 1892 he registered at the National Academy of Visual Arts in Amsterdam.

Although he became proficient at various genres, such as still life and life studies, Mondrian was mainly a landscape painter. His painting technique followed the work of the Amsterdam painter George Hendrik Breitner and the tradition of the Hague School. Around 1870, painters such as Willem Maris and Anton Mauve had shocked the Dutch art world with representations of the Dutch polder landscape painted with unusually broad brushstrokes for the time. Their intention was not particularly to give an accurate representation of their subjects, but rather to capture the atmosphere and the light. Mondrian further developed the atmospheric compositions which his predecessors had created with their broad brushstrokes, and also began to show some interest in the structure of the landscape.

A good example of this is the painting *Summer Night* from 1906-07. This painting shows a Dutch landscape by moonlight. In the foreground we see a

Piet Mondrian, *Summer Night.* 1906-07. Canvas, 71 x 110 cm. Gemeentemuseum, The Hague.

piece of land at the water's edge. The water reflects the silver-grey light of the moon, which is at the top of the painting on the right. The lefthand half of the painting, behind the water, is taken up by trees and a farm painted in just a few brushstrokes. All this is set against a dark grey sky.

In 1909, the Dutch writer / psychiatrist Frederick van Eeden wrote in the journal *Op de hoogte* (Well-informed) about Mondrian's early work: 'There are some truly splendid designs in his earlier period. His vision of nature is majestic and noble. His colours are sometimes magnificent.' This article was written after an exhibition at the Stedelijk Museum in Amsterdam, where Mondrian exhibited work alongside the painters Jan Sluyters and Cornelis Spoor. Mondrian had also sent in some recent work for this exhibition. Van Eeden mentioned this also: 'I have never seen such obviously classic cases of acute decadence before. These are what the medical people call "typical pathological pictures".' A few paragraphs later Van Eeden speaks of '... a dreadful orgy of the coarsest, brightest and most barbaric colours he (Mondrian) could scrape together'.

Mondrian's atmospheric naturalistic landscapes had given way to paintings in bright colours. One of the most noticeable paintings at the exhibition was *Mill in Sunlight* from 1908. This painting depicts a windmill as a prominent feature. The canvas is painted in strokes of bright red, yellow and blue colour, which reproduce the sensation of a windmill in the sunshine.

The rapid change of direction in Mondrian's work no doubt had something to do with the fact that in about 1908 he was developing closer links with contemporary avant-garde artists in the Netherlands.

First of all he came into contact with Jan Sluyters again, who had returned from Paris in 1907. In the French capital Sluyters had seen the latest developments in the field of painting, where colour was playing a prominent role.

Piet Mondrian, *Composition No. 3 (Trees).* 1913. Canvas, 95 x 80 cm. Gemeentemuseum, The Hague.

Piet Mondrian, *Mill in Sunlight.* 1908. Canvas, 114 x 87 cm. Gemeentemuseum, The Hague.

Works by Gauguin, Van Gogh and Toulouse-Lautrec inspired Sluyters to produce colourful, expressive paintings.

Another important acquaintance for Mondrian was Jan Toorop, the doyen of the moderns of that time in the Netherlands. Toorop was well-informed about recent developments in France, and was experimenting with the divisionistic technique, placing powerful strokes of paint of various colours side by side. In *Mill in Sunlight* we see Mondrian using this technique. However it is noticeable that Mondrian went much further in his approach than Toorop had done. The strokes and the use of colour are much more powerful, and the subjects seem to lose themselves in a jumble of brush-strokes.

Mondrian's rather sudden change of direction was not just an experiment; it was a serious matter, as is shown in a letter sent by Mondrian in response to a report on the exhibition by the critic Israël Querido. Mondrian wrote the following: 'I consider that the great masters of former times were very great and their works very beautiful, but in my case you will find that at the present time everything has to be represented in a very different way; even using a different technique. For the present I consider it necessary for the paints to be placed alongside each other as purely as possible, in a stippled or diffuse way. I know this is putting it strongly, but this fits in with the idea behind the principle of representation as I see it.'

According to this letter, Mondrian thought the time was ripe for different means of expression, stating that he was not only concerned with form, but that he wanted to give his works a deeper meaning. In the same letter he also wrote: 'I believe that you are also aware of the close connection between philosophy and art, which is precisely what most painters deny ...'. Mondrian did recognise that connection, and he tried to give his works a more spiritual content. He was not entirely clear on how to do this. He wrote: 'I do not know how I shall turn out, ...' and later in the same letter: 'For the time being, however, I want my work to stay within the normal domain of the senses, because that is where we still live. But art can form a bridge to finer regions: perhaps I am wrong to call them spiritual realms, since everything which still has form is not yet spiritual, so I have read ... But it is still the ascending path, away from the material.'

The idea of a path from material to spiritual realms links in with Mondrian's interest in the doctrine of theosophy. In 1909 Mondrian became a member of the Theosophical Association and remained a member until his death. With a single exception, Mondrian did not use picture-language to point directly towards the teachings of theosophy. However, the idea held by theosophy of an evolution towards a higher, harmonious world is important in Mondrian's work and thought. In his study entitled *Mondrian, Theosophy and Rudolf Steiner* (Mondriaan, theosofie en Rudolf Steiner, 1987), Professor Carel Blotkamp argues that evolution is associated with the concept of destruction, in the sense that destruction of the old forms is a precondition for evolution towards a higher world. The destruction of old forms did have a part to play in Mondrian's work. By destroying the forms as they are perceived in visible reality, it should be possible to create a more spiritual world.

In 1909 and the following year, Mondrian turned his attention mainly towards colour, attempting to elevate objects to a higher plane by using colour in an unrealistic way. He left the shapes themselves more or less intact. During this period Mondrian painted a lot of lighthouses and church towers, seen from a point low down and virtually right up against the surface of the painting, so that they seem to rise up before the viewer.

In 1910, Mondrian was involved in the foundation of a new artists' association called *De Moderne Kunstkring* (The Modern Art Circle), which aimed to exhibit work by contemporary Dutch and foreign artists.

At the first exhibition given by *De Moderne Kunstkring* cubist works by Le Fauconnier, Picasso and Braque were exhibited. These had an enormous influence on Mondrian, as he said himself. Cubism, where objects were dismembered into basic geometric shapes, offered him the opportunity to become free of the 'natural shapes of things'. First of all Mondrian reduced his subjects to geometric shapes in such a way that the original point of departure was still recognisable. In 1912 Mondrian moved to Paris, the cradle of cubism, where he became better acquainted with the work of Picasso and Braque. The cubist works which Mondrian produced in Paris give an impression of intricacy; the subjects have been thoroughly abstracted and disappear into a pattern of planes and lines. In the painting *Composition No. 3 (Trees)* from 1913, the trees are no longer recognisable as such. The painting is built up from geometric shapes in brown, ochre-coloured and grey shapes, partly bounded by dark contour lines. However, Mondrian went further still. In *Composition No. 3 (Trees)* there are still some lines with jagged or curved shapes. In later paintings these have disappeared, and the horizontal and vertical lines form a pattern consisting of mainly rectangular shapes. Between 1914 and 1917 these rectangles were broken open, and the black lines came to form a pattern of intersecting horizontal and vertical black lines.

Although Mondrian's paintings were still based on visible reality, his work had left the 'normal domain of the senses' which he mentioned to Israël Querido in 1909. In a letter written in 1914 to the art teacher H.P. Bremmer, Mondrian was able to be much more specific about what he was doing. He wrote: 'For I construct lines and combinations of colours on a flat surface in order to represent universal beauty as consciously as possible. Nature (or what I see) inspires me, it moves me just as much as any painter and puts that urge in me to make something, but I want to come as close to the truth as possible, and therefore I want to abstract everything until I reach the foundation (still an external foundation!) of things. I consider it a true statement that by not wishing to say anything specific one says the most specific thing of all – the (universal) truth.'

In his striving towards a higher reality, Mondrian was attempting to achieve a universal harmony. According to him, this harmony which was universal or always true could not be expressed by representing 'something specific' or a visible reality, because beauty does not depend on coincidental, external or individual characteristics as in the 'natural manifestation of things'. Mondrian attempted to express this harmony by juxtaposing basic abstract shapes and bringing them into equilibrium with each other. He thus avoided subjects taken from visible reality, which have individual, external and coincidental characteristics, and also avoided associated phenomena such as volume, space and perspective.

In the meantime, Mondrian had been forced to settle in the Netherlands again, because due to the outbreak of World War I he was not able to return to Paris after a visit to his father. In the Netherlands he came into contact with 'like-minded' artists such as Theo van Doesburg, who founded the journal *De Stijl.* At van Doesburg's invitation Mondrian became involved in planning and setting up the journal in 1917, and wrote articles expounding his views about art.

Bart van der Leck, whom Mondrian had met in 1916, was also involved in *De Stijl.* At that time Van der Leck was painting strictly stylised shapes in equal areas of colour against a white background. Van der Leck's work inspired Mondrian to place rectangular shapes against a white background. This can be seen in *Composition with Colour Planes No. 3* (1917). In this painting red, light blue and yellow rectangles are set against a light background. The painting is composed entirely of abstract shapes, and no longer has any source in visible reality. However, one problem is that the coloured planes seem to hover above the background, thus giving a feeling of space which Mondrian did not want. Mondrian found a solution to this problem by anchoring the planes, so to speak, in a regular grid pattern.

In the letter to James Johnson Sweeney mentioned above, Mondrian looked back over these developments and described them as follows: 'This

Piet Mondrian,
Composition with Colour Planes No. 3. 1917.
Canvas, 48 x 61 cm.
Gemeentemuseum,
The Hague.

attitude of the Cubists to the representations of volume in space was contrary to my conception of abstraction, which is based on the belief that this very space *has to be destroyed.* As a consequence I came to the destruction of volume by the use of the plane. This I accomplished by means of lines cutting the planes. But still the plane remained too intact. So I came to making only lines and brought the colour within the lines. Now the problem was to destroy these lines also through mutual oppositions.'

Mondrian succeeded in destroying the lines as well. In 1920 the regular grid pattern gave way to carefully placed horizontal and vertical black lines and different-sized areas of primary colours and shades of white.

Composition with Red, Yellow and Blue is an example of the work which Mondrian was producing around 1920, and which he gradually perfected in the years which followed. In this painting, horizontal and vertical black lines form a large square approximately in the centre, which is a very light grey in colour. Around the square there are narrow rectangular areas of varying sizes in white, black, yellow, red and blue. The horizontals and verticals and the coloured planes hold each other in balance. Any reference to time, space, form or volume has gone. What remains is a clear manifestation of universal relationships.

During the course of the 1920s, Mondrian reduced the size of the coloured

Piet Mondrian, *Composition with Red, Yellow and Blue.* 1922. Canvas, 42 x 50 cm. Stedelijk Museum, Amsterdam.

planes or transected them by lines. In the 1930s the lines were doubled, and during the New York period they became coloured.

In *Broadway Boogie-Woogie* and *Victory Boogie-Woogie* Mondrian added a new and quite significant dimension to his work. The prominence of the lines was broken by using small successive blocks. In both these stimulating paintings, not only is the 'natural manifestation of things' destroyed and a new harmony established through the subtle balance between opposites, but also the static character of the paintings from the 1920s has given way to a dynamic equilibrium.

SASKIA BAK
Translated by Steve Judd.

Church and Ideology in the Netherlands

Religious pluralism

Three factors have made the Netherlands receptive to influences from outside: the absence of a strong Dutch national consciousness, limited surface area and a peripheral geographical position. Culture and the pattern of religious values are also susceptible to these influences. Since the Reformation, Luther and Calvin have gained ground, according to the principle *'cuius regio eius religio'* (the people of a country or region must adopt the religion of their leader). This gave rise to a religious and ideological pluralism, which still exists today.

The religious boundary cuts straight across the Netherlands. The south is largely Roman Catholic and the extreme north-east, Friesland, Groningen and Drenthe (one quarter of the area of the Netherlands), is predominantly Protestant. Until the beginning of the Second World War religious values and norms were dominant. Religion was, from the point of view of the state, so important that each ten-yearly census between 1809 and 1971 contained the question: 'To which denomination do you belong?' If the answer was 'None' the respondent was 'non-denominational'. This is a statistical term distinct from 'unbelieving' or 'non-churchgoing' which would mean, in general, that the respondent did not attend church services.

In the nineteenth century the Netherlands was a 'Christian nation'. In 1909, 5% of Dutch people described themselves as 'non-denominational', 35% were Catholic, 42.2% Dutch Reformed (the original established church) and 9.4% Orthodox Calvinist (a movement which broke away from the established church), and other denominations 6.5%. In 1988 the Central Statistics Bureau *(CBS; Centraal Bureau voor de Statistiek)* produced the following overview from a sample survey: 32% non-denominational; 36% Catholic; 19% Dutch Reformed; 8% Orthodox Calvinist, and other groups and denominations taken together, 6%.

Pillarization

'Pillarization' or 'vertical pluralism' (*verzuiling* in Dutch) is a typically Dutch phenomenon; it has been a feature of the Netherlands since the end of the nineteenth century, when Protestant and Catholic fellow-believers began to organize themselves into groups. These organizations were to be found in political parties, in schools and universities, in hospitals, in homes for the elderly, in the mass media, and even in the trade unions, and led to the development of powerful social networks.

The Socialists, who originally represented the working class, also contributed in part to this 'pillarization'. The liberals, who were predominantly free-thinking humanists, did not. Only the Protestants and Catholics formed true 'pillars', since a pillar comprised all social classes, held together by a single ideology. The Socialists also had an integrating ideology, but this was not based on religion. Pillarization brought a certain degree of immunity from fascist rule during the Second World War, when the Netherlands was occupied by Germany. The pillar system also gave rise to a broad political truce, as the leaders worked together to reach agreement. After the Second World War, the Socialists attempted to change the system. They founded a new political party, the *Partij van de Arbeid* (*PvdA*; Labour Party), which encompassed Protestant, Catholic and humanist working groups. The attempt failed. In 1980 however, the *Christen Demokratisch Appel* (*CDA*; Christian Democratic Appeal) was formed – a fusion of the larger Protestant political parties and the Catholic party. At the time of writing, the Netherlands is governed by a coalition of the *CDA* and the *PvdA*, under the leadership of Catholic prime minister Ruud Lubbers.

Recent opinion polls reveal that only one fifth of the Dutch population, and only one third of all members of religious denominations, is in favour of political pillarization. Pillarization still exists in radio and television although this system, as 'an expression of religious movements' is increasingly under threat from commercialism. Pillarization is still deeply rooted in healthcare, education and farmers' organizations. A Christian trade union, the *Christelijk Nationaal Vakverbond* (*CNV*; National Christian Trade Union) still exists alongside a general trade union, the *Federatie Nederlandse Vakbeweging* (*FNV*; Federation of Dutch Trade Unions), which came into being through a fusion of Catholic and Socialist trade unions.

The position of the so-called fourth 'denomination' in the Netherlands, Islam, is a current issue. Islam and other non-Christian religions sometimes attempt to join the pillarization system in order to further their social and political emancipation. When, some time ago, a Hindustani became a member of parliament for the *CDA*, a public discussion ensued on the issue of whether the *CDA* was still a 'Christian' party. The prime minister, in a speech on 18 January 1992, declared that the non-Christian minorities 'in a manner of speaking, are breaking into the Dutch culture of potato-eaters and coffee-drinkers, so that they may feel themselves to be truly Dutch, and our culture becomes more variegated'.

In contrast to the situation in Great Britain, the Queen of the Netherlands has no authority within any of the denominations. However, just as in Great Britain, the function of the royal family, with Queen Beatrix at its head, is to set an example to the nation. The family is Protestant-oriented, although two of the Queen's sisters have joined the Catholic church. In her Christmas message at the end of 1991, Queen Beatrix spoke about religion and art. She pointed out the importance of spiritual values for Dutch society, which is increasingly influenced by money and economic problems, and seemed to be falling prey to 'commercialization', which even a Christian festival such as Christmas could not escape.

The influence of religion and ideology

In the past peoples' lives were greatly influenced by religion, and although that influence has decreased considerably, experts by no means underestimate its importance today. Religion does not exist in isolation, and therefore cannot be studied in isolation. Religion, denomination and ideology are interlinked. Those who hold a certain religious belief and may or may not be members of a denomination, also vote for a certain political party, receive an education, are unfit for work, or contribute through their occupation to the production process.

It makes a great difference to a church whether its pastors and priests are growing old, or whether they appeal to a younger generation; whether the bourgeois middle class predominates; whether most of its members come from the large towns or the country – which is rarely the case in the urbanized Netherlands of today. Churches, too, are concerned with political problems. Church leaders therefore hold regular discussions with politicians from all parties. Churches are concerned about chronic poverty and social unrest; they seek national and international peace, they speak out against injustice and for those seeking asylum, and further the pursuit of fulfilment in life.

It is said that churches should concern themselves with all these issues, without becoming enmeshed in them; thus religion – and by implication churches – can remain a creative force for our cultural consciousness. Some believers become more detached when a church gives in to a sort of morphological fundamentalism. Churches do, after all, tend to cling to established structures for too long. It is for the sake of creativity and flexibility that these 'detached' believers adopt a very critical attitude. Does a church decline because it refuses to move with the times, or because it *does* move with the times?

Because the Church can only work within a socio-cultural context, it must constantly make people aware of this context, maybe use its own criteria to prize it open and reveal something of the so-called third dimension, which relates to the 'spiritual values' referred to above. The particular way in which a Church functions – in this case the Christian church – prescribes that it is never completely absorbed by its context but, through Christian belief, continues to stand for something special and universal, something different: the story of Jesus in which we can read who 'God' really is, as Van Peursen writes in his essay 'The Future of Church and Religion in the Netherlands' *('Toekomst van kerk en godsdienst in Nederland')*.

Religious Dutchmen and women are more attached to national traditions than their non-believing compatriots, who are mostly from the large towns. They are also more devoted to law and order and to peace. The Lutheran theologian Heinrich Benthem (1661-1723) reported, after returning to Germany, that Dutch churches were dirty, that there was much religious freedom, that there were brothels in Amsterdam for sailors, that children were much too liberally brought up, and that there was a lack of good manners. There was, he claimed, a general lack of orderly discipline and authority. The bourgeois authorities saw to it that the quibblers, the radicals, were not given too many opportunities. Mutual religious stereotypes were preserved through sermons, catechism and regular provocations. This was the situation with religion and the Church in the past, and it is broadly the same today.

The historical heritage

The best description of the relationship between religion, ideology, church and the past has been written by Ernst Zahn, a sociologist born in Czechoslovakia. He originally wrote a view of the Netherlands and the Dutch for German readers, and a Dutch translation of this was published in 1989 under the title *Regenten, rebellen en reformatoren* (Regents, rebels and reformers). In this broad study he considers Dutch society against its historical background. The fact that non-conformism in the Netherlands is not only tolerated but also respected is a consequence of historical developments. There have been many changes in the Dutch spiritual landscape, but there is also much continuity.

It is often argued that bearing witness, the profession of faith, is a national characteristic. In this respect all Dutchmen are 'protestants' – a word derived from the Latin *protestari,* which means to testify in public before a court. In the Netherlands there were, and there are, also 'testifying' socialists and agnostics. In the Netherlands problems such as, for example, the 1992 minorities question, are discussed or debated nationally. Zahn summarizes this mentality as follows: 'In the Netherlands the critical spirit, protest – the spirit of the left if you will – which, in a free democratic society, should be the guardian and not the enemy of the political and social order, has a religious, national and humanist tradition.'

Religion was no opium here, but an inspirational force. 'Even in a period of secularization, latent religious attitudes in the Netherlands continued to be characteristic of the culture and habits of the Dutch. Religion remained a public matter, never a private matter for the individual which did not concern others.'

Anyone landing in daylight at Schiphol airport will see below them the Dutch countryside, divided into countless tiny parcels of land; geometric, Mondrian-like, with a cloud of smoke here and there. *'Da unten am Rhein'* Karl Barth once said, *'das ist eine Ecke wo es qualmt'* ('It's a smouldering corner, down there on the Rhine'). In his essay from 1973, 'A Country of Church Spires' *('Een land vol kerktorens'),* the ecclesiastical historian Jan van Laarhoven gave a stirring commentary on this: 'Indeed, in that estuary of broad, slow rivers the lowland mist mingles with the smoke from the many, many small houses where the Lord is called upon, and the theological gunsmoke which blows in from elsewhere lingers in the air for much longer and forms a gloomy drizzle, which makes the soil fertile enough for a diverse denominational crop. Nowhere are there so many theologians – who know the truth – than in this land of churches and conventicles, of quiet pieties and pent-up debaters; this land of practical tolerance and impractical pedantry. The historian attempting to describe the ecclesiastical history of this country loses count of all the spires, he stumbles over the profusion of rood screens and pays the toll at all those denominational lift-bridges because in this country even God's water is canalized and His fields divided into minute parcels.' As far as religion and denomination are concerned, the Netherlands is a 'counting' nation: nowhere in the world are religious statistics so highly developed and refined. A recent publication recorded a total of no less than 1,100 denominations and groups.

There are state universities in Leiden, Amsterdam, Groningen, Rotterdam, Utrecht, Enschede and Maastricht. The universities in Tilburg and Nijmegen are denominational; both are Catholic. Amsterdam, in addition to its original municipal university, also has the Free / Reformed University *(Vrije Universiteit).* All these institutions are financed by the government. For several years now there has also been a humanist, or so-called 'secular' university in Utrecht, which teaches 'humanist studies'. This institution is also subsidized by the government.

Social research

The trend towards examining this spiritual pattern in its entirety, using sociological research methods, began to take shape after the Second World War, when almost every 'denomination' came to have its own research institute.

Johannes Petrus Kruijt, a teacher from a working-class Zaandam family, and himself non-denominational, studied geography and then went on to research non-denominationalism on the basis of census statistics. In 1933 he obtained his doctorate under Professor Steinmetz at Amsterdam. Kruijt argued that clerical conservatism led to increased secularism. This hypothesis was later upheld by Eduard Schillebeeckx, a Flemish theologian who had been studying the relationship between theology and sociology. Schillebeeckx simultaneously noted an enduring religiosity and a failure on the part of churches: 'It is not the people who are leaving the church, but the churches themselves are no longer to be found where people lead their daily lives.' These words by Schillebeeckx are quoted in *The Identity of Catholic Academics* (De identiteit van katholieke wetenschapsmensen, 1980).

During the Second World War, Kruijt and his wife were baptized and received into the Dutch Reformed Church by the pastor and sociologist Willem Banning. Banning and Kruijt were among the co-founders of ecclesiastical sociology in the Netherlands. The Rotterdam economist George Zeegers set up a Catholic research institute, the Catholic Social-Ecclesiastical Institute *(Kaski; Katholiek Sociaal-Kerkelijk Instituut)*, the only 'confessional' institute still in existence. This institute also carries out research for the Dutch Reformed Church. In 1946 Banning was appointed to the first chair in 'Sociology of the Church', at Leiden, and in 1951 Zeegers was appointed to a chair in Nijmegen. Most Dutch universities have chairs in 'Psychology of Religion' and 'Sociology of Religion', and these have earned the Netherlands an international reputation.

Those wanting to familiarize themselves with the social research carried out on religion since these institutions were founded should consult *Once Again: Religion and Church in the Netherlands: 1945-1986* (Nog Eens:

godsdienst en kerk in Nederland 1945-1986), a sociological bibliography of church and religion in the Netherlands. Published by the Catholic Centre for Documentation *(Katholiek Documentatie Centrum)* at Nijmegen, this describes no fewer than 1,245 studies. Foreign academics have thus referred to the Netherlands as a 'laboratory' for socio-scientific and historical research in the religious and ecclesiastical field.

Recent developments

It is interesting to compare results from a 1966 survey on attitudes to the existence of a God with those from later surveys (both expressed as percentages of the random sample).

	1966	1979	1986
there is a God who is concerned with each person as an individual	48	34	30
there must be some sort of higher power or being which controls our lives	34	40	33
I do not know whether there is a God or a higher being	13	17	25
there is no God or higher being	4	9	13

Church attendance has fallen considerably, but even in the Netherlands it is difficult to coax people out of their 'private little paradises' now that they have television sets. In the year 1990-91, 2.6 million Dutch went out to watch first-division football matches. However, *each week* 2.7 million Dutch people of 15 years and upwards (i.e. 22%) attend a church service. This is still a relatively high number.

Spiritual values and their deeper foundations are therefore of considerable importance in Dutch society today. Four factors have been of importance in recent developments:

1. In recent decades the Catholics, by far the largest group, have undergone a revolution with the introduction of a collegiate church structure. As a result this group has become, sociologically speaking, considerably less distinctive. The Dutch Catholic has become a peaceful and unpretentious figure.

2. A relatively high number of respondents no longer trust the Church, and express this lack of trust in surveys. The *Humanistisch Verbond* (Humanist Society) has discovered that these so-called seculars do not take kindly to being organized. A significant number would not describe themselves as unbelieving, and even vote for the CDA.

3. Furthermore, according to the most recent estimates, almost half a million people in the Netherlands belong to a non-Christian religion. These people

belong primarily to Islamic groups, and now constitute the so-called fourth denomination. Not only mosques, but also schools have been provided for these immigrants, who would now like to be given their own university.

4. Finally, in the new Europe, the Netherlands must protect its cultural heritage. It is obvious that careful consideration is needed to determine how this is to be achieved, and the European Values Study *(Europees Waardenonderzoek)* should provide the comparative framework for this. The Netherlands must not become some sort of 'Germania inferior'.

The Netherlands is a wealthy country which takes care of the poor and oppressed. But material welfare does not guarantee happiness: 'No government can make its people permanently happy. Even the most enlightened policies may have only a limited impact on overall life satisfaction, one that lasts for only a limited time.' (R. Inglehart). In the Netherlands of today health and happiness are still important aims. Ideology and the churches still have a role to play in the fulfilment of those aims.

WALTER GODDIJN
Translated by Yvette Mead.

FURTHER READING

GODDIJN, WALTER, *The Deferred Revolution. A Social Experiment in Church Innovation in Holland. 1960-1970,* Amsterdam / Oxford / New York, 1975.

GODDIJN, WALTER, 'Towards a Democratic Ideal of Church Government in the Netherlands, 1966-1970: a sociological analysis', in: *A Democratic Catholic Church* (ed. E. Bianchi & R. Radford Ruether), New York, 1992, pp. 156-71.

Grounds for Memory

Colonial Literature from the Former Dutch East Indies

The colonial literature of the Netherlands is, with the possible exception of Spanish and Portuguese letters, the most voluminous and innovative of colonial literatures in the Western world. It also has one of the longest traditions. If we restrict ourselves to the literature produced in the former colonial East Indies, now the Republic of Indonesia, we can speak of an uninterrupted tradition that began around 1600 and ended, in a formal sense, at the end of the Second World War. One should qualify this by saying that the true colonial life from which fiction was constructed then ceased to exist, but the minds which contemplated that life were active well beyond 1945. In fact, some would argue that even in the last decade of this century one still finds reverberations of this genre of literature, though I would argue that most of these texts were written by a generation that no longer has any kind of firsthand knowledge of a place and a society that was once known as *tempo dulu* or 'time past'.

This literature that lived for at least three-and-a-half centuries has several unique features. First of all, one must discard the usual notions of what can be called 'literature'. Beginning with the journals of the sixteenth-century mariners, great texts were produced by men who were totally ignorant of aesthetic canons in the European mother country. They also unwittingly established a model prose style: simple, demotic, wary of rhetoric, pungent, and enlivened with striking detail. In the eighteenth century this style was further modulated by the influence of native story-telling and it remained the major mode of colonial fictional representation well beyond the Second World War. It goes without saying that, being the individualistic medium that it is, this literature also includes several exceptions to this stylistic rule; the work of Louis Couperus (1863-1923) being perhaps the best known example.

Dutch colonial literature starts with the prose of the mariners. The journals which such men as Lodewyckszз., Van der Does, Turck and Kackerlack wrote during Holland's fateful first voyage to the Indies (1595-1597) constitute the first significant colonial texts. They provide us with vivid accounts of life on board ship (almost always a most miserable existence), with depictions of unusual sights, sounds and scenery, and with the way those untutored crews dealt with the Other in the shape of various native peoples. The latter was usually a violent confrontation, but as soon as educated men were placed in command relations became generally peaceful but also more curious. Life in the late sixteenth and early seventeenth century was rough and human conduct matched it. This is well known, but there is also the lesser known fact that some of these voyagers were courageous men with minds eagerly inquiring after new facts and alternative modes of existence. Such a man, for instance, was Frederick de Houtman (?1570-1627). Although his brother's crass conduct (Cornelis de Houtman was the commander of the first two voyages to the Indies) caused Frederick to be imprisoned in Achin for two years, he compiled the material for the first European attempt at a Malay lexicon and phrase book, studied the stars of the southern constellations, and recorded life at the court of his jailer, the Sultan of Achin. Frederick de Houtman's phrase-book represents the beginning of Dutch linguistic investigation of Indonesian languages which, in terms of the colonial era, culminated in Herman Neubronner van der Tuuk's work during the second half of the nineteenth century and the publication of his awesome Kawi-Balinese-Dutch dictionary, published posthumously between 1897 and 1912.

Georg Everhard Rumphius (?1628-1702) (Collection Letterkundig Museum, The Hague).

This element of intense curiosity and eagerness to learn remained strong during the seventeenth century. What might at first glance seem pragmatic texts for information gradually disclose merits which we are now more likely to classify as artistic. For instance, the poetic muse did not fare well in the colonial Indies until the two decades prior to the Second World War, yet one will find a most delicate lyrical disposition in Rumphius's prose descriptions of Moluccan flora and fauna. His large *Herbal* (Amboinsche Kruydboek, published posthumously between 1741 and 1750) is not only an irreplaceable standard text for tropical botany, but also a treasure-trove of nature poetry. Because modern scientific nomenclature did not exist in Rumphius's time, is was necessary for him to describe plants in nontechnical language. He had to picture them and convince his readers of the excitement he had felt when he first encountered them. His reverence for the humblest of organisms can also be found in *Ambonese Curiosity Chamber* (D'Amboinsche Rariteit-kamer, 1705), in which Rumphius (?1628-1702) described tropical shellfish, shells, minerals and precious stones.

The one major prose-text of the eighteenth century is similarly a mixture of the informative and the entertaining. Published between 1724 and 1726, the descriptive history entitled *Old and New East Indies* (Oud en Nieuw Oost-Indiën) by a divine called François Valentijn (1666-1728), has been mined for information about the VOC or the 'United East Indies Trading Company' and its management of the colony. But throughout the voluminous work (comprising about 5,000 pages) one will find fascinating descriptions, excellent narratives and acerbic portraits of contemporaries, all in a style that rivals the best prose written at that time in Europe. Valentijn's writing has all the virtues of the mariners' prose, combined with a sense of humour and a good eye for the peculiar and the picturesque. Despite his faults (he shamelessly stole material wherever he could find it) Valentijn loved gossip and was a master of anecdotal prose. He constantly interrupts himself to tell a good story, even if it has nothing to do with the matter at hand. There is, for instance, the tale of how a shoemaker tricks a legal official, his social superior; the story comes in the midst of a report on how sumptuously the Dutch lived in Batavia. And there is an incident on the island of St Jago when a Portuguese steals the hat and wig of the ship's assistant; and a scene aboard ship when the steward, Faro, tries to hang on to a large pot of suet on a tossing and bucking ship. He falls down and can't get up because he keeps slipping on the suet while being blown about by the wind; it is a scene of slapstick worthy of Chaplin. And I cannot help thinking that Valentijn's observation about the teeth of the Ambonese is a dig at his compatriots. He tells us that some things the Ambonese do would 'misbecome' the Dutch, such as their 'long nails (which they) redden with Lack (which is otherwise called Alcanna by the Arabs)', but this is not true about their 'white and clean teeth, which is very common among them, and they despise many Europeans who have teeth that are yellow or covered with a blue growth, and in this they undoubtedly surpass us'.

The eighteenth century did not produce much memorable art, except for Valentijn, but it is remarkable for its society. Unlike any other Western colony, the Dutch East Indies rapidly became Asianized during the late seventeenth century and for the duration of the eighteenth century. The upper echelons of society in Batavia (now Jakarta) became thoroughly *Indies* (to use an English word that comes the closest to the Dutch *Indisch*) because the VOC had a policy which encouraged its male employees to marry or live with Asian women. These women and their mestizo offspring were readily granted legal status as Europeans and very shortly after its establishment the Company stopped subsidizing Dutch females to travel to the Indies. Conversely, a Dutch man married to an Asian or Eurasian woman could not return to the Netherlands as long as his wife and their children were alive. Eurasian daughters often married newly arrived Dutch men who soon occupied important positions (competition was fierce, but so was the death rate); and since few sons lived to adulthood, and those who did were prohibited from advancement if their mothers were Asian or Eurasian, wealth and influence were passed on via the women to kin acquired by marriage. We have, therefore, a rather unique situation in that for nearly two-thirds of its history, Dutch colonial Mestizo society was the elite ruling class, with women as the real powerbrokers. This Indies society disdained European mores and preferred to be Asian in practice and appearance. They copied the grand style of living from Javanese society, wore the practical local garb of *sarong* and *kabaya,* bathed several times a day (a practice abhorred by the Dutch), adopted domestic slavery from Asian society, and generally indulged in the ease and hedonism which they copied from the Asian upper classes and for which they were severely criticized in Europe. Religion became virtually irrelevant as a social force, while money and status dictated social intercourse. Jean Gelman Taylor made the important observation that from 1645 (which is only 35 years after the first governor-general was dispatched from Holland) to 1808 (when Daendels assumed office), not a single person was appointed governor-general who had not had long and sustained experience in the Indies. Hence for a century and a half the ruling elite was for all intents and purposes independent of Holland and created its own distinctive society and style of living.

Stamp issued in 1987 to mark the centenary of Multatuli's death.
The quotation from Multatuli reads in English: 'Man's vocation is to be human'.

Mestizo power declined during and after the British interregnum administration of Raffles from 1811 to 1815. After the colonies had been restored to the Netherlands in 1816, the ruling emphasis shifted back to Europe and the Eurasian elite, now a large and ever-expanding number of people, moved to landed estates in the interior of Java. Though they had lost political power when European reforms were introduced after the Napoleonic era, they had also permeated colonial society. Mestizo culture could not be denied because it was this culture that became synonymous with the meaning of the word 'colonial' when one looked back at *tempo dulu.*

Specific elements of Eurasian life became part of the colonial literature and arts that began to flourish once again in the second half of the nineteenth century. Some of these characteristics were hedonism, sensuality, liberal sexual mores, hospitality, violence, stubborn individualism, emotionalism, irresponsibility and an inclination for passion. With the possible exception of recalcitrant individualism, none of these aspects were especially favoured in Dutch society or its literature. Two totally different societies had evolved, but as long as the colony produced a profit, eccentric 'colonial' behavior was gladly suffered with tolerant hypocrisy. In terms of culture, an independent kind of literature was gradually becoming known and kept on developing quite separately from European imperatives. Since it had no idea of what aesthetic innovations were in fashion at any given time, colonial literature had the rare luxury of evolving freely though, to be sure, it sometimes confessed to a lack of tradition. It had one, but didn't know it yet. Colonial literature was not really mapped and codified until the middle of the twentieth century. Be that as it may, the important point here is the ignorance of European cultural tyranny: it permitted colonial literature to try innovations which standard literary orthodoxy in Holland would not dare to consider until much later.

Maria Dermoût (1888-1961) and her two children in 1912 (Collection Letterkundig Museum, The Hague).

A case in point is Eduard Douwes Dekker (1820-1887), a nineteenth-century writer who, under the name of Multatuli, became Holland's best-known writer. That he is also a colonial author reminds us of the remarkable fact that Dutch colonial literature produced four acknowledged masterpieces of modern Dutch letters: Multatuli's *Max Havelaar* (1860), Louis Couperus's *The Hidden Force* (De stille kracht, 1900), E. Du Perron's *Country of Origin* (Het land van herkomst, 1935) and Maria Dermoût's *The Ten Thousand Things* (De tienduizend dingen, 1955). This, to my knowledge, is not equalled by any other Western literary tradition.

Dekker's masterpiece, which launched his career as Multatuli and introduced the modern period of Dutch literature, was called *Max Havelaar.* Published in 1860, it possessed a style and form which had not been seen before. The style – which is the nineteenth-century continuation of the mariners' prose – was based on the rhythms of spoken language and was perfected by Dekker in long letters he wrote during his career as a colonial official in the Indies. It scorns empty rhetoric, is wildly innovative in its syntax and original in its diction. Multatuli's prose is the voice of a passionate individual who ignores any limitations imposed by society, politics, or culture. This highly unorthodox novel is a Romantic document of great power that dazzled its contemporary audience with its virtuoso display of fictional voices. Quite apart from its revolutionary message, *Max Havelaar* changed Dutch letters once and for all.

Another innovator came out of the Indies a couple of decades later. The novels of P. A. Daum (1850-1898) were the first realist fiction in Dutch literature. They depict colonial society of the late nineteenth-century in a sympathetic but honest way. Daum does not obfuscate; he depicts the foibles and sins of life on Java just as straightforwardly as he praises its virtues. In *From Sugar to Tobacco* (Uit de suiker in de tabak, 1885) and *Ups and Downs of Life in the Indies* (Ups en downs in het Indische leven, 1892) Daum gives us an insider's view of how rich planters lived. They could acquire great wealth in a short time and lose it just as quickly. They lived a life that was far more uninhibited than anything Holland could imagine and the difference in social values is illustrated by the fact that what the Indies and Daum considered normal swearing or normal sexual references in his novels, were bowdlerized by Dutch publishers when some of the novels were finally accepted in the Netherlands. In a series of connected novels, Daum showed how one got ahead in what had become a rigidly bureaucratized ruling elite that was controlled from The Hague. The Peter Principle worked just as well for colonial incompetents as it does for today's lightweights in business and government. In the novel that bears the name of its protagonist, *H. van Brakel* (1888), Daum gave a most affecting portrait of the decline of a European; decline and disillusion remained major themes in colonial literature. Van Brakel is an alcoholic who destroys his career and his life but it is a measure of Daum's superior skills as a novelist that the reader is never permitted to hate this kind but weak engineer. *Guna-Guna* (Goena-Goena, 1889) and *Number Eleven* (Nummer Elf, 1893) exhibit the daily life of Indies society; the authenticity of Daum's depiction has been praised by experts on more than one occasion. Daum attacked the hypocritical attitude of the Dutch in Europe in *Indies People in Holland* (Indische mensen in Holland, 1890). The novel makes it quite clear that Indies money never stank but that the people who had earned that money were said most definitely to smell. If one wants a realistic picture of what colonial life was like toward the end of the nineteenth century, Daum's ten novels are as trustworthy a replica as one could hope for. They are eminently readable today because Daum also deliberately cultivated a forceful and direct style which avoided those rhetorical excesses which can quickly date a work of fiction. This did happen with those writers of fiction, mostly women, who produced soap-operas set in the tropics, replete with intrigue, sexual innuendo, moonlight and perfumed night air. They sold well at the time but are now only perused for sociological detail.

Only two twentieth-century authors completed their life's work before the demise of the colony during the Second World War. The more important of these two was also the most influential colonial writer of the present century. E. du Perron (1899-1940) was perhaps not the best novelist, poet, or essayist of the first half of the twentieth century but in the aggregate he affected more people and more aspects of twentieth-century colonial literature than anyone else. He also has the distinction of being the first major colonial author to have been born and raised in the tropics, a fact that makes a great deal of difference to how that society and its environment are experienced and interpreted. Du Perron's short life symbolizes a condensed version of the fortunes of the tropical colony. He came from a wealthy family of landed gentry who indulged him royally. He enjoyed the usual complement of servants and indifference to education, and even when his parents had moved to Europe continued for a while a life of unencumbered plenty.

But Du Perron's parents did not manage their money well and, aided by unscrupulous tradesmen and the stock-market crash, their fortune rapidly dwindled. The father committed suicide, the mother died soon after and the son found himself penniless. For the decade or so that remained to him, Du Perron lived from hand to mouth while supporting himself as a writer and a journalist.

When he returned for three years during the thirties he discovered that the Indies of his youth, the colony previously described as living according to eighteenth-century virtues, had turned into an efficient imperialism that was a business before it was a way of life. The colony was also agitating to become an independent republic. Du Perron met and talked to some of the Indonesians who, after the war, would become prominent figures in Indonesian political life. He sought out and encouraged many other people, contributed to liberal journals, helped writers get published, wrote introductions, started one intellectual magazine after the other and constantly kept tabs on anyone he considered worthy of attention. Du Perron's correspondence is formidable. Meanwhile he began the effort to promote colonial literature as a separate and distinct genre. He did so first with a published anthology and was planning several more. He fought to enshrine Multatuli's reputation as a colonial official as well as an author in four polemical books and, most importantly from a literary point of view, he published a large and important novel entitled *Country of Origin* (Het land van herkomst, 1935). Du Perron's prose was right in line with the main tradition that began with the mariners. For instance, he called a collection of his poetry *Parlando* (a term used in music to indicate that the performer should present a musical text as if speaking), and all his published work is written in that mode. *Country of Origin* was an innovative hybrid of a novel. No one at the time knew how to place it, not realizing that the Dutch obsession with categorizing had never been of any importance in Java. The novel pits the old Indies against the Europe of the thirties and finds the latter wanting. A careful reading discloses that for Du Perron, despite all his misgivings, the former Indies, the Indies of his youth, was a form of Romanticism, not the sentimental indulgence of false emotions, but the genuine inspiration known to any other European community except the Netherlands. Besides the fact that emotionalism would find no favourable response in Holland, Du Perron also found that in interbellum Europe intellect had outreasoned intuition and emotional exhilaration, while the masses had elected the viscera and intolerance to power. Yet Du Perron had also discovered that his Indies no longer existed and that the present colony had become very much like the Europe he preferred not to inhabit. In other words, during the short span of his life he had lost both worlds, lived a homeless life, and had to accept the hard truth that he could only be housed by his own self. Du Perron's life and work not only became symptomatic of the colonial literature produced two decades later but also turned out to be generally prophetic for the second half of this century.

Edgar du Perron (1899-1940) in Tsjandi Sewu (1920) (Collection Letterkundig Museum, The Hague).

One of the writers Du Perron discovered and encouraged was more than a decade older. Like so many colonials prior to the twentieth century, Willem Walraven (1887-1943) came to Java as a soldier and stayed. After many failed attempts at business, he finally managed to make a living from journalism. Walraven had married a Sundanese woman and *lived* what other people could only discuss as the uneasy union of east and west. Veering between hatred and devotion, discriminated against by his own kind yet not considered a full-fledged member of his wife's people, Walraven represents a most melancholy example of the colonial tragedy. His work also reiterates the non-traditional aspect of colonial literature which states that literary treasures are to be found outside what custom has staked out. Besides some very fine stories, Walraven's literary legacy is represented by his letters. He was a compulsive correspondent who 'was only happy when he was writing'. In these missives from his own loneliness, one will find one of the most authentic voices in colonial literature prior to the Second World War. Walraven's messages of exile were known to only a few at the time, but anyone who read them felt as if he had caught a glimpse of their individual pain. Walraven died in a Japanese concentration camp. His belated friend and promoter Du Perron died on the day the Dutch armed forces surrendered to the German invaders.

Beb Vuyk (1905-1991) and her son Hans Christiaan in 1934 (Collection Letterkundig Museum, The Hague).

Just before the war started in Europe, Beb Vuyk (1905-1991) published a barely fictionalized account of the primitive but magical existence a pioneer could once lead in the tropical archipelago. Most aptly called *The Last House in the World* (Het laatste huis van de wereld, 1939), it describes the difficult but independent life led by Vuyk and her husband on the remote island of Buru in the Moluccas. There they tried to make a living from producing kajuputih oil but, more importantly, far removed from the strictures of modern society and an imperial bureaucracy, they managed to live life as an adventure. This novel as well as the two fine stories, 'Journal of a Journey by Prau' *('Journaal van een prauwreis')* and 'Way Baroe', narrate events in a present that had already been overtaken by history. The narratives seem almost magical in their uniform illumination of a place still unmarred by progress. Vuyk's variations on a theme she formulated as 'the wild green smell of adventure' – and indeed her prewar fictions dazzle with green – are poetic without ever becoming sentimental, joyous without being euphoric, and uncomplicated without being simple. These modest epics of a life that was still dangerous are valedictory praise for a time and a place that would never be again.

The greatest production of colonial literature dates from after the Second World War. Memory truly is the mother of invention. Now that the colony was irrevocably gone the processes of reclaiming it imaginatively had been set in motion. Not only were more individual texts being written, but order was applied to what hitherto had been a seemingly amorphous mass of testimonies. Du Perron had already sensed a pattern and had tried to formulate a sequential development, but it was not until Rob Nieuwenhuys (born in Java in 1908) produced a series of responsible anthologies and in 1972 his monumental literary history of this genre, *Mirror of the Indies* (Oost-Indische Spiegel, third, revised ed. 1978), that this quite unique and rich body of work had finally been codified in a coherent fashion. Dutch colonial literature now existed as a totality, as a specific complement to a European literary tradition: individual, unusual, with its own ways of addressing human destiny. Nieuwenhuys had also wrested these texts from investigators interested in anything but literature. He proved they could stand on their own, that they had their own tradition, and that they need not apologize to anything the European home country had produced. In fact, as I already indicated, its colonial literature produced some of Holland's masterpieces. One of these is the beguiling novel entitled *The Ten Thousand Things* (De tienduizend dingen, 1955) by Maria Dermoût (1888-1961).

An Indies person born and raised like Du Perron and Nieuwenhuys, Dermoût fashioned a mesmeric narrative out of turbulent life in the Moluccas, the same region Beb Vuyk had written about. The structure of *The Ten Thousand Things* is centred on an older woman, Felicia, who once a year, on All Soul's Day, commemorates those who she feels have been murdered, like her son. One is easily deceived by the hypnotic style, but this novel is just as violent as *Country of Origin,* not to mention Daum's, Vuyk's, Friedericy's or Alberts's fiction. This may not seem noteworthy today, but violent narratives were unusual for Dutch literature; vehemence of any kind was a rarity, at least until after the Second World War.

Dermoût's work is distinguished by a repetitive and languid style which owes its unique rhythms to Indonesian story-telling. Also Indonesian is her reverence for objects, no matter how small, and being able to convey the possibility of their magical significance, something known as *pusaka* in the archipelago. *The Ten Thousand Things* is a masterpiece not only because all of these elements are presented in a moving fictional story, but also because the book offers a hard-won wisdom, one that wants us to understand life and creation as a whole, without hierachical values. And yet, no matter what one says about Dermoût's work, there always is a residue of the unrevealed, a suggestion of mystery. Like all enduring works of fiction, there is no final explanation of *The Ten Thousand Things.*

Mystery is also the hallmark of the baffling stories A. Alberts (1911-) published in 1952 under the title *The Islands* (De eilanden). Alberts had been a government official on Java and Madura and only began to write and publish after the war. The same is true for Friedericy, Dermoût, and others. Alberts's modernist fiction distills all the previously mentioned elements into an essence that is so concentrated that it can be viable in small amounts. All of Alberts's fiction is unfashionably short and invariably enigmatic. His sober, almost deadpan prose is stripped of all rhetoric. It seems like the final distillate of the mariners' prose and, should therefore, be transparently simple. But Alberts created a style of prose that baffles when it seems most limpid and achieves a resonance of meaning quite as profound as Beckett's. The Indies of *The Islands* is reduced to basic elements such as green, water, heat, and stone, and is plagued by incomprehension and virulence. The tropical archipelago finally became a myth, a country of the mind, a realm of the imagination.

H.J. Friedericy (1900-1962) on the porch of his house in Soenggoeminasa (Collection Letterkundig Museum, The Hague).

A great deal more can be said about Dutch colonial literature. Since the war there has been an explosion of primary literature about and learned commentary on the erstwhile tropical colony. All the authors mentioned published a great deal more. Nieuwenhuys, for instance, published a fine group portrait of an Indies family (*Faded Portraits;* Vergeelde portretten, 1954) which continued a genre established by Daum and Du Perron. Since Nieuwenhuys's novel there have been many similar domestic explorations because the family is central to the emotional life of the Indo-European community. Both Vuyk and Nieuwenhuys published somewhat fictionalized recollections of life in the Japanese concentration camps. This particular sub-genre expanded dramatically after 1945, but Vuyk's and Nieuwenhuys's work remains unassailably superior, especially the latter's *A Bit of War* (Een beetje oorlog, 1979). One should add that Nieuwenhuys published a large number of articles, anthologies, introductions, essays, and collections of old photographs over the past four decades, and is still doing so. His latest publication, *Sinjo Robbie* (1992), is a memoir about his youth; the book includes for the first time a discussion of the undeniable eroticism of life in the tropics. Given the prudent history of Dutch letters prior to the Second World War, it is no surprise that this controversial topic was seldom seriously acknowledged.

Besides the so-called 'camp-literature' the second half of this century has also seen a considerable number of publications by people who were too young by the end of the war to be cognizant of it but used whatever material was passed on to them, and by people who are descendants of the Eurasian community that was forced to migrate to the Netherlands. I would hesitate to call this *colonial* literature; it is rather a kind of European literature which *uses* life in the tropical archipelago as any writer will use anything whatsoever if it suits his or her purpose. But be that as it may, the former Indies in the role of the uncensored domain of the mind has produced first-rate narratives, including such a masterful achievement as Jeroen Brouwers's *The Flood* (De zondvloed, 1988).

Dust-jacket of the English translation of Rob Nieuwenhuys's collection of stories from Indonesia.

Dutch colonial literature is not a poor relation of mainstream Dutch letters. This extensive literature, with a tradition at least three-and-a-half centuries old, developed *contingluously* with Western literature, acquiring its own specific themes, mandating its own preferred style, developing its own distinctive echoes. The actuality of the life that fed this writing may be gone but the oeuvre it wrought has not dated. At the most minimal level, colonial literature is necessary because for a long time the greater emphasis has been on the political, social and historical aspects of that ever-receding past. But understanding an actual experience comes down to smell, touch, visual shocks, comes down to the emotions and the senses. This is something that the sciences, be they social or otherwise, fail to perceive but which literature will always cherish if it does not wish to be relegated to the boneyard of theory.

E.M. BEEKMAN

LIST OF TRANSLATIONS

THE LIBRARY OF THE INDIES

Publisher: The University of Massachusetts Press, Amherst, Mass.
General Editor: E.M. Beekman

The Poison Tree: Selected Writings of Rumphius on the Natural History of the Indies (Tr. E.M. Beekman). 1981.
BRETON DE NIJS, E., *Faded Portraits* (Tr. Donald and Elsje Sturtevant). 1982.
MULTATULI, *Max Havelaar: or The Coffee Auctions of the Dutch Trading Company* (Tr. Roy Edwards). 1982.
NIEUWENHUYS, ROB, *Mirror of the Indies: A History of Dutch Colonial Literature* (Tr. Frans van Rosevelt). 1982.
ALBERTS, ALBERT, *The Islands* (Tr. Hans Koning). 1983.
DERMOUT, MARIA, *The Ten Thousand Things* (Tr. Hans Koning). 1983.
SCHENDEL, ARTHUR VAN, *John Company* (Tr. Frans van Rosevelt). 1983.
Two Tales of the East Indies: Vuyck, Beb, 'The Last House in the World' (Tr. André Lefevere) & Friedericy, H.J., 'The Counselor' (Tr. Hans Koning). 1983.
DU PERRON, E., *Country of Origin* (Tr. Francis Bulhof and Elizabeth Daverman). 1984.
COUPERUS, LOUIS, *The Hidden Force* (Tr. Teixeira de Mattos). 1985.
DAUM, P.A., *Ups and Downs of Life in the Indies* (Tr. Donald and Elsje Sturtevant). 1987.
Fugitive Dreams. An Anthology of Dutch Colonial Literature (Tr. E.M. Beekman). 1988.

ANTHOLOGIES

Insulinde: Selected Translations from Dutch Writers of Three Centuries on the Indonesian Archipelago (ed. Cornelia Niekus Moore). Honolulu, 1978.
Memory and Agony. Dutch Stories from Indonesia, collected and introduced by Rob Nieuwenhuys (ed. E. Krispyn). Boston, 1979.

POSTWAR FICTION WHICH EMPLOYS THE INDIES

BROUWERS, JEROEN, *Sunken Red* (Tr. Adrienne Dixon). London, 1990.

ew

Fairy Tales for the Low Countries

About Marlene Dumas, a South African Artist in the Netherlands

In 1984 Marlene Dumas (Capetown, 1953-) painted a self-portrait. In this painting, her most exhibited work, we see the head of a young woman, her chin resting on her right hand. Dumas painted the portrait from a polaroid photograph. The photograph shows more of the setting than the painting; it shows us that Dumas is sitting in the front seat of a car, and has turned to face the photographer sitting in the back. Her hand rests on the back of the seat.

Apart from omitting her surroundings, Dumas made few alterations to the snapshot. Only the colours have been changed: she has given herself bright orange hair and ice-blue eyes. Dumas called her self-portrait *Evil is Banal.* This title, and the knowledge that this is a self-portrait, colour our interpretation of the painting. But these two clues still leave scope for differing views of it. Some art critics claim that Dumas has painted not only herself but an archetypal woman – and a negative one at that: The Evil Woman, sin incarnate. Others claim that Dumas is angry because she herself is banal: there is nothing unusual about her appearance, she resembles any other attractive blonde woman. Photographs and paintings usually serve only to intensify the resemblance between people. They do not show the unique, but the general. A photograph of someone grimacing is usually dismissed with the argument that it is not a good likeness, yet such facial expressions are perhaps more personal than a composed face. It has also been claimed that Dumas' use of the title *Evil is Banal* is a reference to her South African background: by being born white in South Africa she was born evil.

Most critics have interpreted the title in a more general way. They believe Dumas is trying to say that evil cannot always be recognized. Anyone could be a murderer. In 1991 Dumas drew a portrait of Hitler which she called *Evil is Banal. A Male Version,* thereby strengthening her reference to fascism with the title *Evil is Banal,* which was borrowed from Hannah Arendt.

However, the interpretation of the painting which most pleased Dumas ignored all these references. The punk singer John Lydon (Johnny Rotten) saw Dumas' painting at the major exhibition *Bilderstreit* in Cologne. Lydon thought it a beautiful painting, even though he did not know what it meant. He thought Dumas looked like a woman who did not care whether others loved or hated her.

Marlene Dumas, *Evil is Banal.* Canvas, 125 x 105 cm. Stedelijk Van Abbemuseum, Eindhoven.

The fact that Dumas was so amused by this interpretation is characteristic of her relationship with her paintings. One of the most important themes in her work is interpretation. She called her retrospective exhibition at the Van Abbe Museum in Eindhoven (Spring 1992) *Miss Interpreted.* Although the artist appears to be pushing the viewer in one particular direction, she much prefers to mislead. Dumas herself wrote about her paintings of the fairy tale figure Snow White: 'The viewer feels at home in the story: satisfied that he knows what it is all about. But that feeling cannot last because he becomes aware of the conflict between the elements'. Dumas does not want to remove that conflict. She would most like her paintings to be viewed in the same way as the English nursery rhymes she learned as a young girl in South Africa. In a nursery rhyme things which would be impossible in daily life happen casually, sometimes only because they rhyme. In a nursery rhyme, a little girl can go swimming without going near the water:

Mother, may I go out to swim?
Yes, my darling daughter,
Hang your clothes on a hickory limb
And don't go near the water.

Marlene Dumas, *Waiting (for Meaning).* 1988. Canvas, 50 x 70 cm. Kunsthalle zu Kiel.

Marlene Dumas pursues the same freedom in her art. She dislikes the search for a meaning which, once found, renders the painting superfluous. Form and content, word and picture, title and painting; these must stay together. In 1988 Dumas painted a nude woman who is lying on her back on a table. She called it *Waiting (for Meaning).* In 1992 she wrote: 'They are looking for Meaning as if it was a Thing. As if it was a girl, required to take her panty off as if she would want to do so, as soon as the true interpreter comes along. As if there was something to take off.'

Dumas often paints subjects – such as attitudes towards the genitals – which Dutch artists have, until recently, ignored. During this century, nude pictures have been rejected as *kitsch.* Of course, this applies particularly to the female nude. In the history of art there are almost no portrayals of men which are both aesthetic and erotic. According to Dumas, the body of Jesus Christ is still the most erotic portrayal of the masculine in the visual arts. In 1987, Dumas herself ventured to paint a male nude. She painted a very pink man, reclining on a stretched-out cloth. We see the man from the side, from head to foot. His arms are behind his head, he invites us to look at his body. Yet his penis, to which our gaze is naturally drawn, is not erect. Dumas called the painting *The Particularity of Nakedness.* In this painting she was concerned with the experience of tenderness. She was shocked by the criticism the painting received. A woman called it a 'homosexual painting'; a man thought it a failure because it consisted purely of horizontals. 'Both parties wanted him erected one way or the other', Dumas later wrote. Perhaps this is why she later went on to paint people without sexual organs.

Marlene Dumas began her career in South Africa drawing 'bikini-girls'. While attending Johannesburg's Academy of Art she moved on to abstract art, which was, as elsewhere, the prescribed movement in South African art academies during the seventies. But she was not content to neglect important emotions. These are difficult to express in abstract art. In the seventies she tried to record her emotions in abstract drawings, but this proved to be impossible. 'In 1977 I made a drawing while I was crying', she told me in

Marlene Dumas, *The Particularity of Nakedness.* 1987. Canvas, 140 x 300 cm. Stedelijk Van Abbemuseum, Eindhoven.

Marlene Dumas, *The Turkish Schoolgirls.* 1987. Canvas, 160 x 200 cm. Stedelijk Museum, Amsterdam.

an interview in March 1992, 'I was suffering from the pangs of love. But you couldn't see that in the drawing. So I called it *Love hasn't got anything to do with it.*' According to Dumas many visual artists leave the expression of great emotions such as pain, sex and love to the media. In order to express these, Dumas needed subjects. She once again turned to figurative art.

Dumas' breakthrough in the Netherlands came when, in the mid-eighties, she instilled new life into an old genre, the portrait. Her portraits of mostly unknown people – her friends and acquaintances, first recorded with a polaroid camera – abound with feeling, although those portrayed never give away all their secrets. What Dumas knows of them we can only suspect, but through her talent our suspicions become strong ones, of grief, desperation, lust and pain.

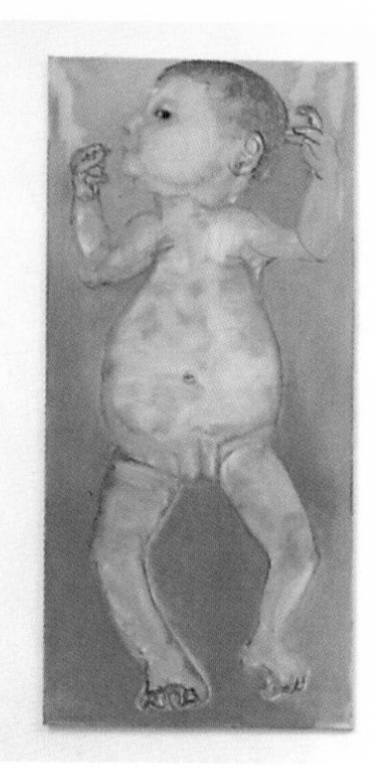
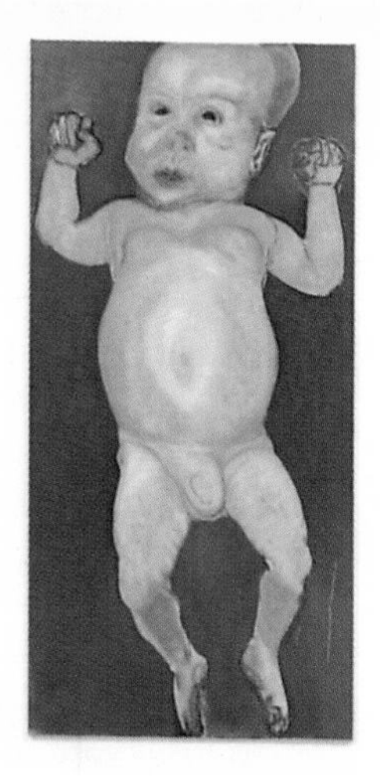
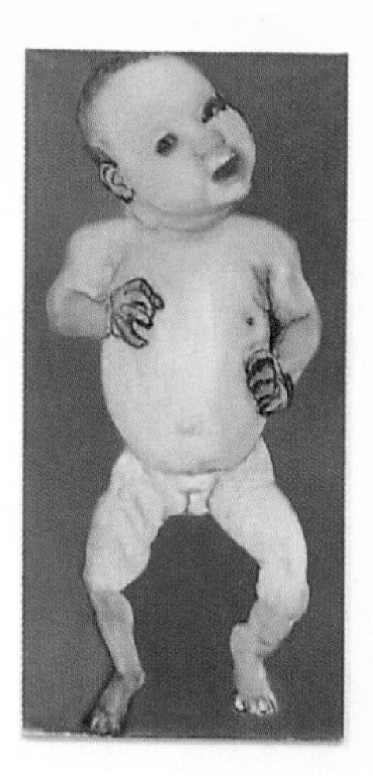
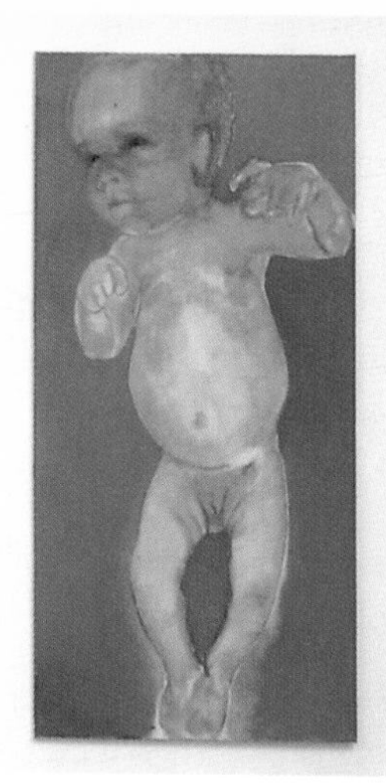

Marlene Dumas, *The First People (I-IV)*. 1991. Canvas, (4x) 180 x 90 cm. Collection De Pont Stichting, Tilburg.

In 1987 Dumas began to paint group portraits of people familiar to everyone: a class of schoolchildren with their teacher; lanky schoolboys in uniform. The people in the group portraits are even more anonymous than those in the individual portraits; their role is not devised by Dumas herself, but by society. The poses and expressions are familiar, but Dumas sometimes alters or intensifies them. A little boy in shorts is given extra-white legs, faces are left blank, and the painting as a whole is cast in a particular colour. In this way Dumas adds value to the photographs. She sees it thus: 'With photographic activities it is possible that they who take the picture leave no traces of their presence, and are absent from the pictures. Paintings exist as the traces of their makers and by the grace of these traces. You can't TAKE a painting – you MAKE a painting'.

Dumas' inspiration often comes from everyday life. The series *The First People* is particularly disturbing: four portraits of babies, painted two years after the birth of her daughter in 1989. The babies, who are the colour of corpses, with the distended stomachs of the starving and pronounced sex organs, look so frightening at first sight that it seems as if the artist has deliberately made them ugly. But Dumas believes she has painted reality: 'The television *Pampers* baby has become the norm. That is why motherhood comes as such a shock. You don't realize what babies look like in reality.' In 1986 Dumas had already made a series of drawings of babies, which she called *Fear of Babies.* These babies look less unpleasant than the four in the portraits she painted after her own child was born; in this sense Dumas is a realist.

Dumas has made cheerful portraits of slightly older children, such as the beautiful *In the Beginning* from 1991. In this painting we see a toddler, dressed only in a little red jumper, drawing on the ground. From the title we know that this must have been one of her first attempts. It is probable that this painting is also a self-portrait of Dumas, reflecting the pleasure she derives from painting. Perhaps it is this to which her warning about the danger of art refers: 'Art is not meant for children. Like poison and medicine it should be kept out of reach.' The artist admits that she is sometimes afraid that she can no longer draw something simply for pleasure; not because she is afraid of being misunderstood, but because so many images already exist. 'You can't produce art simply because it gives you pleasure' she claims. For that reason she sometimes draws in secret. She takes time off from art.

In addition to these subjects from close to home, Dumas also extracts material from newspapers and magazines. This material sometimes has political overtones. She has produced a large painting of the Nuremberg trials, and portraits of South African women. Yet these works contain no political message. Dumas wants to discover whether the image of a crying woman in a painting has a different meaning from when it appears in a newspaper. These paintings do indeed say something about the power of the various media, and about Dumas' talent as a painter: one looks at a photograph in a newspaper for only a few seconds at most before turning the page, but the same picture on a museum wall can make one stand still in front of it for a long time. Perhaps this is why Dumas is not afraid to acknowledge her sources. On rough paper, in the catalogue of her major exhibition in the Van Abbe Museum, she set down a databank. This databank consists largely of groups of reproductions of paintings and illustrations which, for one reason or another, belong together. The databank begins with a series of recumbent, mostly nude, men and women: provocative beauties from paintings, a man shot dead, whose torso is bare, and Michael Jackson in his oxygen tent. The caption under the latter reads: 'From Captain to Sleeping Beauty'.

On other pages there are photographs of adults and children standing in circles holding hands. This usually indicates dancing, as in Matisse's famous painting, but on the same page Dumas has inserted a photograph of a procession of people affected by river-blindness in South Africa. The connections Dumas makes in her databank are based on similarities of form: for example, she combines a painting by Mondrian, filled with bars and crosses, and a photograph of a military cemetery, with its stiff rows of crosses extending as far as the eye can see. Many will dismiss as superficial the link between Mondrian's bars and the military graves. But for Dumas such similarities are a rich source.

Marlene Dumas, *The Dance*. 1992. Canvas, 90 x 180 cm. Collection F. Wisman, Utrecht.

In her latest works Dumas is less concerned with the interpretation an image can evoke. The titles have become simpler, and anecdotal rather than enigmatic. On the large canvas *The Dance,* from 1992, we see four little girls, two black and two white, holding hands in an empty room. Dumas has painted them with their backs to us. A figure has been drawn in chalk on the ground in front of them. The title gives nothing away, but it is probably an angel. Are the girls dancing round it? Are they performing a ritual? We cannot say. But we can accept this, because there are enough other things to look at. The painting is obviously taken from a snapshot. The position of the little girl on the left tells us this. She has turned away from the circle and is looking towards the door. Is someone entering the room? It does not matter. We are glad that the artist was able to capture the little girl's curiosity.

Dumas paints attitudes and situations which have probably never been captured before. This, too, she has been doing for some time. A good example is the little girl who is kneeling and watching, watching, watching. Once again, the title of this canvas gives us a clue: *TV Trance.*

Although Dumas has lived in the Netherlands since 1976, she still does not feel Dutch, particularly where her art is concerned, although she is regarded as such in the Netherlands. According to the press, Dumas was one of the three 'Dutch' artists who took part in Jan Hoet's *Documenta IX* in Kassel. For this exhibition she painted, among others, portraits of Hoet and the other exhibition organisers.

Dumas admits that living in the Netherlands has changed her work. It has become 'quieter'. She uses fewer sensational images. According to Dumas the existence of an artist such as Jeff Koons – who began by chromiumplating vacuum cleaners and later exhibited photographs of himself and his wife Cicciolina during lovemaking – would be unthinkable in the Netherlands. The Dutch are too respectable, too careful for that. Dumas also has doubts about the plethora of regulations for the visual arts in the Netherlands. The result of working by government order, and assessment by various planning authorities, is art which is unadventurous and takes no risks. In particular, the regulation which stipulates that 1% of the construction costs of new government buildings must be spent on art, has led to many futile embellishments. In 1991 Dumas took on such a commission for the first time, for the psychiatric institution *Het Hooghuys* in Etten-Leur. Dumas painted portraits of the residents. However, unusually for this type of commission, she allowed the residents to have a say in how art would be used to embellish their building. They could choose how they wanted to pose for Dumas. 'These people did not ask for art. I want to show them as they choose to present themselves to me.'

It is apparent, from a letter written in 1991 to the Icelandic artist Sigurdur Gudmundsson – also resident in the Netherlands at the time – that Dumas finds her work for the Netherlands useful. 'Let us make mountains for those who have no mountains. Let us invent incredible stories and sagas for their structured landscapes. Let us sow their sea with vermin, resurrect their extinct species. Let us exploit misconceptions.'

BIANCA STIGTER

Translated by Yvette Mead.

FURTHER READING

Miss Interpreted. Marlene Dumas, Eindhoven, 1992.

Indonesia and the Netherlands

A Renewed Interest

In the period from 1945 to 1963, that is to say from the proclamation of the Republic of Indonesia up to the termination of the conflict over Western New Guinea (Irian Jaya), the Dutch had to a great extent lost interest in their former colony. However, in 1963 Irian Jaya was finally annexed by Indonesia and shortly thereafter, still under the régime of President Sukarno (1901-1970), political and diplomatic relations were restored. Especially after the communist coup of 30 September 1965 and the subsequent assumption of power by President Suharto (1921-), there was an increasing improvement in relations between the two countries. To implement its economic recovery plan the Suharto government sought help from western countries and Japan. At the request of the Indonesian government, the Netherlands became the chairman of IGGI (the Inter-Governmental Group for Indonesia), which was formed in 1967. As a result, the former ruler acquired for the next twenty-five years an important role in the spectacular economic development of Indonesia, although Dutch development aid remained comparatively limited in financial terms. After a hesitant start Dutch investments in Indonesia later increased to such an extent that the Netherlands has now overtaken France and Germany in this respect.

Bilateral contacts were quickly intensified, both at government level and also through all sorts of private initiatives. A cultural agreement between the countries, concluded in 1968 and ratified in 1970, opened up possibilities for a variety of exchange programmes in the fields of science, art and sport. Numerous Indonesians received grants to take courses or do research in the Netherlands. In the context of cultural cooperation a Dutch department was set up at the *Universitas Indonesia* in Jakarta; while the *Erasmushuis,* an annex of the Dutch embassy in Jakarta, provided more practically oriented courses in the Dutch language, as well as an information service, for which there proved to be still considerable demand.

Interest in Indonesia also increased greatly in broad areas of Dutch society. The crisis in political relations during the period 1945-1963 and the anti-Dutch policy of Sukarno had led to a negative attitude in the Netherlands towards the former colony. But after 1965 the tide began to turn. An important part in this was played by the 'East Indian Dutchmen', those born and bred in the Dutch East Indies. They included a large number of so-called 'Indos', half-castes of mixed Indo-European parentage. In the post-war years these people had sought a safe haven in the Netherlands and had initially turned their back on their 'far-off fatherland'. But gradually these groups began to discover Indonesia anew, prompted by a mixture of nostalgic yearning for *tempo dulu*, the 'good old days', on the part of the older people, and curiosity on the part of the younger generation about their unknown 'Country of Origin' (the title of a celebrated novel – also translated into English – by Edgar du Perron (1899-1940), himself an Indo-European).

However, even in circles with no traditional ties with the colonial era, Indonesia was attracting ever-increasing attention. This found expression in various ways. Indonesia became the Dutchman's favourite non-European holiday destination; every summer all flights to Indonesia were – and are – fully booked with tourists both young and old, all of whom discover or rediscover the country in their own way.

Then there is the interest, at various levels, in the language, history and culture of the former colony. Nowadays every Dutch provincial town of any significance has courses in *bahasa Indonesia,* the national language of Indonesia. A national television course in this language attracted tens of thousands of participants. In many places in the Netherlands amateur groups play *gamelan,* the traditional music of Java, which also forms the accompaniment to the famous shadow puppet theatre, the *wayang*. Exhibitions and courses about aspects of Indonesian art and culture draw disproportionately large numbers of visitors, as do performances of Indonesian dance, theatre and music.

A similar development is to be observed at university level. After the fifties and sixties, during which hardly any students enrolled for Indonesian studies, the seventies saw a change in this field too. Dozens of students now come to Leiden every year to study Indonesian languages and literature, whilst numerous students of, for instance, anthropology and sociology, history, archaeology and history of art at various institutions of higher education choose Indonesia as their special subject. Thanks to the possibilities of field research in Indonesia itself, which are provided for in the cultural agreement between the two countries, such study need not be restricted to research in libraries and archives. Young research workers can acquire a substantial knowledge of the country, the language and the culture through personal experience. For this reason, and also because of the unique collections in museums and libraries, the Netherlands can maintain its position as the European 'centre of excellence' in the field of Indonesian studies.

The number of publications about Indonesia appearing in the Netherlands, both academic and popular, books and periodicals, is remarkably large. Indicative of the present attitude is the fact that the annual book week in the spring of 1992 had Indonesia as its theme: there were hundreds of publications of every kind, scale and quality, both new and reprints. So-called 'East Indian' *belles-lettres,* novels and stories with a colonial East Indian-Indonesian background, form one of the most flourishing categories in Dutch literature. It is certainly no coincidence that Pramudya Ananta Toer (1925-), the novelist who is blacklisted in Indonesia itself on account of his left-wing activities prior to 1965 and who has spent more than fourteen years in prison, should be so popular. His extensive oeuvre appears rapidly in Dutch translation and some of his books are among the Dutch bestsellers.

It may be said without exaggeration that many Dutchmen have very close ties of many kinds with Indonesia: historical, emotional, scientific, artistic, touristic. Events and developments there are followed with great interest, although strangely enough the press, notably the daily papers, provides a minimum of current information.

On the part of the Indonesians the interest is much less intense. For a certain group of Indonesians the Netherlands is important as a source of knowledge of their own culture and history, because of the information about their country accumulated in Dutch libraries and archives. For some groups of academics (primarily historians and lawyers) knowledge of Dutch is still essential in order to make use of these sources. In a few areas of Indonesia (Ambon, North Celebes) and in certain circles in other parts of the country Dutch still plays a limited role in the social intercourse amongst the older generation, but it is in fact a vanished or vanishing language. As far as the Indonesians are concerned there are few or no emotional ties with the old 'mother country'.

In March 1992 the cooperation between the Netherlands and Indonesia was somewhat unexpectedly subjected to heavy political pressure. On 25 March President Suharto issued a declaration, proclaiming that Indonesia no longer wished to receive development aid from the Netherlands. The role of the Netherlands as chairman of IGGI also came to an end. This decision was due to irritation aroused by the critical attitude taken by, in particular, the Dutch Minister of Development Aid and chairman of IGGI, Jan Pronk, toward human rights policy in Indonesia. The direct consequences of the decision were not limited to cooperation at government level. A variety of technical projects being carried out by private enterprise with the financial backing of the government had to be terminated where no alternative source of funding could be found.

The decision also had far-reaching consequences for cultural and scientific cooperation between the two countries. It appeared that this, though coming under the competence of other Ministries, particularly the Ministry of Education and Science, was financed from the Development Aid budget and was thus also affected by the Indonesian decision. This meant that all sorts of current programmes had to be terminated. Indonesian graduates studying in the Netherlands had to return home, and some scientific research projects came to an abrupt end.

But from the beginning the Indonesian government had emphasized that it had no intention of terminating economic, scientific and cultural cooperation between the two countries. On the contrary, it said that by the very fact of removing the one-sided 'aid' element this cooperation could develop much more healthily and positively now that it was between partners who were on an equal footing.

In the second half of 1992 both parties demonstrated their desire to put these good intentions into practice in new and concrete forms of cooperation, for which reciprocal ministerial visits laid the foundation. Thus in September 1992 the Dutch Minister of Education and Science, Dr J. Ritzen, visited Indonesia, where he concluded outline agreements with his

Indonesian colleagues: Dr Fuad Hassan for Education and Science and Dr Habibie for Research and Technology. Dr Fuad Hassan subsequently paid a return visit to the Netherlands. These visits were followed by the exchange of official delegations. On 12 December 1992 a detailed programme for cooperation in 1993 and 1994 within the framework of the Cultural Agreement was finalized and approved. It covers a wide field of scientific and cultural activities, with more attention being paid to science and technology than in the past. Another important feature is that the planning and organisation of specific programmes is left as far as possible to the relevant bodies themselves. The financing is also primarily a matter for the institutions themselves, where necessary with government backing. The Dutch Minister for Education and Science has in the meantime made substantial funds available for this purpose from his own budget.

Thus at the beginning of 1993, after a tumultuous and confusing 1992, the prospects for wide-ranging intensive cooperation between the two countries on a new basis appear to be favourable after all. There is in any case no lack of good will.

A. TEEUW

Translated by Rachel van der Wilden.

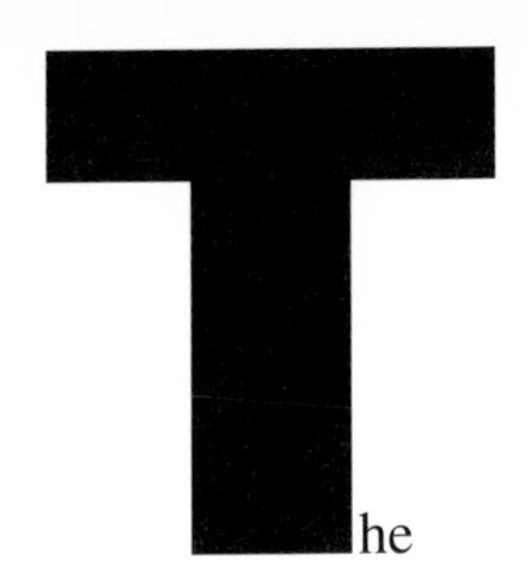

The Great Leap Forward

Dance in the Low Countries: the Advantage of a Lack of Tradition

Amsterdam on an evening in June, 1992. Two small figures on the immense stage of the *Muziektheater*. The sole piece of decor – a gigantic chandelier – makes them seem even smaller. The boy (Jean Emile) looks at the girl (Fiona Lummis), who for the time being finds him unworthy of a glance. She looks back only when it suits her. They shuffle around slowly, getting closer and closer to each other. She remains the inaccessible princess on the pea, he is much suppler, slipping willy-nilly into strange gyrations of the hip in his passion to thaw the ice queen.

Not much actually happens, but what does, takes place with a commanding sense of timing and proportion. The boy wipes his hand, almost unnoticed, before grasping hers. They look back for a fleeting moment, then stand still. *Andante* is over. Two people have moved very subtly for ten minutes on an endless stage. It looks so simple. Yet afterwards the world seems a little bit different.

The hall is sold out for this Hans van Manen programme in the *Holland Festival,* and will remain so for the entire one-month run. Hans van Manen (1932-) has been a choreographer for the past thirty-five years, and has grown in stature to become one of the Netherlands' best known living artists. This is unusual for a choreographer, especially in the light of the fact that he does not pander to public taste.

The *Holland Festival* made him a central figure in their programme. They showed him as choreographer to the large companies: *Nederlands Dans Theater* and the *Nationale Ballet,* but also as a maker of modern dance for smaller groups, and finally as a photographer.

For he is all these things rolled into one. His versatility is typical of the generation which determined the post-war shape of modern dance in the Netherlands. The two other great choreographers of his generation are also doubly talented. Rudi van Dantzig (1933-) is the author of the succesful novel *For a Lost Soldier* (Voor een verloren soldaat, tr. 1991). Toer van Schayk (1936-) is a painter as well as a choreographer.

December 1991, a festive get-together in the stylish *Koninklijke Muntschouwburg* (Royal Mint Theatre) in Brussels. The opera company announces that it is now the permanent home of Anne Teresa de Keersmaeker (1960-) and her troupe, Rosas, which becomes the company-in-residence; *De Munt's* offer of hospitality will not only make it possible for them to develop new works but also to study their classics again.

This is an act of justice to the finest choreographer Belgium has ever produced. But also a remarkable gesture, because De Keersmaeker will certainly not dance to the opera directors' tune. She is not the kind of choreographer who can easily be asked to create a divertissement for an opera.

The standard of dance in the Low Countries is a high one. This has been the case for some time now. Almost long enough for it to seem the most normal thing in the world that tens of thousands of people come to see dances by Hans van Manen. Almost long enough for there to seem nothing special about a choreographer in her early thirties getting a key position in Belgium's most prestigious art institution.

And yet it is not just a matter of course that choreographers such as Van Manen and De Keersmaeker occupy the focus of attention. Anyone who came to the Low Countries in the seventies religiously intent upon seeing a dance performance would have been hard pressed indeed. One could go to Brussels to see the renowned Maurice Béjart (1927-) and his Ballet of the XXth Century. He was at the height of his powers, setting the standards for new developments in ballet and was the founder of *Mudra,* a school considered for quite some time to be one of Europe's finest dance institutes. In Antwerp, Jeanne Brabants's (1920-) *Ballet van Vlaanderen* (Ballet of Flanders) maintained high standards of classical ballet. But these two groups were oases surrounded by a vast desert. The great leap forward was still a long way off.

The situation in the Netherlands was not much better. At the time, the *Nationale Ballet,* which had traditionally concentrated on a classical repertoire, added modern pieces under the new leadership of Rudi van Dantzig. In The Hague, the *Nederlands Dans Theater* was laying the foundations through trial and error, for its present eminence. In the Netherlands twenty years ago, apart from the two major companies, you could count the number of good dance performances on one hand. Timid attempts were made at modern dance by dancers who had studied in New York. Then there was *Scapino,* a company which was at that time youth-oriented. But nothing in the Netherlands and Flanders then indicated they would be among the leaders of modern dance in the 1980s and 1990s.

This blossoming of dance in the Netherlands is largely due to the amazing coincidence that a single generation produced three extremely talented choreographers: Rudi van Dantzig, Toer van Schayk, and Hans van Manen. They were the ones responsible for turning the *Nationale Ballet* and the *Nederlands Dans Theater* into companies with international reputations. Reputations which, by the way, are due to the quality of the performing artists. For a long time the art of dance in the Netherlands had been a matter of choreography much more than of virtuoso dancers.

Of the three, Rudi van Dantzig is the most Dutch. Even though he comes from a socialist family, his sense of guilt, his social engagement and his nostalgia for the innocence of youth all betray a Calvinist streak. He is sometimes called the 'parson' of dance, which has stuck as a nickname. His style is based on classical technique, though blended with a great deal of the expressionism of Martha Graham. He is essentially a narrative dance maker, whose choreographic works often refer to current events in society, relentlessly pointing out to his audience the dangers of environmental pollution, greed for power and egoism. Much of his best work such as *Monument for a Boy Who Died* (Monument voor een gestorven jongen) and *Four Last Songs* (Vier letzte Lieder), was done in the sixties and seventies. Certainly, in his later work his social engagement threatened to get the better of the dance component.

After more than twenty years as director of the *Nationale Ballet,* Rudi van Dantzig stepped down in 1991 and was succeeded by the American Wayne Eagling. At present it still remains to be seen whether he will afford his predecessor the opportunity of regularly creating new works for the company.

Anne Teresa de Keersmaeker (1960-) (Photo *Antwerpen 93*).

Toer van Schayk is an artistic brother to Van Dantzig. Their thematic choices have often shown striking resemblances, so much so that on a number of occasions they have even collaborated on a choreography. But Van Schayk does not allow his engagement to show in his work so explicitly. He is a more whimsical and elusive choreographer, with a sharp eye for detail and a curious sense of humour. His approach to dance is that of a visual artist or painter, employing plastic movements hitherto seldom seen in dance. His *pièce de résistance* is considered to be his 1982 piece called *Landscape* (Landschap), a full length ballet relating the history of a piece of land through dance and decor.

In many ways, Hans van Manen is their counterpart. He too could be regarded a typically Dutch choreographer but more in the sense of *De Stijl* or the painter Mondrian, a man of the clear line and the balanced division of surfaces. This work has a timelessness achieved by few others and is of constant high quality. The Van Manen retrospective held in 1992 attests to this. His early work stands up perfectly alongside his later pieces. The years too have not dulled the subtle humour that runs through his ballets like a thread. By now, his work has been included in scores of companies' repertoires. *Adagio Piano* (Hammerklavier) and *Great Fugue* (Grosse Fuge) are regarded as postwar classics.

In the mid-seventies, Jiri Kylian (1946-), a Czech by birth, was asked to become leader of the *Nederlands Dans Theater.* It turned out to be a brilliant move. He made the *Nederlands Dans Theater* into an elite group with extremely talented – mostly foreign – dancers. His own development as choreographer went hand in hand with his group. At first he made extremely lyrical, flowing ballets, usually set to the music of Central European composers. For the past few years he has embraced a more abstract and adventurous dance idiom.

The *Nederlands Dans Theater* is also of interest as a business venture. It is the only dance company in the world to have its own custom-made building, the *AT&T Dans Theater,* designed by Rem Koolhaas and completed in 1987. The company maintains a succesful formula whereby three groups perform under the name NDT. Special choreographies are tailor-made for each group. NDT1 is the large group led by Kylian, NDT2 consists of young dancers who are studying to get into the first group, but who are a separate entity and enjoy an international reputation in their own right. NDT3 was

Hans van Manen, *On the Move* (Photo by Hans Gerritsen).

formed in 1991 and is made up of older dancers for whom new work is made by choreographers such as Kylian, Van Manen and William Forsythe.

Of great importance to the development of dance in the Netherlands has been the recent appearance of performing venues in the major cities. The AT&T *Danstheater* in The Hague (1987) already mentioned, the *Muziektheater* in Amsterdam (1986), home to the *Nationale Ballet,* and the Rotterdam Municipal Theatre (1988) all have the same dimensions.

Typical of the Dutch dance scene is the rich variety of smaller dance troupes that have sprung up alongside the large ones since the 1970s. Unlike in many other countries, the larger groups do not lead a totally separate existence to the smaller ones. Hans van Manen in particular regularly choreographs for smaller groups, while the NDT sometimes reciprocates by commissioning choreographies from the smaller companies.

Hungarian born Krisztina de Châtel (1945-) settled in Amsterdam in the 1970s. Her first choreographies were characterized by their extreme austerity and great fidelity to a form once chosen. She would have her dancers clash with some kind of obstacle, a wall of earth slowly ploughed under, a battery of powerful wind machines, four glass walls moving closer to one another threatening to squash the dancers like goldfish in a shrinking bowl. Her recent work is more open in character. More than in the past, she now utilizes the personalities of her dancers and the differences between male and female. *Føld* and *Dualis* are among the best pieces modern Dutch dance has produced. She has recently been commissioned to choreograph a new piece for the prestigious *Muziektheater* in Amsterdam.

If dance in the Netherlands is relatively cherished and cared for like a hothouse plant, in Flanders the various groups have to contend with weather conditions more like those of an open field in order to survive. For a long time scarcely any state funds were available and venues that wanted to programme dance were few and far between. Many Flemish choreographers first made their mark in the Netherlands.

The vacuum left when Béjart went to Lausanne in 1986 is a case in point. His place was taken by the American Mark Morris, whose frivolous choreographies never really caught on in Brussels. Béjart's departure also led to the gradual dismantling of the *Mudra* school, Belgium's only serious dance academy. Only the very strong were able to survive in that hostile climate, but those who did gained worldwide recognition.

The kind of dance now setting the pace in Flanders is surprisingly young, scarcely a decade old. It is being led by choreographers who made their international breakthrough in their mid-twenties. Dance in Flanders was scarcely hampered by tradition, and was able to exploit this fact to its own advantage; dance has been re-invented in Flanders in the last decade. This has resulted in an unexpected measure of success and international acclaim. Anne Teresa de Keersmaeker, Wim Vandekeybus (1963-), and Jan Fabre (1958-) are award winning choreographers, much sought after by the major festivals; choreographers who from the very outset presented themselves as citizens of the world.

Flemish dance, like Flemish theatre, is very popular in the Netherlands. The work of the three choreographers just mentioned is greatly appreciated and admired and their groups perform there regularly. It is as though the Dutch recognize something they themselves lack in their southern neighbour's vocabulary of movement, tending as it does towards extremes. The opposite is hardly the case. Venues in Belgium show little interest in Dutch

Jiri Kylian, *Forgotten Land* (Photo by Joris Jan Bos).

Jiri Kylian, *Forgotten Land* (Photo by Hans Gerritsen).

dance. The Dutch tendency to see themselves in perspective, (*relativeren* as the word is in Dutch, trans.) has few adherents in Belgium.

At the forefront of current Flemish dance is Anne Teresa de Keersmaeker, trained at Béjart's *Mudra* school. Her first professional choreographic work, *Phase* (Fase), brought her immediate acclaim. A duet for women which was impressive because of its close affinity to the compelling music of Steve Reich, extreme attention to detail and the dancers' willingness to work to the point of exhaustion. From the very beginning she set such high standards for herself, that only a fierce effort could achieve them.

In the years that followed De Keersmaeker would prove herself an extremely musical choreographer, but her taste would gradually broaden. *Rosas Dances Rosas* (Rosas danst Rosas), *Elena's Arias, Bartok / Notes* (Bartok / Aantekeningen): each new choreography was an attempt at extending the boundaries of herself, her dancers, and the audience. The introverted passion of her earlier pieces has gradually developed into a more extrovert, richly varied form of dance. Even so, to this day, many everyday movements lie at the heart of her choreographies, and, set in a new environment, take on new meanings. Her dance suggests meaning, but never imposes it. In this regard she is the standard bearer of a contemporary expressionism.

In her case, it is virtually impossible to single out any peaks of quality or success. Each of her works sets a standard for modern dance, and each does so with a different emphasis. *Ottone Ottone* and *Stella* are more theatrically scored, her most recent pieces *Heartland* (Achterland) and *Ore* (Erts) remain closer to dance. Her vocabulary of movement has grown enormously in the past ten years. Her vocabulary and style has spawned many followers, though rarely within Flanders.

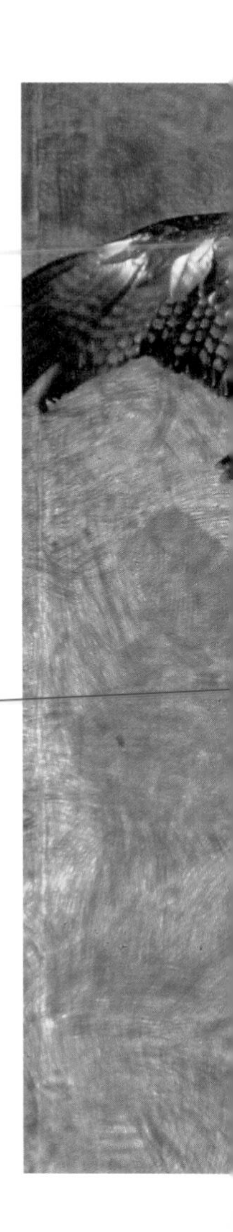

One production was all it took to establish Wim Vandekeybus's reputation. His first full length production, *What the Body Does Not Remember,* was an immediate hit. All over the world, audiences – largely of the young – were recognizing themselves in the grim chain of childhood memories in which fierce kicks and leaps alternate with intimate details, such as a gorgeous dance for the hands alone. It is a physically demanding kind of dance at the cutting edge, with flying leaps and heavy falls to the floor. Anyone with a sloppy sense of timing, or who does not jump high enough, will be cut to pieces, that is the message. The performance seems to be structured along the lines of a series of children's games, in which the rules become clear to the audience as the dancers perform.

He has continued this line with his group *Ultima Vez* in *The Bearers of Bad Tidings* (Les porteuses de mauvaises nouvelles). His third large scale production, *Always the Same Old Lies* (Immer das Selbe gelogen) is a cautious reconnaissance in another direction. The physicality is still there, but there is now also room for moments of poetic stillness.

Jan Fabre is known mainly as a visual artist, but his two essays in choreography justify his position among the *crème de la crème* of Flemish dance. His *Dance Sections* (Danssecties), originally intended to be integrated into the opera trilogy *The Minds of Helena Troubleyn,* can be seen as a direct challenge to classical ballet by the visual, plastic arts. Twelve female dancers in formation perform nothing but the basic positions of classical ballet, and do it so relentlessly and meticulously that the spectator is forced to focus his / her attention on the slightest variation. It is movement bordering on standstill. The skin of aesthetics, set, ornament, variation is casually peeled away in order to penetrate to a core hard enough to maintain itself in the face of arbitrariness. As though one were flying over a city at a great height, and only as one approached did it become evident that it was teeming with life.

Fabre has made other pieces since *Dance Sections.* One of them is called *The Sound of One Hand Clapping* for William Forsythe's Frankfurt Ballet. A full-length triptych, in which the chaos of everyday life is surrounded by a lucid, symmetrical, ballpoint-blue world-according-to-Fabre. He continues to work as a visual artist and in theatre. It would be a great loss to the art of dance were his contributions to choreography to be limited to the present pieces.

Meanwhile, an infrastructure for dance is being created in Flanders. Theatre *deSingel* in Antwerp is staging trendsetting dance from anywhere and everywhere. De Keersmaeker has found a permanent home in Brussels, as has her fellow artist, the Walloon Michele-Anne de Mey, whom she has known from the outset of her career. Fabre and Vandekeybus have their own organizations to give them a solid base. The other, smaller, groups can, in the meantime, show their work at festivals and in various theatres in Flemish cities.

At the moment, the position of Flemish dance is rather similar to that of Dutch dance at the beginning of the eighties. A canon has not yet been formed, but a few groups and choreographers now have some solid ground under their feet.

What is remarkable is that contemporary Flemish dance is being shaped – if we except De Keersmaeker – by those with no formal education in dance. This holds for Wim Vandekeybus and Jan Fabre, but also for the second echelon led by Alain Platel (1956-) and Marc Vanrunxt (1960-). Their work owes its quality not so much to technical dance genius, as to the unbridled energy with which it seeks out extremes and for the rigour with which it dispenses with convention. This radical attitude can be felt wherever their work is perfomed.

Flemish dance is a dance of extremes which, like the rose of Jericho, can blossom in the desert.

ARIEJAN KORTEWEG
Translated by Scott Rollins.

Jan Fabre and Eugeniusz Knapik, *Silent Screams, Difficult Dreams* (Photo *Antwerpen 93*).

Belgian Federalisation

Belgium was born of a divorce. In 1814 prince William of Orange had been assigned, as a reward for his services during the preceding wars, the Kingdom of the Netherlands, which included, as well as the former United Provinces, the former Austrian Netherlands. In this Southern part of the United Kingdom of the Netherlands the nobility and the bourgeoisie were Catholic and Francophone. In 1830, after fifteen years of strife-torn cohabitation with protestant Holland and spurred on by the upper classes and clergy, the South rebelled against the North and founded its own state.

The new Belgian state did not revert to the structure of dukedoms and counties which had prevailed under the Ancien Régime but retained the administrative structure which had been introduced by the Revolution and subsequently by Bonaparte. Belgium became a centralised unitary state. In the northern provinces (Flanders) the population spoke various dialects belonging to the Dutch language group; in the southern provinces (Wallonia) the Walloon and Picard dialects, which belonged to the French language group, were spoken. In the capital, Brussels, the two language groups co-existed. Throughout the whole country the elite spoke French.

The constitution stipulated that language use was a matter of individual choice but in fact the whole country was administered in French. French was the sole language in parliament, government, the civil service, the army, the courts, the universities, secondary education and in business and commerce. Flemings had to learn and to speak French if they were to pursue a career. The use of French was a status symbol. The Walloons could make a career for themselves in their own language throughout Belgium; they had no need to learn Dutch. Dutch was maintained in Flanders at primary school level and it was this which ultimately prevented the complete gallicisation of the Flemish population.

Flemish opposition to the dominant position of French and the Francophone elite quickly developed. Intellectuals from the petty bourgeoisie and the middle class who had received their education under the United Kingdom of the Netherlands refused to accept the elimination of Dutch from public life. They pointed to the beauties of the language, the art and culture of Flanders and Brabant in the past and delivered the first blows in a 'language battle' which would last for over a century.

Teachers and literary figures in particular began to influence the people and to inculcate a 'Flemish national consciousness'. They gradually succeeded in making the Dutch-speaking population aware of its 'Flemish identity'. This also had repercussions in Parliament where in the second half of the nineteenth century an increasing number of representatives fought for equal recognition of Dutch in public life.

As the realisation dawned on the Francophone population that the official recognition of Dutch might ultimately force them to learn the language, at least those of them who were in public service, a fierce opposition grew among them to this threat of general bilingualism. As early as 1860 it was being argued that Flanders and Wallonia should be separated, with the aim of protecting Wallonia from potential penetration by Dutch. In the cities of Flanders also the Francophone bourgeoisie was not prepared to abandon its language of culture in favour of a Dutch which was still strongly marked by dialect. In Brussels, the capital of a country administered in French, which was preoccupied with gallicising its Dutch-speaking population as quickly as possible, the Flemish Movement encountered deep hostility.

The strongest opposition, however, developed in the south, where a well organised Walloon Movement sprang up which demanded that French remain the official language and opposed the principle of equality for French and Dutch in Belgium. Around 1900 a pro-French tendency became apparent, which put forward the idea that the Walloons were French and that Wallonia ought to become part of the great French Nation. Other Walloons proposed a complete administrative separation between Flanders and Wallonia, which, they thought, should each have their own parliament and could only co-exist in a federal state.

This new Walloon attitude was most clearly expressed by the socialist statesman, Jules Destrée, who published a controversial Open Letter to king Albert in the *Revue de Belgique* (Belgian Review) in 1912. He wrote: 'Your Majesty, permit me to speak the truth, the whole and terrible truth: there is no such thing as a Belgian. (...) You reign over two peoples, there are Walloons and there are Flemings, but there are no Belgians.' Destrée's letter became one of the documents of Walloon history.

Meanwhile the Flemings had steadily increased their parliamentary representation, partly as a result of the extension of the suffrage. From the 1870s onwards a series of acts was passed which required the use of Dutch in Flanders in the courts, public administration and, later, in secondary education and the army.

Following the First World War, Dutch became the medium of instruction in the state university in Ghent in 1930 and separate language groups were phased in in the free universities of Leuven and Brussels. This made it possible to produce an elite educated exclusively in Dutch.

At the same time the Flemish parties, which had gained official parity for French and Dutch, proposed the introduction of a bilingual administrative system throughout the whole country. These proposals met with a rejection by the Walloons. Wallonia wished to remain exclusively Francophone. This Walloon rejection was a turning point in Belgian history. It caused Dutch speakers to decide to develop Flanders into a monolingual area. Subsequently new language laws in the thirties led to the implementation of monolingualism in administration and education in both Flanders and Wallonia. Brussels and its suburban municipalities were required to operate a bilingual system.

On the eve of the Second World War a consensus had been reached that the Dutch and French-speaking communities should both be granted 'cultural autonomy'. The German invasion in May 1940 put implementation of this plan into abeyance.

After the end of the occupation, the issue was taken up again. The process was speeded up by the deep divisions between the Flemish and Walloon community at the end of the war concerning the behaviour of the king, Leopold III, during the occupation. The Walloon community was critical of the king for what they judged to be his collaboration and failure to give a lead to the Resistance. The Flemish community, on the other hand, supported the king's decision to remain in the country during the occupation and to seek to shield the people, as he saw it, from the worst excesses of the enemy. It was finally decided, after a referendum in 1950, that Leopold should formally give up the throne in favour of his elder son Boudewijn, the present king. Both sides recognised that the structure of the state needed to be adapted to cope with the divergent opinions, behaviour and desires of Flemings and Walloons.

A research centre was established by law in 1948 as the result of a bill introduced by the Walloon MP Pierre Harmel (1911-), later prime minister and foreign minister. This studied Flemish-Walloon relations and presented a series of notable conclusions to Parliament on 24 April 1958. The Centre recognised the existence within Belgium of Flemish and Walloon cultural communities and declared that Brussels was the common property of both.

These conclusions laid the foundation for the passage of a new programme of language legislation in the sixties. The border between the language areas was recognised in law in 1962 and fixed as an inviolable administrative border.

In 1970 there was an important revision of the Constitution. This was announced to the Chamber by the then prime minister Gaston Eyskens in the following words: 'The unitary state with its structure and method of operation which is currently legally in force has been rendered obsolete by events. The communities and the regions must take their place in new state structures, which are better adapted to the actual situation in the country.'

The constitutional structure of the country was altered quite fundamentally. The constitution stipulated that there should henceforth be four language areas (Dutch, French, German and the bilingual capital Brussels), three cultural communities (Dutch, French and German) and three regions (Flanders, Wallonia and Brussels). Communities and regions had separate councils composed of the representatives in the national parliament who thus had a 'double mandate'.

The revision of the constitution met needs which had become increasingly pressing since the end of the Second World War. The desire for cultural autonomy had become stronger in Flanders. In Wallonia, where there was no language problem, a strong desire for economic self-determination had developed. Traditional industries which had brought prosperity to Wallonia in the nineteenth century had become out-dated. The closure of the coal mines and the crisis in the steel industry had caused serious social problems. Walloon politicians and unions thought that the national government and private capital in Brussels were turning their backs on Walloon problems. They also, therefore, though for different reasons from those of the Flemings, began to demand self-government. Both tendencies, the cultural in Flanders and the economic in Wallonia, coalesced in the demand for federalisation of the unitary state.

The running-in period of the new institutions in the seventies showed that both Flemings and Walloons wished to go further down the road to dividing up the country. In 1980 the constitution was revised once again. In Flanders cultural self-government and social and economic autonomy were entrusted to the same bodies. For the Francophone community and Walloon region these spheres of autonomy were placed under different bodies. The old councils were restructured into a sort of parliament. Executive power for regional matters was entrusted to Executive Bodies which acted as real governments. Power at the regional level was extended and strengthened.

Even this constitutional revision did not end the process of federalisation. In 1988-89 the constitution and laws were further amended. In the first phase the powers of the regional institutions were considerably extended; in the second phase these institutions received relatively broad financial funding and powers.

Because the nationally elected representatives still had seats in the regional assemblies – the double mandate – this constitutional revision was likewise not considered as the final phase in the process of federalisation. In 1989 the centre-left cabinet of Wilfried Martens attempted to introduce further amendments but failed. The elections of 24 November 1991 ended the ten year premiership of Mr Martens. The incomplete reform of the state was passed on to his successor Jean-Luc Dehaene.

At the end of 1992 Belgium is a state in which three linguistic and cultural communities are recognised: Dutch, French and German. The country is divided into three regions: Flanders, Wallonia and Brussels. The national government remains responsible for general administration, Finance and the Budget, Overseas Aid and Social Services.

The structure and operations of the state rest, however, in large measure on the duality of the Communities and the Regions. The Communities have responsibility for education, culture and issues concerned with 'personal welfare'. The latter comprise health care policy, social welfare, reception and integration of immigrants, care for the disabled and elderly, protection of minors and social rehabilitation of offenders.

The Regions are responsible for land use planning, quality of the environment, nature conservation, housing, water management, certain economic matters such as regional aspects of credit, energy and employment policy, and public works.

The Communities and Regions are jointly responsible for certain matters, for example scientific research and administrative supervision of the provinces and municipalities.

Apart from education, the residual powers rest with the central government. Economic and domestic policy matters are divided between the central and the regional level.

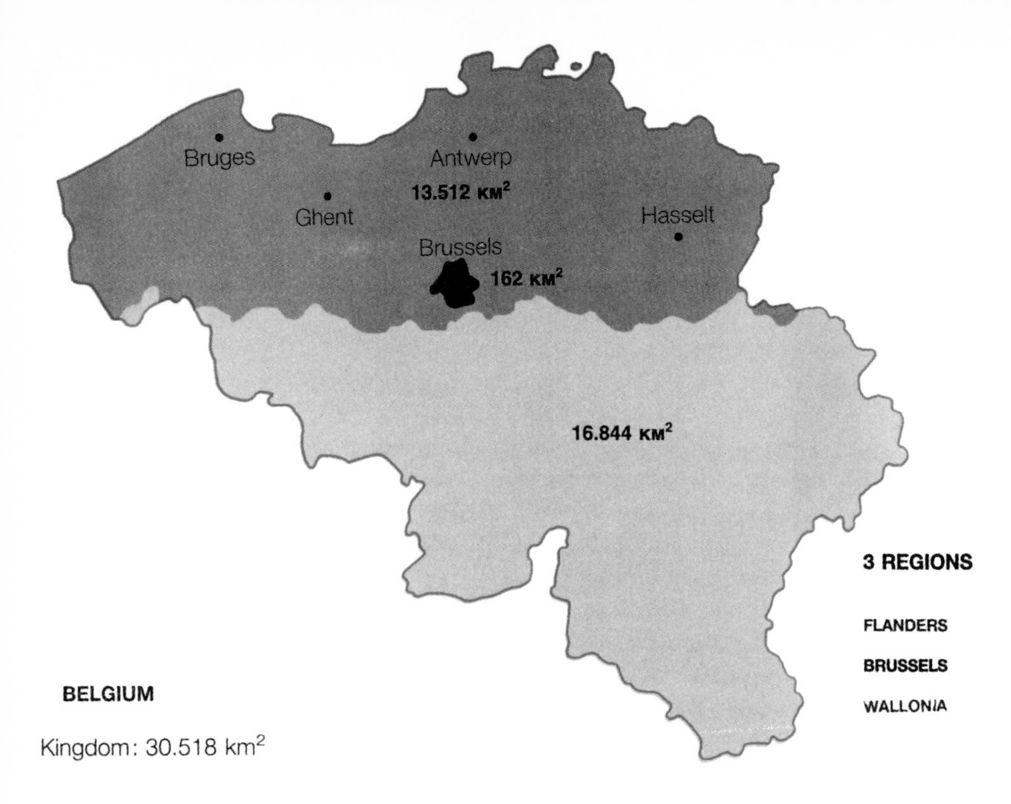

In the Brussels region (the 19 municipalities of the metropolitan agglomeration) the Dutch and French-speaking communities act independently on education and issues of 'personal welfare' but act jointly on other responsibilities. The Brussels Region has its own Executive and Council.

The Brussels Metropolitan Region has the same regional powers as the Flemish and Walloon Regions. Certain community powers (including cultural matters and education) which have not been assigned to the Dutch and French Communities are exercised by specific institutions in the Brussels Region.

The German-speaking community has an elected Council and an Executive, which have responsibility for cultural and personal welfare matters and for education. The territory of the German-speaking community belongs to the Walloon Region. The German-speaking community and the Walloon Region can decide by a process of consultation to have certain responsibilities of the Walloon Region carried out by the institutions of the German-speaking community.

The Arbitration Court was established in 1980 and had its powers extended in 1988. It is a special court outside the judicial structure. It has 12 members, 6 lawyers and 6 former MPS. The Court has responsibility for laws (national legislation), decrees of the Communities and Regions and ordinances of the Brussels Metropolitan Region. It ensures that each legislative body remains within the bounds of its competence. The judgements it gives are final and binding on everyone.

Flanders has a population of 5.8 million, Wallonia 3.3 million, the Brussels Region 930,000 and the German-speaking community 60,000. The Flemish Region is also the economic power house, responsible for 75% of Belgian output.

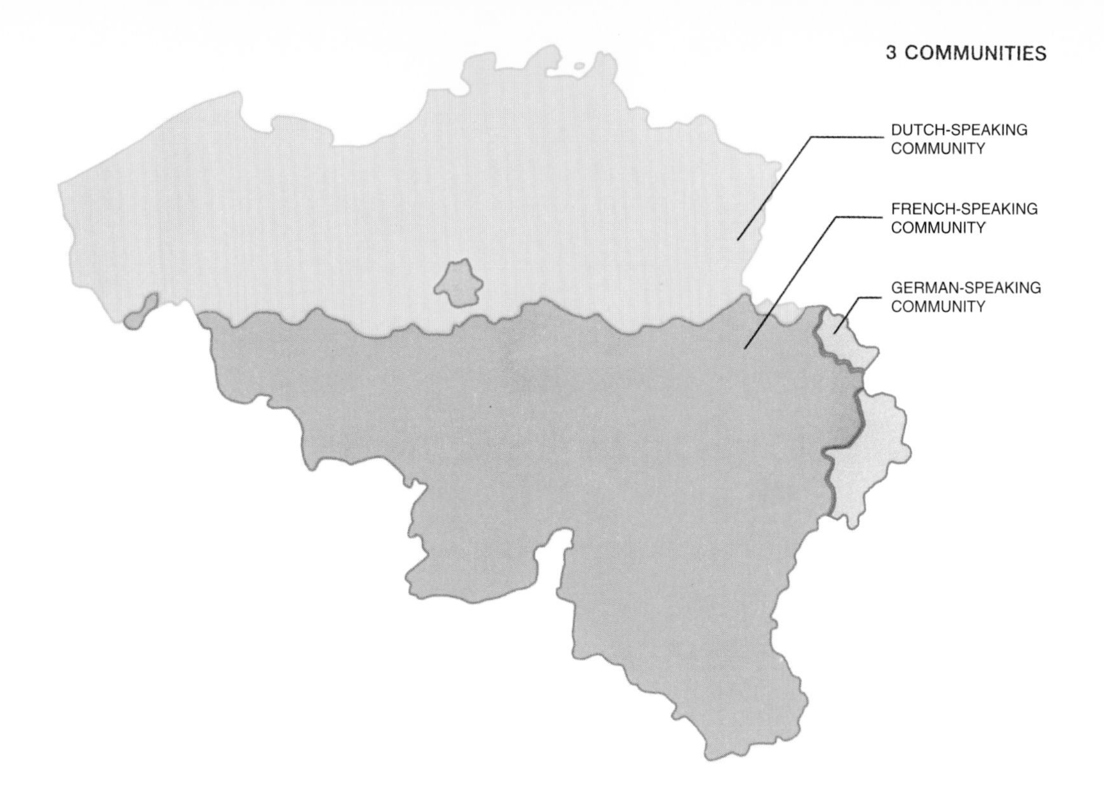

Federalisation is still in progress. The desire for greater autonomy continues to grow in both Flanders and Wallonia. If this tendency continues Belgium may become a confederal state. Luc van den Brande, Minister-President of the Government of Flanders, has already expressed a similar opinion on this matter.

At the beginning of 1993, the national parliament has revised the constitution once again. Article 1 now reads that Belgium is a federal state. The bilingual province of Brabant, which straddles the language boundary, will be divided into two provinces, Flemish-Brabant and Walloon-Brabant. The double mandate (national and regional) of the members of parliament will be abolished. After the next elections, the federal parliament will be completely separate from the independent regional parliaments. The Communities and Regions will have the right to enter into international treaties. The evolution towards a Belgian confederation does not seem to be grinding to a halt.

MANU RUYS
Translated by Lesley Gilbert.

FURTHER READING

SENELLE, ROBERT, *The Reform of the Belgian State,* Vol. V no 198, 1990. (Memo from Belgium, Views and Surveys, Ministry of Foreign Affairs, 1000 Brussels).

The Flemish Movement. A Documentary History 1780-1990 (Edited by Theo Hermans. Co-editors Louis Vos and Lode Wils), London & Atlantic Highlands NJ, 1992.

reations of Earth and Fire

The Ceramics of José Vermeersch

José Vermeersch, *Figure.* 1968. Canvas, 100 x 100 cm. (Photo by Sergyssels).

José Vermeersch, *Self-portrait.* 1948. Canvas, 31 x 36 cm. (Photo by Sergyssels).

Flanders has an artistic tradition which has continued and developed almost organically, right up to the present day, and some of the elements found in contemporary artists can be explained in historical terms.

A good example of this is the West Flemish painter and sculptor José Vermeersch. He was born in 1922 in Bissegem, a small town not far from Courtrai, where at the age of twelve he began his studies at the Academy of Fine Arts. During the early years of the war, he attended the Antwerp Academy to improve his painting, and after the liberation of Belgium in 1945 he returned to West Flanders. One of his tutors was Constant Permeke (1886-1952), a leading figure in the expressionist movement in Flanders, who nevertheless had little stylistic influence on his pupil. Rather, Vermeersch seemed to want to contradict his master's expressive power by

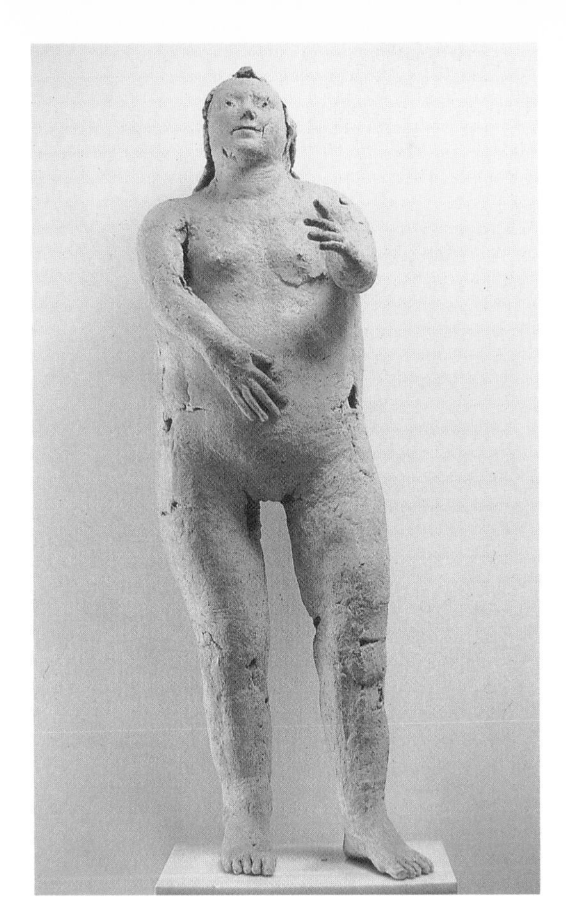

José Vermeersch, *Reno's Sister*. 1968. Ceramic and pink engobe, H 138 cm. (Photo by Sergyssels).

José Vermeersch, *Renaldo's Brother* (detail). 1969. Ceramic, H 64 cm. (Photo by Sergyssels).

voicing a quieter, more inward expression. Later however, in the late sixties, he was to take the stirring emotion found in Permeke's work and include it in his own style.

Vermeersch married shortly after finishing his studies, and several years of financial hardship followed. He was forced to look for work in the building materials industry, where he specialised in producing ceramic tiles for open fireplaces. Whether by coincidence or not, ceramics were later to play a fundamental part in his artistic career. He began painting again in 1962, and the first ceramic sculptures appeared a year later. During the ensuing period he alternated between painting and sculpting, but in the last twenty years it is mainly as a sculptor that he has made his reputation, and he has become well-known internationally in that capacity. In 1992, an exhibition of his paintings at the Museum of Fine Arts in the town of Mons in Wallonia (South Belgium) met with widespread admiration, because many people thought that Vermeersch had discovered a new discipline.

Although painting forms an essential part of his creative capacity, José Vermeersch is still best known as a sculptor who has chosen the difficult material of ceramics as his medium. Artists who use this material are usually to be found in the field of applied art. Those who dare to go further and use it for sculpture generally produce small or medium-sized pieces, since firing the clay is a precarious business and the average kiln cannot take large pieces. Firing larger pieces of work in several parts can cause

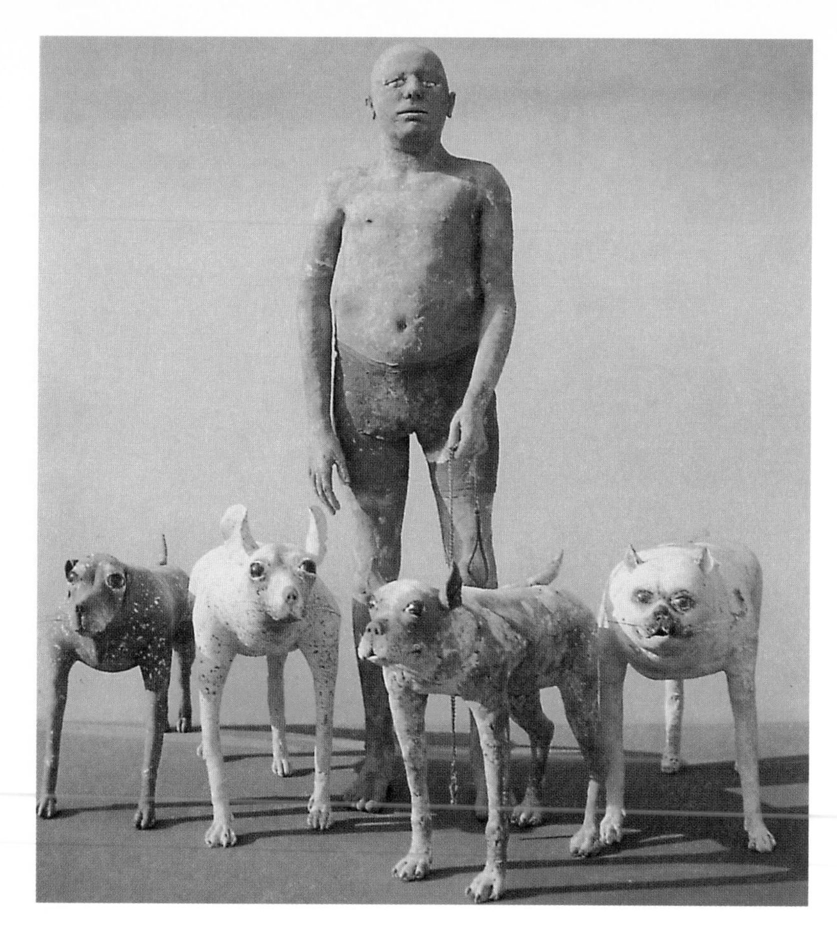

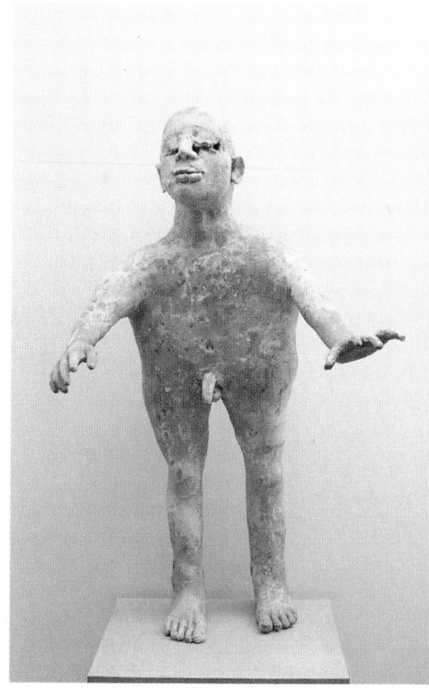

José Vermeersch, *Standing Figure.* 1970. Ceramic, H 84 cm. (Photo by Sergyssels).

José Vermeersch, *Medan with Dogs.* 1973. Ceramic, H 145 cm. & 55 cm. (Photo by Sergyssels).

problems when it comes to assembling and fixing them together. What is more, different firings rarely produce exactly the same shades of colour, so that the unity of the piece is broken. Vermeersch was aware of these technical problems, and he solved them by constructing his own large kilns, based on a principle used by the earliest civilisations. In 1979 he organised an autumn camp for young people in his own district, where he demonstrated this primitive method using a so-called field kiln, a kiln dug into the ground. He has produced about one hundred sculptures using this method.

While the technical side of ceramic sculpture is an important and difficult area, what the artist is trying to achieve is more important still. It was a natural consequence of Vermeersch's development as a painter that he should move out into the third dimension. His interest in the Italian fresco painter Giotto can be seen in a number of the portraits, and especially self-portraits, which he has produced over the years. In contrast with the more emphatic use of colour for which he opted later on, the self-portraits are almost always painted in delicate shades, and the typical colour of ceramic fits in with this pattern. When he occasionally produces sculptures in polychrome, he personally does not think it enhances their expressiveness. Part of the meaning he wants to invest in his statues comes from the natural colour of his material.

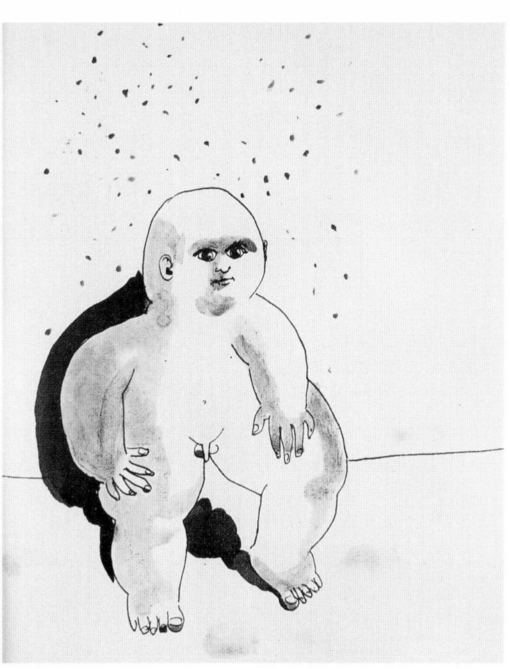

José Vermeersch, *Seated Woman with Dog*. 1974. Ceramic, H 100 cm. & 55 cm. (Photo by Sergyssels).

His theme is intentionally a limited one, but it is no less universal of that: the human and the animal. He almost always portrays human figures naked, because he wants to show them free of the influence of cultural connotations. Clothing indicates rank, class and background, and it adds something to the person which covers, conceals and falsifies. A person is born naked, so nakedness can also be seen as a symbol for life. The figures of Vermeersch hide nothing, and they are rarely beautiful in the classical sense. They present themselves with all their faults, and these are not hidden: quite the contrary. The human shapes are not deformed but they are not very pretty either – they have lived, and so they do not fit into the canon of the classical Greek ideal of beauty. In short they are archetypes of the physical human image, as it is also portrayed by the American photographer Diane Arbus. This feeling comes out even more strongly in the torsos, where the body is merely a shape, depersonalised, almost abstract, a universal object which is known but not named.

The posture of the figures is also important. Sitting or standing they emanate a certain dignity, despite their physical imperfections, similar in a way to Egyptian sculptures from the Middle Kingdom. Their dignity does not disguise the shabbiness which always goes with nakedness, but rather elevates it to a universally recognisable image of the human. Prudishness is put aside in order to penetrate to the essence of the human being – a kind of

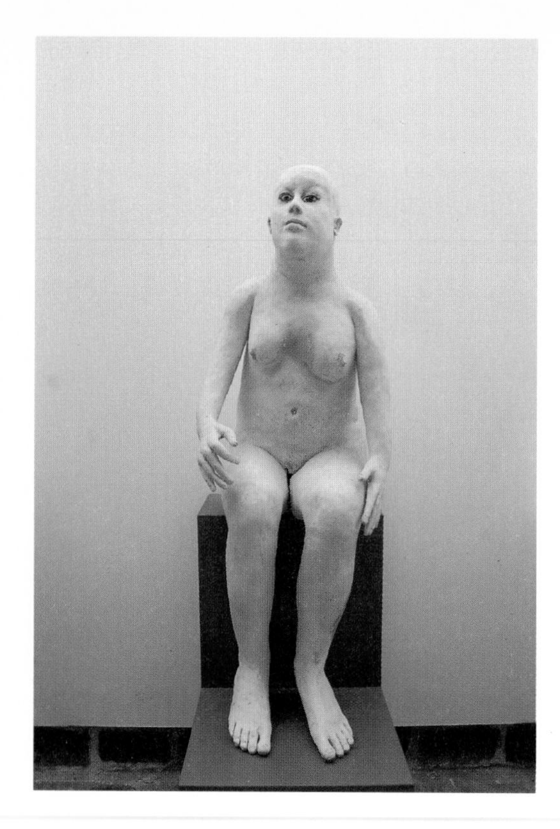

José Vermeersch, *Seated Woman.* 1988. Ceramic and white engobe, H 104 cm. (Photo by Sergyssels).

José Vermeersch, *Seated Woman with Dog.* 1992. Ceramic, H 90 cm. & 30 cm. (Photo by Sergyssels).

dignified helplessness in a world where everything has become an illusion and where the things that make people exciting – mind, character, impotence and capacity for love – are ignored.

The human figure is often portrayed together with a dog, and there is a clear association between the two. The dog is man's best friend. The animal and the human each continue where the other leaves off, and both are portrayed as naked: the animal because that is its natural manifestation, and man because he wants to present himself in the same way. Here the dog is not a pet, but a being of equal value, with his own characteristics and feelings. He too is a universal phenomenon, since he is of no specific breed or variety. He and man belong together, equally anonymous and equally timeless. Vermeersch has succeeded in portraying this timelessness in an inimitable way, which fits perfectly with his material. Here both man and animal are created anew from the earth, that primal material which becomes as fragile as man, but which is hardened by fire – a symbol of life experience. One thing which is noticeable about this artist is that he always

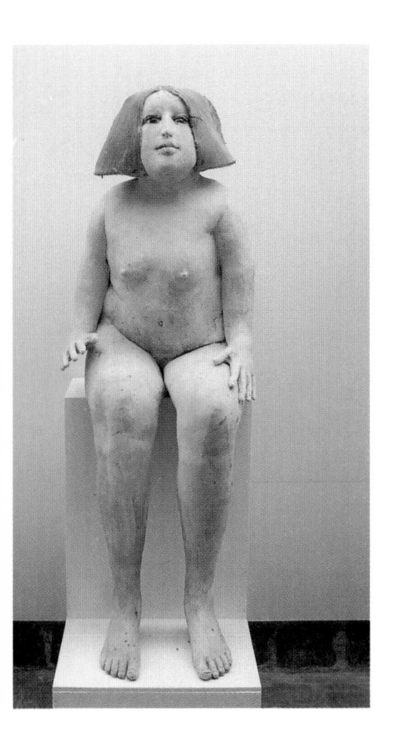

José Vermeersch, *Seated Woman*. 1992. Ceramic, H 120 cm. (Photo by Sergyssels).

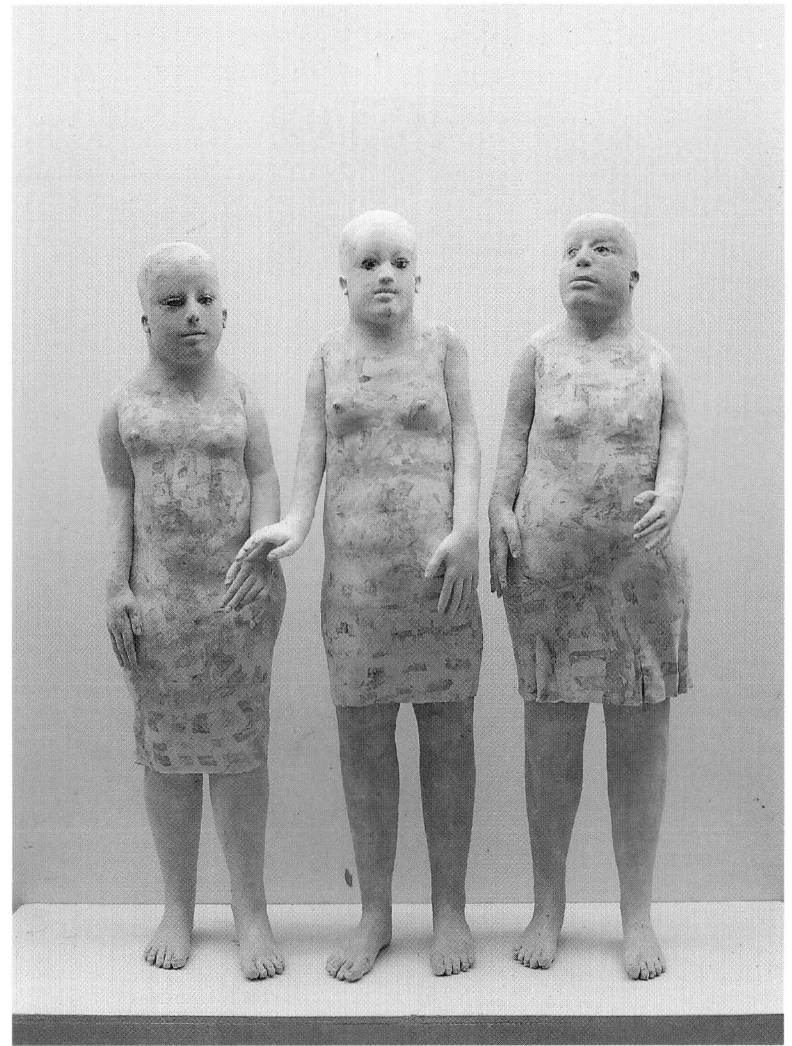

José Vermeersch, *The Three Sisters*. 1993. Ceramic, H 3 x 130 cm. (Photo by Sergyssels).

approaches his characters with gentleness, respect and a certain sense of tenderness.

Within the context of contemporary Flemish art history, José Vermeersch is a unique figure. The way he uses his fragile material to express his feelings is both classical and contemporary. The classical elements are: a certain monumentalism, a quest for balance between quiet contemplation and exuberance, a certain irony hidden beneath the surface and a joy in handling his material. He has also succeeded in using ceramics as a comprehensive means of expression within the Flemish tradition, and he manages to use his medium to transpose universal shapes into a contemporary vision of modern man.

LUDO BEKKERS
Translated by Steve Judd.

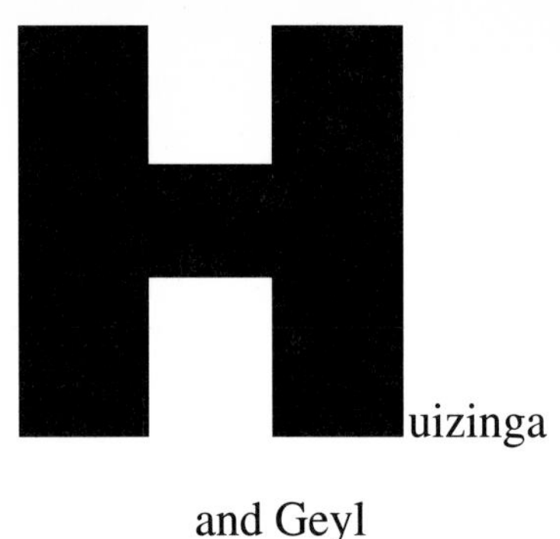

uizinga and Geyl

A Portrait of Two Dutch Historians

Surely all of us have occasionally participated in discussions about who was the greater philosopher, Kant or Hegel, the greater composer, Bach or Beethoven, the greater painter, Velasquez or Rembrandt. Such discussions are for obvious reasons largely irrelevant but they sharpen the mind and may give pleasure. In the case of Johan Huizinga and Pieter Geyl, however, the two historians presented in this essay, the question does not arise. Huizinga's achievement was more valuable than Geyl's. But why then this double portrait? Primarily because between the two world wars and during the first decade thereafter both were considered abroad to be the best representatives of the Dutch historical profession and both wrote books and essays which were widely read by the general public inside and outside the Netherlands. But there is another side to it: although roughly contemporaries and both roughly to be characterized as Dutch liberals, they nevertheless reacted differently to the circumstances they had to live through. It is the contrast between the two men that makes it interesting to study them in a single article.

Huizinga's life was unexciting. He was born in 1872 in Groningen, studied Germanic philology and linguistics at his city's university – where his father taught physiology – and in 1897 wrote his doctor's thesis on an aspect of Old Indian literature. He then became a history teacher at a secondary school in Haarlem, but was also allowed to give lectures in the University of Amsterdam on the ancient history and literature of India. In 1905 he became professor of general and Dutch history in Groningen. At that time his published oeuvre consisted of fewer than 200 pages and none of them related to the subject he was now expected to teach. Yet one publication on medieval town history in Holland was in preparation, and this obviously sufficed to justify what on the face of it was an eccentric appointment. Huizinga was then a happy man, happily married, thanks to his wife financially secure, with a growing family and a position in life he thoroughly enjoyed. He did not publish widely, but in 1911 and 1912 he wrote an excellent long article on the 'origin of our national consciousness' and in 1914 his book on the history of Groningen University in the nineteenth century appeared, a book commissioned by the University which was then celebrating its tercentenary. This is a marvellous, most elegantly written work. Never before had Dutch cultural history in the nineteenth century been described and analysed on such a scale and in so witty and perceptive a manner. The lightness of its touch, and the sympathy with which Huizinga depicted the life and work of many of his predecessors without for one moment forgetting that most of them did not rise to dizzying heights, lend it a charm that is as fresh now as it must have been in 1914. It is the work of a happy man.

In the summer of 1914 Huizinga's wife died and he was left alone with five young children. This totally changed his existence. He did not remarry until 1937. For a quarter of a century Huizinga, withdrawn into his study, cultivated his sense of loss (increased by the death of one of his sons in 1920). Deep worries about the World War and what he took to be the ravages it caused in European culture changed him from the modernist he was into a conservative who feared that history was taking the wrong track and heading towards disaster.

Huizinga's general conservative attitude was not reactionary. His own historical work was not at all old-fashioned. On the contrary, old-fashioned critics considered it too innovative. His inclination towards pessimism did not burden his style, for this remained remarkably light even in books or essays of considerable complexity. His sorrow, moreover, did not hinder his creativity. In 1914 his book on Groningen University came out. In 1915 he accepted a call to Leiden where he taught 'universal history', that is, all history since the fall of the Roman Empire except Dutch history for which there was another chair. He did so until November 1940 when the University was closed down by the Germans, who had conquered the Netherlands in May 1940. One of the subjects he dealt with in his first lectures at Leiden was American history. As a result he was able to write a book with penetrating and well-informed essays on the United States. It appeared in 1918. In 1919 he published his *The Waning of the Middle Ages* (Herfsttij der Middeleeuwen), his largest and his most famous book. In other words, Huizinga published within five years three substantial works about totally different subjects, each of them in its own sort a masterpiece and all highly original in their approach.

The Waning of the Middle Ages is regarded as Huizinga's major work. Over the years it was translated into (in that order) English, German, Swedish, Spanish, French, Hungarian, Italian, Finnish and other languages. It was read by a cultivated general public that enjoyed the accomplished poetic style and the force of the images which, though presented in vivid detail, served the broad philosophical interpretation put forward by the author. Here solid and profound scholarship was made to serve the purpose of the imaginative writer. Among professional historians the book undoubtedly had some influence; mostly in Germany, but later also in France where from the 1930s Huizinga was hailed as an innovator who prepared the revolution in historiography which younger French historians attempted to bring about, with some success. Yet Huizinga, who took the value of his writings for granted but did not seek to establish a school, was rather embarrassed by such enthusiasm, and it is easy to see why. After finishing the book he was occasionally led by outside pressure – it was not easy for a well-known publicist to escape from the duty to give public lectures – to return to the subject but he did so with some reluctance. His interests were wide and varied. Although obviously a historian of culture, he did not develop a method to be used by himself or others in relation to all subjects which drew his attention. His approach was too personal for this; moreover, it changed from case to case.

In *The Waning of the Middle Ages* Huizinga studied the decline of medieval civilization, apparent in fourteenth and fifteenth-century Burgundian court culture notwithstanding its conspicuous pomp and richness. Although Huizinga appreciated the art of the so-called Flemish Primitives, among them Jan van Eyck, as one of the greatest achievements in world painting, he did not accept that it should be characterized as a product of the incipient Northern Renaissance, as was done by many of his contemporaries. In his view it bore the features of the general late medieval civilization of Northern France and the Low Countries, and this was a civilization at its end, unable or unwilling to step outside the boundaries defined by its predecessors in the thirteenth century. In the thirteenth century medieval culture had realized its full potential. In its scholastic system it had found ways to explain the order of the universe and the microcosm; in its Gothic church architecture it had succeeded in giving concrete shape to the truths and values revealed by religion and philosophy. During the fourteenth and fifteenth centuries this solid framework was maintained. Its intellectual profundity and aesthetic quality, however, was threatened by the exuberance of the later generations. The original themes were not further developed but popularized, trivialized by an immense volume of allegories, symbolism, crude details. A civilization, so Huizinga suggested, declines when it stops expanding and exhausts its energy in endlessly rehearsing the same truths, explaining them over and over again and proving them right by the most banal analogies and examples.

Though publications continued to flow from his pen during the 1920s, all of them valuable, some of them fairly substantial, Huizinga seemed to suffer from a loss of direction. His attempt to write a large book on twelfth-century civilization as a sort of counterpart to the work of 1919 miscarried and he abandoned the project in 1930. After that date he began to collect material on a totally different subject: the element of play involved in culture. Culture, he thought, begins as play. After satisfying their elementary needs, human beings fill their spare time by playing together. This is the origin of culture. Culture begins as play, that is, as a series of acts which are not necessary for assuring the survival of societies and individuals, but are constricted by rules and performed with dedication and a certain element of competitiveness. It may be singing or dancing, it may be ritual, it may be fighting, bodily fighting or fighting in words. From such beginnings the whole fabric of refined culture springs, and to be lasting culture should remain loyal to at least two aspects of this origin: it should cherish the element of play and, because it has to do this, keep to the rules without which play is impossible. In his short but dizzily erudite *Homo Ludens* (1938) Huizinga explored this theme in the entire history of mankind. The book earned astonished respect, was much translated (an English edition appearing in 1949) and widely read. Yet it probably does not possess the enduring quality which made *The Waning of the Middle Ages* a classic.

Homo Ludens contains a moral lesson. Huizinga condemned contemporary culture for having become intolerably serious, totally undisciplined and just as overloaded as late medieval culture. He made a plea for self-control, modesty, respect for ethical values and other virtues which seemed to get lost in the gigantic production of all sorts of wild vagaries and fashions. This links *Homo Ludens* with the pamphlet-like book he had published three years previously under the title *In the Shadow of Tomorrow* (In de schaduwen van morgen, 1935; English edition 1936). In its subtitle Huizinga indicated that he wished to give a diagnosis of 'our' age's spiritual suffering. It is a highly subjective and angry book, a catalogue of instances of cultural barbarism and repellent cynicism. It is not a scholarly work. It was an immediate success, a best-seller, the only one in Huizinga's oeuvre. Part of its popularity was probably due to the fact that the book, though it left out politics, was in a sense thoroughly political all the same. It must have been clear to all its readers that the general cultural degeneration which Huizinga diagnosed was in his view particularly virulent in countries ruled by totalitarian systems of government. Obviously the book could be interpreted as an attack on Nazi and Bolshevik ideology.

Huizinga was not merely a sober scholar; he was a sensitive man whose approach to the subjects he studied was both analytical and divinatory. Though perfectly capable of rational argumentation and of positivist research he was more than ready to let himself be guided by intuition and inspiration and often had the impression of establishing direct contact with past reality. During the 1930s his inclination towards a form of mysticism (a mysticism, however, which was perfectly controlled and by no means exuberant) brought him very near to a positive experience of divine providence, that is to say, he not only came to value Christianity as a necessary antidote to the decline he thought to see around him but to accept the reality of God's will. He used this insight in his interpretation of Dutch history. For the emergence and survival of the Dutch nation, he declared in some strange but intriguing essays, it was hard to find a rational explanation. Nor do the inexhaustible richness and beauty of Dutch seventeenth-century civilization, especially its painting, easily lend themselves to being understood in terms of historical development, there simply being no preparatory factors discernible which could be said to have made the whole phenomenon possible. As a result Huizinga looked with almost religious awe at Dutch existence and achievements. In Huizinga's view Holland was a unique case. It could not be explained. It was there to be admired as a gift from God.

Huizinga had a difficult time during the German occupation. He died on 1 February 1945, a few months before the German defeat in May. His reputation was high. Soon after the end of the war friends and pupils decided to prepare a definitive edition of his works and despite the chaos, the poverty, the shortages of that period they succeeded in publishing with remarkable expedition the nine volumes of his *Collected Works* (Verzamelde werken, 1948-1953). His writings are still often discussed and the recent publication of his correspondence (3 vols., 1989-1991) has renewed interest in his ideas and his personality.

Pieter Geyl (1887-1966) was like Huizinga a nationalist, but of a different complexion. Huizinga's emphasis was on gratitude to providence for having

Pieter Geyl (1887-1966) in the fifties. This photo was dedicated to G.J. Renier, his successor at University College London.

Portrait of Johan Huizinga (1872-1945).

allowed the Dutch to become and remain a nation, Geyl admonished his readers to feel pride at Dutch greatness. In his study of 1912 'on the origin of our national consciousness' Huizinga had shown that Dutch nationhood was an ambiguous concept. If the Burgundian dukes and their Habsburg successors had managed to unite the Low Countries more firmly than in fact they did, one single nation might have emerged out of what we know now as Belgium and the Netherlands with, consequently, a national feeling relating to the whole area rather than the seven provinces of the Dutch Republic alone. Geyl agreed with this view, but only to a certain extent. Huizinga attached far greater importance than Geyl to the aspect of state building; there are passages in his work in which he interpreted nations as the products rather than the producers of states. So for him the rise of the Dutch nation was no problem: when the Dutch Republic came into existence during the late sixteenth century it was quite natural that a form of national consciousness developed firmly tied to that new state. Geyl, however, adopted the view that not the state but language is the foundation of nationhood. As the Dutch language was spoken in the northern provinces which later became the Dutch Republic and hence the present monarchy as well as in some of the provinces excluded from the Republic and eventually part of the independent Belgian state, there was something deeply wrong with the history of the Low Countries. Nature, Geyl propounded, had predestined all the Dutch-speaking provinces to form one national state. This did not happen.

The Dutch Republic did in fact become a nation, but a truncated one. The Dutch-speaking provinces in the Southern Netherlands (generally called Flanders) were quite unnaturally joined with the French-speaking provinces (generally called Wallonia) into an artificial political entity (generally called Belgium). This was a tragedy for all concerned, brought about by the military outcome of the Revolt of the Netherlands – the result, therefore, of outward circumstances, not of natural development.

Geyl was fifteen years younger than Huizinga. He went to school in The Hague and studied history, Dutch language and literature at the University of Leiden. In 1913 he obtained his doctor's degree in history with a dissertation about a seventeenth-century Venetian diplomat residing in The Hague. That same year he moved to London as the correspondent of an influencial liberal newspaper *(Nieuwe Rotterdamsche Courant).* He did not remain a journalist for long. In 1919 he was appointed to a new chair of Dutch Studies at University College London. In 1936 he returned to the Netherlands as professor of modern history in the University of Utrecht. He had long been waiting for an opportunity to leave Britain, where he had become a respected scholar and teacher but, for obvious reasons, did not find a large audience for the ideal he cherished most: the so-called emancipation of Flanders.

Some years before 1914 Geyl had decided to support Flemish efforts to break the supremacy of the French language in Belgium. In Flanders only the Dutch language should be used in the administration, the courts, in business, the schools, the universities, for Dutch was the original language in that area and the mass of the people still spoke it. In innumerable articles in the press, in lectures, meetings, committees, Geyl fought to further this cause. But apart from involving himself in discussions relating to practical politics, he set himself the task of demonstrating the fundamental unity of all the Dutch-speaking provinces and the tragedy of its disruption in the form of a long narrative. Between 1930 and 1937 he published three volumes of his *History of the Low Countries* (Geschiedenis van de Nederlandsche Stam, partly translated in English 1932-1964), that is, of the Northern as well as the Dutch-speaking parts of the Southern Netherlands. Then the project halted. He had reached the year 1751; only in 1959 did he bring his narrative forward to 1798, but he had then enlarged the scale to such an extent that it was clearly impossible to continue the book in this manner. Yet although a failure in the sense that it was left unfinished, and moreover rather unequal in quality, Geyl's work had an enormous impact both on the general reader and on his fellow historians. Since Geyl's intervention it was no longer admissible to repeat the tired and complacent views about the age-old contrast between Belgium (including Flanders) and Holland which had for so long obscured past and present reality and caused deep misunderstandings.

At the time of Huizinga's death in 1945 Geyl was a well-known and powerful personality in the Netherlands. Under the German occupation he had behaved courageously. He was appreciated for his originality, and feared for his outspoken criticism of views he disagreed with. He was a formidable polemist and so enormously energetic that few were able to keep pace with him. He enjoyed a solid prestige outside the Netherlands. His book on *The Revolt of the Netherlands* (1932) was a text much studied by British and American undergraduates; learned articles in English historical journals had given him the reputation of being a serious scholar. But he had not yet become as famous as Huizinga was. Abroad, it was only after the war that Geyl rose to the status of a celebrated and influential author. He owed this to his critical assessment of one of the books which made the greatest possible impression at that time: A.J. Toynbee's *A Study of History,* largely written before the war (6 vols. 1934-1939) but immensely popular only after it.

Geyl started his attack on Toynbee's system in 1946 and continued it when further volumes were published. It is impossible to indicate here the full extent of the discussion. Two points may suffice. First, Geyl objected to Toynbee's ambition to explain the whole course of human history and showed that his results were by no means based on empirical research, as he claimed, but on a preconceived scheme. More important still, he passionately criticized Toynbee's pessimism as to the future of Western civilization. Toynbee prophesied – or gave Geyl the impression of doing so – the fall of Western culture and of its dominance, whereas Geyl maintained his firm belief in its continuing vitality. Thanks to these elements the debate was raised to the level of a controversy not only between two professional scholars but between two views of life, two attempts to make sense of history with the purpose of defining basic attitudes in relation to a generation's expectations and ambitions. Given the widespread pessimism of the post-war years and the widely felt veneration for Toynbee's majestic achievement, Geyl's attack – firm but polite, though in the course of the years becoming more strident – was courageous and he was much admired for it. He had in the long run many followers, and thus exercised concrete influence in one of the most complicated and fundamental intellectual discussions of the 1940s and 1950s. This made him famous. What side would Huizinga have chosen had he lived to witness the debate? It is difficult to say, but he might well have felt far greater sympathy for Toynbee's religious point of view than Geyl, who was an agnostic, did.

Geyl's work, though at least three times as large as that of Huizinga, is narrower in scope and less profound. But it is in many respects innovative; it is lively, extremely readable and forceful. We owe him a great debt. In a warm tribute to him (1958) A.J.P. Taylor wrote that Geyl 'represents the ideal to which historians strive … He has the air of a historian when he simply crosses the street. Even when he is wrong (and I think he is sometimes), he is wrong as only a historian can be.'

E.H. KOSSMANN

LIST OF TRANSLATIONS

JOHAN HUIZINGA:

Dutch Civilization in the Seventeenth Century, London, 1968.

Homo Ludens. A study of the play element in culture, New York, 1970.

America. A Dutch Historian's Vision from Afar and Near (ed. H.H. Rowen). New York, 1972.

The Waning of the Middle Ages. A study of the forms of life, thought, and art in France and the Netherlands in the fourteenth and fifteenth centuries, Harmondsworth, 1976.

PIETER GEYL:

Debates with Historians, Groningen, 1955.

The Revolt of the Netherlands, 1559-1609, London, 1958.

The Netherlands of the Seventeenth Century, 2 vols., London, 1961-1964.

History of the Low Countries: Episodes and Problems, London, 1964.

‘O, this is a place!’

Aspects of the English World of Guido Gezelle

Guido Gezelle was born in Bruges on 1 May 1830. After his studies for the priesthood, he became a teacher at the school in the preparatory seminary at Roeselare. His efforts to emancipate the Flemish language and its literature from the hegemony of French and of Dutch from the Netherlands, were of great importance to a generation of students who would later make him into a symbol of the Flemish Movement. His first romantic and religious volumes of poetry, *Flemish Poetical Exercises* (Vlaamsche dichtoefeningen, 1858), *Churchyard Flowers* (Kerkhofblommen, 1858) and *Poems, Songs and Prayers* (Gedichten, Gezangen en Gebeden, 1862) were exceptional in their free metrical style and lyrical expression. During his years in Bruges from 1860 to 1872 where he was a professor at a seminary for English students and later curate of the parish of St Walburga, he was especially active as a prosewriter, folklorist with the weekly *Rond den Heerd* (Round the Fireside) and razor-edged ultramontane journalist in the polemics of Belgian politics. Troubles

The work of Guido Gezelle (1830-1899), has repeatedly been linked with both British and American literature and culture. And not without reason. After all, Gezelle was not merely a writer in the native tradition of religious literature dating back to the seventeenth-century Reformation, he was also associated with an international cultural movement of Catholic revival of his day. With regard to England this means that his poetry and prose show affinities to the so-called Oxford Movement which in a spiritual sense provided a significant response to the scepticism of the Victorian Age. The publication of Gezelle's remarkable translation of the then hugely popular *Hiawatha* by Henry Wadsworth Longfellow, merely reinforces this ‘English connection’. Speculation concerning this has continually been supported by Gezelle's biography, which shows that the poet and priest had contact with England for virtually his entire career.

Flemish Anglophilia

The young Gezelle, educated for the priesthood in the predominantly Catholic West Flanders of the nineteenth century, was exposed very early to the continental idea of the day that England was a country to which missionaries should be sent. For that matter many of the buildings in the ‘medieval’ city of his birth, Bruges, bore witness to the history of English Catholicism. It is symbolic that he should end his career as the chaplain of the renowned English monastery there, founded in 1629 by a community of Canon nuns belonging to the Windesheim congregation which had fled from England to settle ultimately in Leuven. Ever since the sixteenth century Bruges, along with such towns as Douai and St Omer in northern France, had been one of the centres of those English concentrations that had sprung up on the continent in response to the banning of catholicism in Anglican England. After the French Revolution refugees began a movement in the opposite direction, attempting in turn to convert the Anglican world. The young and extremely idealistic priest, Gezelle, wanted nothing more than to join in this tradition and this adventure.

**arising from this caused him to move to Courtrai in 1872 where again he held a number of minor clerical positions. This gave him the opportunity to return to his beloved activities of philology and poetry. He also wrote occasional verses for an extensive circle of acquaintances. He founded a magazine, *Loquela* (Language, 1881-1895) for the study of his native tongue and published a number of technically superior collections of poetry in which he explored natural phenomena in a highly individual idiom and very personal rhythms: *A Garland for the Year* (Tijdkrans, 1893) and *A Wreath of Rhymes around the Year* (Rijmsnoer, 1897).
He spent the last year of his life back in Bruges where he passed away on 27 November 1899.
In 1901 an important volume of previously unpublished poems appeared posthumously, entitled *Last Poems* (Laatste Verzen).**

Bruges had an extensive so-called English colony: Anglicans – to the Catholic authorities a veritable missionary zone in their own midst –, but later also a great many resettled Catholics, some of whom, from the 1850s onwards, would also introduce the artistic ideas of the neo-Gothic revival. It was at the preparatory seminary at Roeselare that the student Gezelle was really introduced to anglophilia: the educational institute had a separate department or course *('cours')* for English students. Letters have shown that the linguistically talented Gezelle was much sought after by the English lads, *'assiégé par les Anglais',* and through the exotic tales and testimonies of heroic pioneers there gradually developed a virtual propaganda campaign on behalf of the missions in England and North America. When Gezelle returned to Roeselare in 1854 as a teacher, it was obvious he would be put in charge of the English students. And there he became friends with Joseph Algar, Master of Arts at Oxford, who on an intellectual level opened many doors for Gezelle. Until 1860, Gezelle engaged in relentless activities on behalf of England. In a relationship characterized by great openness, friendship and trust, he counselled the rather turbulent group of English students, including the non-Catholics, both materially and spiritually. With some of them an extensive correspondence developed; concerned mothers in England entered into correspondence with the 'guardian of their boys'. Reinforced by the news of a shortage of priests in England, and supported by the enthusiastic letters of former students who were participating there in the 'great work in the Lord's vineyard', Gezelle developed an unrelenting campaign among his pupils to recruit missionaries. It was a world of idealism, emotion and wishful thinking, as well as one fraught with diffi-

Guido Gezelle (1830-1899) around 1860.

culties with parents and government authorities. Gezelle received many letters from young 'missionaries', expressing both their hope and their confusion after their confrontation with a totally unfamiliar, hostile world.

The odd thing about Gezelle's position was his inability to realize his own dream. His definitive departure for England remained an unfulfilled expectation, interiorized in a number of texts (letters and poetry). He and those around him were for a long time convinced that he would receive permission to go. Repeated, denied requests made to the Bruges episcopate by Gezelle and others do not seem to have dampened his enthusiasm. In 1861, he wrote to the Dutch man of letters J.A. Alberdingk Thijm that the latter could not imagine how Flemish youth was burning to realize the papal ideal of conversion 'as far as the four corners of the globe'. It was in this atmosphere that Gezelle had been working since 1856, translating Longfellow's 'Mondamin', the fifth canto from *Hiawatha,* and the famous poem 'Excelsior', texts informed by a highly ultramontane, anti-Protestant spirit. If it had to be done in this manner, then Gezelle wished to take part in the heroic reconquest of England (and thus the world) as a poet, an act which he and many others felt was an appropriate reciprocal gesture to those who had spread Catholicism on the continent.

Gezelle's 'English' career continued beyond 1860. Inspired by the English school system, which, among other things, allowed students more freedom, and together with his friend Algar, he co-directed a kind of English department of the Bruges college. In 1861 he became vice-rector of the English Seminary, originally a private initiative by a wealthy Catholic convert, John Sutton, but which since its founding in 1859 had been as much a product of cooperation between Bruges and Westminster. Gezelle then came into contact with the English clerical hierarchy, even with Cardinal Wiseman, and now directly prepared the English recruits, who were willing, as we read somewhere, 'to spend time, labour, anxiety and care on their duty'. Gezelle, by then a parish priest in Bruges, remained also after 1865 closely linked with England. He was not only spiritual guide in the private lives of English families, but also a kindred spirit in a circle of resident foreign artists and archaeologists (James Weale, Thomas Harper King, William Brangwyn, a.o.) who, inspired by the ideas of Augustus Welby Pugin would greatly influence Flemish neo-Gothicism as practised by Jean Baptiste Béthune, Louis Grossé, Jacques Petyt, among others.

Sacred poetry

In a letter dated October 1861 Algar warned his friend Gezelle: 'Don't let your Anglomania be carried too far.' It is a small indication of the fact that Gezelle, confronted with the sober and rationally inclined Algar, still adhered to a strongly romantic, idealistic realm that was no doubt far removed from Victorian England. Someone like Gezelle, from his vantage point in Flanders in the 1850s-1860s mainly had an eye for the euphoria that accompanied Catholic emancipation. That specific situation (small missionary communities, often made up of immigrants) demanded the establishment and expansion of a local rural church with a large contribution by educated lay people. This was diametrically opposed to the establishment of

Frederick William Faber (1814-1863) (Collection Guido Gezelle Archief, Bruges).

The English Seminary, Bruges.

a central governing hierarchy (1850) and the worldwide evolution of an ultramontane Catholicism. In fact, Catholic England in the 1850s was riven with controversy. An important role in this was played by the so-called Oxford Movement, originally a kind of counter reformation within Anglicanism, intended to rid it of excess Protestantism. From 1845 onwards it formed the axis of the English variant of a liberal Catholicism striving to raise the intellectual level and freedom of thought of English Catholics, with John Henry Newman as its leading exponent.

It is not always clear to what extent the West Flemish priest Gezelle was aware of these situations, and how far he was capable of expressing any sympathy he may have had for a more liberal form of Catholicism. We know from witnesses that Gezelle both knew and read Cardinal Newman (whom Gezelle's former student Hendrik van Doorne says Gezelle considered 'The New Man'). From fragments and a manuscript of an unfinished poem we know that in 1879, when Newman's honour had been restored by the hierarchy, Gezelle began translating the *Dream of Gerontius* (1960), well-known in English Catholic circles. Anyone who reads Gezelle's work, however, will encounter mainly those figures from the same English circles who more strongly adhered to the authority of superiors within the Roman Catholic Church. Furthermore, in its mental outlook, Gezelle's work strongly resembles that of the members of the Oxford Movement in their resistance to a secularized world and their rediscovery of the lost institutional power, spirituality and piety of the 'Gothic' Middle Ages. It is also remarkable that, just like Gezelle, John Keble and Frederick William Faber made the link with poetry. In contrast to a poet like Gerard Manley Hopkins, who regarded this relation as problematic, for these poets religion and poetry were extensions of one another. In both areas of experience there is room for the discovery of the sacred via the profane, for the interest in devotion, liturgy, ceremony and tradition.

It is understandable therefore that Gezelle too was interested in the 'sacred poetry' of Keble and Faber. It is no coincidence that Gezelle's own first volume of poetry, *Flemish Poetical Exercises* of 1858, contained a translation from Faber's *Hymns* (1849). Also, it is sufficiently well-known that the atmosphere around the 'confraternity', a secret society set up by Gezelle for his pupils at the Roeselare minor seminary to promote sacramental devotion, showed striking affinities to the ideas espoused in Faber's *All for Jesus* (1853), a work which circulated among Gezelle's students. In this connection, it is not surprising that Gezelle was euphoric when writing to his favourite student Eugeen van Oye from Arundel, where he had been staying as chaplain to the Duchess of Norfolk, recalling the place where Faber situated his *Ethel's Book; or, Tales of the Angels* (1858): 'I am in the very place where 'Ethel' lives, at the residence of the Duchess of Norfolk, the mother of the child for whom Ethel's book was written. I have dined with Ethel, spoken to her, heard her speak. I know the houses where the real children lived that are described by Faber; I know the history of Ethel's book. O, this is a place! a Catholic duchess in England is something indeed!'

Longfellow

The similarities mentioned above do not alter the fact that there are also great differences between Gezelle's own poetic practice and that of Keble, for that matter probably England's best selling poet of the nineteenth century. Gezelle's own poetry undergoes a perilous adventure with language, while Keble's, which incidentally is more poetic treatise than actual poems, is more of a blend of theology, devotion and apology in which spontaneity is subdued.

With a poet like Gezelle the situation is somewhat different. This is obvious when we examine Gezelle's most important translation work from 1886 – we shall not consider his prose translations of such Oxford Movement authors as John Mason Neale and Charlotte Yonge – , his poetic version of *The Song of Hiawatha,* an epic poem by the popular American poet, Henry Wadsworth Longfellow. The exotic tale of a mythical hero, a kind of Messiah bestowing peace and prosperity upon his people, based on hybrid elements from Indian oral culture, was enormously popular in nineteenth-century Europe. Only a year after its American publication, Gezelle in 1856 was one of the first to translate the fifth canto, 'Hiawatha's Fasting', which because of its theme and symbolism (the creation of maize) must certainly have appealed to the young, religiously inspired poet. It is notable that the epic continued to fascinate Gezelle.

Gradually, however, the emphasis shifted from the functionality of the theme to the work of translation itself. He prompted student poets from his surroundings – such as Hugo Verriest and Emiel Lauwers – to try their hand at translation and was in turn stimulated by their results into improving his own 'rendition'. The results of 1886 approached the ideal Gezelle himself had posited in a letter to a colleague (his name is Eugeen de Lepeleer) who in 1889 had just embarked, following in Gezelle's footsteps, on a translation of Friedrich Wilhelm Weber's *Thirteen Lindens* (Dreizehnlinden, 1878). 'You've stuck too close to the German text,' wrote Gezelle, 'you must forget about it, and once it's forgotten, you must polish your own work and file it down *ad amussim*'. For his own literary, aestheticizing translation Gezelle sought his own idiom and rhythm which indeed often make one forget the original. At the end of the day, for Gezelle, as for many other great and professionally competent poets all too aware of the existence of other texts, translation was ultimately a matter of one's own artistic achievement. This puts into perspective our (nonetheless necessary) search for parallels and connections, including those between Gezelle and England.

PIET COUTTENIER
Translated by Scott Rollins.

The Evening and The Rose

I've many many an hour with you
    been sharing and enjoying,
and never has an hour with you
    been for one while annoying.
I've many many a flower for you
    been picking out and plucking,
and, like a bee, with you, with you
    the honey from it sucking;
but never an hour so dear with you,
    so short enduring ever,
but never an hour so sad with you,
    when you and I must sever,
as the hour when so near to you,
    that *evening,* with you seated,
I heard you speak and spoke to you
    what our souls repeated.

Nor was a flower so sweet by you
    discovered, culled, elected,
as which that *evening* shone one you,
    and to me was affected!
Although, for me as well as you,
    – who will this harm be curing? –
an hour with me, an hour with you
    be never long enduring;
although for me, although for you,
    however bright and blowing,
that *rose,* and yet a rose from you,
    not long its prime was showing;
still long will guard, I vow to you,
    unless it all forgoes,
my heart three dearest pledges: YOU,
    THE EVENING – and – THE ROSE!

(1858)

Translated by Paul Claes and Christine D'haen.

BAUR, FRANK, 'Bio-bibliografische inleiding' (Bio-bibliographical Introduction), in: *Guido Gezelle. The Song of Hiawatha. Jubileumuitgave van Guido Gezelles volledige werken* (Guido Gezelle. The Song of Hiawatha. Jubilee Edition of Guido Gezelles Complete Works), Amsterdam, 1930, pp. 235-269.
COUTTENIER, PIET, 'Gezelles onvoltooide vertaling van Newmans *Dream of Gerontius*' ('Gezelle's Uncompleted Translation of Newman's *Dream of Gerontius*'), *Gezelliana,* XIII, 1984, pp. 106-116.
LEEUW, BOUDEWIJN DE, a.o., *De briefwisseling van Guido Gezelle met de Engelsen 1854-1899* (Guido Gezelle's Correspondence with the English 1854-1899), Ghent, 1991.
D'HAEN, CHRISTINE, *De wonde in 't hert. Guido Gezelle: een dichtersbiografie* (The Wound in the Heart. Guido Gezelle: A Poet's Biography), Tielt, 1987.
GEZELLE, GUIDO, *Mijn dichten, mijn geliefde* (My Poems, My Beloved) (Anthology, ed. Piet Couttenier), Ghent, 1992.
HOLMES, J.D., *More Roman than Rome: English Catholicism in the Nineteenth Century,* London / Shepherdtown, 1978.
NUIS, HERMINE VAN, Guido Gezelle. *Flemish Poet-Priest,* New York, 1986.
PERSYN, JAN, '*The Song of Hiawatha* in het spoor van Longfellow' ('*The Song of Hiawatha* in Longfellow's Footsteps'), in: Gezelle, Guido, *The Song of Hiawatha. Tijdkrans. Verzameld dichtwerk 3* (The Song of Hiawatha. A Garland for the Year. Collected Poetry 3), Antwerp / Amsterdam, 1981, pp. 9-40.
RICHARDS, BERNARD, *English Poetry of the Victorian Period 1830-1890,* London / New York, 1988.
WESTERLINCK, ALBERT, *Taalkunst van Guido Gezelle* (Guido Gezelle's Art of Language), Bruges / Nijmegen, 1980.

IN TRANSLATION

GEZELLE, GUIDO, *The Evening and the Rose. 30 Poems translated from the Flemish by Paul Claes and Christine D'haen,* Antwerp, 1989.

Visiting Professor

by Cees Nooteboom

Let's pretend for a moment that I'm not me; that has its uses on occasion. I'm going to pay myself a visit. My room number is up in the thousands, and to reach it I have to enter a Stalinist building with staircases, lifts and corridors. Behind every door people are in furious pursuit of knowledge: this is Berkeley. My memory has scattered a trail of crumbs, so I'm able to find my room. But that wasn't what we agreed: I was going to pretend I didn't know myself, to try and see the room where I have spent these past months as if it were a stranger's. That's not difficult: it is a strange room, which I took over from someone who taught Yiddish, and before that it belonged to the Department Chairman, a Hesse specialist. The result is an odd combination of Hebrew and Gothic lettering, since each of them left behind whole walls full of books, plain Yiddish and plain German, but also Gothic Schillers and Goethes, Yiddish-Hebrew dictionaries, shelves-full of spiky characters I cannot read. This room was my constant, and my meagre pile of Dutch colonial literature, which sits as incongruously in the German Department as Yiddish, could not make much impression. Malevolent books in fierce, unread rows, yearbooks of the 'Schillergesellschaft', the serried ranks of the *Publications of the Modern Language Association of America, The Big Book of Jewish Humor,* a *History of Norwegian Literature, Dramen in 5 Teilen, German Quarterlies, Monatshefte,* all pristine, unread and hence a little resentful and vindictive. I tried to ignore them. *Et in Academia ego,* and it was an instructive experience. How do people cope who spend their whole lives in an environment like this?

Lino on the floor, metal-framed windows, steel desks. Walls like custard pudding that has been standing too long. Six paces from the door to the window. The hatstand with the Jewish scholar's orange jacket on it. There was something about that jacket. Far more than the books it symbolised an absent owner, as though he might return at any moment to claim his room. It hung menacingly on a hanger. It was a character, that jacket, orange, smouldering, dead. It didn't like me, that was obvious. On the desks I wasn't using there were boxes full of exam papers, still reeking of anxious student sweat. That was the world inside. Outside was quite a different story. On the left stands a building which looks like the Reykjavik Egyptology Museum.

'ZOOLOGY', it says, between two griffins sitting on their haunches. Smoke issues constantly from the roofs: somebody is cooking mummies. On the side walls there are ox skulls with laurel wreaths (sorry, *I* can't help it). Aren't you mixing up your tenses, Professor Nooteboom? You talk about a building that *stands* but something that *was* quite a different story. No, I'm not mixed up: for months the lush lawns stretching from that building to below my window were strewn with students in their libidinous innocence, reading, sleeping, testing each other, acres of Californian bodies, young, unimaginably healthy, lying between Zoology and me like a 'memento vivere'. What else? A library, a tall flagpole flying the American flag, tall spruces and eucalyptuses, distant hills, lust, but all gone now. Now it is winter even here. The students have disappeared from the campus, the magnolia petals lie at the foot of their trees like pink snow, fog shrouds the hills, it's vacation time, the building is empty. I have packed my books and am alone again amid Gothic and Yiddish; in a few day's time all sign of my presence here will have gone, the room will grow back over my closed episode like the jungle enveloping an explorer's camp.

'What was it like?' my friends will ask when I get back, and I shall find it quite hard to answer. Well, what *was* it like? My first steady job since I once worked in a bank in Hilversum in 1951 (or thereabouts). I was as scared of it as a gypsy of a rented house, but it was better than I expected, though I couldn't help finding it odd seeing the same people in the same place every day. I know that's how things are in the real world, but I'll never get used to it. Besides, it creates odd relationships between people: they are not married to each other and yet they spend large parts of their lives in the company of other people not of their own choosing.

What about the lessons? Of course I should say lectures, but all I have ever had myself were *lessons,* so I'll go on calling them that. They weren't too bad, or rather, I enjoyed them. Hard work, especially at first, but as the semester wore on, more and more fascinating. At the beginning I talked about my own work, again something I have not much experience of. The students had read my books, in published form and in manuscript. Any tendency to take a detached or abstract approach was soon shot down with a 'Hey, when do we get into the meat of the book?'. One isn't accustomed to thinking of one's collected writings as *meat,* but the question was instructive. I was most anxious about their reaction to the book I had written when I was the same age as they were now, *Philip and the Others.* I have always had a problematic relationship with that book myself, embarrassment at my painfully obvious innocence at the time, at the visibility of the writer, who just happened to have the same name as me. Their reaction was important to me because my American publisher had suggested bringing out a translation, but I couldn't make up my mind. On the one hand there was the wise dictum of my fellow-author Harry Mulisch, who in a similar case had decided 'that he had no right to forbid a young writer (the writer he had once been) to publish a book'. On the other hand there were the thirty-odd years that had elapsed between then and now. It needed only a glance in the mirror for me to see how long that was. The students found it no problem at all. An old man's false modesty was of no concern to them, they felt rather that the young writer that I had been needed defending against the stale old hack, and that is what happened.

The following topic, Dutch colonial literature, involved quite different problems. For years Massachusetts University Press has been publishing a wonderfully produced collection in English, edited by E.M. Beekman. Everything from Beb Vuyk to Friedericy, Alberts, Du Perron, Couperus, Van Schendel, Rumphius – a monumental series. And yet it wasn't easy. People of my age can still reel off the list of all the islands in the 'Emerald Girdle'[1], words like *dessa* (village), *kampong* (native quarter), *babu* (children's nurse), *residèn* (Dutch district commissioner) are familiar to us and though we may not have been there at the time, we still have a certain notion, even if derived only from literature, of 'what it was like'. But what can you do with a generation that has only a vague idea of where present-day Indonesia is in relation to the rest of Asia and when you talk of 'the Indies' is more inclined to think of 'India' than 'the Empire of the East Indies', that hasn't a clue what colonialism was really about and looks at you as though you are telling them weird fairy stories when you give them an outline of colonial relationships. In fact, their bewilderment was immediate, because I had hung up a map of the Netherlands, the Dutch East Indies and the world, and they simply could not comprehend how that crumb stuck in front of Germany, which itself was not very big, had kept such a vast empire together with a few wooden ships (which took such an unbelievably long time over the journey!). 'Must have been pure bluff', said one of them. To say nothing of nuances like *indos* (Eurasians) and *sinjos* (native boys), the relationship between the Dutch district commissioner and the native 'regent' as depicted in, for example, Louis Couperus's novel *The Hidden Force,* the difference between Ambonese, Dayaks, Javanese and Minangkabauans, relations among the Javanese nobility and other matters that the average American (or German, or Spanish) student has never heard of. That was the first lesson I learned, that you must never assume that what you take for granted is equally familiar to someone else. The wonderful photo collections compiled by Rob Nieuwenhuys, like *Pictures from the Dutch Raj,* which were luckily all in the library, were a great help. The students were mesmerised by the photo of Paku Buwono IX in court dress, wondered whether the Javanese had allowed themselves to become the tools of the Dutch, and hence whether the regents should not be seen as collaborators. They were on the side of the nationalists, made it clear to me that 'we' should of course never have got involved (in colonialism), but that they were not holding me personally responsible. That was the least of my problems, it was more complicated answering such pertinent questions as: 'What was the exact layout of a colonial house?', 'What was the chain of command?' and 'What was the exact function of the Council of the Indies?'. I learned a lot. In his *Lectures on Literature,* Nabokov analyses a number of works from world literature (Proust, Mansfield, etcetera) by giving visual representations of plans and situations. That sounds very simple, but it gets difficult when you try it for yourself. The first chapter of *The Hidden Force* opens with a walk that the commissioner, Van Oudijck, takes around his post at Labuwangi. Assignment: construct a map of the centre on the basis of that walk from the commissioner's house, down Long Avenue, past the Secretary's house, the girls' school, the notary's house, a hotel, the post office, and so on, and when you have done that draw

1. Description coined by Multatuli in his novel *Max Havelaar* (1860).

a plan of the Van Oudijck home, if only to get a better impression of the topographical piquancy of Leonie's adultery.

The American university is a world in itself. From my window everything for miles around, as far as the eye can see, is part of it, libraries, faculty buildings, a stadium with swimming pools, private parking spaces patrolled by merciless parking wardens, a faculty club where you can eat and drink, places for receptions. And between all those buildings mohair carpets in a specially retouched green, the celebrated lawns that the student body lounges on (see above). Two thousand professors, the minimum possible number. Temporarily I was one of them, a *visiting professor,* someone who has just dropped in for tea. On one solitary occasion someone actually called me 'professor' – it's enough to scare the life out of you. Once, at the opening of the academic year, I also had to don a gown and put a strange, heavy biscuit tin on my head, with a tassel which I could see dimly out of the corner of my left eye. I keep the photo carefully hidden. I look like someone else, a black, canonical part of myself, someone who knows all about structuralism and deconstruction and could never write a poem. It was a splendid gathering, though. The real Professor of Dutch pointed out the Nobel Prize winners to me, and identified the headgear and the *hoods* (a kind of multi-coloured silk shawl that is worn over the shoulders, the colours of which indicate the university where one gained one's doctorate). I liked the Italian bonnets best, black velvet chef's hats which revealed the kind of wisdom that was being cooked up in the skulls beneath. It was one of the few occasions where I strode along at full speed, if only because I had the feeling that I might be hauled out of the line at any moment and exposed in front of the troops.

Meanwhile I pondered on the wisdom contained in all those heads and the rampant forms it can assume. I did not need to fantasise, a glance at the endless mass of stencils that floated through my building advertising lectures was sufficient. 'Goblet and Skull: a Goethean Answer to Faust's Cognitive Dilemma', 'The Occult in Mörike', 'The Stream and the Frozen Moment: Images of Stasis in Faulkner's Prose', a river of specialist knowledge flowing incessantly through the corridors. Behind every closed door bubbles a source which in turn will be referred to in another publication, everyone becomes everyone else's footnote, in the depths of the building lie the bodies of the dead writers who once provided the original text for all these self-propagating palimpsests, a verbal nuclear reaction which forces you to shield your writer's soul in lead if it is not to be scorched. I didn't know exactly how I was supposed to feel among the birds of paradise, crows, peacocks and toucans around me, like a sparrow or a phoenix or simply an unclassified bird which would suddenly fly off again without ever having made a sensible remark about Christ and Antichrist in *Paradise Regained,* Sansovini's *Concetti Politici* and their Indebtedness to Machiavelli or the Absurdist Element in Early Icelandic Sagas.

Apart from my students, I was really most fond of the lunatics wandering around the campus. I am using the word 'lunatic' in its sense of 'holy fool'. Thrice holy the man in his bobble suit who lay on the ground every afternoon at about midday and put on a black blindfold. When it rained he spread a paper-thin plastic sheet over himself, but was determined to lie there, as though he were bound to obey the laws of some distant constellation in order to keep the cosmos in equilibrium. Sometimes he silently directed the non-existent traffic for a while, earnest, well-groomed, tanned, a *young executive* who simply wanted to go through life in a suit with multi-coloured bobbles on it. Holy too the singer who couldn't sing, with a straw hat, plastic tape recorder, plastic microphone, practising Sinatra songs with unrelenting seriousness, the complete antithesis of song, grating words, hackneyed tunes, no one dared to listen. He too had his regular times, as did the Awkward Philosopher, who drew a large audience every day and in his strange garb satirised current affairs in America, like Socrates in Athens. A satirist who missed nothing, you could see his words penetrating the young heads. Reagan's new arms and old intestines, AIDS and national morals, the chemical analysis of Coca-Cola and help to the Contras, chronicles of ordinary life. Like the man in the bobble suit he didn't ask for money, or rather it was simply not possible to give them any, they were driven by other compulsions, they appeared as if under contract, absurd scarecrows in a world in which one is brought up to be a winner.

My house sat on top of Grizzly Peak. Behind it a huge, rolling nature park. Berkeley lay stretched out at my feet and beyond in the distance, across Berkeley Bridge, in full array, were San Francisco, the bay and the Golden Gate. I miss that view, the wide horizon, the endless variations of light and mist and sun and time of day, I shall never find anything like it again. At first it was unnerving, because in the summer the whole coast around San Francisco is cloaked in sea fog. Getting up, I saw the world from an aeroplane, a grey carpet of clouds which one assumed was hiding the otherwise fabulous view. It was weird, starting the day with no world at all. The only sign of life was up here where I was: an avocado tree outside my bedroom window, with rectangular, harsh green, dew-laden leaves, motionless. Behind it a tree with silvery flaking bark and bright-red berries, the breakfast tree of a spotted woodpecker. He woke me every morning with his drilling, systematically working over the whole trunk with his geometric eating pattern. Usually I would creep out of bed and look at him, at his head beating its loud tattoo. We could call it work, but for us that term doesn't include eating. I wondered what he did the rest of the day. Did he have other trees? By the time the fog cleared he was already gone, as sunlight pierced the thinning mist. Islands, bridge arches, distant skyscrapers emerged from their bridal attire, the world was called back into existence and I could even see Berkeley Pier, the headlights of the cars on the freeway, the dense, slow-moving stream towards Oakland and the stream moving in the opposite direction towards Sacramento. I had a car too, and because there were sometimes two of me I had two: without a car it is impossible to get around. In order to get to the University I had to go down Marin, a street that plunges down almost vertically like an arrow into the abyss. The speed limit was 15 miles per hour. For the faint-hearted there was an alternative route, a maze of confusingly named streets which wound its way slowly downwards, in which it was easy to lose your way. It was a smart neighbourhood, with huge houses in enclosed gardens, lots of elderly people in children's clothes, blue-rinsed grandmothers just able to see over the steering wheel, on their way to the supermarket at ten miles an hour in huge, ancient jalopies. Anyone who can no longer drive is finished, has had it. One's last car is a harbinger of death. I had such a car. A friend knew an old Jewish lady who wanted to get rid of her car because she wasn't allowed to drive any more. To get rid of it, but not to just anyone, after all she had been given it by her husband in 1962, and in the intervening twenty-five years had driven only 53,000 miles in it. I was summoned for an audience. She was ninety-three, tall and stately. Mrs Stanford. She spoke with an accent which one can imitate but not transcribe: it contained echoes of a whole vanished Europe. During the war her husband had lived in hiding in Amsterdam and had died in America, the name Stanford came from a later marriage, but that husband was dead too now. Coffee, Viennese biscuits. The word 'Amsterdam' had had a definite effect, brought about a shift in the apparatus of language and history. She asked if we could speak German; America evaporated outside the windows, inside it became the Germany of 1910, 1930, of a family with big department stores and great social status, and then, with the fateful thickening of afternoon conversations, the other Germany, the Germany of hate, flight, the death of the family, exile, and the peace of this afternoon in Berkeley and the conversation with a man who considered himself old but was considered young by her, a man from a city where her husband had escaped with his life, someone who was going to buy her car. I was shown them, car and husband, the festive moment of the gift, she herself transported back in time, aged sixty-eight, her hair still black, happy laugh, the dead husband, and gleaming silver-grey, breathtakingly modern, the Buick Skylark with its sharp tail fins, its grey-blue leather, its chrome perfect for Humphrey Bogart movies. So, it was time for me to buy it, it was in great shape, but I mustn't drive down Marin in it, that was too dangerous. And did I want to take a test drive? The price was 400 dollars, how much was that in 'goolden'? Just over eight hundred 'goolden' for a museum piece, a silver shrine on wheels from the year when I was twenty-seven. I sat in the driver's seat, there was play in the steering, the car swayed, rocked a little, but when I accelerated it purred up the hill as though it had been made yesterday. 'Grüssen Sie Ihre Frau Gemahlin', she said as I left, as though it were obvious that there was such a person, and I didn't bother to correct her because the sentence was unforgettable; I must take it with me into the next century to see if there were someone left, in the depths of Tibet, to whom one could still say, 'Grüssen Sie Ihre Frau Gemahlin'. I christened my new car Mrs Stanford, but nobody in the land of freedom would insure me, unless I got a California driver's licence. They 'had no record of me', demanded exorbitant sums. Finally the University had pity on me and a strange company took me under its wing when I promised I would only use the car to drive to and from campus. That was how I got around, like someone from another age. Every day I negotiated the slalom of the smart streets and made my way to the fields of Academia like a real human being, a poet among the professors, someone who taught students what *guna guna* (magic) was, while the spirit of Louis Couperus looked on contentedly and the orange jacket waited doggedly for the moment I would finally get the hell out of there.

June, 1987

From *The World a Traveller* (De wereld een reiziger, De Arbeiderspers, Amsterdam, 1989, pp. 197-206).
Translated by Paul Vincent.

Cees Nooteboom (1933-) (Photo by Paul Van Den Abeele).

Cees Nooteboom

Cees Nooteboom (1933-) made his prose debut in 1955 with the novel *Philip and the Others* (Philip en de anderen), a poetic, melancholy account of an adolescent's journey through France. It is a classic wanderer's story about the search for one's own identity, which places it in the tradition of works like Alain Fournier's *Le grand Meaulnes.* Themes like 'time' and 'memory', which are to recur with a deeper philosophical resonance in Nooteboom's later work, already feature in this first novel. In the story 'Visiting Professor' (1989), Nooteboom characterises his attitude to his début as follows: 'I have always had a problematic relationship with that book myself, embarrassment at my painfully obvious innocence at the time, at the visibility of the writer, who just happened to have the same name as me.' However, he took to heart his fellow-writer Harry Mulisch's 'wise advice', that one should not repudiate work once published, and the book has been reprinted – and appeared in translation.

In 1956 Nooteboom's first collection of poetry, *The Dead are in Search of a Home* (De doden zoeken een huis), appeared. The underlying motif is death and is clothed in a traditional poetic form, with long lines, separate stanzas and rhyme. In later collections a more experimental approach to form gains the ascendancy; the emphasis now falls on poetry as artefact, as can be seen from the title of the omnibus *Constructed Poems* (Gemaakte gedichten, 1970). The theme of death is developed further and is given an added dimension by 'time' in its various manifestations. The poet strives to grasp time, movement, the chaotic nature of life. Formally this has a sobering effect: the poet retreats into the position of an observer who distances himself as much as possible from himself, – ideally the 'I' of the poet should disappear as a subject from the observed world.

Although Nooteboom regards himself as first and foremost a poet, and has been acknowledged as such, it was as a writer of prose that he first achieved really wide public recognition. Two directions, two genres can be distinguished in his prose work: on the one hand the novels and stories, and on the other the literary travelogues.

Nooteboom's breakthrough as a novelist came in 1980 with *Rituals* (Rituelen), which was awarded the F. Bordewijk Prize in the Netherlands and in the USA the 1982 Mobil Oil Pegasus Prize for the best non-American novel. *Rituals* is a very complex novel, with parallels, mirror effects, double bottoms, disruption of the normal linear time sequence, and hence different levels of meaning. The underlying theme is the possible attitudes people can adopt towards the phenomena of life and death, the chaos of existence and the passage of time. The narrator (or narrative agency) is a somewhat aloof observer, afflicted by a rather melancholy, nihilistic view of life, who is trying to chart a number of key moments in his progress towards full consciousness. The conclusion is that every ritual performed in order to confer meaning on human actions is intrinsically meaningless. *Rituals* is also a novel about time, in which the central question is how 'time' operates in experience and memory. This also focuses on the problem of writing: how can one capture what is amorphous, chaotic and fleeting? However, *Rituals* is also a novel about a particular span of time: the years between 1953 and 1973, from French existentialism to the modern Amsterdam of the 1960s and 1970s. In the short novel *A Song of Truth and Semblance* (Een lied van schijn en wezen, 1981) the problem of the relationship between fiction and reality, imagination and memory is concentrated in a writer engaged in writing a story containing characters from the last century. However, the characters the writer creates become so real that he begins to doubt his own existence. *In the Dutch Mountains* (In Nederland, 1984), Nooteboom's most 'fantastic' novel to date, is also concerned with writing, but also with fairytales, road-building and 'reality'. His attachment to his second homeland, Spain, also plays an important role in the book, which was awarded the Dutch Multatuli Prize (1985). Similarly, *The Following Story* (Het volgende verhaal, 1991) is a tale of transformations, possibilities, dreamlike visions. It describes the (imagined?) sea voyage of an ex-Classics teacher (hence the wealth of Classical references), who under a pseudonym writes fairly banal, or at least emotionless travel stories – a subtle touch of irony.

Between 1957 and 1960 Cees Nooteboom wrote travel pieces for the magazine *Elsevier;* from 1961 to 1968 for the daily *De Volkskrant,* and thereafter for *Avenue.* He introduced the literary travelogue into Dutch journalism and literature, making it a fully-fledged genre, focusing on real locations and events – all over the world – but at the same time creating space for the observer's subjective vision. Not that his work is devoid of emotion: he is often concerned to convey impressions, evoke an atmosphere – which ties up with the themes of his poetry and prose fiction. Over the past decades Nooteboom has published various collections of travel stories, the most recent anthology of which is *The World a Traveller* (De wereld een reiziger, 1989), in which anecdotes, observations, essays and memories are strung together by Nooteboom with exceptional erudition to form an often ironic whole. In 1992 he produced *The Long Route to Santiago* (De omweg naar Santiago), a most impressive compilation of earlier journeys to Spain, supplemented with new experiences and illuminated with intriguing photographs by Simone Sassen. This is Spain as one would have liked it to remain.

Nooteboom made a great impact with his impressions of the momentous changes in Germany. In February 1989, at the invitation of the German Cultural Exchange Service, he took up residence in Berlin, where he planned to finish a novel. However, the writer was overtaken by 'time' and 'history': he witnessed the collapse of the Wall, and reported on its tumultuous aftermath. The result is his *Berlijnse notities* (Berlin Notes, 1990), which won him the *Preis des 3. Oktober* in Berlin, so called in celebration of the date of German reunification. In 1992 his whole oeuvre was honoured by the award of the Constantijn Huygens Prize.

FRANS DE ROVER
Translated by Paul Vincent.

LIST OF TRANSLATIONS

Rituals (Tr. Adrienne Dixon). Baton Rouge, 1983; London, 1984; Harmondsworth, 1985.
A Song of Truth and Semblance (Tr. Adrienne Dixon). Baton Rouge, 1984; London, 1990.
Mokusei! A Love Story (Tr. Adrienne Dixon). Amsterdam, 1985.
In the Dutch Mountains (Tr. Adrienne Dixon), London / Baton Rouge, 1987.
Philip and the Others (Tr. Adrienne Dixon). Baton Rouge, 1988.
The Knight Has Died (Tr. Adrienne Dixon). Baton Rouge, 1990.
The Following Story will be presented at the *Frankfurter Buchmesse 1993.*

The Mauritshuis

From City Palace to National Museum

One of the most important museums in the Netherlands is the Mauritshuis in The Hague, which today houses the Royal Picture Collection. It was originally the private residence of John Maurice (Johan Maurits), Count of Nassau Siegen, who built it between 1637 and 1644 and used it to house the collection of objects he had assembled during his time in Brazil. After his death the house was used for various purposes until it finally became a museum in 1822.

The building

Carved in the floor of the Mauritshuis, in front of a portrait of John Maurice (1604-1679) himself, is a Latin text which sums up the versatility of the man. The translation reads: 'John Maurice, Count of Nassau, Governor of Brazil, illustrious military commander, architect, patron of the arts'. During the Stadholdership of Frederick Henry, John Maurice led the Dutch army to many successes. He struck up a close friendship with Constantine Huygens, the prince's private secretary, a real humanist with a great interest in the plastic arts and a cultivated musician, poet and architect. John Maurice was also acquainted with Jacob van Campen, the well-known architect and painter.

John Maurice bought from Frederick Henry a plot of land at the corner of the Hofvijver in The Hague, then the seat of the court, to build a house on. The plans were drawn up in 1634 by Jacob van Campen in consultation with John Maurice and the construction was put in the hands of the architect Pieter Post. Huygens was building his own house nearby at the same time, and when the Dutch West India Company sent John Maurice to Brazil as Governor it was only natural that his friend Huygens should supervise the further progress of the building.

When 'Maurice the Brazilian' returned to The Hague in 1644 his house was ready for him. It was built in the 'Dutch Classical' style with the flat surface of the walls divided by regular massive pilasters and ornamentation taken from Greek and Roman architecture. For the interior he,

The Mauritshuis in The Hague.

The Golden Room (Photo by Daniël van der Ven).

as it were, recreated Brazil, with the aid of a large number of objects which he had brought back with him and which he displayed all over the house. His collection consisted of natural and man-made curiosities, precious and other types of stones and shells, weapons and artefacts, stuffed animals, furniture and paintings. The paintings in the entrance hall must have been particularly striking. They depicted South American landscapes with animals and exotic tribes taking part in native ceremonies.

Alas, John Maurice's collection was broken up. He himself gave away most of it as a diplomatic gift. Today the museum's only reminders of that time are one work by Albert Eckhout – *Two South American Tortoises* – and a handful of Brazilian landscapes by Frans Post; both these painters actually accompanied John Maurice on his journey to Brazil.

John Maurice lived in the house for only a few years before being appointed Stadholder in Cleves. After that he rarely visited it. After his death in 1679 the house was used as an ambassadorial residence. A fire in 1704 totally destroyed the interior and only the external walls remained. Fortunately it was decided to restore rather than demolish it. One striking product of this 18th-century reconstruction is the Reception Hall, known as the Golden Room because of its decoration; this is now the oldest part of the interior. The paintings on the walls and ceilings are by the Venetian artist Giovanni Antonio Pellegrini, who visited The Hague in 1718. On the walls female figures in grisaille represent the four elements, while on the ceiling are portrayed the Sun God Apollo and Aurora, the Goddess of the Dawn, with Night fleeing before them.

In the 18th century the Mauritshuis was used for various purposes, including as a wine store and a prison; then it was eventually decided to turn it into a museum for the royal picture collection. At the opening in 1822 the Government Gazette announced: 'The Royal Collection of Paintings may now be visited on Wednesdays and Saturdays from 10 until 1 by anyone who is properly dressed and is not accompanied by children.'

The history of the collection

The nucleus of the Royal Collection of Paintings is the Orange collection, which had modest beginnings. Frederick Henry (1584-1647), the art-loving son of William of Orange, added considerably to it. But his daughters married German princes, which meant that a large part of his collection ended up in Germany. Something similar happened to the estate of William III (1650-1702), who was both King and Stadholder. After his death art treasures from his palace of Het Loo were sold at public auction in Amsterdam in 1712. The stadholder William IV (1711-1751) added more Dutch 17th-century masters to what was left of the collection. Perhaps his best known purchase is *The Young Bull* (1647) by Paulus Potter. Amazing for its sheer size, it is still one of the best known works in the Museum.

The basis of the current collection was assembled by Stadholder William V (1748-1806). Starting from that formed by his father William IV, he built up a unique collection of some 200 works; his preference, like his father's, being for Dutch 17th-century pictures. National pride and his own connoisseurship influenced his choice. He bought single masterpieces and occasionally whole collections, such as the Slingelandt collection in 1768, which contained three Rembrandts. The most valuable work in the collection was bought in 1766 – *Adam and Eve in Paradise* by Rubens and Jan Brueghel the Elder cost 7,350 guilders; a huge sum for that time.

In 1774 William V began to bring together his pictures, including those from his country residences at Het Loo and Soestdijk, in a gallery in The Hague. This was open to the public at set times during the week, thus creat-

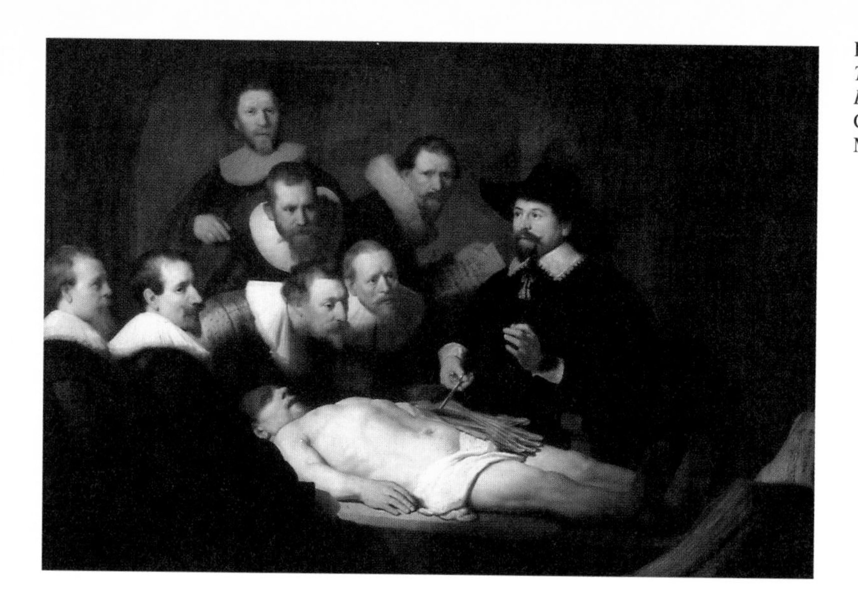

Rembrandt H. van Rijn, *The Anatomy Lesson of Doctor Tulp*. 1632. Canvas, 169.5 x 216.5 cm. Mauritshuis, The Hague.

ing what was in effect the first museum in the Netherlands. However, although he was then only 23 years old, William v never added anything more to his collection.

In 1795 the Stadholder's collection was seized by the French and taken to the Louvre in Paris. After the fall of Napoleon King William I (1772-1843) had the pictures brought back from France and presented them to the nation. But he also ensured that many further masterpieces were added to the Royal Collection. For example he gave instructions for the purchase of Rembrandt's *The Anatomy Lesson of Doctor Tulp* (1632). He made sure the Mauritshuis got this work by forbidding its public sale. The first of the three Vermeers in the Museum, his *View of Delft,* also entered the collection through William's efforts. In 1822, when it was bought, very little was known about the artist. Later it was in the Mauritshuis that the French art critic Thoré-Bürger 'discovered' the genius of the now world famous 'Sphinx of Delft'. But even in 1882 Vermeer was still so little known that his *Young Girl in a Turban* could be bought for a trifling sum. Now it is one of the works for which the Museum is best known.

New acquisitions were not confined to works from the Golden Age. The Flemish Primitives were enriched by the acquisition of *The Lamentation of Christ* by Rogier van der Weyden. The attribution of this work was long contested; but scientific research has now removed the last remaining doubts about it.

Successive directors of the Mauritshuis have steadily built up the collection. Abraham Bredius, the controversial Director from 1889 to 1909, was an inspired art lover and collector. He had a special love for Dutch 17th-century painting – and for Rembrandt in particular. He bought officially, but he also bought regularly on his own account works which he then offered on permanent loan to the Museum. When he died he left them to the Museum, which in this way gained no fewer than six Rembrandts.

He was also responsible for the purchase of *The Goldfinch* (1654), a signed and dated work by Carel Fabritius, Rembrandt's most renowned

Johannes Vermeer, *View of Delft*. c.1661. Canvas, 98.5 x 117.5 cm. Mauritshuis, The Hague.

pupil, which is one of only eight pictures definitely attributed to Fabritius; Bredius bought it in 1896 in Paris because of its unusual subject – a chained bird perched on its feeder.

The Mauritshuis has frequently received important gifts and bequests. Only recently, a number of individual gifts enabled the purchase of the *Portrait of Constantine Huygens and his Wife,* probably by Jacob van Campen. The close relationship of Huygens and van Campen with the building of the Mauritshuis made this a particularly prized acquisition. The collection now consists of nearly 1,000 pictures and *objets d'art,* of which some two-thirds are permanently on public display.

Although the building no longer fulfils its original purpose as a private residence, the interior retains an intimate personal atmosphere, which reminds you of that time. As you walk through the rooms and ante-chambers you will find a collection of Flemish Primitives, portraits by Holbein, Flemish masterpieces from the time of Rubens and Van Dijck and of course the art of the Dutch Golden Age in all its glory. A 17th-century palace is just the right environment for such a princely collection.

MARJAN VAN ZIJTVELD
Translated by Michael Shaw.

Picturing Dutch Culture

It has been a pervasive and limiting assumption of the study of art history that meaning takes the form of 'iconicity' – that the sense that pictures make is located in the meaning of people or objects represented. In the study of the predominantly secular and non-narrative Dutch art of the seventeenth century this has been coupled with the assumption (one with ancient precedent) that such meaning or sense is a message, instructionally intended: you may delight in the people and objects in pictures, but are meant to attend to the moral instruction which they offer. The model for such pictures has been located in emblem books. It was a major accomplishment of the work of Eddy de Jongh to discover the relationship between certain motifs in Dutch painting and the images accompanied by texts in the popular emblem books. Images so conceived lend themselves to words, they originate with texts in mind.

The 'reality effect' peculiar to much Dutch painting has persuaded many viewers that this art registers how things are or how they were. Art historians have argued that things are not what they seem to the eye – they are devised with meanings in or (if hidden) out of view. But the notion that Dutch pictures are therefore only apparently real (because they have hidden meanings) or selectively or subjectively real (because the painted world is creatively chosen and one person's view) is misleading. For, along with the appeal to moral meanings, it effectively suggests that we can bracket or bypass the pictorial mode itself – the reality effect – so basic to these pictures. Painters make paintings not meanings. It is to the mode – the reality effect – that I turned my attention. And it was with reference to this pictorial mode that I tried to ground Dutch painting in its culture.

It was while looking at Vermeer's *Art of Painting* that I began to consider another manner of interpretation. The map depicted by Vermeer does not signify a longing for former political unity, nor is it a sign of the vanity of worldly concerns, it is a piece of painting. A painter painted a map and incidentally signed his name on it as its maker. This painted map first drew my attention to the link between painting and mapping at the time. The map-painting relationship can be described as a matter of *format:* the absence of a positioned viewer as if the world came first before the viewer; the absence of a prior frame; a formidable sense of surface on which words along with objects can be inscribed. It can also be described as a matter of *function:* maps as pictures and picture-like maps were both engaged in gaining knowledge of the world. I had the good luck to find a painting by Jan Christaensz. Micker where Amsterdam was laid out on the surface like a map but with unseen clouds casting shadows on it. It provides what might be called the missing link which demonstrates the close relationship existing at the time between painting and mapping.

Paintings were like maps, but they were also like mirrors: when Kepler, in his study of the mechanism of the eye, defines *to see* as *to make a picture,* he provides a model for the particular relationship between finding and making, between nature and art, that characterizes much painting in northern Europe. The operation of the eye is, so he proposed, like a camera obscura – and this illustration of its operation is a good analogy to a picture like Vermeer's *View of Delft.* Like so many Dutch pictures, this is produced in an age of observation – the sky is scanned, land surveyed, flora and fauna observed and described. Instead of a direct confrontation with nature, we find a trust in devices, in intermediaries that represent nature to us. The major example of such a device is of course the lens. Painting can be described as another such intermediary.

If we take the pictorial mode – the reality effect – not as hiding moral instruction, but as offering a perceptual model of knowledge of the world, then pictures are related to the empirical interests of this age of observation. The picture takes its place besides the many other devices – the eye, the

Jan Christiaensz. Micker, *View of Amsterdam.* Historisch Museum, Amsterdam.

microscopic lens – which squeeze and press nature so that we can experience (or experiment in the seventeenth-century use of the word) her. The attentive eye and crafty hand of the painter are here related to the eye and hand of the experimenter. Painting itself is like an experiment.

Readers outside the field of art history have been receptive to this analysis: the definition of a mapping impulse brought landscape painting to the attention of geographers and offered new confirmation of their already expanding and problematizing notion of maps as conventional representations. The definition of Dutch painting as sharing a perceptual view of knowledge and an interest in craft with seventeenth-century experimental science has forged links with current studies in the history and sociology of science. Here, too, historians are concerned with the conventional and crafted nature of natural knowledge at the time.

But the academic specialists studying Dutch art remain upset and unconvinced. Indeed it appears to them that I am not even looking at the same objects as they are. Why? I think it is largely a matter of certain professional habits.

Art historians who study Dutch art have made two objections – one basic and one less so. The basic one involves misunderstanding (or simple non-attention to) the place of the word *art* in the title of my book *The Art of Describing* (1983). The book is not about describing but about the *art* of describing. Artifice, one might say, is assumed from the beginning. The phrase 'the art of describing' does not claim that pictures picture the world as it is, but rather the world as it is seen, microscoped, mapped, crafted, in short as it is represented. The argument is that pictures make sense (by which I mean produce understanding) rather than meaning out of the world.

The second objection was their concern about the subtitle: *The Art of Describing: Dutch Art in the Seventeenth Century*. The distinction I drew between two modes – descriptive and narrative, northern and southern, Netherlandish and Italian – had of course been noted in the past. There is a famous remark attributed to Michelangelo which described northern art as an art appealing to women. The distinction was for me at least partly a heuristic device, a way to get away from what I see as the dominance of an Italian or Albertian model of the picture in European writing on painting. I anticipated that exceptions could be found and indeed built them into my account. I defined a mode of painting that can be generally, but is not uniquely, attached to the pictorial tradition of a specific part of Europe. One could say that within each pictorial tradition, northern and Italian, the other is possible: Caravaggio, for example, is Italian by tradition, but descriptive in mode.

What I had not anticipated was the denial by Dutch art historians that there is such a thing as Dutch art! Or maybe, to be fair, that there is *one* such thing as Dutch art. Surely to deny the fact that there is something called Dutch painting is rather like denying that there was an Elizabethan theatre or a Russian novel. From Chardin and Hogarth to Manet, Cézanne, Picasso and Braque, a secular, domestically oriented, realist mode of painting with roots in the Netherlands is a feature of the European tradition of painting.

But Dutchness is not only a matter of painting. It is notable that in the seventeenth century, when travellers and policy makers from abroad repeatedly marvel at the economic miracle of the Netherlands and comment on what seemed to them striking about its society, the native people lacked chauvinism. So many cultural norms were under construction in Dutch seventeenth-century life, and, I would argue, in Dutch seventeenth-century painting: our bourgeois way of living, sense of individuality, and ways of organizing society from banking to the bourse, notions of punishment, civic charity, and most particularly the household and the family. But I am struck by the manner in which Dutch historians, many of them working in the manner of the French so-called Annales group, are wary of making claims specific to their culture. They want their findings about Dutch history not to be Dutch specific, but to corroborate general truths. French historians also, of course, seek general truths in their account of details, but the difference is that Annales historians in France think that it was in France that general social truths were manifest!

Despite the absence of chauvinism, Dutch scholars are protective of their (national?) territory. A catalogue essay for the loan exhibition *Great Dutch Paintings from America* (1991) clearly expressed anger at these paintings as being American loot that had been taken from the Netherlands. But it was not clear what it was that had been taken: do these paintings constitute a common patrimony and if so in what respect? Because they are all painted by Dutch painters or because they were owned by Dutch owners? The remarketing of paintings made for the market is surely only a problem if one feels the paintings have a special place in a culture.

I wonder if the practice of tolerance does not have some bearing on the absence of chauvinism. In the seventeenth century the northern Netherlands was a land receiving many immigrants. It was tolerant, but the price for toleration was conformity, or a fiction of conformity. A kind of low-key conformity covered or protected difference – city from city, province from province, person from person – and allowed nothing to stand out – not even, as it were, a common culture. In this kind of situation to claim something as distinctively Dutch was perhaps to threaten the delicate fabric woven out of different people. A general distinctiveness is divisive if a society is trying to be inclusive. This old suspicion of national pride was given renewed validity during the Second World War.

Now to Rembrandt. There is a consistency about the fact that while insisting on the infinite variety of Dutch art, Dutch art historians are also currently trying to cut Rembrandt down to size. This is being done numerically, as the Rembrandt Research Project sorts out true from false in terms of his actual production, and ideologically, by claiming that major components of his reputation are a nineteenth-century myth. In proposing Rembrandt as an exception to the Art of Describing I fear that I unwittingly accepted the nineteenth-century romantic loner myth. My book *Rembrandt's Enterprise* (1988) was an attempt to see him inside his culture, not outside it. I proposed that one should instead understand Rembrandt as responsible for producing the very values which the nineteenth century associated with him: individual uniqueness; painting as monetary value; as aesthetic aura. These are not anachronistically ascribed to Rembrandt and to his works. They are products of his own enterprise. His is the curious and impressive production of a man who claimed individuality for his own way of painting and at the same time got other painters in his studio to paint in his Rembrandt manner. (Imagine Van Gogh getting a large group of assistants to paint like him,

The Polish Rider. c.1655. Canvas, 116.8 x 134.9 cm. The Frick Collection, New York.
This painting was 'discovered' in 1897 and attributed to Rembrandt. It was signed 'Re'. Recently it has been argued that it was painted by Willem Drost.

even to copy his self-portraits on occasion!) It is not the limits of the real Rembrandt, but his authoritative reach or spread that we are learning about from the Rembrandt team.

If one turns from considering art as creating knowledge to art as creating value, one can see Rembrandt's painting as creating values that have remained basic to European (and American) culture. While we are attending to the important role played by the picturing of culture, it is important to note that the Dutch language does not, and indeed did not in the past, have a word for that enterprise which Rembrandt's painting exemplifies.

In conclusion, let us turn to the home, to the territory of household and family which is the subject of so much of what is called Dutch genre painting. Dutch images of the household have been read as showing how not to behave or, in more recent accounts and with attention to different cases, how in fact people ought to behave. What, if not illustration or moral example about the life of women, was the reason for making such pictures? Why did painters so obsessively paint the house and its inhabitants?

In his fascinating study of Dutch society and culture, *The Embarrassment of Riches* (1987), Simon Schama has described Dutch culture as a consensus reached between opposites, a co-existence achieved between competing value systems. It seems to me that Dutch culture was less settled than Schama implies. I also think that rather than reflecting a culture as Schama thinks, the painting is often in subtle ways constructing it.

Nicholas Maes and Gerard ter Borch – two of the most ambitious painters of the home – are not warning or recommending this or that (nor are they in the newest post and anti De Jongh art historical mode, simply making

Gerard ter Borch, *A Company in a Room.* c.1654. Canvas, 71 x 73 cm. Rijksmuseum, Amsterdam.

skilful paintings). They are examining, through representing, problems in the system of social behaviour. Dutch pictures suggest that the Netherlands – no different from our own world in this! – was stranger and more troubled than Schama allows.

There are some pictures by Maes or Ter Borch which seem to illustrate the system proposed in the writings of Jacob Cats which divides the lives of women into six ages – *maeght* (girl-child), *vryster* (maid), *bruyt* (bride), *vrouwe* (wife), *moeder* (mother), *weduwe* (widow). Ter Borch's *Woman Spinning* in Amsterdam is even related to an emblem illustrating the behaviour of the virtuous housewife. But how did a woman transform herself from *vryster* to *vrouwe,* from the necessarily flirtatious, erotically engaged courting girl into the manager of a household? Maes investigates this doubled or split persona of a woman in a series of distinctive paintings featuring divided domestic interiors with the housewife situated between the flirtatious maid in the kitchen and the refined guests above.

What Maes does by doubling, Ter Borch does by what we can call overlapping. A woman's conflicting roles are now posed as a question of identity: *vryster*-whore. What kind of negotiation is going on in his famous painting in Amsterdam? What kind of courtship is it? Proper or improper? Is this a father admonishing a daughter, as Goethe once wrote, or a young man negotiating to pay a whore? Ter Borch entertains the notion that as the woman in the house behaves like the woman in the brothel so the reverse might be also true. The question is put pictorially by means of his marvellous invention of the splendidly gowned woman seen from the back, her face hidden from view.

Johannes Vermeer, *The Artist in his Studio: Allegory of the Art of Painting*. c.1665. Canvas, 120 x 100 cm. Kunsthistorisches Museum, Vienna.

Simon Schama and others have suggested that there was balance between the good home and the bad – the musicos or brothels as the negative alternative to the orderly household. But perhaps, Ter Borch shows, the problem was that the difference was not clear. For Amsterdam to construct musicos or bordellos on the model of the domestic house is not a demonstration of balance but a testimony to continuing uncertainty about whether there is any difference between the two. It was a problem for women as well as for men.

There is no need to argue the centrality of the household / family to Dutch social and political organization – but this would not necessarily have made it a central subject for painting. It is worth inquiring why it should have become such. An important element is the identification of the painter with the family. In northern Europe painting was celebrated in a familial context: parents, wife, children all take their place in paintings beside the artist. There is a practical basis for this – family members often served the artist as models. But more importantly the family provided the artist's ambience: a room in the house was the painter's working space.

Vermeer's achievement as a painter culminates in the series, done toward the end of his short career, of distinctive representations of solitary women in the household. The women are upright, impressive, self-possessed, separated from both men and children. What is interesting about them is less what they do – mostly traditional women's task like making lace, reading letters, cooking – than how they are represented.

In these paintings Vermeer effectively removes the representation of women from the tensions that concerned Maes and Ter Borch. There is a difference between using family members as one's models and taking the woman in the home as *the* model. While Ter Borch offers us the virtue of a woman spinning, Vermeer offers us the virtue of a woman posing in the home.

Vermeer's pictures have been plumbed for their psychological power – the nuance with which the male painter attends, past the barrier of chair or carpet-draped table, to the self-absorbed woman in view. It has been said that Vermeer overcame his inhibitions to celebrate these women and lets them simply be themselves. That is to treat them as objects of his generous feeling. But there is another aspect to this: the basis of Vermeer's attention to these women rests on the way he takes and represents the house as his studio and the women in the house as his models. (Rembrandt, by contrast, removed his studio from the domestic setting.)

It was argued in the Netherlands of the time that woman's place should be in the home. Jacob Cats wrote that the husband must be on the street to practice his trade while the wife must stay at home to be in the kitchen. But here, as elsewhere in his writings, Cats appears to have been prescriptive rather than descriptive. The house was not only lived in but also worked in by men as well as women. It had not yet become the female domain it was to become in the nineteenth century. Vermeer, then, is not registering the social fact of woman's domesticity, but is producing it himself in his pictures. That is one reason they seem to us not only skilful but also socially valid. Vermeer's pictures of these women are enabled by his acknowledgement of the relationship between the practice of the painter and social practice. There is an element of entrapment about the situation – the condition of female idealization is domesticity. But the artist in the home-studio is also trapped. As so often in European painting (one could, a bit outrageously perhaps, compare Vermeer to Picasso in this) the artist's power is not in his use of, but in his identification with the situation of the women in the studio who are his models.

SVETLANA ALPERS

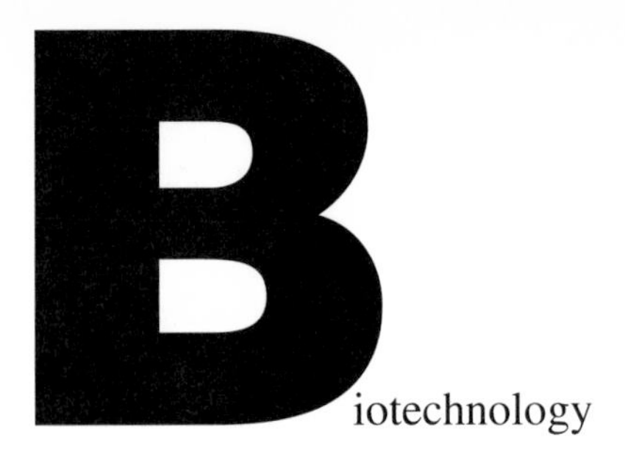

Biotechnology in Flanders

Big in the Microcosm of Cells and Molecules

As soon as biochemists began to grasp the principles of genetics, many Flemish researchers immediately jumped on the boat as well. Today they are still manning the decks and are even playing a leading role in many areas. This is not very surprising, because for centuries Flanders has been the land of beer. Brewers use yeast, which is already biotechnology: making use of the metabolism and biosynthetic abilities of organisms which are specially cultivated for that purpose.

Modern biotechnology goes one step further. It changes the nature of the organisms which are used by altering the DNA molecule deep inside each cell, the blueprint for the production, conversion and breakdown of very diverse biological materials. By making changes to the chemical building blocks of heredity, cells can be restructured so that the proteins which they produce are better suited to people's needs. Useful sections of genetic code can also be transferred from one organism to another. Thus bacteria are equipped with genes which enable them to produce enzymes in fermentation tanks, and man makes use of this in all kinds of processes.

There are only three significant producers of industrial enzymes in the entire world: Novo in Denmark, Gist-Brocades in the Netherlands and the Flemish company Amylum in Aalst. All three are carrying out pioneering work in the area of enzymatic engineering, which is the artificial improvement of existing enzymes. The genetic manipulation of bacteria has long been a routine procedure for these companies. Bacteria are very well suited for this, because apart from the main DNA molecule they also have small rings of DNA containing coding material for less vital functions. These are called plasmids, and they can be removed from bacteria and foreign genes inserted in them without difficulty. If the recombined DNA is later put back into the bacterium, it will carry out the instructions in the new section of genetic code perfectly. It will begin to produce proteins which were previously completely foreign to it, possibly even proteins of human origin.

The genetic enhancement of plants is much more difficult, because their cells do not contain any plasmids which could act as vehicles to smuggle in foreign genes. However there is a bacterium which can infect plants through small wounds on their stems. It does this by inserting a plasmid into the plant cells. Part of the plasmid is then integrated in the DNA of the host cells and causes them to produce substances which serve as food for the bacterium. Using this bacterium, in 1982 professors Marc van Montagu and Jozef Schell became the first in the world to genetically alter plants. In their laboratory at the University of Ghent, they thought up a veritable conjuring trick to demonstrate their technique. They took a bacterial gene for resistance to a certain antibiotic and attached it to light-resistance regulatory genes from pea plants. Regulatory genes do not contain coding material for specific products, but function as a kind of switch for neighbouring genes. When the entire structure was transferred to tobacco plants, the plants' resistance to antibiotics also became light-dependent.

After this astonishing demonstration the time was ripe to convert the results into profits, through the R&D company Plant Genetics Systems (PGS), which immediately signed a cooperation agreement with Advanced Genetic Sciences Inc. in Connecticut. The first usable results followed soon afterwards. In 1985, PGS achieved a world first by equipping plants with a gene which allows a certain bacterium to produce a protein poisonous to insect larvae. The result was plants which produce their own insecticide, one which is completely harmless to people and the environment.

In 1987 there was an equally significant scientific breakthrough in the area of weed suppression. In recent years chemical companies have developed herbicides whose active components are not poisonous to humans or animals, and which are converted into non-damaging substances soon after

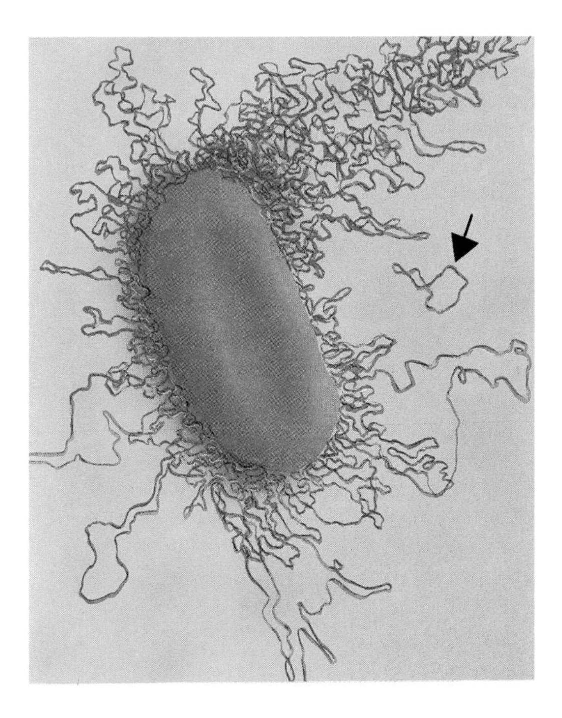

This is what a coli intestinal bacterium looks like under the electron microscope after researchers have caused it to explode so that the DNA has flowed out. The arrow indicates a plasmid.

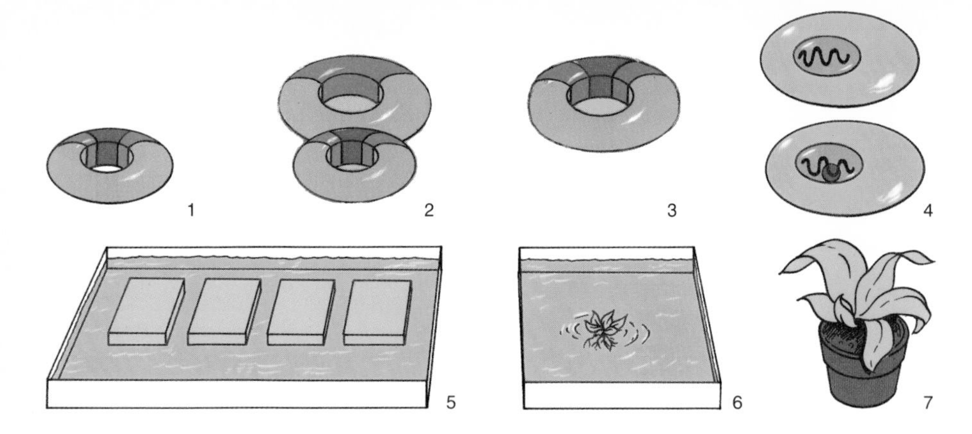

In order to insert foreign genes into plants, the researchers at Ghent devised this procedure: 1. The DNA fragments used by Agrobacterium Tumefaciens to infect plant cells (green) are attached to the gene to be transferred (red) in a Coli plasmid. 2. The plasmid which has been recombined in this way is transferred to A. Tumefaciens. 3. Plasmids can exchange more or less equivalent parts. Thus the fragment with the DNA to be transferred can enter the plasmid of A. Tumefaciens, which is much larger (and therefore difficult to manipulate directly). 4. When the bacterium infects a plant cell, the foreign gene is included in the plant DNA. 5. The infected cells are cultured. 6. A callus tissue grows from the cell tissue. 7. Plants grow from the callus culture, and all their cells contain the new gene.

use. Unfortunately this new generation of weedkillers makes no distinction between agricultural plants and weeds. Where they are used, only certain bacteria can survive, and this is because they produce enzymes which are able to neutralise the active ingredient in the weedkiller. The researchers at PGS managed to take the gene which makes a certain bacterium resistant to one of the new broad-spectrum herbicides, and transfer it to potatoes, tomatoes and tobacco. The plants which had been manipulated survived the application of weedkiller, even if they were given a tenfold overdose, and also passed on their resistance to subsequent generations.

A new process for obtaining hybrid seed

In 1988, all this pioneering work gained the Schell-Van Montagu duo the IBM Science and Technology prize. Thanks to their revolutionary work, PGS rapidly grew to become the unrivalled leader in plant biotechnology in Europe. When it was set up the company had only three shareholders. Now there are twenty, including Volvo subsidiary Hilleshög, Japan Tobacco and the French seed giant Clause (which has in the meantime been taken over by Sanofi). At world level PGS is racing neck-and-neck with American giants like Monsanto and Dupont.

The Ghent team are still a lenght ahead, as became clear when they made the front cover of the top professional publication *Nature* with the biotechnological construction of male sterile plants. The implications of this are tremendous. In many agricultural plants, the female pistils and male stamens are located on the same plant. This hinders cross-pollination, the age-old refinement technique which produces better seed than self-pollination. In order to prevent self-pollination in monoecious plants, the stamens from one of two parental strains have to be removed by hand, which is a labour-intensive process and therefore very expensive. In 1990 PGS unveiled plants which no longer produce pollen. Here a regulatory gene was used which is only active in and during the development of the tapetum, a vital layer of tissue in pollen grains. This gene was attached to the genetic information for a bacterial enzyme which breaks the chain of reactions between a gene becoming active and the formation of the corresponding protein. By inserting this combination into plant DNA, the development of the tapetum became impossible. The plants are male sterile and the pistil can only be fertilised by pollen from a different plant. Upon germination some of the hybrid seed also produced plants which, just like their parents, did not produce pollen. This is no problem at all for plants such as lettuce and chicory, which are harvested for their leaves rather than for their seed.

It is a problem in the case of maize, tomatoes and other plants which depend on the formation of fruit. In collaboration with researchers from the University of California, PGS has also managed to get around this problem. During the process of refinement, plants which had been made male sterile were crossed with normal, fertile plants of the same variety which had already undergone some biotechnological tinkering. They were equipped with the genetic information for another bacterial enzyme which reverses the action of the first one. The gene was attached to the same tapetum-specific regulatory gene. The result was hybrid daughter plants whose reproductive organs work normally again.

Medical biotechnology

All this made Ghent into a worldwide centre for agricultural applications of biotechnology, but Ghent is also at the forefront of medical biotechnology. In 1983 professor Walter Fiers, one of the pioneers of enzymatic engineering, set up a branch of the Swiss biotechnology company Biogen in the shadow of the University in Ghent. Biogen specialised in medicines for use against cancer. In collaboration with a research group in Leuven under the leadership of Professor De Somer, important work was also carried out on the anti-tumour and anti-virus substance interferon, which occurs naturally in the body. The R&D company has been developing biotechnological medicines for the Swiss pharmaceuticals company Hoffmann-Laroche since 1987, and therefore changed its name to Roche Research Gent. Early in 1993, the research team announced in *Nature* that they had succeeded in modifying the protein Tumour Necrosis Factor, produced naturally by the body, so that the body is able to tolerate it even in large dosages. Biotechnologically produced TNF is already being used experimentally in cancer therapy. Administered in large doses it can destroy cancer cells, but in its natural form then also damages healthy cells.

Along with the laboratories of Dr Volckaert in Leuven and Dr Glansdorff in Brussels, Professor Fiers' laboratory belongs to a group of thirty-five European laboratories which are working together within the framework of the *Biotechnology Action Programme* on decoding the DNA of baker's yeast. This project is the European counterpart of the American *Human Genome Project,* which is attempting to chart out all human genes. Baker's yeast was chosen because it is considered something of a model organism in biotechnology. A first chromosome, containing 360,000 chemical building blocks, has already been completely analysed.

It's in their blood

From 1986 a small group at PGS also began to work on biotechnological medicines, concentrating on heart diseases. In 1991 a joint venture called

Corvas International was set up with a Californian research group, with the specific aim of developing a new thrombolytic drug. Less than a year later the Flemish partners in Corvas published an article in *Nature.* They had developed a scientific method which made it possible to calculate the spatial positions of the atoms in a protein molecule out of hundreds of billions of possibilities. In enzymes it is specifically their spatial shape which defines their action, so if the shape is known, it is also known how the enzyme must be changed in order to make it more efficient. In the case of Corvas International it is now becoming possible to develop enzymes which have an even stronger effect on the molecules involved in the formation of blood clots. This research is being carried out in close collaboration with Professor Désiré Collen of the Catholic University of Leuven who was the first to unravel the structure of plasminogen tissue activator. His research opened up the possibility of biotechnological production of this substance, which occurs naturally in the body and is twice as effective at dissolving blood-clots as the old streptokinase. The rights were sold to the Californian biotechnology company Genentech, sixty percent of which is owned by Hoffmann-Laroche. Professor Collen is now working on an improved version, which will be marketed by Corvas International.

AIDS, Alzheimer and the rest

Ghent is also the home port of Innogenetics, which was set up in 1985. This company uses biotechnological techniques to develop diagnostic tests and medicines. Just two years after it was set up Innogenetics unveiled six world firsts at the same time. These included the very first AIDS antigen test, developed in collaboration with the Tropical Institute in Antwerp. The tests which were in use at the time could find antibodies, but the body's immune system does not begin to produce these until months after infection, while the virus's own antigens can be detected within three or four weeks.

Another world first was a test for Alzheimer's disease, which was developed in collaboration with researchers from Antwerp University Institute. Until then it was only possible to diagnose Alzheimer's with any certainty after death, if a brain biopsy showed the presence of accumulations of protein in the brain. It is still not known how these so-called plaques originate. In 1987 British researchers reported in *Science* that patients who develop Alzheimer's at a relatively early age all show the same characteristic on chromosome 21. Later it was found that this was precisely where the genetic information was located for the protein which accumulated in the brain. In the meantime Dr Christine van Broeckhoven from Antwerp University, also writing in *Nature,* reported patients with the early form of Alzheimer's but with no faults in the overactive gene. Only recently, Dr Van Broeckhoven's team discovered a region of Chromosome 14 which proved to contain a much more common Alzheimer gene.

The Centre for Human Genetics *(CME; Centrum voor Menselijke Erfelijkheid)* which was set up in 1966 at the University of Leuven by Professor Herman van den Berghe, (1933-), is now trying to settle the dispute using techniques at the leading edge of biotechnology. One research group in the *CME* is currently 'making' Alzheimer mice by equipping the DNA of mouse

Left: a transformed sugar beet plant. Right: a control plant twenty days after treatment with weedkiller.

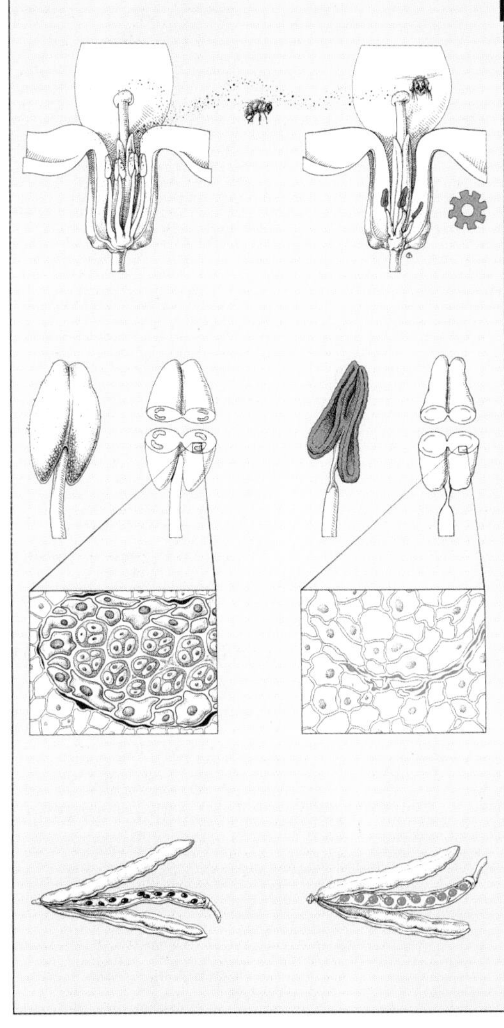

Left: a normal inbreeding strain, with the stamens in which pollen grains develop (below). Right: a plant which has been made male sterile and can only be fertilised by cross-pollination.

embryos with a gene they have constructed themselves, which includes the known mutation of human chromosome 21. In this way the researchers want to find out whether accumulations of proteins also take place in the brains of the transgenic mice. The CME, which is also playing a leading role in unravelling the complex processes which lead to the formation of tumours, has a reputation as one of the most important genetics centres in the world. It is not for nothing that the Centre attracts researchers from every continent. In the microcosm of cells and molecules, Flanders is turning out to be remarkably big. So big that we must offer our apologies to the dozens of research groups and companies which are equally active in biotechnology in Flanders, but which could not be mentioned within the scope of this brief summary.

WIM DAEMS
Translated by Steve Judd.

o

Longing for Paradise

The Poetry of Rutger Kopland

The poems of Rutger Kopland (1934-) are very accessible and inviting, certainly in comparison with much other important twentieth-century poetry. They deal with familiar situations and emotions: taking children for a walk, addressing the beloved, melancholy, the wind turning the pages of a newspaper, etc. The tone sounds familiar too: a conversational pitch, the hesitant exploration of possibilities, and the interrogative form predominate in Kopland's work. One might be tempted to think that the poet Rutger Kopland does not find it easy to distinguish himself from the Groningen psychiatrist R. H. van den Hoofdakker he is in daily life. It sometimes appears as if all this is meant to put the reader at ease among the troubles of the world, as if there is no difference between a poem and a therapy session.

But those who think so are mistaken. Anyone who accepts the invitation to enter into these poems will quickly notice that they are not there to comfort the reader; rather they undermine ease and certainty from the very beginning. This is already the case in the first lines of Kopland's first collection, *Among Cattle* (Onder het vee, 1966), at the very beginning of the poem called 'A Psalm' *('Psalm'):*

The green pastures the still waters
on the wallpaper in my room –
as a frightened child I believed
in wallpaper

The lovely landscape Kopland evokes in the first line would eventually play the part of a primeval landscape as the contours of Kopland's poetic universe became sharper. This poem is, therefore, the germ out of which the whole oeuvre grows. Its role is analogous to that played by the first poem, 'Digging', of Seamus Heaney's first collection, *Death of a Naturalist* (also published in 1966) in this Irish poet's work.

Kopland's landscape is the pastoral representation of Psalm 23 ('The Lord is my shepherd, I shall not want; He maketh me to lie down in green pastures; He leadeth me beside the still waters; He restoreth my soul'). A more idyllic world is hard to imagine, especially if complemented by the words: ‘on the wallpaper in my room’. But Kopland has no use for reassuring convictions, such as those of the singer / composer of psalms, as is already obvious from the fact that he reduces the full sentences of the original psalm to key words in the ‘A Psalm’ that is his own: he is a poet muttering to himself, full of hesitation. When he formulates a full sentence he does so to tell us that his former faith was based on fear and naiveté and, moreover, on a sheet of decorated paper, not solid reality, on wallpaper, not a wall. Wallpaper can be removed, the wall remains. In the same way the lovely representations of a pastoral can be removed without inducing any essential change.

The feelings expressed are therefore not those of being refreshed as in the Biblical psalm, but of being abandoned. This feeling never goes away again: in the final stanza, many years later, the former child now has a child of its own, and that child clings in fear to his father’s hand on a walk through ‘God’s pastures’ where ‘the enormous bodies / of the cattle grunt and snuffle / with peace’. In the next generation, too, feelings of being threatened are bigger than feelings of being at peace. In Kopland’s work the world ‘among the cattle’, on wallpaper or in meadows, is not the pastoral world art has known from time immemorial.

This becomes finally clear in the series of poems Kopland devotes years later, in *Before it Disappears and After* (Voor het verdwijnt en daarna, 1985), his eighth collection, to the World War II concentration camp of Natzweiler in Alsace. The camp, too, is described by means of phrases like ‘very charming landscape’, ‘those green pastures’, ‘those peaceful waters’, ‘peaceful landscape’. Moreover, the camp has been freshly painted, so that it seems as if nothing has happened yet. How paradisical this empty monument to death looks. But it is a paradise from which men have been ejected by a strong arm: it is nothing but landscape. This turns the camp into a metaphor for paradise, rather than paradise into a metaphor for the camp. In Kopland’s vision paradise must have looked like Natzweiler: a world of destruction, and also a world of appearances and deception, a world of ‘as if’. That world of ‘as if’ is identical with the world of the wallpaper from Kopland’s childhood.

This vision of paradise (which is commonly supposed to be lovely and ideal), corresponds to what Kopland wrote in an essay about his own work in which he tried to defend himself against the conviction of many readers that his poems bore witness to a longing for a lost paradise. Paradise, he states, is not a world one should long for at all because relationships in that world are unequal in principle: ‘To me paradise is a tree with a man and a woman under it, and above them somebody who watches what they are doing and knows what they are going to do. The script of their lives has been written. To be known in that way amounts to being nobody, to live in someone else’s shadow, no more, to adhere to the plan of a life, not to design it.’ Kopland’s poems therefore do not express longing, but resistance: many of his poems deal with resistance to being known like this, with anti-mysticism.

Because almost everything Kopland has written is characterized by hesitation, his work can be considered a negation of the words that follow the quotation above in the Biblical psalm: ‘He leadeth me in the paths of righteousness’. Those are the paths of certainty in which Kopland is ill at ease.

Rutger Kopland (1934-).

He prefers the winding tracks that confirm the necessity of the hesitant, the uncertain, the indirect.

Kopland lives in Glimmen, on the border of the provinces of Groningen and Drenthe, in the North East of the Netherlands. The landscape around Glimmen has given him one of his most gripping images for those winding tracks. Few small rivers in the Netherlands wind their way so beautifully, but – and this is the important part – also so invisibly through the landscape as the river called the 'Drentse A', which flows right by his house. In the course of the years he has found the inspiration for many a poem or sequence of poems in this real-life landscape that looks so lovely. The poems range from an almost anecdotal equation of the windings of the river with wrinkles in an old face to the abstraction of a perfect world that has to exist in that landscape, but we shall never know what we should call it since paradise is *passé* ('the wholly undiscoverable answer / to the question which world that is').

Kopland has transformed the meanderings of landscape into meanderings of language: winding sentences full of questions and with every word weighed, moving ever farther away from their anecdotal causes. It is a form Kopland has mastered with increasing perfection over the years. In the period encompassing his debut and the two collections that appeared soon after, *Yesterday's Barrel Organ* (Het orgeltje van yesterday, 1968) and *Everything by Bike* (Alles op de fiets, 1969), Kopland was known as an anecdotal, almost cabaret poet who knew how to delicately touch the sore spots of life with the finger of language. The great popularity of his early work was partly based on a misunderstanding on the part of readers who thought they immediately understood the feelings involved.

Kopland displayed an effortless mixture of the sober and the emotional in playing with genres like the pastoral, the tearjerker, and the anecdote that ends in a punch line. His power seemed to lie in mixing such genres, which allowed him to achieve humorous effects of a melancholy, not a satirical nature. A good example of this is the poem 'Young Lettuce' *('Jonge sla'),* which has achieved great popularity. In that poem a series of melancholy observations is abruptly broken off, allowing Kopland to tap both into a layer of feeling and into a layer of ironic distance in his reader.

Kopland realized the dangers of this too easy identification with the anecdotal layer of the poem: after those three collections he has definitively exchanged easy sentiment, along with the ironic undercutting thereof, for a sharper formulation of his hesitant stance. The anecdotal has been reduced to a minimum, and the suggestive has been increased accordingly. The final line of one of his poems, which has become a slogan, is therefore a valid characterization of Kopland's later work: 'Give me / a question, no answer'.

For Kopland poetry is a way to ask questions, and to keep on asking them. He is not satisfied with the unique and the subjective; by asking questions he wants to find out what we think about life, how we feel, how we observe and how we remember, but also how we ask. Kopland has kept 'digging', in a manner very different from Heaney's, but in poetry of the same quality.

AD ZUIDERENT
Translated by André Lefevere.

LIST OF TRANSLATIONS

An Empty Place to Stay and Other Selected Poems
(Tr. Ria Leigh-Loohuizen).
San Francisco, 1977.

The Prospect and the River
(Tr. James Brockway).
London, 1987.

A World Beyond Myself
(Tr. James Brockway).
London, 1991.

Natzweiler

1
And there, beyond the barbed wire, the view –
very charming landscape, as peaceful
as then.

They would need for nothing, they would
be laid down in those green pastures,
be led to those peaceful waters,

there in the distance. They would.

2
I trace the windows of the barrack huts,
watch-towers, gas-chamber.

Only the black reflection of distance
in the panes, of a peaceful landscape,

and beyond it, no one.

3
The dead are so violently absent, as though
not only I, but they too
were standing here,

and the landscape were folding their invisible
arms around my shoulders.

We need for nothing, they are saying,
we have forgotten this world.

But these are no arms,
it is landscape.

4
The yellowed photos in the display cases,
their faces ravaged by their skulls,
their black eyes,

what do they see, what do they see?
I look at them, but for what?

Their faces have come to belong
to the world, to the world
which remains silent.

5
So this is it, desertion, here is
the place where they took their leave,
far away in the mountains.

The camp has just been re-painted, in that gentle
grey-green, that gentle colour
of war,

it is as new, as though nothing
has happened, as though
it has yet to be.

From *Before It Disappears and After* (Voor het verdwijnt en daarna, 1985)
Translated by James Brockway.

An Empty Place to Stay IX

Just give me the wide, sluggish rivers,
the force you don't see but suspect,
the willows drinking, the senseless dikes,
a dead-still town on the bank.

Give me the winter, the desolate
landscape, the field without signs
of life, the force of resilient heather.

Give me the cat when he's looking
before he leaps, to fight or to run,
to mate or to hunt, when he's looking.

Give me a galloping horse, but one on
his side in the grass. Give me

a question, no answer.

From *An Empty Place to Stay* (Een lege plek om te blijven, 1975)
Translated by Ria Leigh-Loohuizen.

A Psalm

The green pastures the still waters
on the wallpaper in my room –
as a frightened child I believed
in wallpaper

when my mother had said prayers for me
and I had been forgiven for one day more
I was left behind among
motionless horses and cattle,
a foundling laid in a world
of grass

now that once again I have to go
through god's pastures I find no path
to take me back, only a small hand
clasped in mine that tightens
when the enormous bodies
of the cattle grunt and snuffle
with peace.

From *Among the Cattle* (Onder het vee, 1966)
Translated by James Brockway.

Young Lettuce

I can stand anything,
the shrivelling of beans,
flowers dying, I can watch
the potato patch being dug up
and not shed a tear – I'm
real hard in such things.

But young lettuce in September,
just planted, still tender,
in moist little beds, no.

From *Everything by Bike* (Alles op de fiets, 1969)
Translated by James Brockway.

The Valley

1
You see us again sitting in the grass;
those faces of ours, looking
as though they were seeing something
that makes them extraordinarily happy,

like the faces of the blind, unaware
of how they are seen, unsuspecting, looking
at their own secret.

In my notes you read very little
of this, I simply wrote:
been to the valley again, looked a long time,
it was still there.

2
And then you see again what
we were sitting looking at:
grey edge of the wood, the wickerwork
fencing drenched in twilight,
about us the very slightly undulating
soft-green meadows and in the hollow
the little row of spindly alders straying
along the invisible stream.

Then this is what must have made us
so extraordinarily happy.

3
You see how often these photographs have
been
looked at, how often, too, the slip of paper
has been read, on which was written it was still there,
how spotted and thumb-marked they are.

That whole perfect world that must be
there – the wholly undiscoverable answer
to the question which world that is.

From *Before It Disappears and After* (Voor het verdwijnt en daarna, 1985)
Translated by James Brockway.

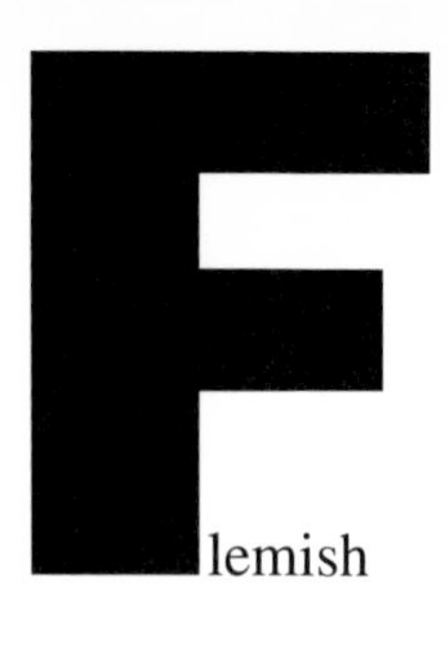

Flemish

Tapestry

Hand-woven tapestries were produced on vertical or flat looms, following patterns drawn to the same scale as the fabric. The warp is completely covered by the weft, which determines the hues and pattern. A characteristic of tapestry is that the threads are woven in only where required by the design. Tapestry was expensive to produce because the weaving progressed very slowly and the materials (mainly wool, or gold and silver thread) were expensive. Nevertheless, the rate of production in Flanders was high and the tapestry trade was a lively one.

Tapestries depicted geometric motives, flowers and plants, gardens and boscages, native and foreign fauna. Many heraldic tapestries were also produced. Pictorial tapestries, too, were made from early times: scenes from the lives of Jesus and the saints, as well as tableaux from the Old Testament, mythology and antiquity. There were also many genre scenes, scenes from courtly romances, and symbolic and allegorical images.

The earliest historical evidence of tapestry weavers in Tournai, Ghent, Bruges, Brussels, Oudenaarde and especially Arras, dates from about 1300. Arras became the most important centre from about 1390. One surviving series of tapestries – namely the *Life of Saints Piat and Eleuthere* in Tournai Cathedral – can definitely be said to originate from Arras; it was woven in 1402 in the workshop of Pierrot Feré. The whole composition is confused and unclear. The busy background, the barely visible sky, the rich architecture, the fern-like leaves, the small trees with their gnarled trunks, the profusion of small flowers in the foreground, the highly-curled hair of the figures; all these are features not only of Arras tapestry, but also of all Flemish tapestry before about 1480. The destruction of Arras in 1477 brought an end to its flourishing tapestry industry.

After the mid-fifteenth century Oudenaarde, Enghien and Brussels increased in importance, but it was at Tournai in particular that high-quality tapestries were woven. The flourishing school of painters there was undoubtedly partly responsible for this. One of the most prominent tapestry weavers and dealers was Pasquier Grenier, who died in 1493. The *Alexander* tapestries, now in the Palazzo Doria in Rome, and the *Seven Sacraments* (New York, Glasgow) were probably produced under his super-

Julius Caesar wearing the imperial crown in the senate, shortly before his death. Tournai, c.1470. Detail of a tapestry from a series entitled *The Life of Julius Caesar,* 432 x 750 cm. Historisches Museum, Bern.

vision. The *Caesar* tapestries (Bern) and the *Life of Saint Peter* (Beauvais) were also manufactured at Tournai. There are striking similarities between Tournai tapestries and the earlier Arras wall-hangings. Yet Tournai work contains more round flowers than earlier work, and the plants are more systematically incorporated into the composition. In some examples, a very narrow border surrounds the central image. The industry began to decline towards the end of the fifteenth century.

The *Trajan and Herkinbald* tapestry (Bern) was produced in Brussels between 1450 an 1460. It was woven after the design of Rogier van der Weyden's *Judgement* tableaux, which had once hung in the city hall there. The composition of *The Adoration of the Magi,* also in the Bern museum, is equally reminiscent of Van der Weyden's work. The great *Passion* tapestry (Brussels) probably originates from the workshop of Gilles van de Putte. The archaic depiction of trees, plants and rocks leads us to conclude that it was woven between 1460 and 1480. In addition, the arrangement of the flowers in the foreground shows similarities to the tapestries mentioned above. The archives reveal that the heraldic tapestry of Philip the Good and Charles the Bold (Bern) was woven in about 1466 by the Brussels weaver

Jan de Haze. This clearly illustrates the capabilities of the Brussels tapestry industry at this time, and demonstrates that certain motives and characteristics of style were not unique to a particular workshop or town, but common to all Flemish tapestry.

From 1480 onwards Brussels became the most important centre in the Southern Netherlands, and remained so until the end of the eighteenth century. It was here that, at the end of the fifteenth century, a very characteristic tapestry style developed, which enjoyed unprecedented appreciation for some three decades. The role of Jan van Rome in this development remains unclear. The figures in the *Herkinbald* tapestry (Brussels) are woven after his design. These, and the figures in other pieces of the period, are depicted in judicious mode; they are extraordinarily stately in their luxurious robes with deep sculptural folds. There is little perspective in the composition, which is arranged more decoratively and logically than previous compositions. A few flowers can still be seen in the foreground, while the various scenes are separated by pillars.

As a result of serious malpractices in tapestry production, the magistrates of Brussels issued in 1528 a decree which stated that all large and costly tapestries should carry a municipal mark and a weaver's mark; this was reissued in 1544 by the central government. The various centres of production nevertheless managed to retain their traditions, clientele, and quality. 'Oudenaarde', 'Brussels', 'Antwerp' tapestry; these names denote not only origin but also appearance, typical features and quality. During this period, and even more so in the seventeenth century, cartoon painters became increasingly important. Tapestry weavers concentrated more and more on interpreting designs and, later, on reproducing these cartoons as precisely as possible.

Italian influence in Flemish tapestry increased with a number of commissions from Italian patrons, in particular Pope Leo X. The most important commission from Italy was the series *The Acts of the Apostles,* commissioned from Pieter van Aelst. The cartoons were painted by Raphael and his fellow artists. The tapestries in this series were interpreted as frescoes, and were therefore given perspective. The sky is broad and open, the clothing plain and unembellished. The border too, with its scenes from the patron's life, constituted a break with the leaves-and-flowers tradition. It was impossible for the weaver to follow the cartoons exactly; but Pieter van Aelst, an experienced weaver, was able to solve this problem. He filled the background and foreground of the *Apostles* tapestry with plants, and adorned Christ's robe with golden suns. The work was highly acclaimed, and this design for the *Acts of the Apostles* was used in various Flemish workshops until well into the eighteenth century.

Brussels cartoon painters also produced important work in the sixteenth century. Bernard van Orley was the leader of Dutch Romanism in tapestry; his influence as a cartoon painter was far-reaching and enduring. Through his talent and imagination, his sense of the monumental, and through his knowledge of Raphael's work, Bernard van Orley led tapestry into a new age of prosperity, without completely breaking with gothic tradition. He produced designs for the *Passion* tapestries (Madrid), the *Hunts of Maximillian of Austria* (Paris) and the *Life of Jacob* (Brussels) and the *Life of Tobit.*

Jacob recovers Joseph in Egypt. Brussels, second quarter of the 16th century. Tapestry from a series entitled *The Life of Jacob,* 420 x 670 cm. Woven in Guillaume de Kempeneere's workshop, after a cartoon by Bernard van Orley. Koninklijke Musea voor Kunst en Geschiedenis, Brussels.

We know of several cartoons by Pieter Coecke van Aelst, who worked for many years in Antwerp and spent the last years of his life in Brussels. These are his patterns for the *Life of Joshua* (Vienna), and the *Life of Saint Paul* (Vienna and Munich). His work is less restful than that of his contemporaries and his figures are strongly emotive, yet elegant. He also paid more attention to border decoration. Michiel Coxie lived in Rome for many years and used the work of Raphael as a model, even acquiring the nickname 'the Flemish Rafaël'. His known work consists of a *History of Adam and Eve, Cain and Abel,* and *Noah and the Ark* (Krakow). The cartoons for the series the *Conquest of Tunis by Charles V* (Madrid) were commissioned from Jan Cornelisz. Vermeyen, who had himself joined the campaign. The series *Vertumnus and Pomona* (Vienna) is also attributed to him.

Little is known of the activities of other cartoon painters from the second half of the sixteenth century. The last decade of that century appears to have seen a strong reaction against the stylistic ideas of the past. The tapestries of the late sixteenth century are less orderly, flatter, and more confused. The horizon is placed quite high. This points to a revival of ideas current around 1500. Because of this lack of readability, monumentality, freshness and colour values, the late sixteenth-century work is of inferior quality to that produced in the mid-century.

It is evident that Brussels weavers in particular contributed a good deal to the new success of the tapestry industry; among them the De Pannemakers, the De Kempeneers, the Dermoyens, the Geubels, to name but a few. Their work was not sold locally, but at the tapissiers' house in Antwerp, where weavers from other towns also brought their work to be sold. The export of tapestries, too, played an important part in the prosperity of the industry.

The tapestry industry fell into a sharp decline in the crises which followed the religious upheavals in the Netherlands: revolt and repression; the stagnation of trade; the closure of the port of Antwerp; the emigration of many weavers and cartoon painters. Not until the late sixteenth century did the industry begin to recover, flourishing once more in the decades which followed.

In 1617 Pieter Paul Rubens was commissioned to paint the cartoons for a *History of Decius Mus.* In 1621-22 he made sketches in oils for a *Life of Constantine,* destined to be woven into tapestries in the Gobelins in Paris. His designs for a *Triumph of the Eucharist* were better adapted for tapestry: more figures – some richly clad – embellish the available framework. There is less depth in the composition, which is separated from the outside world by a narrow frame. In the *Life of Achilles* the frame has lost its independence and has the appearance of a window through which the spectacle may be viewed. The technical means at a weaver's disposal were often inadequate; it was difficult, using wool and silk, to equal the virtuosity of the master's brush and to reproduce the muscular bodies in all their strength.

Rubens' apprentices and successors began to adopt a more relaxed attitude. They took more account of the possibilities open to the weaver. The giant figures gradually disappeared and heavy frames were replaced by borders of flowers and leaves. Everything became lighter and flatter. The same development can be seen in the tapestry cartoons of Jacob Jordaens,

The Bear Hunt. Brussels, c.1645. Tapestry from a series of *Hunting Scenes,* 332 x 333 cm. Woven in Everard Leyniers and Hendrik I Reydams's workshop, after a print by Antonio Tempesta. Koninklijke Musea voor Kunst en Geschiedenis, Brussels.

who trained as a water-colour painter. In about 1620 he began to paint cartoons. He designed cartoons for the *Odyssey*, the *History of Alexander the Great, Country Life,* the *Proverbs,* the *Riding School* and *Famous Women of Antiquity.* His compositions are usually balanced and well adapted to typical tapestry style.

In Brussels, Oudenaarde, Lille, Beauvais and Aubusson many wall-hangings known as *Tenières* were woven, depicting peasant fairs and countryfolk returning from the market or from their work. It is possible that these are merely in the style of the seventeenth-century painter David II Teniers. However, it is certain that he, and in particular his son David III Teniers, supplied cartoons for heraldic and allegorical tapestries.

At the end of the seventeenth century, French influence in Flemish tapestry-weaving became more noticeable, particularly in mythological and historical scenes, and this influence increased even more during the eighteenth century. The cartoons had to be precisely woven; even the frame of the painting was closely copied.

Despite the large demand and the high production in the seventeenth century, the decline of tapestry as an art form had already begun. Woven silks, velvet and later painted canvas and wallpaper were increasingly being used for wall-coverings. Gold leather in particular was becoming more and more fashionable. Tapestries were less suitable for houses with many, though smaller rooms. In addition there was growing competition from foreign tapestry workshops, usually state manufactories, encouraged by the high

Parkland with Animals.
Oudenaarde, beginning of the 18th century.
279 x 482 cm. Koninklijke Musea voor Kunst en Geschiedenis, Brussels.

tariffs on imported Flemish tapestries. Flemish production was indeed rationalized to a certain extent, and tapestry retained its good name, but this was not sufficient to overcome the problems. For this reason weavers attempted to adapt their designs to foreign tastes. Sometimes this even led to the copying of foreign tapestries, but the decline continued nevertheless.

After 1750 the end came quickly. In 1772 Jan Baptist Brandt's workshop in Oudenaarde closed. Jacob van der Borght's workshop in Brussels was still active and in 1785 he produced four less prestigious tapestries depicting the *Legend of the Holy Sacrament of Miracles* for the Church of St Michael there. He died on 13 March 1794; the workshop was closed and the contents sold. This signalled the end of that once-famous Flemish art form. For more than three centuries, Flemish tapestry weavers – in particular those in Brussels – had not only delivered work of great artistic value, they had also been prominent in various European countries.

Not until the second half of the nineteenth century, when all types of arts and crafts enjoyed a revival, was some interest again shown in the vanished craft of tapestry-making. Two centres emerged: Ingelmunster and Mechelen. In 1857 Count Charles A.C. Descantons de Montblanc, Baron of Ingelmunster, in association with the brothers Henri and Alexandre Bracquenié, set up the Manufacture d'Ingelmunster close to the Baron's castle. The Bracquenié brothers originated from Tournai, where they had worked in the Piat-Lefebvre carpet factory. In 1821 they left for Paris where, three years later, they set up the Firma Bracquenié with weaving workshops in Aubusson and Felletin. They first met Baron de Montblanc at the world exhibition in 1850, where they were exhibiting old wall-hangings. Together they formulated a plan to resurrect the Flemish tapestry industry, and agreed to work together for twelve years. This was in keeping with the nineteenth-century desire to provide work for the poor of the Ingelmunster region, who were fairly familiar with linen-weaving techniques. After the Baron's death in 1861, his widow carried on his work. When the twelve-year agreement ended the Bracquenié brothers withdrew from the enterprise and, some time later, opened a new studio of their own in Mechelen. From 1869 the weaving shop at Ingelmunster was run by the Baron's sons, Albéric and Ernest de Montblanc, together with their mother. However, the enterprise went into gradual decline, and with the destruction of the looms in 1914 it was finally brought to an end.

Over the years various wall-hangings had been manufactured there after the designs of old Aubusson cartoons, as well as boscage scenes and *Tenières.* Between 1858 and 1868 they wove the series of tapestries for the Council Chamber of the *Brugse Vrije.* The Ingelmunster workshops also produced the wall-hangings of the *Battle of Ingelmunster,* after the design of the Polish-Russian painter A.X. Sandoz (1858) and the piece depicting Philip the Fair who, in 1297, granted the Bruges ships a letter of safe passage for the Relic of the Holy Blood (1885). The latter tapestry is remarkable for its attempt at perspective; the lower section with its numerous figures, however, contrasts sharply with the empty space above. These works were costly and therefore destined for the government, the nobility and wealthy citizens. Fewer table covers than wall-hangings were produced at Ingelmunster, although a number of carpets were woven. Tapestries for upholstery, for cushion covers, curtains and interior decoration, were made

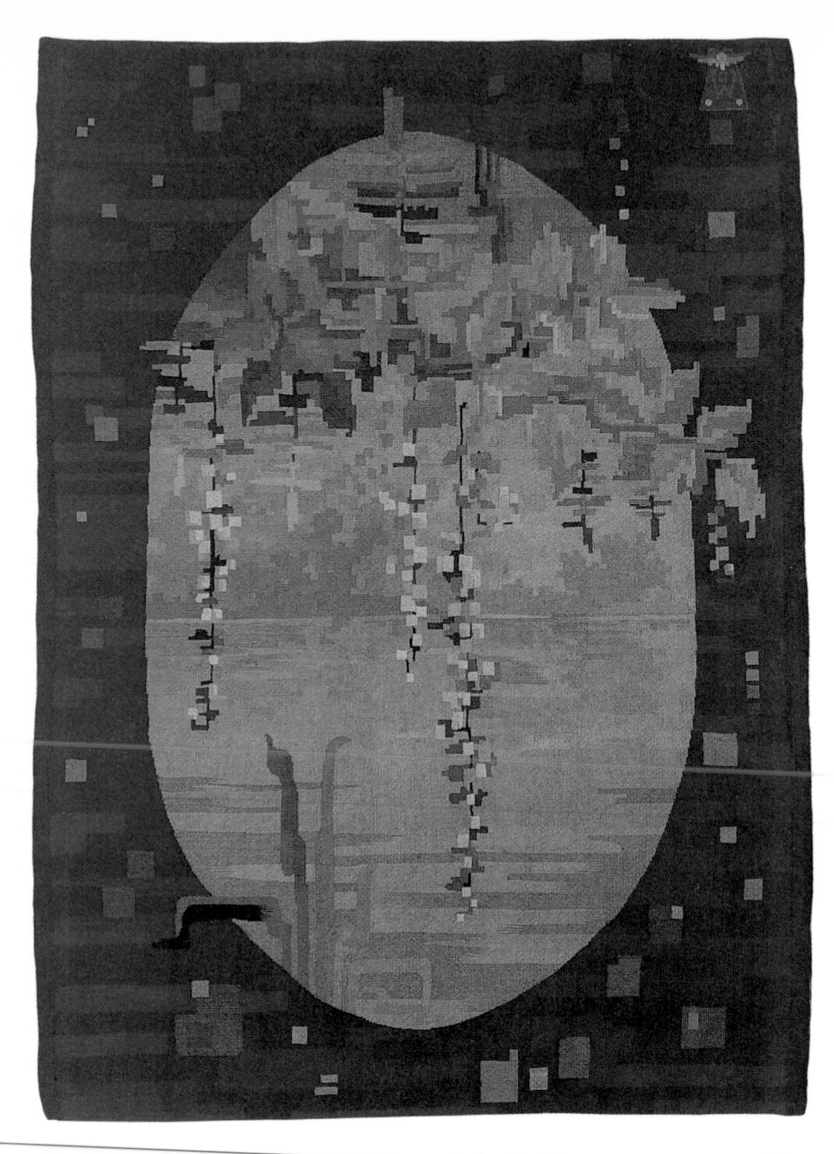

Les Guirlandes. Ghent, c.1925. 105 x 74 cm. Woven in Gaston Woedstad's workshop. Museum voor Sierkunst, Ghent.

throughout. In 1870, with the support of the Belgian government and the city council, the Bracquenié factory was set up in Mechelen. Tapestry weavers from Ingelmunster were employed there, and Henry and Alexandre Bracquenié ran the enterprise. They were succeeded by Alexandre's son, Louis, and by Henry's son-in-law Philippe Dautzenberg. In 1875 Leopold II visited the factory and bestowed upon it the title of Royal, since it had performed such a great service to the country by successfully resurrecting the tapestry industry. There were other small family businesses, often run by former employees of the Bracquenié brothers; one such was the workshop of Theo de Wit, opened in 1889. In 1892 Theo's son, Gaspard, was born and by the age of 13 he was helping in his father's business.

Various painters provided cartoons for the Bracquenié firm, the most prominent being the historical painter Willem Geets, director of the local academy. Geets designed the cartoons depicting the ancient trades and the guilds, each symbolized by a figure, for the Gothic Chamber of the Brussels

The Acts of Humanity across the World. Mechelen, 1954. 865 x 1325 cm. Woven in the Royal Gaspard de Wit factory, after a design by P. Nolfs. United Nations Headquarters, New York.

City Hall. The tapestries themselves, considered interior fixtures, are executed in the so-called Flemish renaissance style. Geets also supplied the designs depicting historical tableaux for the senate hall and other official buildings. These designs were transformed into tapestries by the Bracquenié firm. Old designs from Aubusson and Felletin continued to be used alongside contemporary designs, and many Teniers tapestries were woven too.

Contemporaries were not at all merciful in their criticisms of these tapestries and copies of paintings. Increasingly, there were calls for consideration of the function of tapestry itself and its possibilities. De Wit was probably one of the first to restore the honour of traditional tapestry. He used a low-warp loom, made to an improved design. Under the supervision of Canon Thierry a training school was even set up at Heverlee, and there the high-warp technique was employed. A further stimulus to revival was the establishment in 1927 of the Higher Institute for Decorative Art in the Ter Kameren Abbey in Brussels, where a course in hand-weaving was given.

About 1925, several beautiful tapestries were woven at the workshop of Gaston Woedstad in Ghent from designs by Maurice Langaskens and Woedstad himself. Remarkable in this respect is the stylized tapestry *Les Guirlandes,* which has a very modern feeling. The artist was apparently attempting an interplay of colour areas.

The Royal Gaspard de Wit Factory played a more important role in the revival and renewal of tapestry. The manager and owner of the enterprise was an authority in the field. Many hundreds of tapestries were woven under Gaspard's supervision up until his death in 1971, and the designs of Edmond Dubrunfaut, Anne Marie Delvaux, Julien van Vlasselaer and many others were repeatedly used. Until the present day they have made a major contribution to the distribution and appreciation outside Belgium of modern Flemish tapestry.

ERIK DUVERGER
Translated by Yvette Mead.

Newton in the Netherlands

The Dutch have on occasion prided themselves on the Low Countries being the pivot of intellectual and cultural Europe. The extent of the Dutch cultural area may indeed be small in comparison with that of neighbouring countries such as Germany, France and England, but by the very fact of its central situation the Netherlands was thought to occupy a special position. Ideas from the surrounding cultural areas are absorbed, digested and passed on again to others, the Dutch détour thus making possible an intensive cultural and intellectual exchange. This view was especially popular in the first half of this century and was based more on a self-centred neutralist mentality – the Netherlands, with its own particular mission, stood outside the power politics of the great nations, or so people thought – than on an impartial evaluation of its own cultural history. The fact was that, in most cases, cultural exchange between European nations took place in an entirely natural manner without the Netherlands as intermediary; the notion of the Netherlands as the pivot for ideas from other countries was largely an illusion.

But this was not always the case. Instances can be found in history where the Low Countries did indeed fulfil such a function. One such example is the reception and diffusion of the ideas of the English mathematician and physicist Isaac Newton (1642-1727). His ideas, which were the crowning achievement of the Scientific Revolution of the seventeenth century, were diametrically opposed to those which people were accustomed to at that time. Initially, therefore, a great deal of reserve could be perceived amongst leading scientists throughout Europe. It is partly or even mainly thanks to intellectual circles in the Dutch Republic that Newton's ideas were after all accepted in the rest of Europe; Dutch scientists and Dutch manuals were responsible for the spread of Newtonianism through Europe. For once, the Netherlands was indeed the pivot of intellectual Europe.

Yet in the Republic, too, there were grave doubts about the value of Newton's natural philosophy. Just as in other countries, the history of Newtonianism was preceded by the history of anti-newtonianism. The only difference was that here the latter was of comparatively short duration.

The reservations were principally based on the fact that in his great work, the *Philosophiae naturalis principia mathematica* (Mathematical Principles of Natural Philosophy) of 1687, Newton had introduced a notion which appeared irreconcilable with current ideas and views in physics. Newton had advanced the theory that two physical bodies (for example the earth and the moon) mutually attract each other (he called this force attraction or gravitation), but without giving any mechanical explanation for this phenomenon. However, in the seventeenth century such an explanation was a *sine qua non* for any proper account of physical phenomena. People were no longer satisfied with what they considered to be all sorts of purely verbal elucidations derived from Aristotelian natural philosophy; they had determined that natural phenomena could be explained only in terms of the pressure, push or collision of physical bodies. For one body to act on the other, direct contact was always necessary; influence through a void, or '*actio in distans*', was inconceivable and therefore scientifically unacceptable. Various systems of natural philosophy had been formulated on the

Isaac Newton (1642-1727) by L. Delvaux. Museum voor Kunst en Geschiedenis, Brussels (Photo ACL, Brussels).

Willem Jacob 's Gravesande (1688-1742) (Photo Atlas Van Stolk, Rotterdam).

basis of this premise. The best known was that of the French philosopher René Descartes, laid down in his *Principia philosophiae* (1644), which was regarded as the model for the mechanistic natural philosophy of the seventeenth century. Descartes proceeded on the assumption of a completely filled space, but there were others who preferred to assume that there were small particles of matter (we should say atoms) in an otherwise empty space. But the only explanations which everybody accepted were those based on the effects of contact between these small particles. And it was precisely on this point that Newton diverged from the orthodox mechanistic views of the seventeenth century: his gravity was indeed effective through the void, here it was indeed a question of *'actio in distans'*.

It is therefore quite understandable that Newton's *Principia* could at best count on a mixed reception among leading scientists in Europe. The assessment of Christiaan Huygens (1629-1695), around 1690 still the uncrowned monarch of European natural philosophy, was typical. In principle, an anti-Cartesian work such as Newton's could be assured of a positive reception from Huygens. In his earlier years he had been a staunch supporter of the Cartesian doctrine, but as he grew older his doubts increased; he became less and less convinced that Descartes' theories were always correct. Moreover, Huygens was well acquainted with English natural philosophy. He had been in England, and maintained close contacts with the Royal Society and a number of English physicists. However, Huygens was sharply opposed to Newton's conception of gravitation. He wrote to the German philosopher

Leibniz: 'I am not at all happy with the explanation which Mr Newton gives us for the tides, nor with all the other theories which he bases on his principle of gravitation, which seems to me absurd.'

Other people in the Republic were of the same opinion. The Leiden professor Burchardus de Volder (1643-1709), who like Huygens had excellent contacts in English scientific circles and was himself in correspondence with Newton, could not be won over to Newton's new ideas, despite his admiration for Newton's mathematical genius and his increasing reservations regarding the Cartesian system. The best Newton could count on was an obligatory reference to his contribution to experimental science, such as the mention made of him by the well known Leiden medical professor Herman Boerhaave (1668-1738) in his academic orations in the period round 1700; but in these cases Newton was always referred to in the same breath as numerous others, of whom Bacon and Boyle could expect much more sympathy from Boerhaave. In this initial period, positive interest in Newton's unorthodox ideas was only to be found amongst those on the fringes of the scientific world.

It was only around 1710 that any change began to take place in the mainly hostile attitude of Dutch scientists. A particularly acrimonious dispute between Newton and Leibniz about priority in the discovery of differential and integral calculus led incidentally to increasing discussion of Newton's theory of gravitation. Newton's opponents tried to destroy the credibility of his claims in the mathematical field by demonstrating the absurdity of his ideas in the realm of natural philosophy. However, these tactics only resulted in Newton's ideas receiving more attention, being seriously discussed and also, for the first time, beginning to gain supporters.

An important role in this change of attitude was played by the *Journal littéraire,* which was published in The Hague. In 1712 and 1713 one of the editors, Willem Jacob 's Gravesande (1688-1742), originally a lawyer, but keenly interested in mathematics and natural science, published some articles in which he attempted to find a way out of the senseless wrangling between the supporters of Newton and of Leibniz. In this context 's Gravesande also included a discussion of Newton's natural philosophy.

One reason why the *Journal littéraire,* in particular, sought to play such a mediatory role, was the fact that the paper was in part run by French Huguenots who had fled to the Republic after Louis XIV's revocation of the Edict of Nantes in 1685. It was greatly in the interests of the Huguenots to help maintain and strengthen the Anglo-Dutch coalition against France, which had been formed when William III crossed to England in 1688. In this connection it was also to their advantage to encourage intellectual contacts between the Republic and England. Thus the particular political constellation of the time was a crucial element in the Dutch role as go-betweens in disseminating Newton's ideas in the rest of Europe.

But all this would still not have been enough if Newton himself had not produced a second edition of his *Principia,* adding a new general discussion *(Scholium Generale)* in which he attempted to remove the objections to his principle of gravitation. More emphatically than in his earlier writings he stated that his new principle was purely a mathematical notion, that is to say a notion which *described* the phenomena without at the same time giving a deeper *explanation,* whether in the mechanistic or the non-mechanistic sense. He did not intend to venture such a speculative explanation: 'I do not feign hypotheses', he wrote. In fact he believed that the physicist, too, should be satisfied with the mathematical description of the phenomena observed; it was not given to man, but reserved exclusively for God, to penetrate deeper into reality.

Newton thus not only removed some of the misunderstandings, but also made his modest, almost positivist point of view into a programme with a broader, even religious purport. To fathom the ultimate structure of the world was no longer the objective of physics; such a desire was on the contrary a sign of *hubris,* an attempt to penetrate a realm which God had reserved for himself. The emphasis was all on the phenomena to be observed and their interrelationships, not on the hidden structures behind them.

With this explanation of his natural philosophical standpoint Newton associated himself with an anti-rationalist trend in the Republic's intellectual life which was becoming apparent in the same period. Instead of the rational scrutiny of nature, people began to lay ever increasing emphasis on the pure observation of, and sometimes even humble reflections on, the wonders of nature. This change was manifest in, amongst other things, the rise of so-called physico-theology, a movement within popular physics in which natural phenomena were interpreted as proof of the omnipotence and providence of God. The existence of an all-wise Creator was deduced from the visible method and order in nature; nature, so people thought, could be interpreted as a second revelation of God. This way of thinking had made considerable headway in England at the end of the seventeenth century; from there it had been propagated in the Netherlands, though here it also had original Dutch representatives. There was such a degree of correspondence between this movement on the one hand and Newton's natural philosophy on the other hand, that the popularity of the one was conducive to the popularity of the other.

After the publication of the second edition of the *Principia* the spread of Newtonianism in the Republic gained momentum. A pirate version of the second edition had already been published in Amsterdam in 1714. In leading journals there was suddenly a great deal of interest in the work of Newton and his followers and one by one the universities were converted to Newton's point of view. Boerhaave began to praise Newton to the skies and in 1717 the long vacant chair of De Volder was filled by the appointment of 's Gravesande. As secretary to the Dutch diplomatic mission in London he had made Newton's acquaintance in 1715, and since then had been completely won over to the Newtonian philosophy. In 1720 he was already publishing his Leiden lectures under the self-explanatory title *Mathematical Principles of Physics, Confirmed by Experiments. Or an Introduction to Newtonian Natural Philosophy.* At that time he had the reputation of being the person best able to explain to a public not fully versed in the mathematical niceties of the *Principia* what the significance of the work was and what results Newton had achieved. Not only did students from the Netherlands and abroad come to listen to his explanation, but such a well-known intellectual as Voltaire also came to Leiden especially to follow 's Gravesande's lectures. Those who could not come to Leiden could acquaint themselves with 's Gravesande's views in other ways, for his books had been translated into many languages. And not only *his* books, but also those of other Newtonians, such as his pupil and fellow-professor Petrus van Musschenbroek (1692-1761), whose works achieved if possible even greater popularity.

Did scholars such as 's Gravesande and Van Musschenbroek merely pass on what they had discovered in Newton, or did they set their own stamp on it? The latter is certainly the case. As can be deduced from the title of 's Gravesande's book, the Dutch Newtonians tried above all to steer clear of the knotty problems of higher mathematics and convince their listeners and readers of the truth of Newton's views through experimental demonstration. In the writings of a man such as Van Musschenbroek we may even detect a definite Baconian tint to a natural philosophy which was in essence strictly mathematical. This not only made a concession to the powers of comprehension of students and others with enquiring minds, but also forged a link with the prevailing physico-theological trend. And thus Newton, divested of the difficult mathematical figures and formulae, began his triumphal progress through Europe. This is how Voltaire, after his return from Leiden, presented Newton to his French readers; and this is how the Italian abbot Algarotti presented Newton to his female readers in his highly popular *Il Newtonianismo per le dame* (1737).

K. VAN BERKEL
Translated by Rachel van der Wilden.

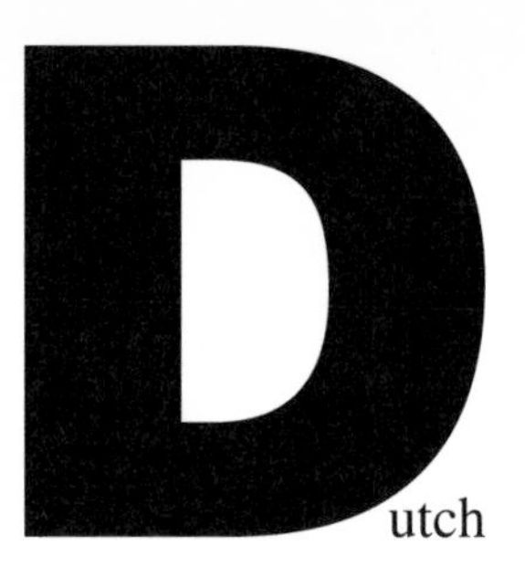

Dutch

Painting

A Personal View

In January 1993 I went to the Netherlands for three days in order to see two exhibitions in Dordrecht and Amsterdam. I flew to Schiphol and took the direct train to Dordrecht. It was a grey, overcast, wet day and as the train travelled the length of the Randstad I found myself, almost unconsciously, observing the landscape between the towns through the eyes of seventeenth-century Dutch painters. Rembrandt's etching of the Omval, Jan van Goyen's monochrome vistas, Philips Koninck's cloud-filled skies, Salomon van Ruysdael's river landscapes and even, although there was no sunlight, Cuyp's views of his home town of Dordrecht seen across the River Maas all came to mind as I glimpsed fields, rivers and distant churches. Even to someone like myself, who has been professionally concerned with Dutch art for twenty years, it is still possible to be surprised by its truthfulness, by the penetration with which Dutch artists observed and represented their surroundings and their contemporaries. This is hardly an original observation and there is of course much else to reflect upon and study in Dutch art, yet it remains the overwhelming impression of Dutch art for the novice and the specialist alike.

Efforts were made, especially in the 1970s, to lay stress upon the intellectual sophistication of Dutch art, a process which began with genre painting and moved on to still-life and landscape. Complex patterns of thought and allusion were identified in Dutch paintings and their elaborate construction and didactic intentions analysed. It was a movement which in books and articles I applauded, and indeed participated in. Much was discovered about the way in which paintings were viewed in the seventeenth century but, on the other hand, many overambitious claims were made. That interpretative tide has now turned and the search is on for a renewed critical language in which to describe and analyse the truthfulness of Dutch art, its prime characteristic and the quality which sets it apart from the art being produced elsewhere in Europe during the seventeenth century. It is a truthfulness which extends not just to the landscape, the townscape, and the settings of domestic life but also to human behaviour and the factors which control it.

I took up the post of Curator of Dutch and Flemish Painting at the National Gallery in November 1971 at the age of twenty-three. Appointment to such a position at that age was in line with the Gallery's policy of appointing young curators – those with promise rather than achievement – who were then trained in the procedures, structures and mores of the institution. This is a policy which has since been abandoned – and I am one of those who has urged its abandonment – and new curators now bring both experience and academic achievement to the Gallery. My first degree at Oxford was in Modern History (which in Oxford means post-Classical) and I took specialist papers in Dante and fifteenth-century France. For the latter I attended classes on fifteenth-century French painting and manuscript illumination at All Souls College with the distinguished Belgian scholar of medieval manuscripts, L.M.J. Delaissé, who for many years had been on the staff of the Bibliothèque Royale in Brussels. He was a remarkable teacher, an inspiration to many young English art historians during his all too few years in Oxford. It was Delaissé's teaching which inspired me to study the history of art. His enthusiastic exposition of the archaeology of the book, as we sat poring over the books of hours themselves in the gathering twilight in Duke Humphrey's Library in the Bodleian, was thrilling. As well as these few classes for undergraduates, Delaissé taught a postgraduate diploma in the History of Art which covered Early Netherlandish painting and manuscript

Philips Koninck, *An Extensive Landscape with a Road by a Ruin.* 1655. Canvas, 137.4 x 167.7 cm. The National Gallery, London.

illumination as well as contemporary developments in France. This was a year's course and after its completion, I enrolled with him as a doctoral student to write a dissertation on the Master of the Rohan Hours, that remarkably expressive illuminator, probably from the Lower Rhine, who was working in Paris in the early fifteenth century. I had scarcely begun my work when the job at the National Gallery was advertised and I was fortunate enough to be appointed. I had never studied seventeenth-century Dutch art, had never visited the Netherlands and could not read Dutch (although I had studied German at school). Gregory Martin, who had been my predecessor at the National Gallery, had published his catalogue of the Flemish paintings in 1970. Neil MacLaren, his predecessor, had published the Dutch catalogue ten years before and so it was that catalogue which would be the first to require revision. (In the event, my revised edition of the Dutch catalogue did not appear until 1991). My first task, I was told, was to familiarise myself with the collection and I began with the Dutch paintings.

It is my belief that there is no greater collection of seventeenth-century Dutch paintings than that in the National Gallery in London. Since the seventeenth century the British have been enthusiastic and discerning collectors of Dutch paintings and their achievements can be judged in Trafalgar Square today. The heroic period of British collecting was from about 1780 until 1850, at a time when trade and the Industrial Revolution were enriching merchants, bankers, factory owners and landowning aristocrats alike and paintings from Continental Europe were pouring on to the market as a direct consequence of the French Revolution and the Napoleonic Wars. Many of the best of these paintings have found their way by bequest, gift and purchase on to the walls of the National Gallery. The Louvre and the Hermitage have important collections of Dutch paintings but only the Rijksmuseum rivals that of the National Gallery. In a sense the two collections are complementary: the Rijksmuseum has those paintings, notably group portraits, which the Dutch never sold to foreign buyers. It has greater portraits and still-lifes, and a finer holding of Vermeers. But for the great landscape painters – Jacob van Ruisdael, Aelbert Cuyp, Philips Koninck, Meindert Hobbema; marine painters – Jan van de Cappelle, Willem van de Velde, Simon de Vlieger; genre painters – Jan Steen, Gabriel Metsu, Gerard ter Borch; and for Rembrandt himself (excepting *The Night Watch* and the *Staalmeesters*), London has, in my view, the edge. It was with this astonishingly rich and numerous collection that I was to familiarise myself. I began, quixotically, with the Dutch Caravaggisti, reading Nicolson on Terbrugghen, Judson on Honthorst and Slatkes on Baburen, all in English, which was a help, but as I persevered at my Dutch evening classes I was able to read the works of Hoogewerff, an art historian I especially admire, on the Bentveughels and Blankert on Pieter van Laer.

Two developments coincided to make these early years at the National Gallery an especially exciting time to be learning about Dutch painting. It was the moment when the iconological researches of Eddy de Jongh and his colleagues at Utrecht University were being published. His *Openbaar Kunstbezit* volume *Moral Emblems and Amorous Scenes in 17th-Century Painting* (Zinne- en minnebeelden in de schilderkunst van de zeventiende eeuw), in which he outlined ways in which emblem books and prints could be used in the interpretation of Dutch paintings, had appeared in 1969 and

Jacob van Ruisdael, *A Pool surrounded by Trees*. c.1665. Canvas, 107.5 x 143 cm. The National Gallery, London.

his ground-breaking essay on Realism and Apparent Realism was published in the catalogue of the 1971 Brussels exhibition. The fullest and most elaborately worked-out presentation of his approach was, however, the catalogue of the exhibition *For Instruction and Pleasure (*Tot Lering en Vermaak), held at the Rijksmuseum in 1976. Visiting the exhibition and reading the catalogue was an exhilarating experience: there was a sense of an entirely new analytical technique being applied to the study of Dutch painting, immensely rewarding and full of infinite possibilities. I reviewed the exhibition and its catalogue warmly in *The Burlington Magazine. For Instruction and Pleasure* spawned a number of other exhibitions which applied a more or less similar approach to the interpretation of Dutch painting. One of these was my exhibition *The National Gallery lends Dutch Genre Painting,* in which a group of paintings from Trafalgar Square were shown at four regional galleries in England with a catalogue which was heavily dependent on *For Instruction and Pleasure* for its general approach and, indeed, for particular examples. It had the small distinction of being the first publication in English to pioneer this new approach and for this reason the catalogue was found useful by students. Eddy de Jongh was immensely kind to this English follower (and, at times, plagiarist): he talked these problems over patiently and with great seriousness, as we sat in his library in Utrecht and he pulled down emblem books from the shelves to illustrate his arguments. This was an early example of the immense kindness and openness with which I have always been received by Dutch scholars. There is not in the study of Dutch art any of the xenophobia which is sometimes encountered in studying the art of some other European countries in which it is hard for foreigners to establish a foothold. The Dutch genuinely welcome foreign scholars who study their art. They can, however, be very fierce critics of what they take to be superficial accounts of their culture, as Svetlana Alpers and Simon Schama have recently discovered.

The other event of the mid-70s which added to the excitement of learning about Dutch painting was the invitation of Michael Levey, who had become Director of the National Gallery on the retirement of Sir Martin Davies in 1974, to organize an exhibition of Dutch art under the title *Art in 17th-Century Holland.* It was to be general in character, a celebration of the achievement of the Dutch in the Golden Age, and, although there were loans from the Netherlands, it was based on the public and private collections of Great Britain. The preparation of the exhibition provided an ideal opportunity to get to know these collections and to focus attention on little-known masterpieces like the *Allegory of Winter* by Cesar van Everdingen in the Southampton City Art Gallery and Jan de Bray's *Banquet of Cleopatra* in the Royal Collection. I am very pleased that a number of the best paintings from private collections have subsequently been acquired by the National Gallery through bequest and private treaty sale, an arrangement which gives substantial tax benefits to the vendor. Among these paintings are Willem Kalf's *Still-life with the Hunting Horn of the Saint Sebastian's Archers' Guild,* Ter Brugghen's *The Concert,* in my view his greatest secular work, Frans Hals' *Boy with a Skull* and Aelbert Cuyp's *River Landscape with Horseman and Peasants.* The exhibition included silver, sculpture and medals, furniture, ceramics, glass and tiles, and the catalogue included essays on these subjects and on Dutch architecture. It has always been central to my view of Dutch painting that it should not be seen in isolation from the other visual arts. It was an extraordinary privilege to prepare this exhibition, to travel in Britain and the Netherlands selecting paintings and other works of art and then remodelling a large section of the National Gallery to accommodate them. The exhibition, which was on show in the autumn of 1976, attracted – unsurprisingly in view of the popularity of Dutch art and the high quality of the loans – a large number of visitors and I hope that those who came to see Rembrandt were also struck by Christiaen van Vianen's silver ewer, with its rippling basin and auricular rim, and Hendrick de Keyser's marble bust which may show Vincent Jacobsz. Coster.

Shortly after the exhibition I became fascinated by Rembrandt's greatest pupil Carel Fabritius, two of whose rare paintings are in the National Gallery, and wrote a catalogue raisonné of his work. I approached him initially not from his relationship with Rembrandt, as had been usual in the past, but rather from his association with the so-called 'Delft School' after his move to that town in about 1650. Did he serve as a catalyst in the transformation of Delft from a provincial backwater into one of the most original and innovative centres in the Netherlands? This proved to be a very difficult question to answer but I was able to strip away many of the incorrect attributions made to Fabritius, particularly in the early part of this century, and reduce his oeuvre to a solid core of just eight paintings. From that core it has been possible to add more paintings in recent years (although I am sceptical

Jan van de Cappelle, *A River Scene with a Large Ferry*. 1665. Canvas, 122 x 154.4 cm. The National Gallery, London.

of the mass of new attributions proposed by the Rembrandt Research Project). It was also useful to reconsider the documents (in Delft and Amsterdam) concerning Fabritius which had been first published by Bredius and Wijnman and add a few new ones. The book was published in 1981 and I subsequently received my Ph.D. at the Courtauld Institute for this book and a number of related articles. Fabritius' interest in perspective and *trompe l'oeil* effects brought me into contact with two young American scholars, Arthur Wheelock, Curator of Dutch and Flemish Painting at the National Gallery of Art in Washington, and Walter Liedtke, who was shortly afterwards given the same responsibilities at the Metropolitan Museum in New York. Despite their own disagreements about a number of points, they were both helpful and supportive of my project and have continued to be valued friends and colleagues. Fabritius also brought me into contact with two of the elder statesmen of my field of study, Jan van Gelder and Egbert Haverkamp-Begeman. Both gave me immense encouragement and showed me great kindness, reading the manuscript, preventing errors and suggesting avenues of new research. Jan van Gelder died in 1980 but Egbert Haverkamp-Begeman continues to give support not just to me but to countless younger scholars of Dutch art.

It was a great pleasure to be a member of the organizing committee of the exhibition of Dutch history painting, *Gods, Saints and Heroes,* which was shown in Washington, Detroit and Amsterdam in 1980-1. This was a

Gerard ter Borch, *A Woman playing a Theorbo to Two Men.* c.1668. Canvas, 67.7 x 57.8 cm. The National Gallery, London.

genuinely ground-breaking exhibition which not only made visitors aware of this distinct category of Dutch painting but also gave a clear idea of the achievements of Dutch history painters whose work, particularly that of the painters active in the second half of the century, is relatively little known to a broad public. It put Rembrandt's religious paintings, the best known of Dutch history paintings, into a contemporary context. The committee met under the enthusiastic chairmanship of Dewey Mosby of the Detroit Institute of Art who, with Beatrijs Brenninkmeyer-De Rooij of the Government Department of Visual Arts, had conceived the project. The meetings and the subsequent meals I remember as being particularly animated and enjoyable: it was at this time that I got to know Albert Blankert, who has written so well about Haarlem classicism, as we talked about the concept of the exhibition and the selection of paintings late into the night over many genevers.

In the early 1980s I was also working on Anthony van Dyck, an artist whose work and personality I find especially intriguing and sympathetic. Van Dyck is a remarkable example of the instinctual artist: he was a prodigy, who was already producing immensely accomplished work in his late teens and, although he was of course profoundly influenced by Rubens, he did not share his intellectual and antiquarian interests. Rather than adopting Rubens' humanist Stoicism, Van Dyck was an untroubled, devout Catholic entirely committed both as man and artist to the ideals of the Counter-Reformation. My monograph on Van Dyck appeared in 1982 and a number of articles and conference papers were also published at around that time. My interest in the painter has continued: I was invited to contribute to the catalogue of the superb exhibition in Washington in the winter of 1990 and in 1991 organized an exhibition of his drawings in the Pierpont Morgan Library in New York and the Kimbell Art Museum in Fort Worth, and my edition of his Italian Sketchbook is currently being prepared for publication.

In response to a commission from the Dutch publisher J.H. de Bussy I expanded the text of the genre painting catalogue into a book which appeared in 1984 under the catchpenny title (insisted upon by the English publishers, Faber and Faber) *Scenes of Everyday Life:* the Dutch edition used a quote from the poet Roemer Visscher *'Daer is niet ledighs of ydels in de dinghen'* ('There is nothing vain or meaningless in things') as a title which, although closer to the argument of the book, may have been more puzzling than illuminating for the majority of readers. It was also in 1984 that the exhibition *Masters of 17th-Century Dutch Genre Painting* was shown in Philadelphia, Berlin and London (Royal Academy). The project was directed with great drive and flair by Peter Sutton who was then at the Philadelphia Museum of Art and I was a member of the exhibition committee as well as contributing to the catalogue. The exhibition and its bulky catalogue brought the discoveries of *For Instruction and Pleasure* (in a slightly modified form) to a wider, English-speaking audience as well as bringing to a mass public the achievement of Dutch genre painters. Vermeer and De Hooch were well represented – the exhibition had the title *The Age of Vermeer and De Hooch* in London – but so too were far less well-known painters: Jacob Duck and Isaac Koedijk were among the discoveries of this very successful and popular exhibition.

In my continuing cataloguing of the National Gallery's collection, my interests were shifting towards the landscapes and a byproduct of this new interest was the exhibition *Dutch Landscape: The Early Years* shown at the National Gallery in 1986. The exhibition traced the emergence and subsequent development of naturalistic landscape in Amsterdam and Haarlem between 1580 and 1650. It made the important point that drawing and printmaking were far more experimental than painting and that the new naturalism is first seen on paper and only later on panel and canvas. For this reason the exhibition contained many drawings and prints as well as paintings. Essays for the catalogue were commissioned from art historians and colleagues in other, related disciplines. Maria Schenkeveld-van der Dussen wrote about literary accounts of landscape and the economic historian Jan de Vries described the physical transformation of the landscape during these years. The catalogue also included an important essay by an old friend, Margarita Russell, in which she argued persuasively that marine painting was a precursor of landscape painting and that Haarlem was the cradle of both. One subject I deliberately omitted was the iconography of landscape – that is, whether elements within representations of landscape, or indeed the entire landscape painting, print or drawing, can be interpreted in a religious or moral sense. Just as I had been reconsidering my ideas on the interpretation of genre painting at this time, so I had come to the view that landscape painting was not susceptible to this type of interpretation – except in the general sense that the landscape is God's creation and, therefore, sacred. My point of view (expressed by omission rather than argument) was challenged in an essay by Josua Bruyn in the catalogue of a larger and more ambitious exhibition of Dutch landscape paintings (in which there were no prints or drawings) organized by Peter Sutton and held in 1987-8 in Amsterdam, Boston and Philadelphia under the title *Masters of 17th-Century Dutch Landscape Painting*. The crux of this disagreement is the extent to which there is a radical change in sensibility in the years around 1600; whether we should see the art of this period as a continuation (at least in an iconographic sense) of late medieval art or whether something quite new was happening, a new way of viewing the world and representing it. I feel strongly that a new art was being developed, in which the iconographic associations of late medieval images had been largely shed, and I argued this case in a review of the exhibition in the Dutch art historical journal *Simiolus*.

Rembrandt van Rijn, *A Woman bathing in a Stream.* 1654. Panel, 61.8 x 47 cm. The National Gallery, London.

Pieter de Hooch, *The Courtyard of a House in Delft.* 1658. Canvas, 73.5 x 60 cm. The National Gallery, London.

Most recently, I have ventured into the much disputed field of Rembrandt studies. The literature is so immense and the problems so complex that I feel that a long apprenticeship in the other principal aspects of Dutch seventeenth-century painting is a good way of preparing for this work. The National Gallery's Rembrandts, one of the greatest collections of the artist's paintings, had to be catalogued and I undertook a detailed and lengthy study of them with the assistance of two colleagues in the Conservation and Scientific Departments, David Bomford and Ashok Roy. Our results were published in the catalogue of the exhibition *Art in the Making: Rembrandt* in 1988. No other single group of Rembrandts has ever been analysed in such detail: supports, grounds, pigments, binding media and the construction of the paint layers were all studied in detail and the results compared in order to establish patterns in the use of materials and in the artist's procedure. Once these were established, they pointed up anomalies such as those which were found in the smaller portrait of *Margaretha Trip,* of which we concluded that 'we are therefore confronted with two possibilities: the small portrait of *Margaretha Trip* is either an extremely skilful imitation of the work of Rembrandt painted between 1660 and 1818, or an authentic painting whose function and execution have led to considerable physical differences from the larger portrait (of the same sitter, also in the Gallery's collection)'. The findings of this study were summarized in the entries for the Rembrandts in the catalogue of the Dutch School paintings in the National Gallery, a thorough revision and expansion of MacLaren's catalogue, which finally appeared in 1991.

In September 1991 the exhibition *Rembrandt: The Master and his Workshop* opened in the Altes Museum, Berlin, the first major exhibition to be shown in the East since the removal of the Wall. Subsequently it travelled to the Rijksmuseum and the National Gallery, where it was the second exhibition to be shown in the new Sainsbury Wing. The paintings section of the exhibition, which also included drawings and etchings, was organized by a committee of three, on which I joined Pieter van Thiel of the Rijksmuseum and Jan Kelch of the Gemäldegalerie, Berlin. We had two principal objectives: to give a wide public a clear and balanced idea of Rembrandt's achievement as a painter, showing paintings from all phases of his career and of all the subject matter he tackled; and to give an account of the debate about the attribution of paintings to Rembrandt in recent years, a debate principally fuelled by the activities of the Rembrandt Research Project. For the second part of the exhibition, we chose paintings which had until recently been attributed to Rembrandt and suggested a new attribution from amongst the pupils and followers of Rembrandt. This section included, for example, the *Vision of Daniel* from Berlin, which was attributed to Willem Drost and the *Girl at a Half-Open Door* from Chicago, which was said to be by Samuel van Hoogstraten. This section of the exhibition received some criticism and it is certainly true that other and better examples might in certain cases have been found. A number of requests for loans were, however, refused on the grounds that the new attributions were hypothetical and the institutions and individuals who owned the paintings preferred to continue to attribute them to Rembrandt. It is a bold museum director who agrees, as the Director of the Chicago Art Institute did, to lend a painting currently hanging on his walls as a Rembrandt to be exhibited as the work of Samuel van Hoogstraten.

The Rembrandt exhibition was an immense undertaking: it was seen by more than a million visitors in three cities and boasted a large two-volume catalogue and massive sponsorship. By contrast, last year, I brought together Vermeer's *Little Street* from the Rijksmuseum and Pieter de Hooch's *Courtyard of a House in Delft* from the National Gallery's collection in a small one-room display which enabled visitors to explore the subtle relationships and differences between these two canvases, which were painted in Delft within a year or two of one another. It was a very rewarding comparison, which was also to be seen again, at the Rijksmuseum, in the spring of 1993. The Vermeer is a topographically accurate townscape while the De Hooch is an artificial construction of actual elements, but both are based on close observation and naturalistic description. In that sense, both are truthful.

The last twenty-one years have been particularly exciting and important ones for the study of Dutch art. There have been fundamental shifts in our understanding of the categories of Dutch art and profound reassessments of many of the principal artists. These developments have taken place in a series of major exhibitions and in important monographs, of which the single most ambitious is that produced by the Rembrandt Research Project. As a consequence much has become clearer but the debates continue to rage – debates about meaning, technique and attribution. However, what certainly remains constant is our sense that the essence of Dutch art – and the quality which sets it apart from the art of other times and places – resides in its truthfulness both about the world itself and the individuals who inhabit it.

CHRISTOPHER BROWN

Studying 'Single Dutch'? What Next?!

Dutch Studies in the Anglophone World

A growth industry? Undoubtedly. Setbacks? Some, alas, – but fewer and farther between now than in the past. Resounding successes? Most definitely, a string of them. The future assured? Not quite – it's uphill all the way.

At a first glance, the figures look impressive enough. Leaving the Netherlands and Flanders out of account, Dutch is currently taught as an academic subject at around 250 foreign universities, in some 40 different countries. The Dutch themselves, most of whom are only dimly aware of any active interest in their language and culture in the rest of the world, tend to be highly surprised when confronted with figures like these. They are even more surprised when they learn that this interest has been increasing substantially in the last couple of decades. Why, they ask, should anyone choose to study a language like Dutch in the first place? And why should the world show more of an interest now than before?

Those involved in teaching Dutch language and culture at universities across the world, the 400 or so enthusiasts at the chalkface, have become adept at countering such questions by inquiring 'Why not?' and switching to a sales pitch. Viewed from a European perspective, they declare, Dutch is not a minor language, merely one of the smaller among the major languages of the EC. Just look, they argue, at the formidable economic strength of the Low Countries and the enviable stability of their currencies. Consider their prominent role in international organisations. Reflect on the intricate workings of a tightly knit, eminently humanist, famously tolerant society with enlightened intellectual traditions, imaginative social schemes and daring technological feats to its credit. Ponder, they continue, the rich history and the even richer art history of these parts: the medieval and Burgundian splendour of Flanders and Brabant, the awesome wealth and power of the Dutch Republic in its Golden Age, the vast overseas empires of the Netherlands and Belgium of modern times, and the continual presence, whether aligned with the ruling circles of the day or half hidden in the interstices of history, of the artists and painters, from Van Eyck to Van Gogh and all the great names in between. And remember, they conclude, that behind all this, all the time, there is a language, Dutch by name, that provides direct access to this world and allows the outsider to gain a genuinely intimate understanding of this society and its culture. And don't forget, they add almost as an afterthought, that in studying Dutch you're getting two for the price of one, for although the Netherlands and Flanders look alike in certain respects, there are differences between them: sometimes obvious, more often subtle, always significant.

While the detail of the case can probably be refined, rephrased and strengthened in all manner of ways, its hard core is incontestable. Dutch is the third Germanic language and more people speak Dutch than all the Scandinavian tongues put together. In economic terms the Benelux countries carry a great deal of clout in Europe, wholly disproportionate to their limited geographical size. Their contemporary societies are open-minded, cosmopolitan, advanced. They have as much reason as any other nation to take pride in their national past. And both the Netherlands and Belgium have distinctive characteristics of their own.

Dutch Studies, then, ought to be a thriving academic discipline in the world at large. It is, in some ways. In other ways, it is not; or not yet. A closer look at the figures mentioned at the beginning, and the facts behind them, reveals the two-edged nature of the current situation. Some 400 academics employed at 250 different universities suggests a thin spread, with few major centres. Add to this the geographical distribution, which is decidedly uneven: the countries immediately bordering on the Netherlands and Belgium show by far the greatest concentration, with sizeable numbers being found also in South Africa and Indonesia, for good historical reasons. This means Dutch has only a very limited presence in universities in the rest of the world, including most of the English-speaking world. The good news, however, is that generally speaking business is – no, let's not tempt fate: not booming, therefore, but coming on rather nicely all the same. For the fact is that barely one or two generations ago the study of Dutch at universities outside the Low Countries hardly existed. There were isolated enthusiasts, hard-working pioneers, lone wolves and literary scholars. But their impact depended entirely on their personal initiative and persuasive powers. The field itself had little infrastructure, few financial resources, and no continuity to speak of.

Much has changed in the last thirty years, in some cases dramatically. Since the mid-1960s the number of foreign universities offering Dutch has more than doubled. In 1970 the International Association for Dutch Studies (IVN; *Internationale Vereniging voor Neerlandistiek*) was set up, providing a focus and a platform for the rapidly growing community of 'international' university teachers of Dutch. The Association acts as an information clearing-house, provides practical support and services, ensures regular contact with academic circles in the home countries, organises large-scale triennial conferences (alternately in the Netherlands and Belgium) covering all aspects of the language and culture of the Low Countries, and publishes its own thrice-yearly journal *Neerlandica extra muros* – which has doubled its size over the last three years or so. Whereas the first-ever gathering of 'foreign' university teachers of Dutch, in 1962, was attended by all of seventeen delegates, today's IVN conferences have become media events attracting two hundred and more. The Dutch Language Union (*Nederlandse Taalunie*), a Belgo-Dutch intergovernmental organisation founded in 1980 to coordinate the efforts of the Dutch and the (federal) Flemish authorities with regard to language and literature, has identified the study of Dutch at foreign universities as one of its priorities and lends financial support to a range of academic centres and initiatives across the world and to the International Association for Dutch Studies.

How have Dutch Studies fared in the English-speaking countries? In what follows I shall leave South Africa out of the picture, as it is a special case. The country has only recently begun to emerge from a long period of political and cultural quarantine; the first Dutch Studies conference which international scholars felt free to attend was held in Potchefstroom in January 1992. In addition, the close linguistic affinity between Dutch and Afrikaans – the latter being a daughter language of the former – means that the study of Dutch there is markedly different from that in the rest of the world. The focus in the following account will be on Britain, the USA and Canada, with only a few words on Australia and New Zealand. The story, it will be seen, is in most places one of steady, sometimes spectacular growth, growth both in size and in depth, coupled however with a continuing underlying vulnerability. But let us line up some facts first.

We should start with the thin end of the wedge. Australia and New Zealand provide perfect if contrasting illustrations of the precarious existence of Dutch as an academic subject in a world far removed from the home countries. The vital statistics have to do with immigration, financial support, and local university policy. Courses in Dutch language and literature began to be taught in the Department of Germanic Languages at the University of Melbourne in 1942. The section had a full programme and a staff of four in the 1960s – and was closed down in 1992. Among the reasons were the falling numbers of Dutch-speaking immigrants to Australia after the main wave in the 1950s and the loss of affinity of second-generation immigrants with their parents' mother tongue, leading to dwindling student numbers. The final blow came when the Dutch Language Union cut the financial lifeline and the University decided to sacrifice the ailing section rather than risk a drain on its resources. As a result, Dutch has ceased to exist as a university subject on the Australian continent. However, as the Melbourne section closed its doors, the University of Auckland took over the torch and established its own course in Dutch, the first ever in New Zealand. This post too is dependent on the linguistic bond tying an immigrant community to a corner of Western Europe, on at least a measure of external funding, and on the skill and commitment of one person offering a Dutch option as part of a German language and literature programme. It is a fragile base to build on.

Melbourne and Auckland may be unusual cases and, given the conditions, more at the mercy of the elements than most. Still, the same or similar factors are involved in many Dutch Studies departments or sections in British, American and Canadian universities, even if in those countries the discipline has become rather more firmly established and, indeed, has grown and grown. This is true of Canada, and it is certainly true of the United States. In Canada, as in Australia, Dutch immigration took off in the post-1945 period. Dutch was first taught at Canadian universities in the 1960s, starting out as a forlorn extracurricular option in the Department of German at the University of Toronto in 1960. Thirty-odd years on, half a dozen universities and colleges in Canada offer courses in Dutch language and culture in one form or another, membership of the Canadian Association for the Advancement of Netherlandic Studies / Association Canadienne pour l'avancement des études néerlandaises (CAANS / ACAEN), founded in 1971, approaches two hundred, and the *Canadian Journal of Netherlandic Studies / Revue Canadienne des études néerlandaises* has been appearing twice yearly since 1979. The latest chapter in the story of Dutch in Canadian higher education is being written at the large and prestigious University of British Columbia in Vancouver, where a two-year 'Netherlands Studies' component is expected to be added to the curriculum shortly, with the aim of establishing a full four-year programme in due course.

Much of the Canadian interest in Dutch Studies stems from the presence of a large immigrant community of Dutch descent, as it did in Australia, as it does in New Zealand, despite the vast differences in the absolute size of these communities. And in Canada too Dutch is normally taught as an option to undergraduates majoring in German or another language. As a result, there is room for only a limited amount of graduate work and research. Meanwhile the difference in scale and the intense activity within CAANS and its regional 'chapters' has made a crucial qualitative difference. Dutch Studies meetings and conferences in Canada now attract historians, art historians and social scientists as well, and sheer multidisciplinary enthusiasm appears to create its own momentum.

By and large, this is also the situation in the USA, where the scale is larger still. Again, immigration played its part, but this time in a more distant past. Between the mid-nineteenth and the mid-twentieth century around a quarter of a million Dutch people, many of them belonging to the Dutch Reformed Church, settled in the US. While their numbers remained relatively small, they proved slow to assimilate, especially in the Midwest. In the nineteenth and the early twentieth century Dutch courses at Hope College in Holland, Michigan, and Central College in Pella, Iowa, catered for these fiercely religious communities. So did Calvin College (founded as Calvin Seminary, 1876) in Grand Rapids, Michigan, where between them the two doyens of American Dutch Studies, H.J. van Andel and Walter Lagerwey, taught for most of the present century and where Dutch is still on the syllabus today.

Among the American universities, Columbia has had a virtually uninterrupted tradition of Dutch language and literature instruction since 1913. It was here that the first Chair was established, when in 1921 Adriaan Barnouw became the first Queen Wilhelmina Professor of the History, Language and Literature of the Netherlands. The period of real growth, however, did not come until the 1960s, when Dutch Studies components were introduced at the universities of Pennsylvania (1962), California (UCLA, 1963), Indiana (1965), Texas (Austin, 1966), Massachusetts (Amherst, 1969), Hawaii (1972) and Minnesota (1972). Since then the subject has gone from strength to strength, spreading to nearly thirty colleges and universities and spawning a wealth of textbooks and study materials in the process. The American Association for Netherlandic Studies (AANS), a resolutely interdisciplinary grouping established in 1975, currently numbers well over two hundred members, including not only Dutch language and literature specialists, but also comparatists, art historians, church historians, straight historians, political and social scientists, geographers and even musicologists. The diverse interests of the AANS membership are reflected in the International Conferences on Netherlandic Studies which have been held biennially since 1982, moving from one place to another, and increasing in size and diversity with each move. Proceedings of AANS conferences duly appear in PAANS, the Association's Publications series. In a separate development, three universities, Michigan (Ann Arbor), Texas (Austin) and Minnesota (Minneapolis), set up Dutch writers in residence schemes, while Flemish writers were occasionally posted to Iowa (Iowa City); these schemes, however, are currently being reconsidered in The Hague and Brussels, and will be reduced to just one writer in residence, based in New York, the others being diverted to countries in Europe.

The largest centre of Dutch Studies in the USA is at the Berkeley campus of the University of California. The soil had been well prepared here, with departments of history, art history, comparative literature and South East Asian Studies having long shown an interest in Dutch material. Dutch language teaching began at Berkeley in 1959, the Dutch government endowed the Princess (now Queen) Beatrix Chair in 1971, the Belgian government followed suit with a (visiting) P.P. Rubens Chair in 1981. The investments obviously paid off: the university responded with Regents Lectureships for prominent Dutch writers (Mulisch, Nooteboom), the library was designated as the prime focus for Dutch literature and history books (the collection now houses over 100,000 volumes in these two fields alone), and every other year since 1985 the section has been running its own international conferences on Dutch linguistics and literature.

The main collective achievement of those involved in Dutch Studies at American universities has undoubtedly been that they have put the subject on the map in the American academic and scholarly world. An internal communication network has been established: both AANS and CAANS have regular newsletters and a conference circuit. There are good contacts with the home countries, and close relations with associations that have overlapping interests, notably the well-organised Historians of Netherlandish Art, set up in 1983, complete with their own newsletter, conference circuit and excellent representation in the museum world. Moreover, Dutch Studies have gained a modest but relatively secure place on larger platforms: CAANS is present at the Learned Societies gatherings, and Dutch subsections have sprung up at such venues as the huge MLA conventions and the more specialist Kalamazoo Conferences on Medieval Literature. Needless to say, the quality of the discipline benefits substantially both from the exposure itself and from the contact with peer groups.

But there is another side. At just about every American university Dutch is taught in the context of a larger undergraduate programme, as one among several free-floating options, often at elementary to intermediate level only. This leaves little opportunity for in-depth study, for specialisation, for graduate work and research. Many Dutch sections are essentially one-man bands, and the one man or woman in question may have to cover a very wide range, again leaving little room for advanced work. While the spread of Dutch Studies through the American university world shows that the subject is no longer dependent on recruitment among a local immigrant population, isolated one-person posts are naturally vulnerable and may easily be swept away by freak fluctuations in student supply and demand. Most centres receive a measure of financial support from the Dutch Language Union in

The Hague; some, including some large and dynamic ones, may be directly threatened if that support is withdrawn. Clearly, despite the breakthrough and the very real successes of the last couple of decades, consolidation is a long way off.

Broadly speaking this is also the situation of Dutch Studies at British universities, although in Britain, of course, they do things differently. Here it is the historians who have organised themselves, not the art historians. Due perhaps to the dominance of one centre, the subject does not have the equivalent of AANS, CAANS or PAANS. But it does have 'Single Dutch', i.e. a full four-year degree course in Dutch; and more.

When Dutch was introduced at University College London (UCL) in 1919, the post covered Dutch history and institutions as well as language and literature. Indeed its first occupant was the well-known historian Pieter Geyl, who was joined by a literary scholar in 1923. Following a gentlemanly disagreement between these two, however, history remained at UCL and philology went to live a separate life elsewhere in the University, at Bedford College. Here, forty years later, Dutch Studies began to grow rapidly, particularly in the 1970s under R.P. Meijer, whose *Literature of the Low Countries* (1978) has remained the standard survey in English. By this time the Dutch Department, with a staff of five, was offering a four-year 'Single Honours' course focusing on Dutch language and literature. When in 1983 the Department returned from Bedford College to UCL, the expertise available at this institution covered Dutch history, art history, and language and literature. The Centre for Low Countries Studies, set up soon afterwards at UCL, is now running a unique interdisciplinary Master of Arts course in the Culture and History of the Dutch Golden Age. The Centre organised its first international conference in 1989 – an exercise to be repeated at the end of 1994. The journal *Dutch Crossing,* which had been appearing three times a year since 1977, is now issued under the auspices of the Centre, and has expanded from a language and literature journal to encompass, like its Canadian counterpart, the social sciences, history and general culture of the Low Countries as well. Alongside *Dutch Crossing* the Centre has begun to publish the book series 'Crossways', the second volume of which saw the light early in 1993. A Dutch writer in (short-term) residence is set to become a reality at the end of 1993.

Dutch has been taught as part of a degree programme in Cambridge and Liverpool for many years, and nearly a dozen other universities introduced Dutch options in the 1970s and '80s. After London the main centre today is at Hull University, where a new degree programme with a focus on the social sciences and business studies was established in 1976. In Hull, as in London, a four-year specialisation in Dutch Studies is available, although the majority – and it is a growing majority – of undergraduates prefer a combination of Dutch with another subject, be it another language or the flexible and increasingly popular European Studies. At national level the subject is represented now in the Association for Language Learning (ALL), which promotes a variety of modern languages. The historians, with their happy hunting ground in centuries of Anglo-Dutch relations, have a longer tradition: their triennial conferences have been taking place since 1959, the proceedings appearing in print in the series 'Britain and the Netherlands'. The lavish William and Mary Tercentenary celebrations in 1988, which did much to lift the Dutch image in Britain and gave rise to a spate of popular as well as scholarly books, are still producing tremors: in March 1993 the Dutch Prime Minister Ruud Lubbers delivered the first William and Mary lecture in the Cambridge Senate House.

Expansion and growth, both in size and in depth, on both sides of the Atlantic: the pictures are really very similar. Nowhere in the English-speaking world is Dutch taught as a regular secondary-school subject, so as a rule the university programmes assume no previous knowledge of the language and start from scratch. At the other end of the scale, if given half a chance, university teachers of Dutch everywhere in the Anglophone world – and across the globe, for that matter – tend to engage in literary translation or other forms of cultural promotion well beyond the walls of academe. All in all, then, the infrastructure of Dutch Studies in Britain is only superficially different from that in the USA and Canada. In Britain the discipline has a more obvious centre of gravity, located in London. At UCL alone there are seven staff engaged in the field, four of them in senior posts; the nearby Warburg and Courtauld Institutes, which are primarily research centres, also have their Dutch specialists. In all three countries, collaboration across disciplines, linking language and literature on the one hand with history, art history and the social sciences on the other, has evidently benefited all concerned.

This fact is more important than it seems, and it matters in more ways than one. It matters in respect of student recruitment. Given the increasing tendency for students to read Dutch in combination with another subject, Dutch Studies as a discipline needs to highlight its relevance not only in its own terms but also in the context of European Studies and alongside other West European languages. It is worth pointing out to students of foreign languages that diversification beyond French or German means greatly improved job prospects, for there is a genuine need for native speakers of English with a good command of Dutch – and no, it is emphatically *not* true that the Dutch all speak English anyway.

It matters, secondly, with regard to the quality of the discipline itself. The Dutch language is central to any serious understanding of Low Countries culture. Simon Schama has been castigated, and deservedly so, for his lack of close familiarity with the written sources of Dutch culture and scholarship. In contrast, and more recently, Jonathan Israel's bold reinterpretation of the 1688 Glorious Revolution as essentially a Dutch invasion is based crucially on Dutch archive material inaccessible to most Anglophone historians. Art historians, too, may wish to take note: one does not need to subscribe to the iconographic tendency in art history to realise that reading pictures as cultural products involves having recourse to the printed word as well as to the painted canvas.

It matters, finally, for the general visibility of Dutch culture and Dutch Studies in the world. While sadly, and incomprehensibly, neither the Dutch nor the Flemish cultural authorities have shown much awareness of the need to establish cultural centres – of whatever description – in the English-speaking world (the recently-founded Netherlands Institute in New York is a private initiative), it is in most cases left to the academic centres to fill the recognition gap. It is a tall order. And in this respect the language and literature division needs all the help it can get from the historians, art historians and social scientists. Rembrandt opens doors for Dutch Studies, his contemporary the poet and dramatist Vondel does not: the strictly language-bound forms of cultural expression in the Low Countries have remained largely hidden from the outside world. Yet culture and language are interdependent. The study of the culture of the Low Countries cannot be reduced to the Dutch language, but cannot do without it either. That is why, for Dutch culture as well as for Dutch Studies abroad, a collaborative, interdisciplinary approach is both strategically and intellectually the best option.

THEO HERMANS

ADDRESSES:

International Association for Dutch Studies (*IVN; Internationale Vereniging voor Neerlandistiek*) and *Neerlandica extra muros:* Marja Kristel (Administrator), Van Dorthstraat 6, 2481 XV Woubrugge, The Netherlands; fax +31 (0)1729 9925.
Canadian Association for the Advancement of Netherlandic Studies (CAANS): Prof. A. Zweers (President), Germanic & Slavic Languages, University of Waterloo, Waterloo, Ontario N2L 3G1, Canada; *Canadian Journal of Netherlandic Studies* and CAANS Newsletter: Dr Basil Kingstone (Editor), Dept of French, University of Windsor, Windsor, Ontario N9B 3P4, Canada.
American Association for Netherlandic Studies (AANS): Prof. Margriet Bruyn Lacy (President), Dean's Office, Liberal Arts & Sciences, Butler University, 4600 Sunset Avenue, Indianapolis, Indiana 46208, USA; AANS Newsletter Editor: Prof. Tom Shannon, Dept of German, University of California, Berkeley, California 94720, USA; fax: (1) 510 643 5994 and 510 642 4243. Historians of Netherlandish Art (HNA): Kahren Jones Arbitman (President), The Palmer Museum of Art, Pennsylvania State University, University Park, Pennsylvania 16802, USA; HNA Newsletter: Kristin Lohse Belkin (Editor), 23 South Adelaide Avenue, Highland Park, New Jersey 08904, USA.
Centre for Low Countries Studies: Dr Theo Hermans (Chair), Dept of Dutch, University College London (UCL), Gower Street, London WC1E 6BT; fax +44 (0) 71 387 8057; *Dutch Crossing* and 'Crossways': c/o Secretary, Centre for Low Countries Studies, UCL.

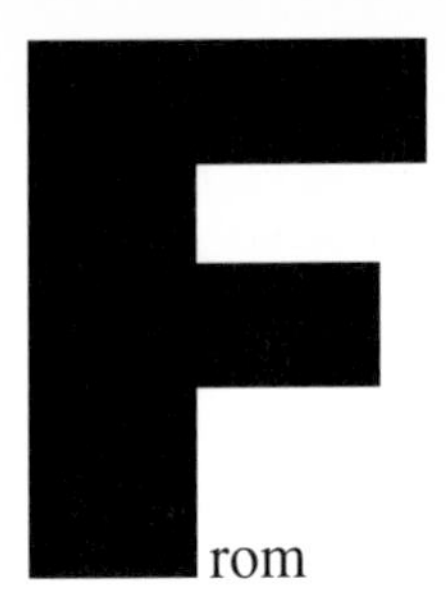

From

First Sight to Insight

The Emblem in the Low Countries

The emblem literature of the Low Countries has become a paradigm in the discourse on European cultural history. But what actually are emblems? Why are they now so widely studied? What is so special about Dutch and Flemish emblem books? Emblem books have literally and metaphorically re-emerged from second-hand booksellers and bibliophile collections to land on students' desks, and that within the last thirty years or less.

Yet emblems are not part of Literature with a capital letter. Not one emblem book has a place in the canon of accepted classics. Emblem art was a temporary phenomenon which eventually burned itself out. The revival which this genre has enjoyed here and there in the post-modern period has little to do with the emblem in its historical context.

1. A fascinating genre

The emblem as a genre has a complex history, and its origins are by no means Dutch. For its development we should go back to the standard model that appeared in France between 1534 and 1560: the emblem consisting of a heading (*motto*), a plate (*pictura*) and a poem, with or without a commentary. The intention is primarily rhetorical; emblems are to make authoritative statements. Referring both to nature (particularly flora and fauna) and to tradition (mythology, the Bible, history, literature) as well as to the everyday human environment, they provide norms and arguments for proper behaviour in an attractive combination of words and pictures. You look, you recognise and you are then persuaded and adopt new insights. So emblem art is a typically humanist activity; it aims at furthering the creation of a new man, specifically by using illustration and word, eye and ear. This dual method of persuasion consists in distilling deeper truths from illustrated data: representation and explanation, display and demonstration, in a pleasing manner. But the artistry of the emblem was not just a question of the quality of the plate and the poetry. The subtler the emblematic edification, the greater was its artistic and persuasive effect. This could for instance be achieved by endowing the combination of motto and plate with an enigmatic quality. The poem then often functions as a convincing solution. Another favoured method was to allow the plate in various ways to contribute to the explanation, for instance by introducing pictorial metaphors or indicative elements in the background. The subtler the reference, the greater its conviction, though this was obviously never arbitrary. Images gain meaning through recognisable analogies. A weathercock can never be a lesson in constancy, though it can ingeniously represent the positive aspects of the politician's vacillation; it is useful 'for indicating the wind directions to those who must use them'.

This enormously successful genre – there were some thousands of editions within a period of about 250 years, the total copies of which must have run into seven figures – seems at first sight to have arisen by pure chance. This occurred in 1531 when a collection of Latin epigrams by Andrea Alciato, a Milan lawyer working in France, which was originally intended for an inner circle of humanists, was provided by an Augsburg printer with a series of woodcuts and published in this form with or without the author's knowledge. To these *poems,* in which the author had derived deeper meanings from the more or less visual descriptions of the subjects in the Greek models he was following, he gave the title *emblemata.* This word, derived from the Greek, refers, after all, to artistic inlays and mosaics of all kinds; the meaningful epigrams also contributed a sort of added value. The addition of plates was an immediate success, and Alciato himself now expanded his collection following this formula. The first authorised edition appeared in Paris in 1534. It became a phenomenal best-seller. Up until 1565 some sixty editions flowed from the French presses in Latin, French, German, Spanish and Italian. Only when epigons began publishing 'similar' little books, was Alciato's title taken over as a somewhat loosely applied name for a particular genre. It was of course only relatively speaking a coincidence. The formula later promoted by Alciato and his Paris printer had its roots in any case in the increasingly popular illustrated literature being adopted in book publishing and elsewhere. It was the significance of the picture that was highly esteemed, as with the vogue for Egyptian hieroglyphs, which were read as ideograms revealing ancient wisdom directly – without explanation: the language of objects. Then there was the infectious fashion among the elite of displaying personal ideals and intentions, often very artfully, in images accompanied by mottos (the *impresa* or device). There was also the prestige of the highly esteemed *poetria* already in vogue among the late medieval *rhétoriqueurs,* the art of fictionalising mythology and fable in order to expose deeper truths. And were *poesia* and *pictura* not, after all, close relatives?

Through their twofold means of communication – pictorial and verbal – the emblem books were immediately (and expressly) aimed at a double market. On the one hand there was the large group of artists and craftsmen, from architects to milliners, whose use of emblems enabled them to offer more meaningful products. On the other hand, there were the readers. For them the genre blossomed out into all kinds of forms – from moralising guides to amorous gift-books, from mystical books of meditation to natural history encyclopedias, from schoolbooks to cookery books, from theological exposition to vulgar classroom levity, from unbridled panegyric to pamphlet and social criticism, from childrens' books to obituaries. It was ultimately an artistic and didactic method (a *genus scribendi)* applicable to all areas of life.

It goes without saying, then, that as an artistic expression of thought this genre provides a remarkably rich source for cultural history. It is in the history of thought and attitudes that it is particularly meaningful: in its formulation of behavioural norms, of upbringing, of giving meaning to things. In current studies there is little apparent evidence of this. Bibliography, editions, genre theory and its application in art and literature are still their main concern. Yet it is very important to understand how the emblem acquires its meanings, how the genre works and how its features distinguish it from other less successful forms of binary communication. But there is more. The way in which the emblem contributed to the development of European civilisation is a boundless and fascinating subject.

2. Emblem art in the Low Countries, or the crown on the genre

It is the graphic quality of the Dutch emblem books that generally accounts for this literature becoming a household word. They are visually extremely pleasing, executed as they were by an impressive line of famous artists and engravers in the sixteenth and seventeenth centuries: from Marcus Gheeraerts to Romeyn de Hooghe via the De Passes, the Galles, the Wierixes, Adriaen van de Venne, Jan Luyken and many others. But most of this artistic fame was probably acquired later, in the circles of bibliophiles and collectors of graphic art. Its 'historical' success was due rather to other factors: the commercial ingenuity and know-how of the printing houses, its social, middle-class character and the fact that ideological movements like the Counter-Reformation in the southern provinces and pietism in the North made ample strategic use of the genre. Finally there is evidence that the emblem in the Low Countries, as indeed in Germany, enjoyed a serious literary prestige. Nearly all the important Dutch writers of the 'emblematic age' – the term is Herder's! – used the genre in some form or other: Jan van der Noot, Daniel Heinsius, Hugo de Groot, Roemer Visscher and his daughter Anna, Hendrik Laurensz. Spiegel, Bredero, P.C. Hooft, Joost van den Vondel, Justus de Harduwijn, Jan Starter, Johan de Brune sr, Adriaen Poirters. Some, such as Jacob Cats and the doubly talented Jan Luyken, even became personified synonyms of emblem art.

2.1. Antwerp: the humanist emblem

Cosmopolitan Antwerp with its distinguished cultural life, its fashionable *rederijkers,* its numerous printers, its scholarly humanists and artists and above all its wealth, is the innovator. Though others showed remarkable enterprise in emblem publishing, it was Plantin, with his workshop at the hub of the Antwerp humanist circle, who set the tradition of Dutch emblem book production in motion. Taking advantage of the crisis in the French book trade around 1560, Plantin's house produced more than a dozen Alciatos for the foreign market in 1565 and the following years. Meanwhile, in 1563, the Hungarian humanist Joannes Sambucus had approached Plantin

Fig. 1 – J. Sambucus, *Emblemata* (Antwerp, 1564). Print of an emblem dedicated to the Roman humanist Fulvius Ursinus. In an English version it reads:
'First reade, then marke, then practise that is good, / For without use, we drinke but Lethe flood ...'
(G. Whitney, *Emblemes,* Leiden 1586, p. 171).

with his fine literary imitations of Alciato (editions 1564, 1566). These were followed, in 1565, by Junius' *Emblemata.* Both these new collections were almost at once spoken of everywhere in the same breath as Alciato's. Thus the Antwerp printing house published at the same time the three most influential works in Latin humanist emblem art, learned, subtle and concerned with moral philosophical edification and its typical topics: the role of Fortuna, human weaknesses (greed, deceit, *voluptas,* folly) and the 'humanist' virtues: integrity, friendship, moderation and conscious loyalty to the community. There is a striking synthesis of all this in Sambucus' emblem on the use of books, in which the humanists' practice becomes itself a cautionary symbol: not the reading of books, but the application of what we read makes us wise (fig. 1). Partly to defray the costs of the relatively expensive woodcuts, Plantin also published Sambucus' and Junius' collections in the Dutch language, with the encouragement of the famous geographer Ortelius and with an eye to the *rederijker* readership and Antwerp's artistic circles. This was the beginning of the noble lineage of the emblem in the vernacular. Later, in 1607 and 1612, the most influential humanist emblem book of the seventeenth century in Europe was to appear in Antwerp: the polyglot *Emblemata Horatiana* by the learned artist Otto Vaenius, the onetime teacher of Pieter Paul Rubens. This book, which systematically rendered Horace's ethical dicta into emblems abounding in neo-stoical wisdom, was to become one of the most popular vade-mecums of European royalty and nobility.

2.2. Cupid at work. The erotic emblem

In the dynamic environment of the young, internationally oriented Leiden University, the erotic emblem makes its appearance around 1600, and this again becomes a brilliant success with far-reaching implications in cultural history. As connoisseurs of classical love poetry, scholars started, as in the Italian renaissance salons, to provide illustrations of Cupid with mottos and epigrams in the vernacular, in a bantering Ovidian or plaintive Petrarchistic manner. This scholarly pastime soon became a profitable trade. Amsterdam printers of popular reading matter (song-books!) soon sensed the market and started vying with one another in the production of collections of *emblemata amatoria. Quaeris quid sit amor* (If you are looking for what love is …, Amsterdam, 1601), written in Dutch by Daniel Heinsius under a pseudonym, is the first in a long series. Though a certain fascination with erotic love was not far removed from this genre in emblem art – we have only to think of the crudely obscene treatment of the theme in German collections written for students – the innovative Dutch amorous emblem books are remarkable for their erudition, their sensitive humour and their refining aims: Heinsius appears as Cupid's Dutch tutor, P.C. Hooft as his secretary. Collections of amorous emblems – printed like music in oblong format for shared use – provided gift books for wealthier youngsters. They served to captivate the hearts of young girls. Their hardy attraction lies in the way in which they give visual form to Ovid's literary conceits and introduce Petrarch's amatory language into the universal language of lovers. Through Cupid's capricious dealings we are given an instructive yet pleasant introduction to the perilous but indispensible Venus: 'purveyor and destroyer of all things'. *Couleur locale* is often of the essence. Where, for instance Alciato depicts love's omnipotence with the classic emblems of fish and flowers – for it rules over land and sea (fig. 2), in Heinsius' amusing *The Trades of Cupid* (Het ambacht van Cupido) this omnipotence is the subject of a nice transposition. The ancient, philosophical idea that love makes the world go round and maintains the harmony of the spheres (Lucretius) is wittily compared here with the trade of the cooper (Dutch: *kuiper*), without whose agency the big barrel of the world is constantly in danger of literally and figuratively falling to pieces. Moreover, the representation of Cupid as a cooper is based on a pun: *kuuper / Cupido* (cooper / Cupid):

Kuypt kleine kuyper kuypt, die alle man doet buygen …
Want waer het sonder u, de weerelt viel in duigen. (fig. 3).

Coop little cooper, coop, bending all to your caprices,
For were it not for you, the world would fall to pieces.

Nudus Amor uiden' ut ridet, placidumq; tuetur?
Nec faculas, nec quæ cornua flectat habet.
Altera sed manuum flores gerit, altera piscem,
Scilicet ut terræ iura det atque mari.

Fig. 2 – A. Alciato, *Emblematum libellus* (Paris, 1542), p. 170: 'Do you see how naked Eros smiles, how gentle he looks? / He has neither torches, nor bows that he could bend. / But one hand holds flowers, the other a fish. / That is to say that he lays down the law on land and sea.'

Fig. 3 – D. Heinsius, *The Trades of Cupid* (Het ambacht van Cupido): Cupid as a cooper, (emblem 2). *Afbeelding van Minne – Emblemata Amatoria – Emblemez d'Amour,* (Leiden, 1619, 2 Pl. 3r)

Fig. 4 – O. Vaenius, *Amorum emblemata* (Antwerp 1608), p. 115. Cupid provides a donkey with wings, thus turning him into a Pegasus. Love refines. R. Verstegen's English legend reads: 'Thear's not so dul an asse but Cupid hath the power, / Through love to whet his wittes, and mend his doltish mynd, / The slow hee maketh quick, hee often altreth kynd, / Hee giveth manie gifts, but mixeth sweet with soure.'

Fig. 5 – P.C. Hooft, *Emblemata amatoria* (Amsterdam, 1611). p. 53: love as hopeless drudgery. The Latin motto goes back to Erasmus' *Adagia.* The plate explains itself. The spinning squirrel symbolizes the lover following the girl. The swans are an attribute of Venus.

Gradually the genre turned its attention more and more to marriage: middle-class morality took over from the gallantry of courtship. The first signs of this occur in the *Amorum emblemata* (Antwerp, 1608) by the above-mentioned Otto Vaenius, the most famous specimen of the genre, which appeared, thanks to exemplary team-work, in three different editions in Latin-Dutch-French, Latin-Italian-French and Latin-English-Italian. This lucrative multilingual product was immediately adopted in Amsterdam (fig. 4 and 5). The ever-increasing moralising tone reached its zenith in Jacob Cats. *The Maiden's Duties* (Maechden-plicht, 1618) is in reality a discourse on love and marriage set out as an emblem book. In *Silenus Alcibiadis* of the same year (the later *Emblems of Love and Morality* – Minne- en Zinnebeelden), Cats, as he himself says, finished Cupid off. Each plate is given an erotic, but also a moral social and religious explanation. 'A triplicate Alciato', Heinsius cheered. Later, adults and the elderly were addressed in the same way as the young had been. Whereas in the Republic it was the erotic emblem that informed the realistic and bourgeois emblem

Fig. 6 – J. Cats, *Proteus, or Amorous Scenes rendered as Moral Emblems* (Proteus, ofte minnebeelden verandert in Sinnebeelden, Ed. Amsterdam, J.J. Schipper, 1658), emblem 28. Peasant couple with onions. Peeling onions, which causes weeping, as symbol of keenness in love, friendship in hard times and tribulation.

books, in the Spanish Netherlands it was a religious counterpart that set the tone. At Archduchess Isabella's suggestion Vaenius now published emblems on 'devotional' love (*Amoris divini emblemata,* 1615): Cupid in a little mantle with a halo. This became a very fertile formula both in Catholic and (later) Protestant circles in the furtherance of a spiritual life.

2.3. Mark, learn and inwardly digest: the realistic bourgeois emblem book

Where familiar realism is dominant in the plates, and where they represent middle-class values, they are often referred to as typically Dutch emblem art. Though the description is somewhat vague and questionable, depending as it does on the 'realism' of the plates, the phenomenon itself is no less interesting for all that. Aesthetically, these volumes are among the finest in Europe in the genre. For the history of life and thought they are often unexplored gold mines. This group includes the tens of thousands of copies of Cats' collections, whose subject matter is still close to humanist emblem books (the fauna and the proverb). Through its tripartite application the genre in his hands becomes a kind of book of life dealing with erotic love, family and upbringing, society, Christian life and death (fig. 6).

A small masterpiece to which recent emblem studies are paying increasing attention is the high-handed *Symbolic Pictures* (Sinnepoppen) by the Amsterdam grain merchant and poet Roemer Visscher, whose home was the centre of a thriving cultural interchange. Visscher had plates made with mottos and provided them with commentaries for his friends, publishing them in 1614. They are all highly original. The prints use an eloquent close-up technique, preferring utensils and instruments whose attributes, application and effectiveness introduce the 'moral'. As has been rightly said: in bourgeois Amsterdam life, norms of behaviour increasingly relied on personal experience rather than classical tradition and the allegorical interpretation of nature. The commentaries were in prose, following the French device books: concise, but very vivid and direct and full of surprising turns of phrase and covert erudition. The tone is often humorous, *ad rem* and satirical – Visscher was not afraid of invective – in the spirit of Erasmus. The mockery in this collection does not, however, muffle its pleasure in being Dutch. The references show a striking interest in the economic sector: earnings and the acquisition of property, and the morality of this. But civil government is also represented in the so-called prince emblems where the deliberate banality of the pictorial material is often inelegantly commonplace. A high official is like a de-lousing comb: he cleanses the land of rogues and adorns it with fine laws. Brooms are extremely useful, but they are made of the hair from the backs of pigs: there's no knowing the origin of magistrates. Visscher also shows a sober piety and middle-class neo-stoicism: the gateway to a Dutch field teaches us the happiness of *kleine vrijheid* (modest freedom): remain lowly and be satisfied (fig. 7).

A solid and even pietistically directed godliness is evident in the splendidly-produced *Emblemata* (1624) by the Zeeland magistrate Johan de Brune sr with realistic plates by Adriaen van de Venne, who was also Cats' illustrator. The originality of this collection consists primarily in its choice of emblematic material: the recreational activities and the lifestyle of the young well-to-do citizen, in which (often erotic) party games figure prominently. There seem to be obvious links with painting (a delicate issue!). Moreover, the explanatory poems are accompanied by erudite, supple, evasive and stylish prose commentaries that herald the advent of the Dutch essay. The ideological tendency reminds one of Cats: the behaviour of the young, the *res publica* and one's relationship to God. Hence, once again, *chacun son goût* (fig. 8).

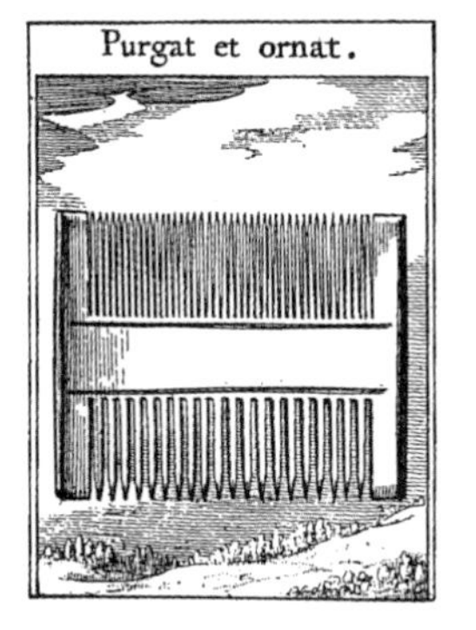

Fig. 7 – Four of Roemer Visscher's *Symbolic Pictures* (Sinnepoppen, Amsterdam, 1614), I, 35 and 9; II, 46 and 6.

Fig. 8 – J. de Brune, *Emblemata or Symbolic Pieces* (Emblemata of Zinne-werck, Amsterdam / Middelburg, 1624), emblem 35: amorous fun on the swing. The author appends a witty essay on the fickleness of the female mind.

In their impressive attempts to revitalise and underpin Catholicism, the Jesuits, and in their train the other monastic orders, made ample use of the emblem. Here it was the Southern Netherlands that set the trend. In contrast to France, for example, where Jesuit emblem art latterly promoted the specific interests of state ideology, the genre became the favoured medium of religious polemic, of education and of personal spiritual growth (of monastics and women in particular). Finalists at the Jesuit colleges even had to devise emblems as edification for their colleagues and to further their competence in Latin and poetry. The Royal Library in Brussels has a unique collection of these often superb manuscripts (which will form part of an exhibition in 1996).

The Jesuits' discussion of the emblem developed into a doctrine that embraced the whole of visual Catholic pastoral theology: pictures are the books of the illiterate and ignorant, they can be easily memorised, they touch the emotions, they have a ritual power, they sugar the pedagogical pill, they enhance concentration and are an important accompaniment to meditation. It was through the Jesuits that the Council of Trent's doctrine on imagery impinged on the theory and practice of emblem art, in the vernacular as well as in Latin. Its effects, therefore, are many and varied.

It was, however, the ardent books on meditation, in the manner of the erotic emblem tradition, that had the greatest impact. Their concentration on personal spiritual growth and individual sanctity and their emphasis on the practical aspects of the religious life apparently fulfilled a need at a time of confessional disputes and dogmatic arguments. Thus the Jesuit Herman Hugo's *Pia desideria* (Pious Desires, Antwerp, 1624) became a European devotional best-seller, to be followed by pietists of various Protestant hue. This had an almost incalculable influence on baroque literature and art. Central European ecclesiastical architecture is but one illustration of this. What now seems to us sentimental, then possessed a powerful eloquence and conviction in its conceits (fig. 9).

3. The Anglo-Dutch connection

One of the largest collections of emblem books is housed, since 1958, in Glasgow University Library. It is named after its founder, the nineteenth-century Scottish aristocrat and scholar Sir William Stirling Maxwell. It has subsequently been considerably enlarged. The Dutch-language section is impressive – a unique set including 84 sketches for the *Symbolic Pictures* – and was by no means fortuitous. Sir William was not just a connoisseur. British emblem art was after all very much under the influence of Dutch examples, and there is little evidence of a reverse trend. It must suffice here to note that this influence pervades the whole history of the genre in Britain from the very outset to its resurgence in Victorian times.

English literary historians are inclined to take the English translation of Jan van der Noot's *Theatre* (1569) as the starting point. The first truly English emblem book was in any case printed in Leiden: Geoffrey Whitney's *A Choice of Emblems* (1586) can be placed in the context of the ethical and political discussions prompted by Leicester's campaign in the Netherlands. Cats' works were much translated in, for instance, the *Pleasant Dialogues and Dramas* (1637) by the dramatist Thomas Heywood, and this continued right into the nineteenth century when with the collaboration of Stirling Maxwell and others, a selection of *Moral Emblems with Aphorisms, etc.* was published in 1860 in London. Dutch cultural historians, confusing cause and effect, associate Cats' success with the 'typically Dutch-Calvinist' mentality. The poet's reception in England (and to a far greater extent in Germany) throws considerable doubt on this interpretation. History repeated itself – translations and editions continuing into the nineteenth century – with Vaenius, particularly his *Horatiana,* selections of love emblems and especially of their religious counterparts: numerous English emblematic devotional books in the style of Herman Hugo – e.g. Quarles' *Emblemes* (1635) – derive from examples in the Southern Netherlands.

For the English commentaries to his *Amorum emblemata* (1608), Otto Vaenius turned to Richard Verstegen, the Antwerp agent for the English Catholic emigrants. He thereupon dedicated the collection to the then most influencial patrons of English literature, William Earl of Pembroke and Philip Earl of Montgomery. This opportunist gesture from the Antwerp poet is symbolic of the Dutch emblem's place in English emblem literature. It is certainly fairly central to it, and though much has been charted, the whole map is still far from complete.

KAREL PORTEMAN
Translated by Peter King.

358 GODDELYCKE WENSCHEN

Infelix ego homo! quis me liberabit de corpore mortis hujus? Ad Rom. 7.

Fig. 9 – Woodcut by C. van Sichem from the second impression (1645) of the Dutch version of Herman Hugo's *Pia Desideria* (Pious Desires): the soul imprisoned in the body.

Useful access to current emblem research is available since 1986 in the journal *Emblematica* (AMS Press, New York).

The following concise reference list contains only a selection of mainly recent English contributions.

On the emblem in general: M. Praz, *Studies in Seventeenth Century Imagery* (Rome, 1964); P. Daly, *Literature in the Light of the Emblem* (Toronto, 1979); Ch. Moseley, *A Century of Emblems* (Aldershot, 1989); M. Bath, 'Recent Developments in Emblem Studies', *De Zeventiende Eeuw,* 1990, 6, pp. 91-96. For Alciato, on whose emblems an immense amount has been published, see W.S. Heckscher, *The Princeton Alciato Companion* (New York / London, 1989) and P. Daly's edition of *A. Alciatus: The Latin Emblems (I), Emblems in Translations (II)* (Toronto, 1985) (with numerous indexes and English translations).
Works in English on the emblem in the Netherlands are understandably less common. J. Landwehr, *Emblem and Fable Books Printed in the Low Countries 1542-1813* (Utrecht, 1988) is a bibliography to be used with caution. Useful for background knowledge: M.A. Schenkeveld, *Dutch Literature in the Age of Rembrandt. Themes and Ideas* (Amsterdam / Philadelphia, 1991) which includes *inter alia* notes on Cats, Roemer Visscher and De Brune. For the application of emblems in Dutch literary life: K. Porteman, 'Embellished with Emblems', in: A. Adams and A. Harper, *The Emblem in Renaissance and Baroque Europe. Tradition and Variety* (Leiden / New York, 1992), pp. 70-89. On Antwerp humanist emblem art: L. Voet, *The Plantin Press 1555-1589* (4 vols. Amsterdam, 1980-1982); K. Porteman, 'The Early Reception of Alciato in the Netherlands', *Emblematica,* 1989, 4, pp. 243-255 and 'The Earliest Reception of The Ars Emblematica in Dutch', in: B.F. Scholz, *The European Emblem* (Leiden / New York, 1990), pp. 34-53. A study of Otto Vaenius' *Emblemata Horatiana* in I. Gerards-Nelissen: *Simiolus,* 1971, 5, pp. 20-63. On the erotic emblem books: B. Becker-Cantarino, *Daniel Heinsius* (Boston, 1978), pp. 55-63; H. de la Fontaine Verwey, 'Notes on the Début of Daniel Heinsius as a Dutch Poet': *Quaerendo,* 1973, 3, pp. 291-308 and 'The Thronus Cupidinis': *Ibid.,* 1978, 8, pp. 29-44. On the twin genres of the Counter-reformation in the Southern-Netherlands: J.B. Knipping, *Heaven on Earth. Iconography of the Counter-Reformation* (Leiden / Nieuwkoop, 1974). A great deal of mainly bibliographical information on Jesuit emblem literature is available in G.R. Dimler's articles in *Archivum Historicum Societatis Jesu* (1976-79); see also his 'The *Imago Primi Saeculi;* Jesuit Emblems and the Secular Tradition': *Thought,* 1981, 56, pp. 25-46. On the Anglo-Dutch connection, see: M. Bath, 'Anglo-Dutch Relations in the Field of the Emblem', in: A. Adams, *Emblems in Glasgow* (Glasgow, 1992) pp. 25-46 and P. Daly, M. Silcox, *The Modern Critical Reception of The English Emblem* (München / London / New York / Paris, 1991). For Victorian emblem literature: K.H. Höltgen, *Aspects of the Emblem. Studies in the English Emblem Tradition and the European Context* (Kassel, 1986). *A short title catalogue of the emblem books and related works in the Stirling Maxwell Collection* was published by David Weston (Aldershot, 1988).

New Amsterdam on the Hudson

The Dutch Background of New York City

Imagine an island approximately the size of the Frisian island of Vlieland with 571 miles of roads, 102,522 business establishments, 105 banks, 243 hotels, 63 hospitals, 492 churches, 47,669 attorneys, and a population density of 27,000 per square mile. Incredible as this may seem, such an island actually exists. It is called Manhattan Island, at the mouth of the Hudson River in New York State, the central core of New York City; one of the financial, cultural, and intellectual leaders of the world.

As a direct descendant of New Amsterdam, the commercial centre of the Dutch West India Company in North America for most of the seventeenth century, New York City's Dutch background is still apparent in many ways and sets it apart from other American cities. One of these unique characteristics was lucidly expressed in an article about New York high society ('Old Money, New Needs', by Judith Miller in the *New York Times Magazine,* November 17, 1991): 'Perhaps because the Dutch ruled New York society until the early 19th century, the rigid, English-dominated class that led Philadelphia and Boston never created a comparable force in New York City. Indeed, as a great mercantile and financial power dependent on talented new people, New York has always offered relatively fluid access to the ranks of society.'

With the advantage of hindsight it is obvious why New York City has grown into the influential megalopolis that it is today. It meets the three basic requirements of successful real estate: location, location, and location. Manhattan not only offers a natural ice-free harbour midway along the coast of North America, but is also situated at the mouth of the Hudson and Mohawk river systems – for years the sole access to the interior of the continent below the Saint Lawrence River, the main artery of New France.

Despite these obvious advantages, the island was at first ignored by early explorers and traders. Hudson anchored along the shore of 'Manna-hata' upon his return from upriver in October of 1609. However, he was searching for a passage to the Orient and had little interest in the commercial potential of the island. Shortly after Hudson's explorations Dutch traders began to visit the area. In 1613 Adriaen Block's ship *Tijger* was accidentally burned while anchored at Manhattan. Block and his crew overcame the loss by building a replacement ship called *Onrust* – the beginning of the shipbuilding industry on Manhattan.

Activity increased in the area after the formation of the New Netherland Company in 1614. This trading monopoly was licensed by the States General of the United Provinces to regulate trade to this new region and prevent the violence that was growing as a result of increased competition for furs. Although Manhattan most likely served as a base of operations more than once during the trading season, it was the smaller island off the tip of Manhattan that probably attracted the most Dutch traders. As a central base of operations *Nooten Eiland* (today Governor's Island) was ideal because it had all the attributes of Manhattan and was small enough to secure against native attack.

When the Twelve Year Truce with Spain expired in 1621, the West India Company was chartered to carry on the war against Spain in the Atlantic theatre of operations. Modelled on the earlier East India Company, the *WIC* soon sent out expeditions to Africa, Brazil, and North America. New Netherland, which extended from the Connecticut River to Delaware Bay, was to become the Company's northernmost operation. The colony was expected to supply enough natural resources, especially furs, to sustain itself and to turn a profit for the Company.

In 1624, as soon as the Company had raised sufficient operating capital, it sent over some 30 families, mostly Walloons, to secure its holdings in New Netherland. Several families and men were located at the mouth of the Connecticut River, as well as on High Island (today Burlington Island) in the Delaware River. The remaining families were sent up to Fort Orange (present-day Albany), while eight men were left in the Manhattan area, probably on Governor's Island. The settlement strategy was to locate families at the remote trading posts on the three major river systems to form agricultural support communities. In the beginning, Governor's Island served as the central base of operations where the trading ships assembled before returning with cargo to the fatherland.

The following year, when large shipments of livestock arrived, Governor's Island proved to be too small to pasture the animals adequately. The problem was solved by transferring the livestock to Manhattan where there was abundant space. Although some twenty cows died from eating noxious weeds, Manhattan had become the primary pasture of New Netherland. Nevertheless, Manhattan still was not attracting settlers. In fact, according to the instructions for Willem Verhulst, director of New Netherland from 1625 to 1626, he was to strengthen his southern settlement the most (Fort Wilhelmus on High Island in the Delaware) and consider making this location the centre of the colony. Interest in the Delaware probably stemmed from a misconception that this region enjoyed a climate similar to Florida's. Concern over maintaining an ice-free harbour was paramount. However, it soon became apparent that the Delaware could and did freeze over, while Manhattan's harbour remained free of ice.

In any case, it was an event far to the north that determined the suitability of Manhattan as the centre of the colony. In the Spring of 1626 the Mahican Indians, who lived near Fort Orange, persuaded Daniel van Krieckenbeeck, the Dutch commander, to support them in an attack on their arch-enemies, the Mohawk Indians, who lived farther to the west. A few miles from the

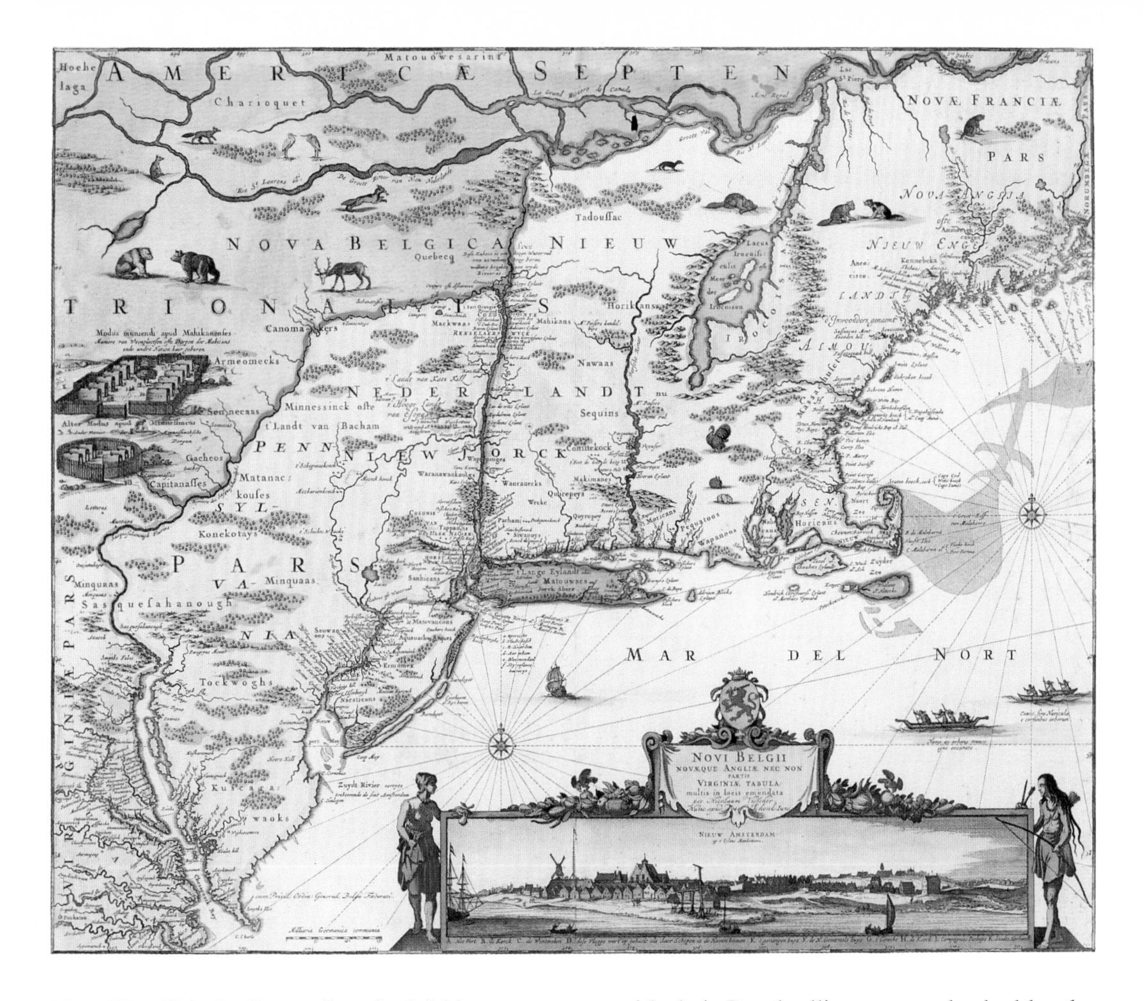

Map of New Netherland by Nicolaas Jansz. Visscher (c.1690) (New York State Library).

fort the Mahican war party with their Dutch allies were ambushed by the Mohawks and soundly defeated. When Verhulst's replacement, Peter Minuit, arrived in the colony in May he immediately sailed to Fort Orange to assess the situation. Minuit decided that matters had become too dangerous to maintain families in remote settlements. His solution was to purchase Manhattan Island, upon which he planned to consolidate all the families from Fort Orange, the Connecticut, and Delaware. Although trading personnel remained at the remote posts, the Mohawks were apparently satisfied by the withdrawal of the families and caused the Dutch no further trouble.

Soon after the purchase of Manhattan Island work began on Fort Amsterdam, which was to protect the inhabitants of the new settlement of New Amsterdam. In the Fall of 1626 the ship *Arms of Amsterdam* returned from New Netherland with news from the North American colony. Peter Schagen sent a report of the ship's arrival to the directors with a brief account of the situation in New Netherland. This letter, which is among the West India Company papers in Royal Archives in the Hague, is as close as one can come to a birth certificate for New York City. It reads as follows:

High and Mighty Lords,
Yesterday the ship the *Arms of Amsterdam* arrived here. It sailed from New Netherland out of the River Mauritius on the 23d of September. They report that our people are in good spirit and live in peace. The women also have borne some children there. They have purchased the Island Manhattes from the Indians for the value of 60 guilders. It is 11,000 *morgens* in size (about 22 acres). They had all their grain sown by the middle of May, and reaped by the middle of August. They sent samples of these summer grains: wheat, rye, barley, oats, buckwheat, canary seed, beans and flax. The cargo of the aforesaid ship is:
7246 Beaver skins;
178½ Otter skins;
675 Otter skins;
48 Mink skins;
36 Lynx skins;
33 Minks;
34 Weasel skins;
Many oak timbers and nut wood.

Herewith, High and Mighty Lords, be commended to the mercy of the Almighty,

Your High and Mightinesses' obedient,
P. Schagen

It is from this letter that the famous and oft-quoted purchase price of $24.00 comes. This figure, of course, reflects the rate of exchange between the guilder and the dollar at the time the letter was first discovered in the late nineteenth century. It corresponds in no way with the actual value of 60 guilders worth of merchandise in the early seventeenth century.

During the early years of the colony New Amsterdam grew slowly. Initially the West India Company directed most of its attention to Africa, the Caribbean, and especially Brazil. Only a small amount of the Company's financial and human resources was diverted to New Netherland. Under the administrations of Minuit, Krol, Van Twiller, and Kieft, New Amsterdam spread from a cluster of houses near the fort northward to approximately present-day Wall Street. As the centre of the colony it served as the entrepôt for commercial activity from Fort Orange on the upper Hudson to Delaware Bay. Ships transferred cargoes of fur and tobacco to the Company warehouse where they were stored until loaded aboard ships bound for the fatherland.

Sailors from various countries, taking shore leave in New Amsterdam, made tavernkeeping one of the most lucrative professions. Governor Kieft remarked once to a visiting Jesuit priest that eighteen languages could be heard in the streets of his city. It has been estimated that approximately one half of the resident population of New Netherland came from places other than the Netherlands. Many were refugees from the Thirty Years' War in Germany, wars between Denmark and Sweden, and the religious wars in France. Thus multi-ethnicity was and has been over the years a characteristic of the area covered by the Dutch colony.

View of New Amsterdam by Jan Vingboons (c.1665) (The Hague, Rijksarchief).

New Amsterdam was a lively seaport town. In addition to the many seamen from all parts of the globe, Indians from the various tribes of Long Island, Westchester, and New Jersey, and Africans, both free and slave, frequented its streets. During the period of Dutch administration, the community at the tip of Manhattan Island was witness to many exciting events. Although Wouter van Twiller's tenure as director of the colony is often characterized as one of stagnation and torpor (a paucity of documentary sources for his administration is partly responsible for this assessment), several dramatic events occurred that must have stirred the populace.

In April of 1633 an English ship, the *William,* put into New Amsterdam's harbour. Its skipper was Jacob Eelckens, who had served with Dutch trading cartels in the Hudson River before the formation of the *WIC*. His experience in navigating the river and familiarity with native customs and languages in the Hudson Valley made him a distinct threat to Van Twiller when he requested permission to trade at Fort Orange. The *WIC* could not admit competition from foreign powers and still remain a monopoly. When denied access to the Dutch fur trade, Eelckens proclaimed that the land in any case belonged to the English king. After some weeks in harbour, the *William* managed to slip free and proceed up the river. Van Twiller eventually sent several ships in pursuit. They forced Eelckens to return to New Amsterdam where he refused to comply with Van Twiller's demand to surrender his cargo of furs. Matters returned to normal when Eelckens departed for London.

The English would continue to threaten New Netherland, not only because of its proximity to New England and Virginia but also because the Dutch controlled the most important fur trading routes south of New France. A few years after the episode with Eelckens, the English sent a force from Point Comfort, Virginia to seize the Dutch fort and trading post on the Delaware River. Since Fort Nassau (present-day Gloucester, NJ) was only garrisoned during the trading season (May-September) the English were able to occupy it without bloodshed. As soon as Van Twiller heard of this

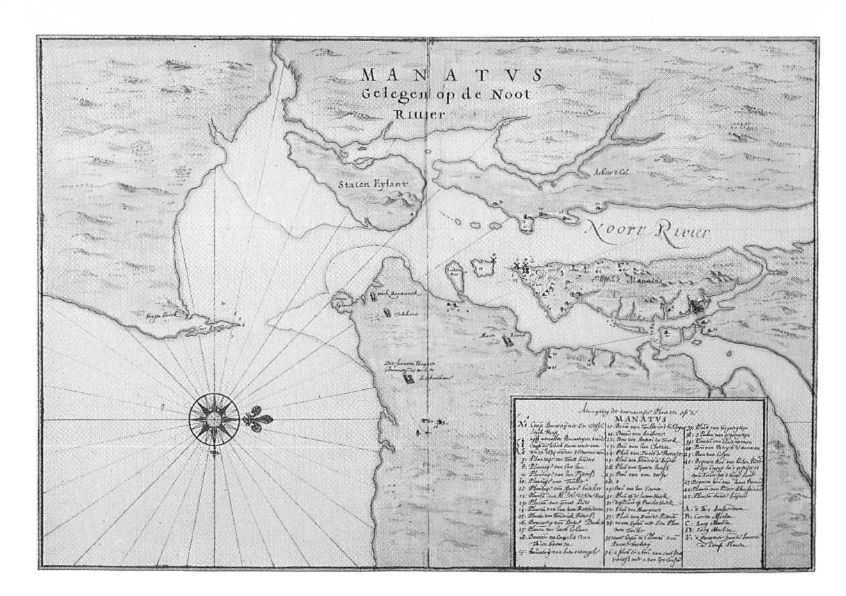

Manatus Map by Jan Vingboons (c.1639) (Library of Congress).

intrusion into the South River region of New Netherland, he sent a military force by sea to recover the fort. The Dutch were aware that whoever controlled the Delaware could also control the fur trade behind Fort Orange. The English soldiers surrendered without incident and were brought to New Amsterdam. They were eventually brought back to Virginia by David Pietersz. de Vries who was sailing to the Chesapeake on business. Once again an English incursion into Dutch territory had demonstrated to the people of New Amsterdam the tenuous nature of their settlement on Manhattan Island.

The civil war in England during the 1640s reduced the threat from this external force; however, it was soon replaced by disruption from an internal force when Van Twiller's successor as director of the colony, Willem Kieft, became involved in a devastating Indian war. These hostilities, which laid waste Dutch settlements in New Jersey and on Staten Island, and gave rise to numerous brutalities against the Indians, introduced New Amsterdam to a wartime situation replete with refugees and casualties.

Kieft's misadventures with the native population led to his removal as director of the colony in 1647. His replacement was Petrus Stuyvesant, newly married to Judith Bayard, daughter of the Walloon minister in Breda, and newly fitted with a wooden leg. As governor of Curaçao, Stuyvesant had lost his right leg in an assault on the Spanish held island of Saint Martin. Stuyvesant had been selected for the position of director-general of New Netherland as much for his administrative abilities as for his reputation as an aggressive military commander.

Stuyvesant arrived before New Amsterdam on May 11, 1647 in grand style. He sailed into the harbour accompanied by a ship that he had captured from the Spaniards off the coast of Curaçao. His administration lasted seventeen years; a period of time during which New Netherland began to attract more settlers and develop into a busy commercial centre with trade connections throughout the Caribbean and along the coast of North America. During Stuyvesant's tenure as director-general New Amsterdam was granted the rights and privileges of a municipality and experienced near hysteria from rumours of invasion.

When the English Civil War (1642-1648) was resolved in favour of the Parliamentarians, Cromwell attempted to improve England's commercial interests around the world by limiting the Netherlands's ability to complete. The so-called Navigation Act, which allowed only English ships or ships of the country of origin to carry goods to England, led to the first Anglo-Dutch War (1652-1654). The war in Europe soon threatened to spill over to New Netherland. In the Spring of 1653 a delegation from New England visited Stuyvesant in New Amsterdam with accusations that he had incited Indians to attack settlements in Connecticut. The New Englanders left abruptly for a conference in Boston when the charges were denied, leaving the impression that military action would follow. Stuyvesant immediately began strengthening defenses throughout the colony. It is at this time that he initiated the building of the defensive barrier along the northern edge of New Amsterdam, which is remembered to this day as Wall Street. In Boston, attempts to form a united New England force to attack New Netherland failed, deflating the possibility of invasion. When word reached the city of peace between England and the Netherlands in 1654, the news was celebrated with a huge bonfire and a day of prayer and thanksgiving.

Portrait of Peter Stuyvesant, attributed to Henri Couturier (New York Historical Society).

Once again the resolution of external problems was followed by a series of internal problems. In 1638, during Kieft's administration, the crown of Sweden sanctioned the planting of an colony in the Delaware, on land claimed by the WIC (present-day Wilmington, Delaware). Although dissatisfied with the situation the Dutch managed to coexist with little friction. However, when the Swedes captured the Dutch stronghold and trading post of Fort Casimir on Trinity Sunday of 1654 plans were laid for the elimination of New Sweden. In the summer of 1655, after Stuyvesant returned from a trading mission to the Caribbean, he began to assemble a force for the Swedish expedition.

On Sunday, 5 September, after church service, the invasion force of seven ships carrying over 300 soldiers left New Amsterdam. New Sweden's defenses were no match for Stuyvesant. He quickly brought the Swedish colony under Dutch control; however, operations on the Delaware were disturbed when news reached the Dutch encampment that Manhattan and the outlying settlements in New Jersey and on Staten Island had been attacked by a large force of Indians. Ostensibly the Indians were searching for a man who had shot an Indian woman for stealing peaches in his garden. However, some officials in New Amsterdam suggested that the Swedes were behind it. Although little damage was done on Manhattan Island, the settlements in New Jersey and on Staten Island were laid waste; there were many casualties and many hostages in Indian hands. Once again New Amsterdam was full of refugees and the smoke of burning farms hung in the air.

Despite these problems with the Indians, the Dutch colony began to grow rapidly. The new influx of settlers and increased commercial activity was propelled by the loss of Dutch Brazil in January of 1654. Once Brazil ceased to consume most of the Company's resources, more attention was devoted to strengthening the colony in North America. However, as New Amsterdam was growing into a major commercial centre between the English colonies of New England and Virginia, it attracted the attention of the newly restored Charles II, king of England, and his brother James, duke of York and Albany. Both were eager to enrich English commercial operations at the expense of the Dutch.

In 1664 Charles granted his brother James extensive territories in North America, which included the Dutch colony of New Netherland. In September of the same year, without a declaration of war, a naval force under the command of Richard Nicolls demanded the surrender of New Netherland. Fort Amsterdam and Fort Orange surrendered without resistance; however, Fort New Amstel on the Delaware (formerly Fort Casimir), belonging to the city of Amsterdam, refused to surrender and had to be taken by storm. The easy capture of the colony was replicated in 1673 when a Dutch fleet retook the colony. It remained in Dutch hands until the end of the third Anglo-Dutch war when it was returned to England as part of the peace settlement.

By the time New Amsterdam became New York, the city already had a rich and exciting past. A period when the attributes of its namesake in the Netherlands were steadily being transferred to the New World. Amsterdam, the financial, cultural, and intellectual leader of Northern Europe in the seventeenth century, and haven for refugees displaced by European wars, had laid the foundation for the ascendancy of New York City as financial, cultural, and intellectual capital of the world, and primary port of entry for millions of European immigrants.

CHARLES GEHRING

SOURCES:

GEHRING, CHARLES T., *New Netherland Documents,* (Council Minutes 1651-1656), vols. 5 and 6, Syracuse, 1983 and 1993.

PHELPS STOKES, I.N., *The Iconography of Manhattan Island, 1498-1909,* 6 vols. New York, 1915-1928.

VRIES, DAVID PIETERSZ. DE, *Korte historiael ende journaels aenteyckeninge van verscheyden voyagiens in de vier deelen des wereldts-ronde, als Europa, Africa, Asia, ende Americka gedaen,* Linschoten-Vereeniging, volume 3, 's-Gravenhage, 1911.

Warmth in Cold Stone

The Architectural Paintings of Pieter Saenredam

If you close your eyes in the Dutch Painting gallery of a great museum and allow your built-in thermometer to guide you, the warmest glow in the room will lead you to Rembrandt. Rembrandt used the reddest, warmest palette of any Dutch painter. His subjects are fuller of flesh and blood and emotion. His large figures emanate body heat that you can feel across the room. Some like it hot.

And some like it cold. Walk to the coolest spot and you will find your way to the distinctive realm of Pieter Saenredam (1597-1665). When you open your eyes, the first thing you see will be the empty interior of a stripped and whitewashed Gothic church. Peering through the arches and down the aisles, you will discover diminutive figures, bundled up in overcoats against the chill, doing not much of anything. You will be impressed by the artist's abilities in perspective (the coldest, most calculating skill in art), and captivated by the transparent design of his composition, the restraint of his colouring. If your reaction is typical, Saenredam's minimalism will remind you of Dutch Calvinism, a religion of renunciation. You will see him as an arch-realist who was nonetheless a poet, an artist who transferred visual facts onto panel so precisely and with such dedication that his work acquires an unintended and therefore all the more touching beauty. If this was your image of Saenredam, you would be in good company, the company of thinkers like Roland Barthes and Umberto Eco. Eco associates Saenredam's work with the concept of 'materialistic ecstasy'. 'Saenredam's cathedrals', he has written, 'speak to us of the dumbfounding silence of a metallic and material light, pure appearance that celebrates itself'. A beautiful thought. But is it true?

If you were conducting your experiment in the Louvre, the Saenredam before you would be an interior from 1630 of the *St. Bavokerk* or Great Church in Haarlem. Built in the late fourteenth century as an overgrown parish church, the *St. Bavokerk* became a cathedral when Haarlem was made a bishopric in 1561. This status was lost in 1578, when the town government fell to the Reformed party. Since then, it has been run by a church council which sees to it that only Reformed services are conducted, alongside other appropriate activities.

Pieter Saenredam,
View across the choir of the St. Bavokerk, Haarlem, from north to south, with a fictive bishop's tomb.
1630. Panel, 41 x 37.5 cm.
Musée du Louvre, Paris.

The draughtsman took his stance against the northeast pier of the crossing of nave and transept. A bleak light streams through the southern windows opposite, casting dim shadows in the vaulting and across the floor of the nave. From right to left, step by step, the picture space grows shallower. The view through the first arch on the right pierces the interior to the street wall of the Brewers' Chapel. There, even after the Reformation, the mighty brewers' guild retained an upstairs office. Two men are looking at something on the wall. An everyday scene, perhaps. In the middle arch our gaze is stopped at the outer wall of the side aisle, to which a small organ is attached. A group of men dressed in medieval costume stands in conclave, attended exotically (was this too everyday?) by a little boy with a turban and sword.

That brings us to the leftmost arch, which is closed at the nave itself by a wall adorned by a plaque and coat of arms, in front of which is the kneeling statue of a bishop. Here Saenredam uses his powers of persuasion to lend verisimilitude to a view that never existed. No such statue ever stood in the *St. Bavokerk,* no such inscribed plaque. The arch was never closed off by a wall. Yet, so convincing is Saenredam's manner that even specialists have been fooled. In 1910, the Utrecht archivist Samuel Muller Fz., in his absolute belief in Saenredam's realism, went so far as to affirm that if Saenredam painted a wall and statue, he for one was prepared to believe they were there

Pieter Saenredam, *Crossing and nave of the St. Odulphuskerk, Assendelft, from the right side of the choir.* 1649. Panel, 50 x 76 cm. Rijksmuseum, Amsterdam (on loan from the city of Amsterdam).

even in the absence of other evidence. (But there *is* other evidence – all of it negative). As recently as 1976, the distinguished American art historian Walter Liedtke, unable to conceive of a positive connection between Saenredam and Catholicism, wrote that the Latin inscription – which unequivocally praises the 'true (Catholic) doctrine' of the bishop – was anti-clerical.

Once having been apprised of these facts, we may be inclined to tell ourselves that there was something fishy all along about the left part of the painting. The statue looks as though it might have been invented by Saenredam, after all. It is also placed rather strangely, isn't it? The plaque clearly refers to the bishop, and seems to hang directly above it, even being cut into by the mitre. But if we reconstruct the space, we see an altogether different situation. The front of the statue base is aligned not with the blind arch and not even with the column abutting it, but with the base of the middle column. The monument is located in the middle of the nave, at a considerable distance – and at a diagonal – from its inscription.

That was an early painting. By the next time he painted a bishop's statue, sixteen years later, Saenredam was more accomplished at the seamless integration of what was there and what was not. His *Choir of the St. Janskerk, 's-Hertogenbosch* in the National Gallery of Art in Washington contains no inconsistencies between the second and third dimensions. It breathes the air of unimpeached authority that only the testimony of a professional observer

Pieter Saenredam, *Choir of the St. Janskerk, 's-Hertogenbosch.* 1646. Panel, 128.8 x 87 cm. National Gallery of Art, Washington, DC (Samuel H. Kress Collection).

can convey. One has to be familiar with Dutch history to know that in 1646 the *St. Janskerk,* which Saenredam shows with its altar set for the mass, had long been Protestantized. And one has to be a specialist in Dutch painting to know that the *Adoration of the shepherds* that serves as altarpiece is a Saenredam concoction based on a much smaller painting by Abraham Bloemaert (1564-1651), with different figures and from another church.

Before you reverse your first impression altogether, and decide that Saenredam was a Jesuit sophist in disguise, let us admit that the picture of the artist as a close observer and a Calvinist is not altogether erroneous. He *was* more of a Calvinist than a Catholic, and his depictions of buildings *are* more reliable than unreliable. Our aim in jolting you with the above exam-

Pieter Saenredam, *The old Town Hall of Amsterdam.* 1657. Panel, 64.5 x 83 cm. Rijksmuseum, Amsterdam (on loan from the city of Amsterdam).

ples was to make it clear that neither of those two principles – Calvinism and true-to-life representation – was a guiding light to Saenredam the painter. Nor were any of the other parts of his artistic personality that have sometimes been taken for the whole: devotion to architecture, fascination with painted space, urge to be alone and not bothered by people and their demands.

That last attribute is perhaps the most appealing. Which of us does not sometimes dream of shutting ourself off from others, following our own creative instincts to the limit, and winning immortality in the process? Something about Saenredam's art gives us the feeling that this is what he did. The wish has been projected onto him by some of his admirers, including, we suspect, Umberto Eco, with his 'materialistic ecstasy'.

Cruel as it may be to dispel that captivating image, our scholarly conscience allows us no alternative. Our research has revealed a Pieter Saenredam who was not only a man of flesh and blood but also a social being like the rest of us. His art was not a hobby, a private vision, or a bid for the attention of posterity over the heads of his contemporaries. It was an occupation that meshed with his apparently very satisfying life as a burgher and a professional.

Saenredam was born for a life in art. His father Jan Saenredam was one of the foremost engravers of Holland in an age when engraving was considered a high-ranking artistic technique, and when the engravers of the

Pieter Saenredam, *Interior of the Nieuwe Kerk, Haarlem, from west to east.* 1652. Panel, 65.5 x 93 cm. Frans Hals Museum, Haarlem.

Netherlands were acknowledged to be the best in the world. Jan was a star pupil of the legendary Haarlem artist Hendrick Goltzius (1558-1617), and when Goltzius gave up the engraving burin for the painter's brush in 1600 Jan found himself at the very top of his profession. Tragically, he lived for only another seven years before succumbing at the age of 42 to a lung disease.

Pieter, an only child of nine at the time, could not well have known how highly his father was regarded in Haarlem, Amsterdam and all the farflung art centers of Europe where the publishers of those cities sold his prints. What would have made more of an impression on him is how important he was in the village where they lived, Assendelft. Jan was an elder of the church council and the cousin and adopted son of the sheriff, a mighty official answerable only to the lords of Assendelft in their castle. The sheriff, Pieter Jansz. de Jonge, was a leading figure in a clan of officeholders all over the *Zaanstreek* – the soggy countryside north of Haarlem, with its rich grazing land and shipyards. From the mid-sixteenth century on, they filled not only high village office throughout the area, but also occupied administrative and engineering positions for the Water Board and preached to the Reformed communities of the region.

After his father's death, Pieter was taken by his mother to Haarlem, where he was apprenticed to a painter and began working his way up to the status of a master artist. Yet his descent from those petty lords of the *Kennemer-*

Pieter Saenredam, *The Mariakerk and the Mariaplaats, Utrecht, with a view of the Domtoren and the Buurkerk.* 1662. Panel, 110.5 x 139 cm. Museum Boymans-van Beuningen, Rotterdam.

land muck stood him in good stead all his life. Through marriages with Haarlem patrician families, Saenredam's relatives made their way into the burgomastership of the city where he lived. It was to these connections that he owed his own election to the deanship of the Haarlem painters' guild, a post which he filled energetically and activistically, and his entrée into the circles of the wealthy Haarlem regents in whose collections we encounter the first mention of several of his paintings of Haarlem churches.

We do not subscribe to a deterministic view of the formation of individuals or society. Yet we cannot help observing how well Pieter Saenredam's life fitted the mould pre-shaped by his family background. This painter of churches and town halls was the son of an artist and the cousin of men who ran town halls and churches, and spoke from their pulpits. He embraced this inheritance, let it fill his life with people and their needs, and in turn filled it with meaning in his art.

No more eloquent demonstration of the interweaving of art and social life can be imagined than Saenredam's interior of the church of Assendelft, now in the Rijksmuseum. It depicts a building for which the artist's father and uncle were responsible during their lifetimes, and in which his cousins preached. The lords of Assendelft, to whom they answered (and for whose chapel his father painted a panel), are present in the painting in the stone of their family tomb on the right and the wood of their bench of honour on the left. Between those two markers, in the floor, is a slab engraved 'Here lie the remains of Jan Saenredam, celebrated engraver, Pieter de Jonge, sheriff of Assendelft for 44 years, his son Gerrit de Jonge, doctor of jurisprudence and attorney'.

Dear Umberto Eco, is Saenredam's loving depiction of this stone and wood and slate a testimony to materialism, to appearance celebrating itself? We beg to differ. Saenredam's artistry, inherited from his father, was dedicated to his father's memory and to the interests of the people in his life. Those interests *were* sometimes material. Saenredam painted the town hall of Amsterdam for the burgomasters who met there; the New Church in Haarlem for regents who served on its council; the *Mariakerk* in Utrecht for families who derived benefices from its ancient chapter. In doing so, he obviously took pleasure in evoking light and space and surface and in his own skill in the mechanics of representation. But his art, like the art of any traditional society, celebrated not material appearances but human interests. And the longer you look at it, the warmer it gets.

GARY SCHWARTZ AND MARTEN JAN BOK

FURTHER READING

SCHWARTZ, GARY & BOK, MARTEN JAN, *Pieter Saenredam. The Painter and His Time,* London, 1990.

An Artist in Remembering

The Work of A.F.Th. van der Heijden

In 1977 a certain Patrizio Canaponi made his literary debut with a collection of short stories, *A Gondola in the Herengracht* (Een gondel in de Herengracht). The content of the stories and the press releases concerning the author suggested that the book was a thinly disguised autobiography of an Italian turned Dutchman. It later appeared that this had all been a hoax. Behind the name Canaponi had been concealed a young man by the name of A.F.Th. van der Heijden, born in 1951 in the village of Geldrop in Brabant. Why this masquerade? With his predilection for an extravagant style, the budding writer Van der Heijden must have felt more at home in the land of opera decors and baroque facades than in down-to-earth Holland.

After publishing the short novel *The Revolving Door* (De draaideur) in 1979 Canaponi fell silent for four years. When he reappeared he had removed his mask. Canaponi was dead, Van der Heijden had taken up the pen himself. And with the change of name a totally different writer emerged. While an affected style had been the hallmark of Canaponi's work, Van der Heijden now manifested himself as an author who combined a robust sense of style and structure with a storyteller's talent. In the four years of comparative silence he had written the first volumes of a sequence of novels entitled *Toothless Time* (De tandeloze tijd).

Although *Toothless Time* has not yet been completed (four out of the planned six novels have so far appeared) we already have before us a remarkable amalgam of *Bildungsroman,* chronicle of our times, and stream of consciousness. Van der Heijden surveys several decades of life in the Netherlands from the perspective of the life of his hero, Albert Egberts, born in 1950. The years of reconstruction after the Second World War, the rise of the welfare state, the social and political upheavals of the sixties, and the growing disillusionment of the seventies all go to form the backdrop against which Albert Egberts's story is told. But Egberts does not occupy centre stage in all the novels. In *The Cocks' Advocate* (Advocaat van de hanen), part four in the sequence, the alcoholic lawyer Quispel plays the leading role, with Egberts appearing only towards the end of the book, and then as Quispel's rival in love.

In the prologue, *The Battle of the Blue Bridge* (De slag om de Blauwbrug), the point from which the past was viewed was 30 April 1980, the date of Queen Beatrix's investiture in Amsterdam. For Albert Egberts, a car thief addicted to heroin, the day is of special significance. It is his thirtieth birthday, the age at which one leaves one's youth behind forever. Yet he feels that he has not yet achieved anything. He is an outsider who observes life from the sidelines and has absolutely no sense of involvement in the demonstrations against the housing shortage which take place on the day of the investiture.

Albert's conviction that he is incapable of action has its roots in his inclination to escape into his memories. He has developed a mental technique whereby he creates the illusion of extending his life by a succession of flashes of memory. He replaces what he calls 'living in length', the normal chronological forward movement of life, by 'living in breadth', a form of living that cuts through the boundaries of time and space, and pays no heed to the straitjacket of the calendar.

Memories not only offer a refuge to which one can flee when day-to-day reality becomes too oppressive, they are also a rich source of material for the imagination. In this respect Van der Heijden shares his character's interest. But a writer has to arrange the memories in such a way that they acquire meaning. So there is one important difference between Van der Heijden and Egberts. While the first has to work hard to achieve his goal, for the second everything remains merely imaginary. Does not Albert Egberts say that his thoughts will never be committed to paper? His contempt for concrete results is doubtless the outcome of his preference for 'living in breadth'.

Now that he derives a far more substantial satisfaction from extending his life by means of a chain of memories Albert places relatively little value on material gain, even in the shape of a work of art. Frittering away his time in idleness, he thinks: 'June had about forty days and each one of those forty days was a repetition of the one before. Even the fact that the first twenty grew longer and the second twenty shrank passed unnoticed. This month of June was in its entirety "one longest day".

Apart from looking deep into that day I really did nothing. Instead of absorbing rapid impressions my senses were open like a camera on that one perfect day for forty days, and the result, I now see, is astonishing. The shadows in the garden have a sharper outline than they have ever had in reality. In the unusually fierce sunshine the grass of the flowerbeds shines like sugar. Nothing moves – not a leaf, nothing. Even those very small white butterflies, otherwise miracles of mobility, hang motionless like blossoms between the bushes. The conifers look like massive stone cones. On the line three or four clothes pegs immortalized … A perfect daguerreotype.' What is striking about this passage is how aestheticistic and hostile to reality Albert's observations and perceptions are. They characterize him as the future junkie seeking oblivion.

After the publication of the prologue, *The Battle of the Blue Bridge,* and the first novel in the cycle, *Parents Falling* (Vallende ouders) at the end of 1983, the second *The Warning Triangle* (De gevarendriehoek) appeared in mid-1985. In *Parents Falling* we follow the hero in his search for the lost days of his youth.

Albert Egberts moves deeper and deeper into his past until he reaches the place where he lived from his third to his sixth year. At that point his memories begin to turn once more towards the present. Although the third volume, announced under the title *Snowy Night in September* (Sneeuwnacht in september), has not yet been published we may assume that it will take us back to the point of departure: the hero's addiction to heroin and how that came about.

After publication of *The Warning Triangle* it looked as if Van der Heijden had shelved the *magnum opus* for a time. In 1986 *The Sandwich* (De sandwich) appeared, a short novella commemorating two deceased friends, and in 1988 *A Day of Life* (Het leven uit een dag), a fantasy about a world in which people only live for twenty-four hours. Both were interludes. What links these two books with the rest of Van der Heijden's work is their readability and their contemplative nature. In *The Sandwich* the dual *in memoriam* is an introduction to the notion that death is the real artist, because by rounding something off, he gives it meaning. Moreover death guarantees a second life, that of the work of art.

In *A Day of Life* everything in human existence is unique and unrepeatable, just as in a book. However, what presents itself in fiction as a one-off event is the concentrate of a collection of similar events, facts and experiences. Within the confines of the story all these singularities acquire a symbolic weight. One of the characters acts as a mouthpiece for this notion: 'When something unique occurs, there is no material for comparison. So our response to what we see is often an image, a metaphor.'

With the advantage of hindsight we may say that *The Sandwich* and *A Day of Life* were a run-up to *The Cocks' Advocate,* which came out at the end of 1990 as the fourth (!) volume of *Toothless Time.* Although in this novel Albert Egberts has been pushed into the background, his role is more that of a writer than in the earlier books. In order to underline this, Van der Heijden has provided a contrasting character, Ernst Quispel. Quispel is a young, successful lawyer, acting on behalf of a group of squatters who are nicknamed 'cocks' on account of their punk hair style. Quispel's social commitment is a pretence, as becomes painfully clear when one of the squatters is found dead in a prison cell. The 'cocks' advocate' is then conspicuously absent, being on one of his drunken binges.

Quispel's alcoholism, an echo of Albert Egberts's drug addiction, is a kind of artistry in caricature. The lawyer believes that he must give shape to the euphoric impulses that seize him every few months by going on a lengthy pub-crawl. In his memory he has arranged his alcoholic excesses like a gallery of works of art. This is of course self-deception, for Quispel's oeuvre is dissipated as rapidly as the vodka he consumes in large quantities.

Even when Quispel does put pen to paper, he is incapable of producing anything lasting. He gets no further than writing replies to advertisements in the personal column in an attempt to realize his erotic fantasies. Writing is for him a 'slow masturbation, but with a pen in the right hand'. The aphorism is not restricted to Quispel alone. Since as a caricature of the artist he is a reflection of Albert Egberts, and so by extension of Van der Heijden himself, the devil's advocate indirectly criticizes artistic creativity in general, embracing the Freudian view of art as a form of sublimated sexuality, and the artist as an impotent lover seeking compensation. The theme of impotence recurs again and again in *Toothless Time.* What is the illusory 'living in breadth' if not a flight from reality?

Quispel's phantoms have become a reality from which he can no longer escape. The cocks he encountered as an illusion in the prologue have now assumed the form of squatters who remind him of his betrayal: just as Peter denied his Lord to save his skin, so does the lawyer Quispel drop his imprisoned client for fear of loss of face and reputation. *The Cocks' Advocate* has much in common with Malcolm Lowry's *Under the Volcano;* there too life is portrayed as an intoxication that has expanded to utterly insane proportions. Firmin's brother Hugh remarks that if civilization ever sobered up for a couple of days, on the third day it would be dead of remorse; a statement that would serve Quispel equally well.

To his shame Quispel is forced to admit that reality does not always live up to the demands made by our aesthetics. Reality and his ideas sometimes collide so violently that even his drink-sodden mind is scarred. The origins of his love for his wife Zwanet lay in his desire to compensate for an injustice he had done her. When she is raped and comes to him to seek help, he suspects her of a subtle form of pretence: of wanting to bind him to her by arousing his sympathy and lust. 'The trouble was that real feelings – pain, fear of death, humiliation – were often expressed in such a way that they lost their credibility or at least became deceptive, because the signs of emotion seemed to be laid on too thick, and hence became theatrical. Or because those signs were distorted, and then seemed to express something entirely different; pleasure instead of pain or, in the case of extreme sexual excitement, pain instead of pleasure.'

Because things are not what they seem, the world begins to look like a stage. Reality and theatre change places, become so completely intermingled that the onlooker, in this case Ernst Quispel, is incapable of determining what is genuine and what is feigned. His failure to establish the right relationship to the mingling of style and genre which leads to the confusion of semblance and reality is one of the main reasons for Quispel's addiction to alcohol.

This ambiguity between the real and the theatrical is one of the paradoxes that twines itself around the cocks' advocate like ivy round an oak tree. He himself is acutely aware of it in his name which in Dutch can mean the wagging of a dog's tail, but also the lash of a whip. Alcoholism is not merely the means of deadening physical pain, pain is the necessary condition, the fuel to ignite happiness. Yet, oddly enough, this happiness gives rise to a sense of emptiness; there is literally no end to Ernst's happiness, and he is left with an insatiable appetite that manifests itself in excessive womanizing. Quispel is the Don Juan of whom a good judge of human character once said that he was the most sterile and thus the most impotent of all lovers. 'The more women he fucked, the chaster he felt.'

Quispel's happiness is so all-embracing and stifling, even, that he is forced to acknowledge that his pact with the demon drink has landed him beyond the borders of reality. An excess of euphoria is unnatural, 'He suddenly knew what made happiness so poignant, and so unbearable. Death. The impossibility of death. The absence of the idea of death.' The rose-tinted delirium into which Quispel drinks himself is just as dull as the hell of an eternal life in which everything repeats itself, or as a world in which

Dionysian heights and tragic depths are absent. Quispel sees himself as the artist of total intoxication, thereby forgetting that nobody can be an artist without knowledge of death. Van der Heijden himself is fully aware of this, as is clearly demonstrated by the novels *The Sandwich* and *A Day of Life* which appeared as interludes to *Toothless Time*.

Initially it seemed that Van der Heijden had chosen 30 April 1980, the day on which the prologue to *Toothless Time* begins, as the date when this review of the past would end. But in *The Cocks' Advocate* we find ourselves midway through the eighties, and Van der Heijden has let it be known that he intends to continue looking at the world through the eyes of his alter ego Albert Egberts until the year 2000. A saga dealing with time and memory that takes an advance on the future is surely unparalleled in literature.

JAAP GOEDEGEBUURE
Translated by Elizabeth Mollison.

A.F.Th. van der Heijden (1951-) (Photo by Wenda Hasselaar).

Extract from *Parents Falling*

by A.F.Th. van der Heijden

Living in breadth ... After having lived almost all that time in Nijmegen 'in length', I realized once more what it meant.

Once more I could picture my accumulated memories as a mountain that was growing bigger at its base: a mountain worn away by erosion. When I closed my eyes, it rose up before me ... The peak, as the oldest part, as the *beginning* of the mountain, was the most worn away.

My life had taken that course: from the peak down into the valley, constantly gathering more moss and rolling stones, absorbing more and more ... Memory was how I could try to find the way back.

The peak was wrapped in clouds, mist and darkness. A little further down a perpetual ice age prevailed: memory could find no footing there. Lower down, rocks sticking through the ice provided some purchase. But rocks were rocks: impassive, silent as gravestones. God knows what they covered. Not a plant did my memory find there, not a blade of grass, nothing that lived or moved ...

Still further down the slope at the tip of an enormous tongue the ice was beginning to melt. Here memories started to flow. They formed a stream which quickly reached the coarse sporadic vegetation.

On its descent the water passed the tree-line, alpine meadows, cows, mountain huts, blossom ... The streams swelled and everything they encountered on their way was more and more familiar to me, nauseatingly so.

While I slumped further down in my chair, the sun on my head, my memory had advanced so far up the mountain that it could see the roofs of the houses like red spots far below in the valley. Frighteningly clear.

There lay the ever expanding city, a broad river running right through its heart. My deepest point. That was where I belonged. There I knew everything inside out. Every house (every interior a world in itself, with sideboards, family portraits, brass vases with peacock feathers in them etcetera), all the inhabitants and their feuds and squabbles. It was where I had just come from. It was all very complex there, complex yet trivial.

But look, here is something really interesting ... An insignificant scrubby plant breaking through a crust of ice ... dry moss ... This wasteland interested me *because* I had had to climb for it.

There was no point in going further: higher up there were only bare rock and snow crusts, covering everything for all eternity.

And there above the tree-line of my memory where the air is thin and makes you fall easily, I saw my mother cycling over a never-ending moor. She was following a long, straight cart-track, the two ruts of which came together like train rails on the horizon. The rough purple coir mat of Strabrecht Heath lay stretched out in all directions. Far in the distance were clumps of birches, recognizable only by their dazzling white trunks.

On the back of the bike sat my little sister Mariëtte. In her sky-blue 'Spanish' frock she looked as if she had descended from the firmament above – to which she might at any moment be returned, for she was sitting, strapped in a white leather safety harness, on a seat attached to the luggage carrier by clamps and springs. The ribbons tied in her corkscrew curls were as sky-blue as her dress and the heart-shaped purse hanging from her wrist … At least the *picture* had not suffered from the inroads of time.

Now and then the child turned round, using whatever freedom of movement all those straps and buckles allowed her, in order to see whether her brother was peeking out from behind father's back. Whenever I looked, she laughed, hunching one of her shoulders.

My mother was wearing for the first time a hand-me-down but still new frock that had belonged to her sister, who, though already engaged, was not yet married to her affluent catch. A full yellow ochre skirt with a petticoat under it, for that was 'only proper', my aunt had said.

I was holding on to the flaps on my father's back pockets. He had undone them for me, so that I could get a better grip by sticking my fingers through the buttonholes: a newly invented means of not losing me, which with every revolution of the pedals made his wallet creep up another millimetre out of his right-hand pocket.

Although there was not a cloud in the sky my parents were moving at a brisk rate. The sweat stains under my father's arms were spreading. Perhaps they were only pedalling so hard in order to ride more smoothly over the sandiest parts of the track. Occasionally we encountered oncoming cyclists who rang their bells from afar and hailed us in a friendly fashion as they passed. When they rode over bumps, they cried 'oops' as they were jolted from their saddles into the air.

Running alongside to the right of the track, and just as interminable, was a deep ditch. Its banks formed a perfect V. There was still a little muddy water at the bottom. It was covered by a thick layer of duckweed which looked impenetrable until I saw a frog break through it … only to disappear again after one leap. The two black rents in the weed closed quickly … we were already past the spot.

The sun prickled my scalp and my fingers clung red and sweaty to the buttonholes of the back-pocket flaps. However hard I looked, the green blanket on the ditch yielded no more secrets. The languid silence was broken by the sound of a dog barking bossily.

'Look, Albert,' my father told me. He was pointing over the heath.

I followed his arm and saw the flock of sheep. A black dog was rounding up a few stray lambs. Barking and snapping he drove them back to the flock which huddled closer and closer together. But other lambs were continually breaking away from a different part of the flock. The dog was going berserk.

Then I saw the shepherd. He was sitting on the bank of the ditch lacing up his boots. His staff with its little spade, which flashed a glint of sunshine towards us, lay across his knees. He looked angrily in the direction of his flock and shouted something in a hoarse voice that did not carry far. An old man. As we passed him he rose stiffly to his feet and walked slowly towards his sheep.

My mother also pointed. And my sister looked. By now the dog had leapt on the sheep and was running over their close knit backs as if they were a platform. His paws sometimes slipped deep into the wool or between their bodies, but he managed to jump with great speed from one side to the other of this living stage, barking his commands now here now there. Although the sheep lending him their backs bleated loudly in protest, they pressed ever closer together, digging their hooves in, as if to offer the dog a firmer footing.

All four of us were so absorbed by this enactment of class struggle that we paid scant attention to the track. From the opposite direction a boy of about fourteen was approaching in a cloud of dust. He had smoked his first cigarette on the moor and was now cycling home as fast as he could to throw up. At the spot where he passed us the ruts in the cart-track became broader for a short distance. Unlike the ground we had thus far ridden over here the sand was soft and grey. The boy skidded, his wheels slid down into the sand and both he and his bike fell against my mother who in her turn toppled into the ditch.

My father braked. His bike gave a jolt. My fingers slipped out of the button-holes and I slid off the carrier. I landed hard on my tailbone on the narrow strip between the tracks. A stabbing pain shot up my backbone and for an instant everything went black.

When it became light again, brighter than before, I saw the boy kneeling near his bike in the sand. His face was white. Two bicycle wheels were sticking out above the edge of the ditch. The front one was still turning, the rear one was slowly disappearing. My father stretched his arms out hesitantly towards the front wheel, then towards the back wheel, but to no avail.

'Bert!' I heard my mother's stifled cry. 'I'm being suffocated!' Pull me out!'

'Wait on! Mariëtte first ...!' he said, bending over towards the back wheel which had now disappeared entirely. He dragged it out by the rim and Mariëtte cried out that she had 'poo' in her mouth.

There was I with my own fully-grown pain, and everyone was turning their back on me. It had manifested itself from my tailbone to the back of my head, a revelation, and there was nobody to complain to. My sense of outrage lent me wings – and that was how I was always to remember the scene: like the frog I had seen the same afternoon I sprang up from the ground and clutched hold of my father's leg, so that his own indecisiveness was no longer the only thing hindering his attempts at rescue.

'Me too!' I yelled. 'I've *hurt* myself!'

He tried to shake me off, but I had a good grip on him. His leg jerked under my grasp. I was standing with my foot on his. Dancing up and down, I stared into the depths.

The top part of my mother's body was completely hidden by her upturned skirt. Her legs (strange dismembered things), protruding from the lacy flounces of her petticoat, thrashed at the bike which was preventing her from gaining a foothold. From behind her still came: 'Poo, Mummy ... poo! I've got poo in my mouth!'

When my father dragged the bike with child and all up on to dry land, my mother's legs still trembled in the air, then they bent at the knee and sank. Her skirt wrapped itself around them and so she lay stretched out in the ditch, where shortly after she rose dripping with green and brown scum to become my mother again. She tried to clamber up the steep side, but did not succeed.

'Bert, help me ... do help me ...!'

My father was standing there with the bike and I was hanging on to his leg.

'Me too! ... Me too! ... I've hurt myself too!'

He finally managed to offer my mother a hand between the handlebar and the saddle. Then there she was next to us.

'Oh, my God, just look at that ...' She was holding a muddy panel of her dress up between thumb and forefinger. 'And that poor little thing ... Bert, give me a hankie quickly.'

The shepherd had reached his flock. He stuck his little spade into the ground and a fine spray of sand descended on to the backs of the sheep. The flock scattered and the dog went under in the waves of woolly surf.

The boy got on to his bike and rode off quickly. My father turned around towards my mother and said: 'You're bleeding'.

'Bleed' was a dialect word that confused me. Because our family was bilingual it meant both *'to bloom'* and *'to bleed'* to me. (For bloom in the sense of bringing forth blossom, my father used the word 'blujen'. 'Ullejen pirrenbum bluujt schon.' 'Your pear tree is in full bloom.') In one use the word had something soothing and in the other it made things more dramatic. It made blooming more painful and bleeding less serious. It had the ambiguity of a rose.

'Where ... where?'

'Your arm.'

First she raised her right arm, where there was nothing to be seen. But when her left arm went up, a thin trickle of blood rose at her wrist and ran slowly, slowly down ... It meandered, wound its way down around her arm like an inverted vine ... until it disappeared in her armpit.

There she stood: dirty and draped with strands of slimy green ... when suddenly that beautiful, bright red blood, like a breath of fresh air, volatile as spring itself, began threading its way from her wrist to her armpit. She bloomed.

She couldn't, she mustn't be hurt. She was *blooming,* not bleeding. Something in me emphasized the beautiful and innocent aspect of the word, and hence of what had happened. She laid no claim to sympathy, a claim she had never allowed me either. Sympathy, against which I had to protect her at all costs ... I had to wipe out, cover up, her pain and suffering with my pain and suffering, so that hers should no longer be exposed to any sympathy whatsoever ... Her pain, her *right* to pain had to be wiped off the map immediately ...

I rubbed my tailbone. My disappointment at the rapid disappearance of my pain (the new sensation) gave me strength enough to attract my mother's entire attention to me instantly. I stood in front of her and screamed: I've hurt myself too! Here ...!' And I turned my bottom towards her and laid my hand on the sore spot, which did not hurt at all any more.

From *Parents Falling* (Vallende ouders, Querido, Amsterdam, 1983, pp. 265-271).

Translated by Elizabeth Mollison.

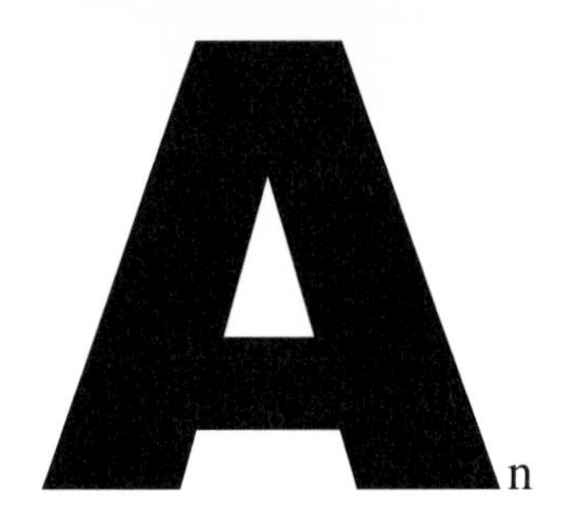

An Anatomy of Dutch Cabaret

Background

Dutch cabaret is unique in the world. That at least is what Dutch people believe. In a country that has always been a melting pot of cultures and influences owing its existence to its neighbours, this cannot be true.

What is true is that Dutch people apparently have strong opinions about what cabaret is and can easily argue whether some theatre performance is really and truly cabaret. The English music hall is not, nor is the American musical or show, nor the French *café chantant.* Cabaret in the Dutch sense is in the first place play with language. The theatrical aspect comes second. The play with language should preferably have some impact, i.e. be part of a political, social or religious statement. We think that cabaret must be about something, and that something is usually ourselves, the microcosm we live in, our ethical and political views, our social opinions. Cabaret must be something personal, and that is why we think that the performing artist must be the creator of its text and songs.

The traditional picture is: only a few people on stage, one of them being the musician, usually the pianist. Their performance consists of an alternation of songs and sketches. The form of songs and sketches is satirical, the content social criticism, and the basis play with words, ambiguity, quotes, imitation.

It is obvious even to a Dutch mind that the definition or demarcation of the style is not clear-cut. The strong opinions however reflect the ongoing discussion about the definition of the form. This discussion in its turn shows the importance of cabaret for the Dutch mind. This importance is all the more confirmed by the fruitful osmosis between cabaret and other performing arts, between cabaret and other art-forms, and between cabaret on stage and cabaret-like performances in other media. The following overview proves this point.

The fifties

Our starting point is the fifties. This decade was dominated by those the Dutch call the Three Greats: Wim Kan (1911-1983), Wim Sonneveld (1917-1974) and Toon Hermans (1916-).

The roots of Wim Kan's career go back to the thirties. Kan's style was not innovative; theatrically he offered nothing new or special. Kan's fame is based on his 'conferences', long one-man conversations with the audience on the hot issues of the time. Play with language was a key element of these conferences.

However, the text was usually written for him, and music taken from well-known tunes of the period. Kan contributed perfect timing, complete control, charm and wit. His trademark was his quasi neutrality. Kan discussed complete Dutch Cabinets on stage without showing any preferences. In later years politicians even felt flattered to be satirized by Kan's subtle irony.

Wim Sonneveld showed a completely different character. He was more the entertainer, someone who liked to dress up, a man who wanted to step outside his own personality and impersonate totally different characters.

Toon Hermans (1916-) in 1980 (Photo by Gaby Hermans).

Wim Kan (1911-1983) (Photo by Fotoburo Stokvis).

Sonneveld won fame through his characters: *Nikkelen Nelis* the street musician, *Frater Venantius* the singing friar and earlier, on radio, *Willem Parel* the organ grinder. Like Kan, Sonneveld was a performing artist who brought to life material written for him. Sonneveld was far less political than Kan, nastier, but also more exuberant and more joyful.

Toon Hermans is the clown of the three. His language is not particularly witty, nor does he show sharp political or social views. He is a man of the people in the sense that he loves mankind and he wants to demonstrate that. So his shows are a mixture of poetry-like reflections, nonsensical entertainment, and French-type songs. They are his own: he writes the texts and he creates the acts. Hermans is at his best in the long-drawn-out acts in which he combines all his talents in playing with the audience. Acts sometimes only exist on the basis of the public and its reactions. Only Freek de Jonge (1944-), a couple of decades later, has proved to be Hermans' equal in this respect.

Sonneveld and Hermans tried their luck on television and that made them really famous. What was recorded and shown was just a plain recording of their one-man shows, but people stayed home to watch and their acts and songs became famous.

Kan hated television throughout his entire life. He stuck to radio and established the institution of the New Year's Eve conference, a one hour monologue in which he discussed the events of the year just past. For years no one dared to compete with Kan in his speciality. Only in the eighties did Freek de Jonge dare to present himself as Kan's successor.

It is the artistic mind that makes Annie M.G. Schmidt (1911-) the mother of Dutch cabaret. Her children's books, musicals, series for radio and television, and theatre plays always break taboos without being rude, unsubtle or would-be witty. The form of Schmidt's work is not particularly cabaretesque, but the content and the atmosphere are. Schmidt illustrates the osmosis mentioned above with her continuous shifts from cabaret-style work to other forms of art.

Van Kooten (l.) and De Bie (r.) in 1976 (Photo by Roel Bazen).

The sixties

As in all other aspects of life, the sixties displayed an eruption of talent, an exploration of technique, a discovery of styles. The demand for art was so extensive that, whatever your talent, when you got onto the stage you achieved success. Thresholds were low and the willingness of the public was great.

The mass media such as radio and television showed their influence. As mentioned earlier, Hermans and Sonneveld explored television, but in a rather traditional way. Annie M.G. Schmidt wrote a special series for television: *Ja zuster, nee zuster* (Yes Nurse, No Nurse), which is one of the best things in her entire oeuvre. Kees van Kooten (1941-) and Wim de Bie (1939-) started on radio as *De klisjeemannetjes* (The Stereotype Blokes) and moved over to television in the late sixties and early seventies.

Television developed its own cabaret series; as, for instance, *Monty Python's Flying Circus* appeared on BBC Television. A good example in the early sixties was the notorious *Zo is het toevallig ook nog eens een keer* (Once Again, by Chance), based on the English television series *That Was The Week That Was.* The programme shocked the religious part of the Netherlands when it compared people's television cult with their religious behaviour. Religion was still a taboo, and television cabaret was prepared to break it.

Nevertheless, none of the television programmes mentioned was as innovative, original and fresh as Monty Python. They were basically television versions of cabaret on stage, as these programmes leaned heavily on the traditional cabaret form of alternating song and text. And their criticism was clear-cut and in most cases harmless. The young rebels were *Neerlands Hoop* (Dutch Hope), Herman van Veen (1945-) and Van Kooten and De Bie. Their influence dominates the second half of our overview and it is only now that new hopes are emerging. These new talents still have to fight the legacy of *Neerlands Hoop,* Van Veen and Van Kooten and De Bie.

Van Kooten and De Bie are probably the most faithful to traditional Dutch cabaret. They aim to criticize society and their main vehicle is language: they typify characters through language, they unmask through

language and they attack the political use of language. Van Kooten and De Bie are very much cabaret artists; meanwhile they've been exploring the possibilities of cabaret on television for over twenty years.

Van Veen is the most poetic and musical of the three. He is not sharp or witty, but his music and songs are. And particularly in his songs and music he is unconventional and innovative. Van Veen didn't remain a cabaret artist. He developed his talent in all kinds of directions, from children's stories to television series.

The seventies

Neerlands Hoop dominated cabaret in the seventies with a series of programmes of undisputed quality; no one could challenge them. Traditional song-sketch-piano cabaret had had it. Now that pop music had become such a dominant entertainment medium, you could not ignore the pop cult if you wanted to appeal to a young audience. *Neerlands Hoop* understood this perfectly and it is no coincidence that with *Neerlands Hoop Express* (1973), undoubtedly the most 'rocking' production up to that time, the success of the duo with young audiences increased enormously.

Apart from *Neerlands Hoop,* alternative forms of theatre were particularly popular. At the point where cabaret and drama meet, a new sort of theatre developed in which the illusion was broken and the 'actors' addressed the public directly. The American theatre clown Jango Edwards established himself in the Netherlands, and with his *Festival of Fools* made an enormous contribution to the development of a climate in which fringe theatre flourished. It wasn't the big renowned theatre companies with their own permanent theatres that set the tone, but the small, often new, theatres, most likely subsidized through universities, that attracted a new, young audience. Performances on the border of drama, music and cabaret dominated the picture of these small stages in the seventies.

Freek de Jonge (1944-)
(Photo by Jan Stegeman).

The fringe theatre was a development that suited the uncommitted political and social climate which followed the pulsating period of the sixties. A development that cleared the way to the small stages beyond the worn and criticized tracks of the official circuit for a young, energetic generation of theatre people. When these theatre people were old enough to take over the torch from their abused predecessors, they themselves gained access to the big stages and the fringe theatre died a silent death. The end of the seventies marked the collapse of fringe theatre and new hope for cabaret in a more recognizable form.

Neerlands Hoop split up in 1979, when Herman Finkers (1954-), currently one of the most celebrated cabaret artists, won the personality prize and was voted 'Most Popular Artist' by the audience at an important national cabaret festival. Bram Vermeulen (1946-) became primarily a (pop) musician, while Freek de Jonge pursued a solo career as a shining example for tens of successors and epigones. De Jonge proved to be more and more a cabaret artist in the original sense of the word, although he draws his material not so much from actual excesses as from more general ethical problems. In the steps of Wim Kan he presented a number of New Year's Eve 'conferences' on television in the first half of the eighties, firmly cementing his already existing fame for the entire Dutch nation.

Brigitte Kaandorp (1963-), Hans Liberg (1954-) and Paul de Leeuw (1962-) were all 1983 finalists in the above mentioned cabaret festival. Together with Herman Finkers and Youp van 't Hek (1954-), they stand in the forefront of the continuous stream of young cabaret artists who have successfully won their place on Dutch stages, very often with much pain and hardship. These young talents often had to go through a very hard time on the so-called youth and community centre circuit before they could expect any public recognition. Jammed between pinball machine and bar – which stayed open during the performance – they were easy targets for a handful of young people who turned their thumbs down anyway. Youp van 't Hek, who founded his cabaret *Nar* (Jester) as early as 1973 and only recently developed into probably the most important cabaret artist in the Netherlands, is typically somebody who won his place on the big stages only with great effort. In his shows, Van 't Hek still radiates the hard worker who wants to score with every sentence and who is the living witness of the message he puts across: don't avoid adventure, choose it and meet the challenge.

Thanks to dogged persistence many artists eventually did make it. The most important cabaret artists managed to gather a crowd of loyal followers, and some of them are worshipped by their own public, in much the same way as one person preferred Hermans and another Sonneveld in the sixties. At any rate, cabaret in the Netherlands is flourishing as never before. Now that video shops compete fiercely with cinemas and the big theatre companies aim more and more at a mature, educated theatre audience, there are plenty of opportunities for cabaret. After the meagre seventies, the entertainment magazines again contain cabaret sections, showing clearly that you can refresh yourself again and again every week with this form of theatre.

Nowadays cabaret is typified by an absence of political and social involvement based on personal experience. The message of the rising talent of the past decade, if there is one, seems to be just a thin layer of veneer. The unpretentious cabaret that aims only to entertain reigns unchallenged. This development may well have started with Herman Finkers and Brigitte Kaandorp, two popular cabaret artists who actually openly emphasize the complete absence of pretension in their programmes. One of the youngest cabaret artists, Marcel Boon, even admits straightforwardly: 'My programme doesn't point the finger at anything as far as contents are concerned.' When present-day cabaret touches upon 'modern' taboos such as AIDS, incest, maltreatment, ethnic problems, it usually doesn't spring from genuine involvement or indignation but far more often forms the easy basis for a non-committal joke. This lack of critical reflection, flirting with taboos as it were, is exactly what some people so strongly reject in the work of cabaret artists like Paul de Leeuw. Discussing socially loaded topics with the sole intention of making an impression can easily deteriorate into tastelessness.

The influence of the electronic media is unequalled in our time. The 'Complete Works' of Freek de Jonge for instance are available in unabridged form on video; moreover, radio and television play a very important role in the exploitation and distribution of the youngest talent. Leading cabaret artists such as Kees van Kooten and Wim de Bie, Paul Haenen, Jack Spijkerman and Paul de Leeuw have their own weekly

Paul de Leeuw (1962-) (Photo by Clemens Rikken).

(satirical) radio and television shows. Recordings of successful cabaret performances are also regularly broadcast. Certain stations will often try to fill the gap created by the disappearance of the youth and community centre circuit, in cooperation with a number of theatre agencies. The last mentioned initiative is taken through the so-called *cabarestafette,* a formula that gives the younger and older winners of various festivals the opportunity to present themselves to a wider audience. A small number of them get the chance to perform for a national audience through television.

Cabaret also makes its influence felt through interaction with the printed media. Of course, there has always been a movement from literature to cabaret. From the sixties onwards, poets and song writers in the Netherlands have regularly left their desks to play on the stages of the small theatres. However, in the last few years an opposite movement can also be detected: from cabaret to literature. It concerns in particular established names. Following their activities as column writers in a number of national newspapers and weeklies, Kees van Kooten and Wim de Bie, for instance, are regularly at Number One in the Top Ten Lists of books with collections of stories ironically criticizing popular trends in Dutch society. Freek de Jonge too moves more often into the literary market; he has published the complete texts of his solo productions and, moreover, written a collection of memories of his youth and a novel. And a developing talent such as Youp van 't Hek is not only active as a sports columnist in a national newspaper, but achieves sales figures publishers just dream about with his collections of stories. Thus success on television and stage appears to have a positive influence on the literary activities of the great cabaret artists.

This development proves that Dutch cabaret still hasn't lost its unique position among other forms of art in the Netherlands.

JOS NIJHOF AND PAUL VAN DER PLANK

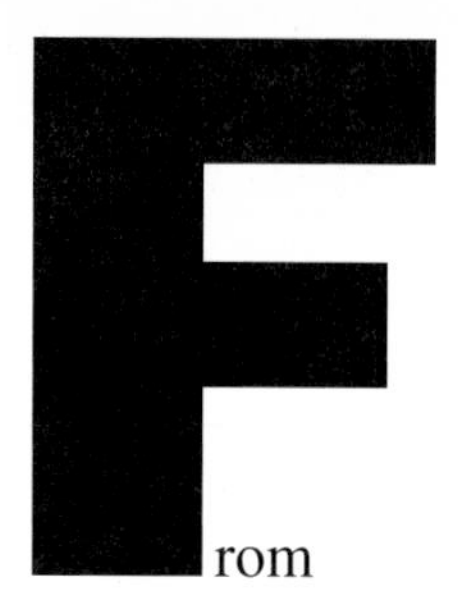

From the Message to the Medium

The Poetic Evolution of Paul van Ostaijen

Along with the disruption of the values and of the very image of the Western world by philosophy, psychology, ethnography, the exact sciences, industrial development and the resulting political-social crises, the years 1910-1920 saw the birth of a vast movement that injected new life into the arts and literature of Europe and America. It sprang up more or less simultaneously in a number of major cities (Paris, Rome, Milan, Munich, Berlin, London, Moscow, Leningrad, then Zurich and New York) and expressed itself in great movements like futurism, cubism, expressionism, dadaism, surrealism, etc.

At the end of the nineteenth century, Belgium and Holland had played a leading role in the creation and spread of art nouveau and of symbolism and it was into these that the avant-gardists sank some of their roots. We think, for example, of Fernand Khnopff or Jan Toorop, of Maurice Maeterlinck or Louis Couperus. In the twentieth century, however, these regions were on the whole more passive and peripheral. If before the 1914-18 War they opened their minds to the 'new spirit', including futurism, they themselves were not the birthplace of any major movement – apart from Mondrian's neo-plasticism. In the literary field in particular, the neo-romantic and realistic tendencies of the end of the nineteenth century long continued to put their stamp on a scene that had often remained fairly provincial despite the efforts of magazines like *De Nieuwe Gids* (The New Guide) in the North or *Van Nu en Straks* (Of Now and Before Long) in the South. As a result, the emergence of a Paul van Ostaijen, a man of cosmopolitan culture and a city dweller through and through, came as a complete surprise and even shocked most of his compatriots. In a Flanders where the priest-poet Guido Gezelle had celebrated piously – and with considerable lyrical power – the flowers and the seasons, and where people were only just beginning to accept the morose abandon of Karel van de Woestijne to the delights of autumn and of self-reproach, the young Van Ostaijen (born in Antwerp in 1896) set the scene for the modern metropolis. Not the type of city which had tragically bewitched his predecessor, the francophone poet Emile Verhaeren, who had celebrated its 'tumultuous forces' in a mixture of hatred and passion which would also be found in the work of numerous German expressionists, but the familiar city with its many day-to-day aspects that surround the strolls, the loves, the work and the leisure of a city dweller happy with his lot.

The War remains strangely absent from his first collection of poems, *Music-Hall* (1916), in which through his love affairs and his fleeting impressions the dandy makes an exhibition of himself, unless he happens to merge into some chance group in the street, the café or the music hall.

Even in his very early verses which recall the French *unanimisme,* we see him beginning to question the traditional poetical language as the refinements and the evanescence of symbolism gradually give way to a more direct language and a free, flowing and concise verse with a dynamism appropriate to its decidedly modern subjects.

An awareness of the political and social realities soon turned Van Ostaijen into a militant in the Flemish Movement and a convinced pacifist. Born during the romantic period of the awakening of European nationalisms and in a Belgium where centuries of foreign occupation and administration had gallicized the upper classes (including those of Flanders), the Flemish Movement had been aiming for almost a century to reestablish the prestige and official use of the Dutch language alongside French. The First World War divided the movement into two camps: those who judged it prudent to await its end before continuing the linguistic battle within the legal framework of a liberated Belgium and those who advocated immediate action, despite – or even sometimes with the aid of – the German occupying forces.

The young Van Ostaijen was one of those 'activists' recruited mainly among university students frustrated till then by the absence of higher education in Dutch. This 'activism', which for Van Ostaijen – as for others – implied social emancipation, in no way excluded pacifism and open-mindedness: it was a question of restoring to the Flemish people their validity and dignity of expression in the chorus of the nations, whose harmony could only temporarily be delayed by an absurd war.

The message of universal brotherhood and the rhetorical speech full of imagery of his second collection of poems, *The Signal* (Het sienjaal, 1918) reflect the humanitarian tendency of expressionism propagated at that time by German avant-garde magazines such as *Die Aktion* and *Die Weissen Blätter,* which somewhat surprisingly perhaps the occupying forces allowed to be imported into Belgium.

The self-taught Van Ostaijen read a great deal and with passion, instantly communicating his feelings about what he read to his friends and, by means of articles, to periodicals in which he very soon began to collaborate. His interest in the art and literature of his time rapidly became the fervour of a proselyte. With an energy all the more combative because the intellectual milieux he addressed – not to mention the others – retained for the most part an unfailingly conservative inertia, Van Ostaijen took up the cudgels for the international avant-garde and for those in Flanders who joined it, sometimes as a result of his influence.

It was with fire that he defended modern art in general and that of his friends in particular: the sculptor Oscar Jespers, the painters Floris Jespers (Oscar's brother) and Paul Joostens, who were soon joined by the German Heinrich Campendonk and others who did not reveal their talent until after the War. Supported by a rapid but selective assimilation of futurist, cubist and expressionist theories, his intransigent yet stimulating criticism soon extended from painting to literature, especially Dutch literature – Hendrik Marsman, Gaston Burssens, Maurice Gilliams, Marnix Gijsen, Karel van de Woestijne – but also German literature (Werfel, Stramm) and French (Jacob, Cendrars, Cocteau, Claudel, Norge, Seuphor and not least Apollinaire). The poets and artists are numerous – Vincent Van Gogh, James Ensor, Else Lasker-Schüler, Francis Jammes, Walt Whitman (whom he calls his 'father') – to whom he pays homage or dedicates verses in *The Signal*. This collection, the title of which no doubt refers to a poem from Whitman's *Leaves of Grass*, can be considered as his happiest and most optimistic book: dealing with all that is young, beautiful and generous in the world, it declares his hope of a pacifist revolution which, springing from transfigured consciences, must conquer the whole earth in a spirit of tolerance and love.

His dreams were shattered when, having fled the possible consequences of his 'activism' after the armistice, he witnessed the suppression of the Spartakist revolt in Berlin – which had tried to establish a sort of communist-inspired, direct democracy under the leadership of Karl Liebknecht and Rosa Luxemburg – and the return of bourgeois order. With no means of support, having left his job at Antwerp Town Hall, he could only count on the financial help of the girl who shared his exile and on the precarious support of a few friends. These were the toughest years of his life. They found expression in a sort of lyrical volte-face, for instead of singing of humanity and passion for life, Van Ostaijen now embarked upon a work of self-destruction and social satire, in a process analogous to the one which replaced humanitarian expressionism with the brutal disenchantment of the *Neue Sachlichkeit* (New Realism) and dadaist derision.

He was to elaborate simultaneously two collections of poems – *Feasts of Fear and Agony* (Feesten van angst en pijn, published posthumously) and *Occupied City* (Bezette stad, 1921) – as well as a series of grotesque narrations. The target of the prose works is usually capitalist society, its institutions, its customs, its prejudices and its representatives, which the writer takes pleasure in plunging into the most absurd situations and the wildest intrigues, to the point where more than once the very principle of narrative, writing and communication is called into question. The essay deviates, drifts off, builds up its own logic which no longer has anything in common with actual experience, or makes way for a digression which proliferates and soon wipes out the intrigue. Trick texts indeed, and subversive because of their subject matter and very essence. Van Ostaijen continued to publish them after his return to Belgium.

As for his poetry, it was reduced, not to silence, but to cries. The standard syntax and prosody give way to words thrown higgledy-piggledy onto the page, in all directions and in different dimensions. This is not the constellation of Mallarmé, nor the joyous accumulation of futurist *mots en liberté*, nor the calligramme of Apollinaire, nor the dadaist montage, nor even the 'concentration' so beloved by August Stramm (Van Ostaijen's favourite German poet), but it is all this at once, torn to shreds and carried along by a fury of negation and despair.

In the nightmare atmosphere of *Feasts of Fear and Agony*, the poet systematically demolishes the illusions, memories and various glad rags that make up his own ego, replacing them with the total, harsh nudity of a beginning that is almost devoid of hope. In a way, *Occupied City* constitutes the counterpart of this process of dispossession and deconstruction, but this time in the outside world, extolled only recently with so much ardour.

However, beneath this chaotic exterior of scenes of war and of occupation and self-scourging, interspersed with sacrilegious prayers and barbarian dances that border on suicide, runs a current of asceticism of which the ultimate objective is 'disindividualization', both in the psychological sphere – subjective and collective – and in the sphere of poetic expression. From now on, only the rejection of individualism, which Van Ostaijen regards as a form of egoism and as the bourgeois value *par excellence,* can enable us to catch a remote glimpse of the possibility of a true revolution, when people 'will have had a bellyful of individualism'. Only disindividualized artistic expression will be capable, by the simplicity and expressive force of its media – form, colours, words – of ensuring a true human communion in the work of art, springing from the subconscious, which the poet regards as the privileged field of intersubjectivity, and therefore the ideal meeting ground. From now on, it would no longer be a question of Van Ostaijen 'communicating' individual thoughts or emotions in a discursive manner, but of creating an 'autonomous' art stemming directly from an 'inner necessity', as required by Kandinsky and most contributors to *Der Sturm,* a 'pure' art, calling only upon its specific means of expression and conceived both as ludic improvisation and as a profound and magic chant, closely related to the mystic ecstasy to which the Abbé Bremond in his turn was soon to liken poetry.

The originality of the poetics of Van Ostaijen, who owed much to the artistic theories of Kandinsky and to the '*Wortkunst*' (Word Art) of the *Der Sturm* group, seems to consist mainly of an attempt to reconcile a simple and obvious form with the expression of the subconscious which the surrealists will aim to achieve in quite a different way. While, in principle, the latter give free rein to an automatic way of writing, Van Ostaijen, wanting to endow the word with as much resonance and expressive intensity as possible once it has emerged from the subconscious, calls into play the selective capacity of reason in the composition. In this way, he intends to create a 'lyrical object' of which the perfect construction, concentrated and disindividualized, requires of every reader a dynamic recreation, where the revitalized words allow us to take a fresh look at things. It is not by chance that one of his most important theoretical pieces of writing is entitled *Lyrical Poetry: Directions for Use* (Gebruiksaanwijzing der lyriek).

Paul van Ostaijen (1896-1928).

Van Ostaijen returned to Belgium in 1921, left again for his military service in occupied Germany, and then settled in Antwerp where he worked in a bookshop. In 1926 he went on to open an art gallery in Brussels with Geert van Bruaene which was a failure. In his poetical evolution towards what he called 'organic' expressionism, he met with little public understanding, for it was mainly the humanitarian expressionism of his own *The Signal* which continued to collect a following in Flanders: after Wies Moens, writers like Gaston Burssens, Victor J. Brunclair, Marnix Gijsen, Karel van den Oever, Achilles Mussche and others, too, followed suit for a time. He therefore found himself more or less alone in trying new formal experiments, together with Burssens who had soon joined him again.

The most representative poem in this last creative phase really seems to be 'Melopee' which Van Ostaijen himself quoted more than once as an example in his writing and his lectures. Its starting point is a 'premise' which is the subject of a series of musical variations and rhythmical shifts. These are held up at a certain point by a 'counter chant', before expanding into an open ending in the form of a question. The personal emotion – in this case a feeling of resigned fatigue in the face of existence – is not expressed directly, but by means of a sonorous and plastic equivalent.

However, at this time Van Ostaijen did not always obey the principle of 'disindividualization': love, death, the quiet force of the trees, the fragility of happiness and the spectacle of some human pettiness could wrest from him an intimate confidence, a cry or a sarcastic remark; but these he quickly transmuted by means of melody and rhythm, yet without divesting them of their expressive power – on the contrary!

Conscious of opening the way for a new form of poetry in Flanders in which the 'sonority' of the simplest words and their magical and ludic power of suggestion were all important, Van Ostaijen intended to publish his new poems under the title *The First Book of Schmoll* (Het eerste boek van Schmoll), ironically borrowed from a famous piano method for young beginners. He died of tuberculosis in 1928 in Miavoye-Anthée before he was able to carry out this project.

The honour fell to Burssens of becoming the first to publish these untranslatable gems, his friend's last verses, in the form of an anthology. Moreover, by his own poetic production, he ensured the continuity of the first avant-garde beyond the conservative reaction of the thirties and of the Second World War, until the appearance of the generation of *Tijd en Mens* (Time and Man) in 1949. Then, in the vicinity of CoBrA and mindful of the surrealist legacy, Claus, Walravens, Van de Kerckhove and other 'experimentalists' took over the exploration of the depths of the language.

PAUL HADERMANN
Translated by Alison Mouthaan.

FURTHER READING

BEEKMAN, E. M., *Homeopathy of the Absurd: The Grotesque in Paul van Ostaijen's Creative Prose,* The Hague, 1970.
BOGMAN, J., *De stad als tekst. Over de compositie van Paul van Ostaijens 'Bezette Stad'* (The City as Text. On the Composition of Paul van Ostaijen's *Occupied City*), Rotterdam, 1990.
BORGERS, GERRIT, *Paul van Ostaijen, een documentatie* (Paul van Ostaijen, a documentation), 2 vols., Amsterdam, 1971.
HADERMANN, PAUL, *De kringen naar binnen. De dichterlijke wereld van Paul van Ostaijen* (The Inward Circles. The Poetical World of Paul van Ostaijen), Antwerp, 1965.
HADERMANN, PAUL, *Het vuur in de verte. Paul van Ostaijens kunstopvattingen in het licht van de Europese avant-garde* (Fire in the Distance. Paul van Ostaijen's Views on Art in the Light of the European Avant-Garde), Antwerp, 1970.
VREE, P. DE & JESPERS, H.F., *Paul van Ostaijen,* Bruges / Antwerp, 1967.
Verzameld Werk (Collected Works) (ed. Gerrit Borgers), 4 vols., Amsterdam, 1979.

LIST OF TRANSLATIONS

Patriotism, Inc. and Other Tales (Tr. & ed. E.M. Beekman). Amherst, 1971.
Feasts of Fear and Agony (Tr. Hidde van Ameyden van Duym). New York, 1976; Toronto, 1976.
The First Book of Schmoll. Selected Poems, 1920-1928 (Tr. Theo Hermans, James S Holmes, Peter Nijmeijer, with an essay by the author, tr. Theo Hermans & Paul Vincent). With a foreword by E.M. Beekman (Introduction by Gerrit Borgers). Amsterdam, 1982.

Song 4

Gibber
jabber
Gibber
jabber
shiver
shiv
c r y i n g
fist
fight fists fight fists
grip
grit
fists clenching

woman of a long time ago comes by
stamps I gave to the boy of the fourth floor

fourth floor?

a human being drops
from
the
fourth floor

tension
trigger calf muscles

leap

jump
drop
dropping
fists leading pain outside
fists seizing pain
fists wringing pain

fists wringing
tatters
ripping
cutting
slash
sob
sickle leg
one two
You
one two
You
sickle leg

a man
an avalanche
plunging plunging plunging
plunges into me
the boy of the fourth floor is laughing

laughing

quivering
fist
tatters to be inside the man
to be inside the boy

Sickle leg traverses me

it

C u t s ——
to cut — across

I
shriek
shrieking
gulping
gibbering
dropping
drop
taut
I am being tightened
You You You

who is You

a man
an avalanche plunging plunging plunging

t o w a n t

What

I want to breathe

I want to be a F I S H

From *Feasts of Fear and Agony* (Feesten van angst en pijn, published posthumously in 1928).
Translated by Hidde van Ameyden van Duym.

Lullaby no 2

Sleep like an ox
sleep like a phlox
sleep like an ox of a phlox
little ox
little phlox
little cookie box
close the lid on the box
I'm asleep

From *The First Book of Schmoll.*
Selected Poems, 1920-1928.
Translated by James S Holmes.

Bersaglieri song

for E. du Perron

A gentleman going up the street
a gentleman going down the street
two gentlemen going up and down
that is the one gentleman goes up
and the other gentleman goes down
right in front of the shop of Henryson and Wenryson
right in front of the shop of Henryson and Wenryson the famous hatmakers
they meet each other
one gentleman takes his high hat in his right hand
the other gentleman takes his high hat in his left hand
the one gentleman and the other
the right and the left the one going up and the one going down
the left going up
the right going down
each with his high hat his own high hat his bloody own high hat
pass each other
right in front of the door
of the shop
of Henryson and Wenryson
the famous hatmakers
then the two gentlemen
the right and the left the one going up and the one going down
once past each other
put their hats on their heads again
don't misunderstand me
each puts his own hat on his own head
that is their right
that is the right of these two gentlemen

From *The First Book of Schmoll.* Selected Poems, 1920-1928.
Translated by James S Holmes.

Chronicle

Contents

Architecture

Rietveld Revisited

To many people Gerrit Rietveld (1888-1964) is known only as the architect of *De Stijl.* When his name is mentioned many of them imagine a three-dimensional version of a painting by Piet Mondrian. This one-sided picture of Rietveld and his work was in need of correction, and for the past few years staff at the Central Museum in Utrecht have been devoting their energies to that task. The fruits of their labours were presented in an oeuvre catalogue and an exhibition which opened at the Central Museum on 27 November 1992.

An inventory was made of all Rietveld's designs, with the aid of various archives, and these were then compared with the finished products. All his houses were visited and clients, residents, colleagues and friends were interviewed. The many hitherto unknown designs unearthed as a result led to a considerable reevaluation of Rietveld's work. The exhibition showed that Rietveld's oeuvre is far more extensive than many people think. In addition it became clear that space, colour, industrialization and prefabrication were the continuing themes of this diverse oeuvre.

As a symbol of the development of Rietveld's work between 1906 and 1963, a series of his chairs placed in chronological order ran through the various galleries like a time chart. The rest of the material was arranged thematically, following as far as possible the chronology of the theme. Rietveld's idiosyncratic relationship with the New Realism *(de Nieuwe Zakelijkheid),* and *De Stijl* also had its place, as did his ideas on public housing and town planning.

The great advantage of arranging the exhibition in this way was that the visitor could see the connection between designs from different periods and disciplines. It became clear that Rietveld developed and applied his ideas in his furniture as well as in his architecture. This applies both to his ideas on space and colour (demonstrated, for example, in the Red-blue Chair and in the Rietveld-Schröder house) and to those on industrialization. Rietveld used pre-fabricated elements in renovating a house as early as 1927. He later developed the idea of a house with a central core block containing a concentration of facilities such as WC, shower, staircase and storage space. This mass-produced core block could be installed in a single operation. In his furniture designs, too, Rietveld allowed for the possibility of mass production. Among other things he designed chairs that were stamped out of just one piece of material in just one operation.

Another theme common to both Rietveld's furniture and his architectural designs was simple, low-cost production. In 1934 he introduced flat-pack furniture, sold in kit form. The wooden summer house that Rietveld designed together with Mrs Schröder was also marketed as a kit. For one thousand guilders (including erection, finishing, and assistance in applying for a building permit) the buyer had a cabin sleeping six people, with a living room, kitchen, and shower.

The Rietveld-Schröder house (built in 1924) in Utrecht.

Gerrit Rietveld, working on a scale model.

Rietveld designed a considerable number of private houses. Their designs show that he was no dogmatist. In contrast to other architects committed to New Realism, he did not insist on rectilinear construction in concrete and glass. Thus we see various of his residential designs incorporating curved lines, thatch and brick. The same flexibility can be seen in the town-planning blueprints Rietveld drew up, particularly from the forties on; he often made a number of very different plans for the same site. Despite his efforts, few of these designs were ever built. Even in the period of reconstruction after the Second World War Rietveld did not get any really large commissions. This may have been due to the predominantly conservative atmosphere prevailing at the time and the reputation he had built up with the Rietveld-Schröder house. The notion that Rietveld, having started out as a furniture maker, would lack technical and constructive skills probably also played a part.

So after the war Rietveld had no choice but to design exhibitions, such as the *Stijl* exhibition in Amsterdam, Venice and New York in 1951. As a result he became more widely known, and in the late fifties obtained a number of large prestigious commissions, such as the Dutch Pavilion at the Venice Biennale, and some public housing projects. Rietveld died on 25 June 1964, shortly after being awarded an honorary doctorate by the *Technische Hogeschool* in Delft.

The exhibition *Gerrit Rietveld 1888-1964* is a superb tribute to a versatile architect and furniture maker. It gives new meaning to the term 'survey'; the visitor leaves the museum with a far broader view of Rietveld than he had when he came.

JANICA KLEIMAN
Translated by Elizabeth Mollison.

The exhibition can be seen at the Guggenheim Museum in New York in the course of 1994.

Henry van de Velde, a European Artist

Henry van de Velde (1863-1957) occupies a special place in the development of twentieth-century architecture and design. By comparison with the big names, he is considered a failure. For a historian this presents a challenge. After all, failure is equated with worthlessness and that is certainly not the case with Henry van de Velde. His failures have turned out to be more than significant.

Henry van de Velde was born in Antwerp. It was clear to him from childhood that he would choose an artistic career, not so much because of the career itself or because he had a definite talent in a particular artistic discipline, but as a means by which to develop freely as a person. A conflict with his father put an end to his initial musical ambitions. Nevertheless, music would continue to be a leitmotiv, even after he had turned to the visual arts. After a brief period at the Antwerp Academy, he threw himself into the adventure of modern art. He joined the progressive groups in Antwerp and Brussels. In the avant-garde art society *Les Vingts* (1884-1894) he became familiar with the work of Seurat. Later on he came under the influence of Vincent van Gogh, which also brought home to him his failure as a painter. His acquaintance with William Morris and the 'Arts and Crafts' design movement in England, however, opened up new horizons. From then on he was to set his art to the service of daily life in a more direct way than was possible with music or painting.

The University Library in Ghent, designed by Henry van de Velde.

In 1895, after his marriage to Maria Sèthe, he built the *Bloemenwerf* house in Ukkel (Brussels) for himself and his young family. He designed not only the architecture and the interior but also all the utensils for it and even his wife's clothes. His plea for a rational beauty, which he made in numerous lectures in Belgium, the Netherlands and Germany, was expressed with conviction in his own house. For many it was proof of his incompetence, for others a hopeful sign of an architecture and design which, far removed as it was from ostentation, returned to the real values.

Bloemenwerf signified a European breakthrough for Van de Velde. In Paris he designed the interior of Samuel Bing's art business, *Art Nouveau,* and won approval at the great European industrial design exhibitions. His own studios in Brussels, however, were a financial disaster. In 1899 he left Belgium to set up in Berlin. There he designed various famous interiors such as that of the Habana company and the hairdressing salon *Haby*. However, the art collector Karl Ernst Osthaus, who was also to become his first biographer, brought him to Hagen to design the interior of the Folkwangmuseum and to build a mansion. Van de Velde also built himself a home there – for the second time. Henry van de Velde's name continues to be associated with Hagen, a new reference point in his oeuvre.

His activities in Germany as architect, designer and author resulted in the founding of an industrial design academy in Weimar in 1906 where Van de Velde also proved his worth as a pedagogue. He wanted to bring about a reconciliation between machines and art. He no longer drew inspiration from existing models, but from the new assignment itself. It was typical of him that he not only wrote the pedagogical programme, but also designed the building. Moreover, the academy was to become the direct precursor of Bauhaus.

The theatre for the 1914 *Werkbund* exhibition in Cologne was a high point in his German period. It was also the finale. As a Belgian in Germany, his possessions were confiscated. He tried to build a new life in Switzerland, but without success. Four years later, he moved to the Netherlands at the invitation of the Kröller-Müller family and built the well-known modest museum on the Hoge Veluwe between 1935 and 1953.

In 1925, at the age of 62, he returned to Belgium full of enthusiasm to start all over again. He founded the *Institute des Arts Décoratifs* in La Cambre, a revised version of his academy in Weimar, became a teacher at the University of Ghent, and started a new career as an architect by building another house for himself. The high point of his career this time was the University Library in Ghent. This late period, too, is often interpreted as a failure and as a negation of his earlier work. But other interpretations are also possible, as is proven by the testimony of the Dutch architect, J.J.P. Oud (1890-1963): 'Henry van de Velde, the architect-pioneer, sets a marvellous example in his relationship with youth ... This man can never grow old.'

In 1947, after the Second World War in which he had played a part in preparing reconstruction work during the Occupation, a disappointed Van de Velde settled in Switzerland again. There he wrote his *Mémoires* by way of an explanation of his failures. He died in Zürich at the age of ninety-four.

GEERT BEKAERT
Translated by Alison Mouthaan.

Antwerp Cathedral (Photo by Gerrit op de Beeck; Antwerpen 93).

The Cathedral of Our Lady in Antwerp

Cleaning the choir stalls.

The large volume produced under the direction of Willem Aerts to commemorate the restoration of the Cathedral of Our Lady in Antwerp, does not deal directly with our actual perception of this imposing building, but takes that perception as the natural starting point for a number of stories connected with it. Little or nothing is said about the physical appearance of the Cathedral or how vital a part it is of the city's image. The beloved is not described as in the Song of Songs, but her fortunes are traced in some considerable detail, and they are varied and rich in colour.

The story is reconstructed in meticulous detail, from the early history of the Romanesque church up to and including the most recent restoration of this largest church in the Low Countries, completed in 1993. However, it deals not only with the story of the building but also with the institutions and the people connected with it, with everything in the way of art treasures that the building has collected or lost during the course of its eventful existence, and everything that still lies hidden underground. All this is covered in a large number of contributions by various specialists. In general, they keep to a sober account of the actual course of events. But it is through that succession or coordination of the facts, lavishly illustrated with scores of documents, that a lively picture of the history of this cathedral church gradually emerges, with the building running always behind and through the events like a watermark. In this way the history of the cathedral is a compendium of the history of the city and of an era. Today we can still sense how much this building and the city are intertwined.

A monograph such as this is also the ideal occasion to examine the uniqueness of Antwerp Cathedral's personality. And in many respects the cathedral is unique, even among its great sisters of the Brabantine Gothic, if only for its imposing dimensions and highly individual proportions, not unimpressive even today, or for its slender north tower. The 'new work' of the Gothic church, on the site of the existing Romanesque church, began in the middle of the fourteenth century with the choir with its gallery and chapels, after which the unique seven-aisled nave and the transept were completed. Building continued until 1521. Then Emperor Charles V laid the first stone of an even greater shrine. The surviving vestiges of the extension to the choir gallery are silent witnesses of a dream which evaporated, the end of an era. After that there was no more building; the cathedral was embellished, altered and restored. And devastated, too. Two iconoclasms and French domination. The building only just survived. It experienced its last flowering during the neo-Gothic era. It was 'repaired and embellished', as Floris Prims wrote, 'according to the requirements and standards of the neo-Gothic which prevailed and flourished at the time.' W.H. Vroom, who studied the financial affairs of the church, notes: 'At a European level the building of the church was one of the most prestigious religious undertakings of the fifteenth and early sixteenth centuries.'

Yet it is even more fascinating if, rather than reading the monograph as the individual story of a building and its institutions, one looks behind this local story for the account of a generic human adventure, in which mankind tries to exceed its own limitations and negate its own insignificance in the tremendous act of building. This is reflected in the first instance in the building process itself – every building is a Tower of Babel – but also in all the various events associated with a building such as this, from the celebration of a rite to the production of endless series of works of art, always pursuing the possibility of creating an image of mankind, albeit under the guise of an image of God.

This universal perspective, where the art-historical approach all too often leads nowhere, shows the data, anecdotes and figures in a different light and they acquire, by their immediate presence, a real significance. From this perspective they do not all become of equal value, but it is possible to compare them one with another. From this perspective, this book with its wealth of information points us beyond itself to the reality of the building as we see it today, resplendent once more. Polemics about the restoration are inevitable, and that is as it should be. But the building is there and will remain there, an inescapable challenge to our intellect.

GEERT BEKAERT
Translated by Alison Mouthaan.

Willem Aerts, a.o., *Antwerp Cathedral*. Mercatorfonds, Antwerp, 1993; 425 pp.

Cultural Policy

The Dutch Language Union

In the Netherlands and Flanders (the Dutch-speaking part of Belgium) Dutch is the official language. Together they make up a language area of over 20 million people. This makes Dutch the third most important Germanic language in the world, after English and German.

In 1980 the Kingdom of the Netherlands and the Kingdom of Belgium signed a treaty which officially recognised that Dutch was the common language of the Dutch and the Flemish. This treaty also provided for the founding of a body to develop the unity of the language, the Dutch Language Union *(Nederlandse Taalunie)*.

The Dutch Language Union is a unique instrument. Nowhere else have two sovereign states entrusted their common concern with a language and with the literature in that language to a joint body by a formal treaty. In the field of language and literature Belgium (Flanders) and the Netherlands have voluntarily limited their sovereignty for the sake of greater unity, so that together they are responsible for the Dutch language. The treaty also ensures that in future decisions to do with language and literature will not be taken unilaterally by one country without other speakers of the language on the other side of the border being consulted.

The Language Union consists of four bodies. Policy is outlined by the Committee of Ministers. This is made up of the Dutch and Belgian ministers of education and of culture. It lays down a common policy for the whole language area and could be called the Language Union's government. The second body is the Interparliamentary Commission, which consists of members of parliament from the Netherlands and Flanders. They can ask the Committee of Ministers to explain the policy followed. The advisory body of the Language Union is the Council for Dutch Language and Literature. It consists of people who have to do with language through their profession or position. They may be linguists or writers or people in publishing, education, the media, libraries, etc. The members are appointed for a limited period by the Committee of Ministers. Lastly, there is the General Secretariat, which prepares and implements policy. This is located in The Hague. The Dutch Language Union gets two thirds of its funds from the Netherlands and one third from Belgium.

The third article of the treaty lists the aims of the Language Union:
a. the joint development of the Dutch language;
b. the joint promotion of knowledge of and correct use of the Dutch language;
c. the joint promotion of Dutch literature;
d. the joint promotion of the study and dissemination of the Dutch language and Dutch literature in other countries.

This is a very wide field, including among other things the joint determination of the official spelling and grammar of the Dutch language, dictionary policy, terminology, and policy as regards the language and Dutch literature in an international context. The Language Union must also promote education and research in the fields of the Dutch language and Dutch literature, and ensure that the language is used correctly in education, the civil service, the mass media and so on. Another important task is that of promoting or organising the teaching of Dutch language, literature and cultural history in other countries and of encouraging the dissemination of Dutch literature, whether in translation or in the original.

Since it was founded, more than ten years ago, the Language Union has published a series of reports, carried out various studies, organised many conferences, produced surveys and provided subsidies, etc. So it has not been idle during this period. Opinions differ as to the results achieved. People who have been working for years in the field of language and literature claim that the Language Union suffers from a very cumbrous administration and that the ministers concerned have shown a lack of political will during its first decade. Those now responsible for policy are aware of this and want to give a new élan to the work of the Language Union, since there is no doubt that it remains an impor-

The Dutch language-area in Europe.

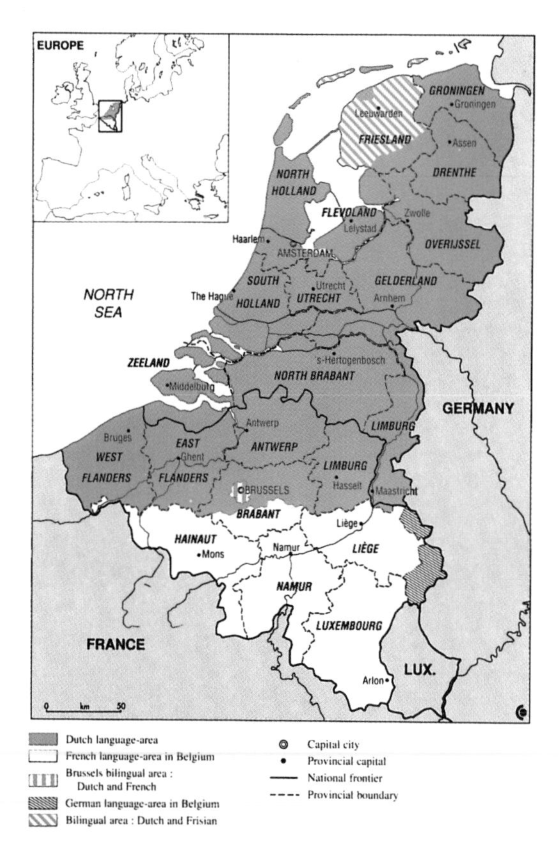

tant institution. A plan has been developed to increase its effectiveness and versatility and to make it a forceful and stimulating factor in the cultural life of the Netherlands and Flanders.

DIRK VAN ASSCHE
Translated by John Rudge.

Address:
Dutch Language Union
Stadhoudersplantsoen 2 / 2517 JL The Hague
The Netherlands
tel. +31 (0) 70 346 95 48 / fax +31 (0) 70 365 98 18

The most important reports and memoranda produced by the Dutch Language Union appear in the series *Voorzetten;* in addition, it publishes a *Publikatieblad* with reports on its activities. Both publications are available form the above address.

The Social and Cultural Planning Office

A Barometer of Dutch Well-being

'To conduct scientific investigations with the aim of producing a coherent description of social and cultural well-being in the Netherlands.' This is in a nutshell the objective of the Social and Cultural Planning Office *(Sociaal en Cultureel Planbureau)* in Rijswijk. This office, established in 1973, is reputed to be unique in the world. It originated from the idea that, alongside a department – the Central Planning Office *(Centraal Planbureau)* – where economic analysis is carried out on behalf of the politicians, there should be a body possessed of the necessary instruments to give an overview of the social and cultural changes occurring in society. For in the nature of things, the politician has not only to make economic decisions, but also decisions about health, education and housing; and these are in turn closely linked to all sorts of behaviour patterns.

The idea for such a body clearly originated in a period when people still firmly believed that society could be shaped, and when, financially speaking, it seemed that the good times would never come to an end. It was thought that human behaviour could be predicted and that politicians could attune their policies to it. This proved to be an illusion. The present researchers of the Social and Cultural Planning Office have therefore distanced themselves from these pretensions. Social reality turns out to be much more obstinate and capricious than the initiators supposed at the beginning of the seventies. Only the name it was given – by analogy with the Central Planning Office – still reminds us of those great intentions.

Nevertheless, since then the Office has built up a solid reputation with its biannual analysis, in which changes in the attitudes and needs of the population are statistically measured. For example: Do youngsters want to live alone, or do they prefer to stay with their parents? This sort of need pattern appears to change very rapidly and it is a matter of great importance to the Office to keep track of these changes, so that politicians may use them to their advantage. The researchers try to chart any trends as soon as possible. An important part of the work consists of dealing with specific requests by politicians with a particular policy-decision to make. In recent years members of the government have very often called upon the Office to provide a basis for a particular financial cut-back. Some time ago, when research showed that small children, legally entitled to attend school, were not always ready for it, the Minister of Education wasted no time in letting them go to school less often. But creating facilities for those children to be looked after elsewhere was out of the question. However, in the view of the Social and Cultural Planning Office, its task is to sketch a coherent picture of the problems, even if politicians then seize on only that element of it which suits their book.

Criticism of the Office often centres on the fact that at first sight the Office is having a second go at things which have already been worked out by the research departments of the various ministries. Yet this criticism doesn't hold water, for the Office's objective is to sketch a coherent picture of the needs. That picture is simply more accurate than those outlined by the separate ministries, which quite often tend to be in competition with one another.

Every two years, the Office publishes a voluminous report (also translated into English) in which all the changes taking place during that period are systematically reviewed. It has an impressive mass of data available for this purpose. It is by nature fodder for politicians and journalists. Here are some examples of the topics to be found in the report: how does crime develop and how does the population react to it? What type of school does the population prefer, and must the (expensive) system of separate public and private (read *Christian)* schools be maintained? What values does the population consider most important? What is the pattern of leisure activities?

The researchers of the Social and Cultural Planning Office sometimes have the feeling that too little is done with their reports. But to a certain extent this is quite understandable, for politics and politicians do not function in a purely rational and scientific way.

The reports of the past four years show that Dutch society is becoming more and more equal. Differences in income have become small. The ideal of equality, professed by most politicians, has largely been put into practice. The latest report indicates that the Dutchman is in general a contented person, but at the same time pessimistic about the future.

PAUL VAN VELTHOVEN
Translated by Annie Goddaer.

Some recent publications of the Social and Cultural Planning Office:

Social and Political Attitudes in Dutch Society (1992)
Social and Cultural Report 1992

Address:
Social and Cultural Planning Office
P.O. Box 37 / 2280 AA Rijswijk
The Netherlands
tel. +31 (0)70 319 87 00 / fax +31 (0)70 396 30 00

The Promotion of Translation in the Netherlands and Flanders

From 1954 until 1990 the Foundation for the Translation of Dutch Literature *(Stichting ter bevordering van de vertaling van Nederlands letterkundig werk)* supported the translation of Dutch and Flemish literature into foreign languages. Two thirds of its financial support came from the Netherlands Ministry of Culture and one third from the Flemish Ministry. Following a number of difficulties with the Foundation, the Dutch and Flemish authorities decided in 1990 to formulate their own translation policies. This meant the termination of the Foundation's activities, and the introduction in the Netherlands and Flanders of separate policies to promote translations from Dutch.

In December 1990 therefore, the Foundation for the Production and Translation of Dutch Literature *(Nederlands Literair Produktie- en Vertalingenfonds)* was established in the Netherlands. One of the Foundation's aims is to promote the translation of Dutch literary works into other languages. It looks primarily to the major European languages (English, French and German) and to the countries with a tradition of translating from Dutch (such as the Scandinavian countries, Poland and the Czech Republic).

The Foundation works mainly with publishers. They receive information, including translated excerpts from Dutch books. An approach from a foreign publisher will be judged by the quality of the work itself, the translator and the publisher. The Foundation also meets part of the cost of translation. In America the approach is through 'Eurosellers'; American publishers are offered books that have already achieved some success on the European book market. English translations so far include Cees Nooteboom's *Rituals,* Connie Palmen's *The Laws* and anthologies of work by Armando, J.M.A. Biesheuvel, W.F. Hermans and other Dutch writers.

In Flanders no new body was set up to replace the original Foundation. The Flemish Ministry of Culture will in future determine its own translation policy, and this differs from the Dutch model. The Flemish Ministry targets its support on the translators. This means that if a translator can produce a contract with a foreign publisher, he will then receive 70% of the translation fee from the Ministry; he receives the remaining 30% when the work is published. The intention is, of course, to provide translators with better payment for their work; but also to gain easier access to foreign publishers through them, and to apply pressure on the publishers to honour their agreements.

Sometimes the Ministry will cooperate with the publishers themselves. In Eastern European countries, for instance, there may be assistance with production costs. It may guarantee to purchase a number of the translated books, thus reducing the publisher's risk. These books are then sent to Dutch departments at universities abroad or to Belgian embassies. The Flemish policy on translations gives priority to translations into English, French or German. There is however considerable interest in other Romance countries and Scandinavia. Recent translations supported by the Flemish Ministry have included works by Hugo Claus, Patricia de Martelaere, Kristien Hemmerechts and Ivo Michiels.

To enable translators to become better acquainted with Dutch literature and its writers, the Dutch Foundation and the Flemish Ministry have introduced the 'Translators' House'. The translators are given the opportunity of staying for a short time in Flanders or the Netherlands. They stay in a comfortable house in Leuven or Amsterdam and receive a grant to cover their living costs.

Although the Netherlands Foundation for the Production and Translation of Dutch Literature and the Ministry of the Flemish Community developed their own policies, they still work together in promoting their common aim. They shared a stand at the 1992 *Frankfurter Buchmesse.* Several promotional leaflets are published jointly. *De Nieuwsbrief Letteren* (The Literary Newsletter), which appeared for the first time in the summer of 1992, is published three times a year. It regularly contains articles on aspects of current Dutch literature and provides specific information on notable recent books in Holland and Flanders and on available translations. In addition *Books from Holland and Flanders,* a brochure with information on recent developments in Dutch literature, is sent to publishers abroad three times a year.

On the occasion of the *Frankfurter Buchmesse 1993,* when the main theme was the Netherlands and Flanders, a German-language *Yearbook of Dutch and Flemish Literature* was published by Hanser Verlag. This contains biographical and bibliographical information on more than a hundred twentieth-century writers in Dutch.

In recent years we can speak of a (relative) success for Dutch literature abroad. There is considerable interest in the work of a number of Dutch and Flemish authors. This is obviously due primarily to the quality of their work; but we can also be sure that recent policies promoting translations in the Netherlands and Flanders must claim some credit for this success.

DIRK VAN ASSCHE
Translated by Peter King.

Addresses:
Foundation for the Production and Translation of Dutch Literature (Director: Frank Ligtvoet)
Singel 464 / 1017 AW Amsterdam / The Netherlands
tel. +31 (0) 20 620 62 61 / fax +31 (0) 20 620 71 79

Ministry of the Flemish Community, Arts Administration. (Director: Robert Elsen)
Koloniënstraat 29 / 1000 Brussels / Belgium
tel. +32 (0) 2 510 34 11 / fax +32 (0) 2 510 36 51

Writers in Residence

Hosting a Dutch writer in residence at a Dutch programme offered at a US university[1] is a bittersweet experience: it can be sweet, but it can also be bitter, depending on the personality of the writer.

Based on my experience, writers in residence (those who, in the past, spent an academic year at universities in Texas, Michigan, and Minnesota) can be located anywhere on a line between two diametrically opposed poles. There are amerophiles and there are amerophobes. The chances of your (and your students') experience being better (or less bitter) tend to be higher with amerophiles, not necessarily because they are amerophiles *per se,* but because their amerophilia enables them to give the US the benefit of the doubt.

Amerophobes, on the other hand, are a bitter experience indeed, simply because they already know everything there is to know about the US before they set foot in it, and because they are utterly determined both not to let any positive experiences they might have (God forbid) undermine their knowledge, and to let any negative experiences compound (confound?) it even more.

Both amerophiles and amerophobes have to cope with the Roosendaal syndrome, so named after the late Dutch entertainer Wim Kan's famous quip: *'de roem houdt op in Roosendaal'* (fame ends in Roosendaal, the city in the Netherlands just above the Belgian border, traditionally considered the watershed between 'us' and 'them').

The Roosendaal syndrome simply means that you were somebody, maybe even a (relatively) big somebody in the Netherlands, and that you are nobody in the US. If you try to convince students of your excellence in spite of appearances, you are bound to run into the fatal question: 'Where can we buy your books?' And in most cases your books are, alas, not available in English. Amerophiles tend to suffer less from the Roosendaal syndrome, again not because they are amerophiles, but because they feel they are somehow able to concentrate for a while not on their selves but on their new environment. Amerophobes, who know everything about that environment anyway, including, especially, the parts of this vast country they have never visited, find nothing to alleviate the gloom they flounder in, and suffer from the Roosendaal syndrome accordingly.

The bitterest case – and the Calvinist Lord has seen fit to visit only one of those on Texas, the unforgettable and soon forgotten Benno Barnard – is when you have to deal with a writer who is hounded by the potentiality of the Roosendaal syndrome even while in Holland, and who has developed boundless arrogance as a defence mechanism.

Both amerophiles and amerophobes also have to cope with the welfare state syndrome. Generations of immigrants, from Albanian goatherds to Laotian mountain people, have come to the US and been able to fend for themselves. Not so Dutch writers. They expect to be met at the airport, without sparing the shadow of a thought for the – after all relatively simple – proposition that the Dutch professor may have a life of his own, and that holiday plans may be part of that life, and they further expect the Dutch professor and / or his assistants to take care of them. Amerophiles soon recognize this as somewhat aberrant behaviour, and strike out on their own, in true pioneer spirit. Amerophobes, on the other hand, see in every US law an attack both on their individual integrity and on the sovereignty of the Kingdom of the Netherlands.

Finally, Dutch writers in residence have to cope with inflated expectations. First, the title 'writer in residence' is not necessarily a first step toward the Nobel Prize. There are many thousands of writers in residence scattered over all US institutions of higher education. Second, Dutch is not exactly a central subject in the US university curriculum, avidly pursued by the best and the brightest of American youth. You have to start from scratch, and teach the language first. Then, as increasingly at the University of Texas, you build up your graduate programme, and if that looks good you will get a trickle of graduate students from other universities, or simply people who want to work with you. The problem is that graduate students taking an interest in Dutch literature, for instance, feel they should learn something about all periods of that literature, not just the works of contemporary writer x, no matter how great and / or near at hand he or she may be.

There are writers in residence who work it out for themselves. My favourite here was (and is) Jan Donkers. Cees Nooteboom is another Dutch writer who has the openness of mind that allows him to overcome the Dutchness which so many among the Dutch flaunt like a combination of a place among the elect and a security blanket. These writers become (very) good teachers, even if they have never set foot in a classroom in that capacity before. They earn the interest and the gratitude of their students, and they have succeeded in the two parts of their mission: to enrich their students and to enrich themselves. Some, like Jean Pierre Plooij, Christine Kraft, and again Jan Donkers even go beyond this and organize Dutch cultural manifestations that actually attract people from all over the campus.

There are other writers in residence who remain invisible, quietly fulfilling the second part of their mission while nobody in the department notices their presence. Finally, there are writers in residence whose doom it is to take Holland with them wherever they go, and not the tolerant and generous Holland of history, rich in cultural achievements, but the petty, wrangling Holland of the contemporary Randstad, rich only in arrogance, self-aggrandizement, and sectarianism. Those who cannot leave that Holland behind when they travel outside of it could at least do the rest of the world a favour and stay there.

It is probably unrealistic to expect writers, especially younger writers, who have to build up their career and their contacts, to stay away from the Randstad altogether for what amounts to nine precious months. The people in Amsterdam who send us writers to reside among us have realized this too. The new formula[2] that has been proposed sounds more promising: send writers on a tour of the US for a few months, let them spend four to five weeks at each university where Dutch is taught, and let advanced students, who have read their work before they arrive, talk about that work with and to them. That kind of experience is likely to be sweet for students; whether it will be for writers depends entirely on them. The US constitution, be it remembered, guarantees – in theory at least – only the *pursuit* of happiness.

ANDRÉ LEFEVERE

1. André Lefevere is Professor of Dutch at the University of Texas at Austin *(eds.)*.
2. It has been suggested to reduce the 'writers in residence' - scheme to one writer in the US (based in New York), while other writers will be staying in European countries *(eds.)*.

Dutch Arts An Introduction to Culture in the Netherlands

For some years now, the Department of International Relations of the Ministry of Welfare, Health and Cultural Affairs in the Netherlands has been publishing a series of booklets in English called *Dutch Arts*. The aim of these copiously-illustrated booklets is to give foreign readers a portrait of the Netherlands through its cultural production.

Dutch Arts is also the title of the first booklet in this series. In a number of short chapters it deals with the following subjects: 'Visual Art', 'Architecture', 'Music', 'Dance', 'Theatre', 'Literature' and 'Film', sketching both the historical framework and the current situation for each of these 'arts'. The editors of the book are hoping in this way to contribute to a better understanding of Dutch culture abroad in the conviction that 'our understanding of man increases with our knowledge of his culture, aided by the images, words and sound of arts'.

Each of the subsequent booklets has a theme. In this way, music, literature, visual art and theatre are extensively covered. The applied arts also receive attention in issues devoted to architecture and design. The booklet entitled *Cultural Heritage in the Netherlands* is slightly broader in scope. Here the authors examine the tangible traces Dutch history has left in its wake – with the battle against the water, the shifting climate between war and peace and the relationship with religion as the formative forces. This journey of discovery provides a broad overview of museums, monuments and libraries.

At the same time, the quality of the booklets' content makes *Dutch Arts* more than a straightforward cultural inventory of the Netherlands. The way in which the themes are approached presupposes a more than superficial interest on the part of the foreign reader. For example, *Theatre in the Netherlands* begins with a theoretical examination of the origins of theatre as a typical product of *homo ludens*. The result is that readers become acquainted with Dutch culture against a general-intellectual background.

The thoroughness of the editors is also apparent from their choice of writers. Each booklet is written by a number of different people who – by virtue of their professional activities – each have a thorough know-

ledge of a particular period or a specific area of the subject in question. Moreover, their contribution is complemented by useful addresses and bibliographical information at the end of the booklets.

Dutch Arts is distributed to a number of foreign museums, scientific institutes and embassies on the basis of a mailing list compiled by the Department of International Relations.

FILIP MATTHIJS
Translated by Alison Mouthaan.

Dutch Arts
Ministry of Welfare, Health and Cultural Affairs
Department of International Relations
P.O. Box 5406 / 2280 HK Rijswijk / The Netherlands

Logo *Schwerpunkt Frankfurter Buchmesse 1993:* 'Flanders and the Netherlands'.

The Netherlands and Flanders at the *Frankfurter Buchmesse*

The 35th *Frankfurter Buchmesse* took place from 6 to 11 October 1993, with the Netherlands and Flanders as the joint focus of attention, the *Schwerpunkt.* The *Frankfurter Buchmesse* is without doubt the largest and most important book fair in the world, attracting exhibitors from 100 countries representing around 8,000 publishers in an exhibition area covering more than 120,000 m². Although this fair is not a major commercial event, since publications may only be sold to book dealers, the *Frankfurter Buchmesse* is irreplaceable as *the* annual meeting place for the international publishing world.

In focusing jointly on the Netherlands and Flanders the *Frankfurter Buchmesse* was, for the first time in its history, giving pride of place to two separate political entities. For the first time, attention focused on a language community which extends beyond national boundaries. Together, the Netherlands and Flanders form the Dutch language-area, and both were seeking to underline this unity by joint participation. This choice was motivated by the growing realisation that far-reaching collaboration is essential in order to protect the Dutch language and Dutch culture in a Europe moving towards unification. One might mention in passing that Dutch is also spoken outside Europe, being one of the official languages of the island of Aruba and of the Netherlands Antilles, as well as of Surinam in South America.

The motto chosen for the *Schwerpunkt* at the book fair was 'The Netherlands and Flanders: open to the world'. This slogan was intended to demonstrate the openness of Dutch-language culture. For the Dutch language-area must not be regarded as an 'island'; it must not only present itself to the outside world, but must also be open to the intricacies of other cultures. For this reason, in the activities which formed part of the *Schwerpunkt* the emphasis was frequently placed on that 'openness', past and future.

Those responsible for the *Schwerpunkt* were keen not to restrict the presentation of Dutch-language publications to literary works. Scientific publications, educational works, children's books and youth literature, art books and even comic strips were also much in evidence. Each day, a special topic or field was highlighted through the organisation of forums, panel discussions and lectures. Among other topics, attention focused on 'feminine literature', the problems of translation, the library system, bookselling, prose and poetry. Some events were even taking place outside the exhibition complex itself. On 6 October, for example, a 'Night of Poetry' was being organised in the *Alte Oper* in Frankfurt. There was room for other art forms too, on the fringes of the *Frankfurter Buchmesse.* In the *Schirn Kunsthalle,* for example, there was a large exhibition of seventeenth-century painting from the Netherlands and Flanders. In addition, Dutch and Flemish groups and companies presented a variety of musical, theatre and dance productions in and around Frankfurt.

The follow-up to the *Frankfurter Buchmesse* will be important. For instance, the literary world is hoping that the number of translations from Dutch will increase as a result of the fair. To date, such activity has been limited, particularly in comparison with smaller languages such as Swedish or Danish. Relatively few Dutch-language books have been translated into English; with the exception of a few big names such as Harry Mulisch, Cees Nooteboom and Hugo Claus, Dutch literature is virtually unknown in the Anglo-Saxon world, even among the cognoscenti. If the overall number of translations were indeed to increase (as already happened in 1992 as a result of a large number of German translations), then the *Frankfurter Buchmesse* has done Dutch-language culture a very great service.

HANS VANACKER
Translated by Julian Ross.

Antwerp Cultural Capital of Europe 1993

In 1993 Antwerp received the accolade 'Cultural Capital of Europe', an initiative of the European Community. In 1992 Madrid was the bearer of this title, and in 1994 the honour will go to Lisbon. The chosen cities offer a cultural programme which can include exhibitions, concerts, theatre productions, film, literature and architecture among other things, each city being free to interpret the project according to its own preferences. The aim of the event is to focus attention on the culture of the chosen city or region, although contributions from other member states of the Community may also feature. With this initiative the EC aims to demonstrate that the Community is more than simply an economic partnership or a gigantic bureaucracy.

The practical realisation of the programme for Antwerp was placed in the hands of Eric Antonis, a man with a great deal of experience who is, among other things, a former director of the cultural centre in the Flemish city of Turnhout and leader of a prominent theatre company in the Netherlands. Instead of dividing the available resources, totalling more than 900 million Belgian francs, among local museums, orchestras, theatres etcetera, Antonis decided to set up his own style of art festival, with the accent on innovative trends. His banner was an overt declaration of war on provincialism.

Major historical exhibitions are a mandatory item on the menu of the Cultural Capitals programme, and Antwerp continued this tradition. These exhibitions attract a large public, and provide visitors with the necessary background information to enable them to understand the traditions and individual nature of a region. The idea in putting Antwerp forward as Cultural Capital was to mark the four-hundredth anniversary of the birth of the baroque artist Jacob Jordaens (1593-1678). A splendid exhibition of paintings and drawings from the world's greatest museums proved that Jordaens fully deserves his place alongside Rubens and Van Dyck. His warm use of colour and candid affinity with the common people are highly original, although the artist's strength waned in his later years and his reputation suffered as a result of the large numbers of soulless canvasses produced by his studio.

The Central Station (Photo by A. van Raemdonck; Antwerpen 93).

Jacob Jordaens, *As the Old Sang, So the Young Pipe.* 1638. Canvas, 128 x 192 cm. Koninklijk Museum voor Schone Kunsten, Antwerp.

As well as exhibitions of medieval altarpieces with their impressive wood carvings, and masks from Zaire taken from the unique collection in the Ethnographic Museum in Antwerp, a testimony to Belgium's colonial past, the programme devoted considerable attention to contemporary visual arts. The city was also permanently enriched by the reorganisation and extension of the Open Air Museum of Sculpture in the Middelheim park, where pieces on display include works by Rodin, Henry Moore, Manzù, Zadkine and many others. Financial problems meant that there were glaring gaps in the collection, particularly from recent decades, and ten artists were accordingly each invited to create a work for Middelheim. They included Richard Deacon from Britain, the Dane Per Kirkeby, Spain's Juan Muñoz, the American Matt Mullican and the Flemish artist Panamarenko. Their work will remain on display in the park beyond 1993.

In the field of theatre and music, 'Antwerp 93' gave commissions to a number of young Flemish composers, directors and ensembles; but celebrated European names were also invited, such as the Frankfurt Ballet with William Forsythe, the French composer and conductor Pierre Boulez and his orchestra, and the German playwright Heiner Müller who directed his highly-praised *Hamlet / Maschine.* An old riverboat was converted and pressed into service as a floating theatre on Antwerp's River Scheldt, giving young artistic talent from fourteen cities (including Barcelona, Los Angeles, Ljubljana, Marseilles, Montreal and Johannesburg) a chance to shine.

An unusual aspect of the Antwerp programme was the attention devoted to philosophy and essay. The British cultural historian Peter Burke, well-known for his studies of the Italian Renaissance, wrote a book specially for the occasion entitled *Antwerp, a Metropolis in Comparative Perspective,* in which he explains Antwerp's rise to power as a centre of influence in the sixteenth century. In addition, a series of *Cahiers* ('Journals') was published containing eighty original texts by novelists, poets, artists, essayists, sociologists, historians, critics, anthropologists and philosophers, dealing with a wide range of subjects including provincialism, uprooting, orthodoxy and the postmodern animal.

In common with all the 'Cultural Capitals', Antwerp carried out an impressive programme of restoration in order to present the city at its best to visitors from home and abroad. The fine nineteenth-century Bourla Theatre, the gothic Cathedral of Our Lady and the Central Station, which is so close to Antwerp's heart, were all completely refurbished. There were also seminars and lectures on the urban problems facing Antwerp and the future development of the old port areas.

This brief review is far from complete. It does, however, show clearly that the organisers were not aiming for spectacular but short-lived success. On the contrary, their contribution will continue to bear fruit long after 1993 has passed into history.

JAN VAN HOVE
Translated by Julian Ross.

To mark the exhibition *Jacob Jordaens (1593-1678),* the following two English-language catalogues appeared:
R.A. d'Hulst, Nora de Poorter and Marc Vandenven, *Jacob Jordaens, Paintings / Tapestries.* Gemeentekrediet, Brussels, 1993; 303 pp.
R.A. d'Hulst, *Jacob Jordaens, Drawings / Prints.* Gemeentekrediet, Brussels, 1993; 140 pp.
Over het Interessante / About the Interesting, a bilingual trial issue journal from the *Discourse and Literature* project, was published in March 1993 by Kritak, Leuven.
Journals 2 *(Wordlessness)* and 4 *(Zoology. On (Post) Modern Animals)* will be published in English by The Lilliput Press, Dublin.

Film

Back to Basics Paul Verhoeven's Instinct for Success

The selection of *Basic Instinct* as the opening film of the 1992 Cannes Film Festival set the crown on Dutch director Paul Verhoeven's success. For the first time since 1968 a film directed by a Dutchman had again been admitted to this competition. Verhoeven (1938-) was the first Dutch director to brave the floodlights on the opening night of the world's most important film festival. The thriller *Basic Instinct* is the third American film made by Paul Verhoeven, who has been living in Los Angeles for the last six years. After *Robocop* and *Total Recall* he may well call himself the most highly paid director in the world, and feel flattered by the titles awarded to him by the American press. 'Sultan of Shock' and 'Attila the Director' are some epithets lavished on the 55-year-old filmmaker whose *Basic Instinct* has produced full houses, ringing cash registers and, this time, also lots of controversy. The film is indeed controversial, even though the puritanical USA tends to get more worked up about it than the Netherlands, where Paul Verhoeven has finally vanquished his old foes in the film world, e.g. the people of the Production Fund who subsidize film-making. The maker of successful films like *What's This I See?* (Wat zien ik?, 1971), *Turkish Delight* (Turks Fruit, 1973), *Keetje Tippel* (1975) and *Soldier of Orange* (Soldaat van Oranje, 1977), was ostracized after *Splutters* (Spetters, 1980), a charged and repulsive portrait of today's Dutch youngsters, fascinatingly drawn, and qualified as 'filth' by the Production Fund people. *Splutters* proved to be a popular success.

During the 1992 Dutch Film Days in Utrecht, Verhoeven was allowed to receive the Prize for Culture. The gross receipts of his new film in the Netherlands surpass those of *Robocop* and *Total Recall,* the spectacular science fiction movies. The first grossed 2,885,000 guilders and the second 5,790,995, and bear in mind that a cinema ticket costs between ten and twelve guilders in the Netherlands. *Basic Instinct* has already grossed fifteen million guilders. These are respectable sums in a country in which the majority of the population goes to the cinema either rarely or not at all. The controversy that raged in the Netherlands about Paul Verhoeven, who used to be known by many as the 'opportunist' and the 'cynic', as the 'man who has to rely on rough effects, and primarily on sex', seems to be dying down. The success of his movies is uncontested.

How are success and controversy linked, really? In 1979 the British movie historian Peter Cowie published his book *Dutch Cinema,* in which he devoted much attention to Verhoeven, who was then still living in the Low Countries and had just finished *Soldier of Orange* (distributed in England by the Rank Corporation under the title *Survival Run).* Cowie compared this film, a war epic centred on queen Wilhelmina's aide, Erik Hazelhoff Roelfzema, with *A Bridge Too Far* by Joseph E. Levine and Richard Attenborough. He concluded that Verhoeven's film 'on practically all counts outranks its rival'. Remarkable praise by an Englishman for the film Verhoeven still considers his best. 'It's the one I feel closest to', he said in a recent interview, and elsewhere, talking about the beginning of his career as a young intellectual stepping into the world of the cinema, the odd man out, he compared

Michael Douglas (m.) and Paul Verhoeven (r.) on the set of *Basic Instinct.*

himself to his soldier-hero: 'I came from the corps, the Leiden student corps of people like Erik Hazelhoff, you know, and landed in the perverted acting milieu ...'

He promptly created controversy, and in his best film he paints a picture of the Dutch people on the eve of World War Two, and immediately after liberation, that did not please too many viewers. Antisemitic feelings, quasi-fascist hazing rituals among students, flowers pressed into the hands of invading German soldiers ... 'Not many Dutch directors would have dared to show all this', wrote Peter Cowie. Here again we are faced with that remarkable, perhaps even dialectic combination of controversy and success in Paul Verhoeven's career. The British film historian informed us that the director was toying with plans to make another big film based on the novel *Success* (Erfolg, 1930) by the famous author Lion Feuchtwanger. That was in 1979, fourteen years ago, and Verhoeven has not made films about success since then, but rather successful films. The benefit of hindsight allows us to interpret the old plan as a good omen. The 'Sultan of Shock', 'Attila the Director', in short, the man who pretends to have made the 'Hitchcock movie for the nineties' with *Basic Instinct,* was forced to run the gauntlet in America. Many called the movie 'inimical to women' and 'homophobic'. There were threats and demonstrations, the press resorted to characterizations like a 'cop and copulation thriller', or even 'a stupid, overheated, sex machine of a movie'. But people were also fascinated by the bizarre, the fantastic and the sensual, the 'nonchalant decadence exhibited by *Basic Instinct*', as Verhoeven's wife put it. And that term, 'decadence', is probably the best characterization, as well as the best explanation of the film's great success. The term has been overused, and certainly misused, but we can understand it as soon as we realize the extent to which the film links up with the motifs and the sentimentalism of nineteenth-century decadent literature.

Verhoeven had shown before that he had a talent for this kind of thing, with his *The Fourth Man* (De vierde man, 1983), the movie that persuaded Mario Kasar of Carolco Productions to commission *Basic Instinct* from him. *The Fourth Man,* based on a novel by Gerard Reve (1923-), links up with books like *Les Diaboliques* (1874) by Barbey d'Aurevilly, and *Contes Cruels* (1883) by Villiers de l'Isle-Adam, French *fin de siècle,* black romanticism. *Basic Instinct* belongs to another culture, to the Anglo-Saxon tradition of the 'Gothic Novel' and the 'Tale of Terror', as the press has already pointed out. One should definitely not try to view it as a kind of realistic film, especially not since *Basic Instinct* works so emphatically with elements taken from the oeuvre of Alfred Hitchcock, particularly *Vertigo,* so outspokenly 'Gothic' and Victorian. This atmosphere is particularly reinforced by the music written by Jerry Goldsmith, so reminiscent of that written by Bernard Herrmann. Scenario writer Joe Eszterhas wanted to see the main character, writer and psychokiller Catherine Tramell, as the 'personification of the Devil'. Others point out a link with the women from *Fatal Attraction* and *The Hand that Rocks the Cradle.* Who still remembers the magnificent story written by Joseph Sheridan LeFanu, Irishman, Victorian, and past master of the 'Gothic Novel' about Carmilla von Karnstein, Count Dracula's female counterpart, foremother of the *'Belle Dame Sans Merci'* Catherine Tramell, bloodthirsty vampire and, maybe not coincidentally, very bisexual indeed?

DONALD UNGER
Translated by André Lefevere.

Daens, or Flanders in the Year 1900

Aalst at the end of the nineteenth century

During the nineteenth century Aalst, a small town in the Flemish province of East Flanders, situated between Ghent and Brussels, was a prosperous industrial centre. As elsewhere in Flanders at that time, the many factories were in the hands of the French-speaking Catholic and liberal (i.e. conservative) elite, who also held political control. The workers, who included many women and children, were paid a pittance which was barely enough to keep body and soul together. They were as good as powerless against this exploitation. Towards the end of the century the Aalst silk factories, in particular, found themselves in difficulties as a result of German competition. Even lower wages and even more female and child labour were introduced, along with factory mergers, in a bid to solve the economic problems. Gradually, however, resistance to the wretched working and living conditions of the workers began to emerge. A number of contrasting elements played a role in this resistance: rich versus poor, Catholic (clerical) versus liberal (anti-clerical) and, last but not least, Flemish-speaking (the working classes, non-enfranchised citizens, lower clergy) versus francophone (the aristocracy, higher clergy and upper middle classes).

In 1893 the *Kristene Volkspartij* (Christian People's Party), or *Daensism,* came into being in and around Aalst. The latter name was a reference to the priest Adolf Daens (1839-1907), whose aim was to see Pope Leo XIII's encyclical *Rerum Novarum* put into practice. The new party, which gained a following throughout Flanders, had its roots in an old Flemish democratic movement with a tradition of struggle against the power of the francophone aristocracy and middle classes, but which had become divided as a result of the first 'war of the schools' in Belgium (1879-1884), a battle about school funding which set free thinkers against Catholics.

The same fate quickly overtook *Daensism,* which as a Flemish and Christian People's Party was unable to project a strong enough image to compete with the Christian Democrats, the socialists and the progressive liberals. The Daensist movement ultimately lost itself in a tangle of purely 'flamingant', militant political, demands, which were of little interest to the Flemish working class.

The Flemish author Louis Paul Boon (Aalst, 1912-1979) is considered one of the most important writers of Dutch-language prose fiction after World War II. He skilfully managed to combine his talent as a narrator with a series of modernist experiments with language and form. In his masterpiece, the diptych *Chapel Road* (De Kapellekensbaan, 1953) / *Summer at Ter-Muren* (Zomer te Ter-Muren, 1956) Boon used an (anti-)novel form to describe social conditions in 19th-century Aalst. Alongside the laborious rise of socialism around the turn of the century, the author also evoked the beginnings of its decline around the 1950s.

In his historical epic *Pieter Daens, or how in the nineteenth century the workers of Aalst fought against poverty and injustice* (Pieter Daens of hoe in de negentiende eeuw de arbeiders van Aalst vochten tegen armoede en onrecht, 1971), Boon used historical material as a basis for describing the rise and fall of Daensism. This 658-page chronicle of the political and social struggle from 1840 to 1920 is written from the point of view of Pieter Daens, the brother of the priest Adolf Daens.

Daens, a film by Stijn Coninx

The film title *Daens,* by contrast, refers primarily to the priest Adolf Daens himself. The young Flemish film-maker Stijn Coninx (1957-) portrays ten years in Daens' life: Adolf Daens arrives in Aalst in 1888, where he revolts against the exploitation of the working classes, but in 1899 is forbidden to wear the cloth of a priest.

Rarely, if ever, has the screenplay of a Flemish film production been so thoroughly prepared. The screenplay was the joint work of the author Fernand Auwera, the film-maker Robbe De Hert, whose films include *De Witte van Sichem* and *Blueberry Hill* and who started preproduction work ten years ago, the French scriptwriter François Chevallier, and Coninx himself. The result is a cleverly constructed film plot. The almost documentary sequences showing the living and working conditions of the working classes, the central plot dealing with the emotionally loaded conflict between Daens and his reactionary opponent Charles Woeste, chairman of the Catholic party, and the attitudes of the clergy confronted with the 'Daens' issue, have been skilfully interwoven by Ludo Troch. The whole is enhanced by the sober colour photography of the highly acclaimed Walter van den Ende. And, above all, there is the successful direction of Stijn Coninx. As well as managing to find suitable locations in Poland, he was also able to extract excellent performances both from the cast and from the technical team. Jan Decleir, for many years one of Flanders' most important stage and film actors, is totally convincing as the rebellious priest Daens. The same goes for the French actor Gérard Desarthe as Charles Woeste, Julien Schoenaerts as Monseigneur Stillemans, bishop of Ghent, and Antje De Boeck in her first role, as well as for the more experienced, young and talented Michael Pas; these last two, as the young *Daensist* and the Ghent socialist, play out the love story within the drama that is *Daens.*

Jan Decleir (far left) as Adolf Daens.

Films of this nature often degenerate into melodrama, but the film-maker has managed to avoid this by occasionally breaking into dramatic moments, in the style of Louis Paul Boon, using ironic accents to bring the scene down to earth. In addition, the sometimes deliberately emphatic music by Fred Brossé ensures that the film goes beyond the level of raw realism. In this way Stijn Coninx manages to get close to what was the crucial element for Louis Paul Boon: a socio-political image of a time which in its essence is placeless and timeless.

Daens, a co-production by Belgium, France and the Netherlands, has won many prizes at festivals of all kinds (it was even nominated for an Academy Award in 1993), and these have earned the film the international recognition it deserves.

WIM DE POORTER
Translated by Julian Ross.

The following novels by Louis Paul Boon have been translated into English:
Chapel Road (Tr. Adrienne Dixon). New York, 1972.
Minuet (Tr. Adrienne Dixon). New York, 1979.

History

The Flemish Movement

Whenever we consider the history of Belgium we are almost immediately confronted with a problem of definition. The state of Belgium dates from 1830. Before 1830 there existed a conglomeration of territories which were governed from the late Middle Ages by the Burgundians, and later by the Spanish Habsburgs. From the eighteenth century, these territories were governed by the Austrian Habsburgs. After a short but rather significant period of French rule, the area formed part of the United Kingdom of the Netherlands between 1815 and 1830.

From very early on, Belgium was divided into a French-speaking area (Wallonia) and a Dutch-speaking area (Flanders). Wallonia, with its industry, was the more dominant of the two until well into the twentieth century; the turning point came in the 1960s. French was also the language of the ruling and intellectual elite in Brussels, the seat of government for the unified Belgian state. The educated bourgeoisie in Flanders also spoke French.

In the course of the nineteenth century an emancipation movement, influenced by linguistic nationalism, began to develop among the bourgeoisie, demanding more attention for the Dutch language. The bourgeoisie wanted the Dutch language to have equal status with French in government, justice and education. Consequently, between 1932 and 1963, a situation arose in which the language of the region became its official language, with bilingualism accepted only in and around Brussels. These developments were accompanied by intense political struggle. Finally, in the 1970s, it became clear that the federalisation of Belgium was inevitable.

This process is documented in *The Flemish Movement. A Documentary History 1780-1990,* using extracts from 96 sources which reflect the various aspects of the Flemish struggle for recognition of the Flemish language and culture. The first text, from 1786, is by the Englishman James Shaw. In his *Sketches of the Austrian Netherlands* Shaw posited that, one hundred years hence, only French would be spoken in Flanders; in fact, a century later, the first language laws were introduced, and two centuries later the federalisation of Belgium became inevitable. The source material, arranged chronologically and meticulously translated into English, consists of two elements. Much attention is paid to the great fighters in the Flemish emancipation struggle, with many extracts from their speeches, pamphlets and books. There are extracts from the work of philologists and men of letters such as Jan Frans Willems (1793-1846) and August Vermeylen (1872-1945), and from the work of socially-engaged intellectuals such as Julius Macleod (1851-1919) and Maurits van Haegendoren (1903-). There are also extracts from the work of politicians such as Frans van Cauwelaert (1880-1961), Camille Huysmans (1871-1968), Hendrik Fayat (1908-) and Gaston Geens (1931-). Alongside these there are extracts representing particular moments in the struggle, such as the first petitions (dating from 1840 and 1856) for greater recognition of the Dutch language in public life. Also of interest is the 1886 Walloon protest against the demand for bilingualism in Flanders. As early as 1932 the legislative foundations had been laid for the exclusive use of the Dutch language in Flemish public life.

Many texts deal with the attitude of the Roman Catholic clergy. The lower clergy supported the Flemish Movement. The episcopacy, on the other hand, had not only long been opposed to the division of Belgium, but also believed that French was the most suitable language for public and intellectual life in the country. The issue of the small German-speaking population in Belgium is not dealt with in this study. The federalisation process is dealt with at length. The concept of federalisation was first mentioned in a pamphlet from 1911 by Jules Destrée, but the process did not gain momentum until after 1970, when it became unstoppable. Socio-economic developments are also interesting. Until around 1960, Flanders was economically inferior to Wallonia, which had a large coal and metal industry. From the 1960s however, Flanders began to take the industrial lead and much Walloon industry, which was outdated and unable to compete with new energy sources, had to close.

Remarkably, although the texts show that Flemings and Walloons were often strongly opposed to each other, they have repeatedly succeeded in solving their disputes democratically. Naturally there were – and still are – extremist political parties, but as yet there has been no violent clash between the two sides.

The book's introduction was written by Lode Wils (Professor of Modern History at Leuven University), and he makes frequent references to the texts. The work was annotated by Louis Vos (Professor of History at Leuven University). Dr Theo Hermans, Reader in Dutch at University College London, was responsible for the selection and translation of the texts. The book contains a bibliography which includes many English works on Flanders.

This study is important for two reasons. First, it enables the English-speaking reader to gain an insight into a continental issue of nationalities, with the two parties concerned seeking a peaceful solution through federalisation. Second, the material may cause the British reader to reflect on Britain's own language-based nationalist movements in Scotland, Wales and Cornwall.

PIETER VAN HEES
Translated by Yvette Mead.

The Flemish Movement. A Documentary History 1780-1990 (Edited by Theo Hermans. Co-editors Louis Vos and Lode Wils). The Athlone Press, London-Atlantic Highlands (NJ), 1992; 476 pp.

Digging into Bruges's Past

Wherever you dig in European soil, you are likely to find ancient relics. It happened to a hotel-owner in Bruges who discovered in his hotel's foundations those of an early medieval chapel! On top of that, archeologists found that in earlier times the Romans had built their fortress nearby; while it was the Vikings who were responsible for the very name 'Bruges', which means not 'bridge' but 'haven'. Today there is a hotel called 'Brygghia'.

Consequently, contemporary tourists will find, within walking distance, a rich store of historical reminders. But do they realise just how much there is to enjoy? Fortunately, we now have at our disposal a magnificent book to serve us as a guide. Its English title is *Bruges and Europe,* and it is also published in Dutch, French and German. The Mercatorfonds (which publishes these volumes) is well-known for its splendid books with their lavish illustrations, and this one is faithful to that tradition. The illustrations are closely related to the text and the authors are as competent historians as they are fine popularisers. They make the reader share their enthusiasm for the city.

In fact, Bruges reflects the European past as a whole, at least during some glorious centuries, since it was a powerful trading centre during the period which the Dutch historian Johan Huizinga called 'the Waning of the Middle Ages'. But it became a sleeping beauty in later days, when Antwerp was in its turn to have its 'Golden Century'. Around 1550 began a decline which was to last until recent times. *Fin de siècle*-artists then found their morose inspiration in dreary Bruges, when even the local administration seriously neglected its task of maintenance and restoration. Why hide it: Bruges has known periods of unequalled splendour as well as centuries of sad decay.

The frontispice of the present volume shows the coat of arms of Edward IV, King of England. The symbol is well-chosen, since that monarch visited the city in 1478, in order to negotiate the forthcoming marriage of his sister Margaret of York with Charles the Bold. Much later, when Charles II had to go into exile, he found a quiet, hospitable refuge here. Both royal visitors left several tangible souvenirs, and it is not by chance that the chapter on Bruges and the British Isles is one of the richest. Relations with France, on the other hand, were full of conflict.

There were practical reasons for those relationships. The three Flemish textile-centres, Ghent, Bruges and Ypres, got their wool from England, so that serious tensions arose with the start of the Hundred Years War. The Count of Flanders was a feudal vassal of the French King, and conflict with the industrial *burghers* of these cities was inevitable. As early as 1302 the latter had been able to inflict a stinging defeat on the chivalrous cavalry from the South, and the first battle of the Franco-English war took place in 1340 near Bruges, at Sluis ('The Sluice'), when the French navy was destroyed there.

But other nationalities will find similar relics of *their* national past. For instance, the Germans with their pride in their mighty 'Hanseatic League', of which Bruges was a pillar, will be pleasantly surprised to come upon an Oosterlingenplaats (Easterners Square), where traders from the Baltic, the 'East'-Sea, had their home. Merchants from Lübeck, Novgorod, Bergen in Norway, and London, set up their common *natio* there.

Nor is this all. If Bruges has been called 'the Venice of the North', this was due not to the numerous bridges in both cities, but to the overland route that linked the Mediterranean to the North Sea. Later on, the Genoese came, and close to the present theatre, one finds the *loggia dei Genoesi,* now called the Saaihalle because of the serge that was sold there. And, by the way, a few steps further on, there was an inn, kept by the Van der Buerse family, where customers used to discuss the prices of goods going in and out. The *beurs, bourse, Börse,* as the continental stock exchanges are called, owe their name to that distinguished family.

Coat of arms of Edward IV, King of England from 1461 to 1483, by Pieter Coustain (Saint Salvator Church, Bruges).

Italy too has left many reminders. Here are hotels called *Lucca* (from the medieval silk-centre), *Portinari* (remembering the best-known representative of the Medici Bank), and *Adorne* (a wealthy family of which one member, Anselm, financed the Jerusalem Church, a remarkable piece of Brughian architecture).

All those 'foreigners' (not forgetting the Portuguese with their close ties to England, and the Spaniards) became respected citizens, and contributed substantially to the municipal Treasury. All these groups were organised into autonomous *nationes,* self-governing entities living under their elected consuls. They felt at home, married Bruges girls and often left their wealth to local heirs. No wonder that one of the contributors to this book, Ms Lori Van Biervliet, writes: 'When you walk through the streets of Bruges, you walk through Europe.' The names are eloquent indeed: English and Walloon Streets, Spanish Quay, Biscay Square, while the Spinola Canal reminds us of a famous Italian general who fought for Spain against the Dutch … And the Cordwainers Street takes its name from Córdoba.

During the great days the English had their *Domus Anglorum* at the Spiegelrei, while the Scottish *natio* was at home in the St Anna district. Much later, in the nineteenth century, the English 'colony' was by far the largest; in 1869 it consisted of 1,200 persons, with their own Bank, Union Club, tea-room and fancy-fairs. But that is another story.

In Bruges, humanists were welcome. Erasmus was here seven times, and called the place, with some exaggeration, *Athenai Belgicae.* Thomas More, too, is well remembered. It was here that he defended his friend's *Moriae encomium.* They both met with an English delegation headed by Wolsey, and enjoyed their discussions with the Spanish scholar Juan-Luis Vives, a Jew who had fled the Inquisition. Vives (whose bust can be seen behind the Gruuthuse-museum) bestowed on Bruges an early Welfare State, introduced by a learned paper: *De subventione pauperum.*

Of course, the present book contains a fine chapter on the so-called 'Flemish Primitives'. Curiously enough, few of them were born here; but such was the radiance of the city that great figures from all walks of life chose it as their residence.

At the same time, numerous men from Bruges went to sea. Some were associated with the explorations which Henri the Navigator organised along the African coast; in those days, the Azores were called 'Flemish Islands'! And a 'Guilhermo de Bruges' was entrusted with the command of the Portuguese fortress at Goa. The same great era both attracted and sent forth the most energetic and the most gifted of Europeans.

This period, when prosperity went together with artistic renovation, lasted for around two centuries. It started when the trade-fairs of Champagne lost their attraction, because the shorter sea-route around Gilbraltar had become safer when the Crusades were over. It came to an end after internal troubles – for some time the emperor Maximilian of Austria was kept prisoner in the house called Craenenburg which is now a café – and the *nationes* preferred Antwerp, since its institutional structures were more liberal and more modern than in Bruges.

When the Spaniards recaptured the Southern Netherlands, Flanders declined rapidly. The most energetic citizens, who had mainly adopted the Protestant faith, emigrated to the North, and the South came under the conformist rule of the Counter-Reformation. While the Northern Republic became a great maritime and colonial power, the future Belgium entered a period of drowsiness, under the domination of a French-speaking group, which, in Flanders, was only a small minority.

The last chapters of the volume deal with the nineteenth century and especially the end of it, when, on the one hand, a neo-Gothic revival had Bruges as its promised land while, on the other, decadent artists found their inspiration in the melancholy of a town where 'grass grew between the cobble-stones'. In both fields, however, British influence was prevalent and reinvigorating. Here the name of the architect James Weale has to be mentioned.

In conclusion: how dreadfully wrong are those who, today, dream of extreme Flemish nationalism, with a sickly distrust of foreign 'corruption'. They should realise that their fatherland was most widely admired when its frontiers were open and its population cosmopolitan.

H. BRUGMANS

Valentin Vermeersch, a.o., *Bruges and Europe.* Mercatorfonds, Antwerp, 1993; 445 pp.

Language

Van Dale, a Concept of Excellence

The Dutch-speaking area has an age-old, rich tradition of lexicography stretching back to the Middle Ages. For centuries, indeed until the nineteenth century, all lexica were translation dictionaries. Only then did monolingual explanatory dictionaries, explaining Dutch words in Dutch, begin to appear on the market. The most comprehensive dictionary of the Dutch language is the – still uncompleted – WNT (*Woordenboek der Nederlandse Taal* or Dictionary of the Dutch language) which was begun in 1852 and has been appearing in various volumes since 1882. The dictionary was begun by the Leiden professor Matthias de Vries. So far, it consists of thirty-seven hefty volumes with a total of 42,000 pages, and provides an extensive inventory of the Dutch language between 1500 and 1921. The completion of this mammoth enterprise, expected in 1998, rests with the Institute of Dutch Lexicology *(INL; Instituut voor Nederlandse Lexicologie)* in Leiden. The *WNT,* the result of 150 years of Dutch-Flemish cooperation, is highly comparable to Sir J.A.H. Murray's *New English Dictionary* (1888-1933), published in a new edition as *The Oxford English Dictionary* in 1933. Both are great scientific dictionaries originating in the nineteenth century and compiled on a historical-philological basis.

Authoritative general dictionaries of English and American bear the names Collins, Oxford, and Webster; comparable dictionaries for Dutch are named after Van Dale, Kramers, Koenen, and Verschueren. The whole quartet may be said to have been derived to varying degrees from the *WNT.* The *Van Dale* is considered the most authoritative of the four, both in the Netherlands and in Flanders.

Johan Hendrik van Dale (1828-1872) was born and raised in the small town of Sluis, in Zealand Flanders, on the Dutch-Belgian border. He died in the town of his birth, where he was headmaster and later keeper of the town records. He had taught himself philology. He is known mainly for the dictionary he revised: the *New Dictionary of the Dutch Language* (Nieuw Woordenboek der Nederlandse Taal), published in 1864. That dictionary, originally compiled by the brothers Calisch, was to be given Van Dale's name with the second edition of 1872. Van Dale did not live to see the publication of his work; he fell victim to smallpox. His work was continued and completed by his student Jan Manhave.The Sluis teacher owes a debt of gratitude to Manhave for the widespread fame now attached to his name, but much more to Dr Cornelis Kruyskamp. Kruyskamp left his mark on the dictionary for many years. He revised every edition from the seventh in 1950 up to and including the tenth in 1976. His successors described him as a discreet, brilliant, and headstrong man with a subtle feeling for language. In the preface to the most recent printing of the dictionary, now commonly called the 'Fat' or 'Big' *Van Dale,* they pay him this compliment: 'It is no exaggeration to say that he made the Big *Van Dale* what it is now.'

The twelfth edition appeared in the summer of 1992. The Flemish linguist Professor Guido Geerts and the Dutch lexicographer Dr Hans Heestermans acted as editors in chief on this occasion, as they had for the previous, 1984 edition. To have the most authoritative dictionary of the Dutch language co-edited by a Fleming and a Dutchman is sound policy: their intensive cooperation emphasizes the unity (in diversity) of the Dutch language area.

The monumental Big *Van Dale,* in three volumes running to about 4,000 pages, is a contemporary diachronic dictionary. It uses 240,000 entries to describe contemporary Dutch vocabulary, but also the vocabulary of an earlier period, generally speaking that of the last 150 years. Readers of newspapers, periodicals, not too specialized journals and contemporary writers are served well by it, as are readers of texts from the nineteenth and the beginning of the twentieth century. Users therefore encounter words like *aidsremmer* (Aids-retarder) and *hoge-snelheidstrein* (high velocity train), but also archaisms like *beurzenknipper* (purse-cutter, now *zakkenroller,* pickpocket) and *smijdig* (bendable, now *buigzaam,* flexible). The Big *Van Dale* mirrors what lives and lived in society. It is therefore first and foremost a descriptive dictionary, but it also has a normative function: it uses labels to indicate whether a word is correct, formal, informal, regional, archaic, historical, vulgar or offensive, among other things.

The twelfth edition contains 12,000 new entries, offers many new meanings for existing entries, and a large number of often surprising quotes and examples. A remarkable innovation is that the etymology of about 37,000 words has been included. The etymology of the adjective *Angelsaksisch* (Anglo-Saxon), for instance, is given as: first part derived from Latin *Angli,* via Germanic. Compare Old English *Angle, Engle,* i.e. coming from *Angul,* derived from *angul* (hook), therefore the hook-shaped region of Schleswig-Holstein.

The editors in chief have given the dictionary a highly informative and clear introduction in which they justify their modus operandi and explain their lexicographical principles. The introduction provides fascinating reading for the non-specialist who wants to understand something of the way in which lexicographers try to get a grip on the complex, recalcitrant, and eternally fluid reality of language. Their general criterion for including a word in *Van Dale* is this: if a word, a meaning, an expression, or an idiom has been current for at least three years throughout the whole linguistic area, it deserves a place in the dictionary, whether or not accompanied by a label such as 'informal', 'ironical', 'anglicism', among others.

An extensive collection of winged words from classical and modern languages and a list of names from Greek and Roman antiquity and from the Bible constitutes an interesting extra. In this way the Big *Van Dale* helps to maintain contact with the sources of our civilization.

This twelfth edition, the first to make use of computerized data bases, is the richest and most meticulous edition of this dictionary ever published. It is also a user friendly edition, thanks mainly to the clear and neatly ordered typography. A very attractive, clear font, aptly named 'lexicon', has been created especially for this edition. The eleventh edition sold 325,000 copies in eight years. It is expected that the twelfth edition will easily break this record. The Big *Van Dale* is an indispensable dictionary for countless lovers of language, crossword puzzles, scrabble, and cryptograms. It will be found in libraries, in the editorial rooms of newspapers, journals, and magazines, and in civil service offices.

The Big *Van Dale* is published by Van Dale Lexicografie bv, a subdivision of the multinational publishing company Wolters Kluwer. Van Dale Lexicografie bv has been managing monolingual and bilingual databases since 1975, with the indispensable help of the computer. Van Dale Lexicografie bv publishes not only the Big *Van Dale,* but also a series of 'Big' translation dictionaries aimed at those who deal with language professionally, a series of concise dictionaries for use at home and in school, and Van Dale's concise library for the language lover, consisting of the *Dictionary of Proverbs* (Spreekwoordenboek) in six languages, the *Comprehensive Dictionary of Synonyms* (Groot woordenboek van Synoniemen) and the *Etymological Dictionary* (Etymologisch woordenboek).

The 'Big' dictionary series consists of six hefty, mutually interrelated translation dictionaries, from and into French, German, and English / American, and a *Comprehensive Dictionary of Contemporary Dutch* (Groot woordenboek van hedendaags Nederlands). The latter contains a well-nigh complete inventory of the last 45 years and forms the basis for the translation dictionaries.

Four editors in chief and 250 collaborators have worked on these Van Dale dictionaries for ten years. Their work produced dictionaries that may well be called the best: they are more topical, comprehensive, reliable, and user-friendly than other contemporary translation dictionaries. The Dutch-English volume, for instance, is unique in the Dutch language area. It contains both British and American English (including American slang) with an extensive account of spelling and pronunciation variants, and also indicates where entries are Irish, Scottish, Canadian, Indian, Australian and South African English.

Van Dale Lexicografie bv is also active in the field of the new media, having recently developed an electronic dictionary, called *Van Dale Lexitron,* a CD-ROM-database that offers more than the usual dictionary: it also contains a spelling guide and provides extensive encyclopedic information. This 'dictionary' meets the needs of various professionals such as translators, journalists, and documentalists.

It was decided in 1975 to use the name 'Van Dale', which symbolizes reliability and quality, as a trade

The Big *Van Dale.*

mark. The books that have been published under that name outshine any other lexicographical work in the Dutch linguistic area up to the time of writing. In addition to all this, Van Dale Lexicografie bv has also walked the path of innovation on the international level.

ANTON CLAESSENS
Translated by André Lefevere.

The Certificate of Dutch as a Foreign Language Not such a Bad Idea

It may not be news to you but it is certainly true: in a united Europe your knowledge of languages is more than ever going to help you make it in society.

Take Dutch, for example, a medium-sized language, the third-largest Germanic language in the world after English and German and spoken by over 21 million people, mainly in the Netherlands and the northern part of Belgium (Flanders). It is therefore of no small importance in a European context or even worldwide, considering the important contribution of these 'low countries' to world trade, history, art and culture.

The fact is that several thousands of non Dutch-speakers both inside and outside Europe study Dutch, some for practical reasons, some for professional purposes and others simply for the fun of it. It is being taught in 246 universities in 37 countries outside the Dutch-speaking areas, among them 31 in the United States, 24 in Great Britain, 17 in South Africa, 5 in Canada, 3 in Australia, 2 in Ireland and 1 in New Zealand. With the exception of Greece, all non Dutch-speaking member states of the European Community offer Dutch at universities, and so do most non-EC countries within Europe. Numerous students of Dutch are to be found at institutions of non-university level, especially in the French-speaking part of Belgium (in the secondary schools for example) and in the French and German border areas of Belgium and the Netherlands. In addition, many immigrants within the Dutch-speaking area take Dutch language classes in specialized institutions.

A considerable number of these learners take part in the examinations for the Certificate of Dutch as a Foreign Language *(Certificaat Nederlands als Vreemde Taal)* so as to have an official proof of their proficiency in Dutch. The setting, organization and administration of these yearly examinations is carried out by a Dutch-Flemish staff, located at the *Université Catholique de Louvain,* at Louvain-la-Neuve, Belgium, under the auspices of the Dutch Language Union *(Nederlandse Taalunie).* The latter is a Dutch-Belgian intergovernmental organization which seeks to integrate the policy of the two countries concerning the Dutch language and literature in all its aspects.

The examinations for the Certificate of Dutch as a Foreign Language are organized on three levels (elementary, intermediate and advanced) each comprising separate tests for the four 'traditional' language skills: reading, listening, writing and speaking. A candidate has the choice of taking an exam for a complete level or for one or more of the separate skills, thus obtaining either a full certificate (when passing all four skills at one level) or a partial certificate. Any test can be repeated at will at a subsequent exam session and a full certificate will be granted after passing the four tests required.

The exams take place once a year on or about the first Wednesday of May. The examination bureau at Louvain-la-Neuve sends the same question papers, cassettes (for listening and speaking) and extensive instructions to the local examiners, usually teachers of Dutch at educational institutions. After the examination, the material is sent back to Louvain-la-Neuve where it is marked centrally by a team of trained examiners. The Examination Commission then decides upon the granting of certificates.

For each examination level the required vocabulary and grammar is laid down and a description of the requirements in terms of verbal ability is available. Thus both teachers of Dutch and potential examinees can form a clear idea of what will be expected. Old exams have been published and can be used as exercise material but the contents of the exams are not based on any specific manual or method prescribed or recommended by the Examination Commission.

Between 1977, when the Certificate originated, and 1992, 34,157 candidates from 32 countries took part. The bulk of these candidates, about two-thirds, were immigrants in the Netherlands and French-speaking Belgians. English-speaking countries taking part were: Australia, Canada, Great Britain, Ireland, the United States and South Africa. The rest of the participants came from countries as diverse and sometimes unexpected as France, Greece, Indonesia, Japan and South Korea.

In 1992, 5,827 examinees presented themselves and there was a significant increase of candidates from English-speaking countries (55% more than in 1991). English-speaking candidates, a total of 665 in 1992 (including those that took the exam outside English-speaking countries), generally do well in the Certificate exams. In 1992 they got 6% more passes than average at the elementary and the advanced levels and 10% more at the intermediate level.

So, if you're an English speaker, have some interest in languages and / or want to get ahead in life, why not go Dutch? After all, many people find it a charming language. Or maybe you have already started? Good choice! Anyway, if you're mastered some of it and feel ready to prove it, obtaining the Certificate of Dutch as a Foreign Language may not be such a bad idea.

MYRIAM GUNS

For more information, phone or write:
Certificate of Dutch as a Foreign Language
Université Catholique de Louvain
P.O. Box 12 / 1348 Louvain-la-Neuve / Belgium
tel. +32 (0) 10 47 29 95 / fax +32 (0) 10 47 49 49

Literature

Mulisch's Intellectual Challenge

Harry Mulisch (1927-) is undoubtedly one of the most talented of living Dutch writers. His work, which has received a number of awards, consists of novels, poetry, short stories, drama, current affairs and essays. There are English translations of Mulisch's novels *The Assault* (De Aanslag, 1982) and *Last Call* (Hoogste tijd, 1985) and the translation of his magnum opus *The Discovery of Heaven* (De ontdekking van de hemel, 1992) is expected in 1995.

Though Mulisch's work is very varied, two constants are clearly present throughout: the Second World War and Harry Mulisch himself. Mulisch's life and work are inseparable, for he regards his life as his source of insight; starting with his first novel *Archibald Strohalm* (1952) he has himself always been the undisputed centre of his work. Mulisch sees his work as a new, self-generated body, a living organism that must outlive him, born of a personal and human longing for eternity and immortality. Within Mulisch's esoteric views on writing, the act of writing is central, because in his opinion the writer only exists in what is written.

The Second World War, the other constant, deeply affected Mulisch's thinking. His father, an army officer in the Great War, was of Austro-Hungarian extraction; his mother was a Belgian Jewess. Mulisch's father collaborated with the occupying forces in the Netherlands during the Second World War, partly to protect his family. These circumstances, so traumatic for the young Mulisch, account for his later comment: 'I *am* the Second World War'.

Mulisch regards contemporary history as an extension of his own life. Consequently, his novels can be read as documentaries. He prefers to select the utopian moments in 'his' history, with the Second World War remaining to the end of time a horrific landmark. Thus in his most successful novel *The Assault* – in which one evening in the Second World War forms the starting-point for a whole lifetime – there are two utopian moments: the Hungarian revolt of 1956 and the massive peace demonstration in Amsterdam in 1981.

The bare observation that Mulisch's work reflects his own times seriously underrates his work, for it is the very multivalence of that work that is its essential characteristic. This kind of book can be read (and even studied) at a number of levels. Thus *The Assault* is a metaphysical novel devised as a classical tragedy that can also be read as a war novel or a psychological novel, or as a poetical novel. That *The Assault* stands in its own right as a gripping – and lucid – tale is amply proved by the film version of it. The film, which concentrated on the element of suspense, even won an Oscar. The novel, however, offers more.

The Assault is only briefly concerned with the attack on a Dutch collaborator during the occupation and the direct consequences of this event for the Steenwijk family, all of whom, apart from the youngest son Anton, are murdered by the Germans. The remainder of the book deals with the effects the Second World War proves to have had on the survivor, Anton Steenwijk, and on Dutch life in general. Psychologically, it follows Anton's development; the way in which he tries to come to terms with this dramatic event in his childhood. Philosophically, the main concern is with the relevance of guilt and responsibility. This philosophical leaning is typical of Mulisch's work.

Mulisch appears to be exclusively interested in mankind: he is preoccupied with probing what animates people in general – not any one unique individual. This means that he is a philosophical writer who is not afraid to tackle the larger questions in life. So the theme of his latest book, *The Discovery of Heaven,* running to more than 900 pages, is the worldwide paganising effect of headlong technological development and its disastrous results for humanity.

Harry Mulisch (1927-).

The Discovery of Heaven opens with a prologue in heaven. The narrator is an angel who is reporting to a superior on the measures he has taken in the world to accomplish his mission. His task was to bring back to heaven the stone tablets containing the Mosaic Law. People no longer pay the slightest attention to these Ten Commandments, so this material evidence of God's covenant has to be recovered as a confirmation of God's decree to withdraw his hand from humankind. To this end, however, an emissary must first be sent to earth to carry out the assignment. This celestial ruse leads to a series of bizarre and often humorous complications on earth; the novel's narrative comes largely from terrestrial beings.

However successful Mulisch's latest novel may be, I still consider *Last Call* to be his masterpiece. It has great pace, the construction is superb and the psychology is profound. *Last Call* tells of the demise of the elderly actor Uli Bouwmeester. In the twilight of his ill-fated life he is invited to perform just once more. In the play 'Heavy Weather' he has to take the part of an actor who is to play Prospero in Shakespeare's *The Tempest*. Of course *Last Call* can be read as a story about the theatre. Alternatively it can be seen as a study of freedom and the lack of it, in which the theatre becomes a metaphor for the world. But as an account of Uli's quest, his search for his destiny, the book is unequalled. The detachment that Uli increasingly achieves as the moment of death approaches makes a considerable impact on the reader.

The significance and the scope of Mulisch's subjects certainly entitle him to a readership beyond his own borders. The reader who overlooks Mulisch's literary complexity with its various facets and inferences is rewarded with well-written and extremely readable stories. But anyone with the interest and ability to compare Mulisch with other great writers and thinkers will have no cause to regret that intellectual challenge.

JEROEN VULLINGS
Translated by Peter King.

LIST OF TRANSLATIONS

'What Happened to Sergeant Masuro?' (Tr. Roy Edwards). *The Hudson Review*, XIV, 1961, 1, pp. 28-49.

'The Powers That Be' and 'Operating Garbage' (Tr. James Brockway). *The Literary Review*, V, 1961-62, 2, pp. 276-279 and 280-282.

The Stone Bridal Bed (Tr. Adrienne Dixon). London / New York / Toronto, 1962.

'The Death of My Father' (Tr. N.C. Clegg-Bruinwold Riedel). *Delta*, V, 1962, 2, pp. 86-97.

'Four Anecdotes on Death' (Tr. Ina Rike). *Delta*, XI, 1968, 4, pp. 5-17.

'The Horses' Jump and the Fresh Sea' (Tr. Adrienne Dixon). In: *Modern Stories from Holland and Flanders* (ed. Egbert Krispyn), New York, 1973, pp. 95-117.

What Poetry Is (Tr. Claire Nicolas White). Merrick (NY), 1979.

Two Women (Tr. Els Early). London / New York, 1980.

Symmetry (Tr. Adrienne Dixon). London, 1982.

The Assault (Tr. Claire Nicolas White). London / New York, 1985; Hardmondsworth, 1986.

Last Call (Tr. Adrienne Dixon). London, 1987; Harmondsworth, 1990.

A translation of *The Discovery of Heaven* is in preparation.

Poetry International Rotterdam

Poetry International started out in 1970 as a small ambitious festival organised by the Rotterdam Arts Council *(Rotterdamse Kunststichting)*. The city on the Maas was to become a free-port for poetry from the whole world and in every language. That was aiming high, and well beyond the then available means. But from the start it succeeded, albeit not without faults and failings. The idea was simple enough: 'To give a hearing to the human voice.' The original intention is clearly expressed in these words and they have been the guiding principle ever since. This meant that the festival had to find its own way and acquire its own character. That way has been marked out by poets from many countries, and the character has been formed by the same host of international poets. In past years, just for one week, an imaginary realm of poetry has been created. Some 900 poets from all over the world, (among them Joseph Brodsky, Seamus Heaney, Derek Walcott and Pablo Neruda), have been guests in Rotterdam. Since that first year they have done more than just read their poetry in their own languages, accompanied by oral and written translations. They have initiated several projects (including the well-known translation project), organised symposia and colloquia and spearheaded such popular events as *Poetry in the Park*, which now attracts roughly 80,000 visitors on a single Sunday. Poetry International has regularly acquired new elements and its scrutiny falls again and again on what surrounds us and determines our lives. It has been fortunate in that it started in a small way and could learn from its mistakes, and that there was an immediate contact between poets and public. Hence the introduction of such projects as *Children Write Poetry*, started by the American Kenneth Koch.

It has been said that Poetry International's festivals are politically biassed. This is a misapprehension that needs correcting. Poets are invited to contribute because of their poetry's place within their own language, not because of their nationality. Race, religion, political leanings or whatever are not considered in selecting them – the only consideration is their poetry. Poets are nominated by poets, not by writers' unions, ministries or embassies. This has often caused problems. Sometimes poets were barred from leaving their countries, or from travelling to the Netherlands, or the situation might be more serious than that. To meet such emergencies the Poetry International Award was introduced in 1979, intended for poets whose work involves them in serious political difficulties. The prize of Fl 10,000 is accompanied by an invitation to attend the festival as soon as the recipient is free to do so. The award has so far been made fifteen times, and in twelve cases it has possibly – sometimes definitely – contributed to the recipient's release. Since 1992 there is also the Ludo Pieters Writer in Residence Fund, which each year enables an author or poet who has difficulty in publishing in his own country to spend an academic year at a Dutch university.

There is evidence in Rotterdam of excursions into combining graphic art with poetry. Artists are regularly involved in the design of festivals and the visual presentation of poetry. Lucebert's line *'Alles van waarde is weerloos'* (Everything of value is vulnerable) has, since 1978, shone in neon lights from a prominent position high above the city. Thousands of tram passengers every day read the words *'Van de maan afgezien zijn we allen even groot'* (Seen from the moon we are all the same size) above a huge portrait of the author Multatuli. The autonomous Poetry International Foundation has been in existence since 1988, and since that time dustcarts have driven round the town with lines of poetry on their sides. It began with twelve new vehicles, now there are some two hundred of them and in the coming months the entire waste disposal fleet will be decked out with lines of poetry. The names of the writer are always given. Sometimes they are world-famous poets; others are not, but equally have something to say. Is there not something of the poet in everyone? Maybe it is the first time in history that poetry is brought from house to house like this. The lines speak for themselves 'Let the earth always be bright, and ever bright the skies' (Rafael Alberti, Spain); 'Our clock points to new times' (Joeli Kim, Russia); 'Sweetly rests the custom of power on the power of custom' (H.M.Enzenberger). We cannot say that these lines have any direct influence on daily life in Rotterdam, that they contribute to any change, let alone to an improvement in living conditions, but they are recognised and accepted. It no longer strikes people as strange. *'Het gedicht is een bericht'* (The poem is a news item) the Rotterdammer Jules Deelder wrote. He did not mean by this that the poet is a messenger, rather that he is concerned with what goes on around us with which we have to live. The Poetry International Foundation now has various offshoots: *Poetry in the Netherlands and Flanders, Poetry on the Road, Poetry International Exchange Programme, Poetry Assists, Poetry International Archives and Documentation Centre,* etc.

In June 1994 the 25th successive Poetry International festival will be held in Rotterdam. The International Advisory Board has already this year given thought to the next 25 years. Is Poetry still as it has been since the first festival in 1970, with all its variety and diverse forms, or is it becoming in some respects more thematic? Several possibilities have been mentioned: Politics, War and Peace, Science, Education, Music, Ballet, Mixed Media, Video, the Business World (ethics for the poet as advertisement writer), Forms of Distribution. The list can be extended with such themes as earth and sky, forms of cooperation with writers and their organisations in developing countries, or support for the poetry now emerging from Central and Eastern Europe. There are plenty of questions and proposals, and the possibility of selective realisation is there too. But whatever else may happen, poetry itself remains central to Poetry International.

MARTIN MOOIJ
Translated by Peter King.

Address:
Poetry International Rotterdam
De Doelen / Kruisstraat 2 / 3012 CT Rotterdam
The Netherlands
tel. +31 (0) 10 413 43 30 / fax +31 (0) 10 433 42 11

'Freedom was the priest riding past on his bicycle with his cassock flapping in the wind.' Lieve Joris and *Back to the Congo*

Two out of the four great contemporary Dutch travel writers – Cees Nooteboom, Adriaan van Dis, Carolijn Visser and Lieve Joris – are women, and they are by no means the least intrepid travellers. Carolijn Visser (1956-) travelled all through China, unhindered by officialdom of any kind, and wrote the sobering *Grey China* (Grijs China, 1982) about it. In the early eighties Lieve Joris (1953-) also braved the not exactly woman-friendly Islamic society of the oil states Saudi Arabia, the United Arab Emirates, and Kuwait. Her description of these societies in *The Gulf* (De Golf, 1986) proved so incisive that the book was immediately reprinted during the Gulf War. It was the first in her series of travel books, soon to be followed by *Back to the Congo* (Terug naar Kongo, 1987) and the beautiful, emotional story of a Hungary bursting at its communistic seams, *The Melancholy Revolution* (De melancholieke revolutie, 1990).

Born in a small Flemish village in 1953, Lieve Joris very early got the idea she absolutely had to leave her place of birth behind and go out into the big wide world. In an essay entitled 'A Room in Cairo' (Een kamer in Cairo), she writes: 'I spent six years gazing at the world through the windows of my Flemish boarding school. Freedom was the priest riding past on his bicycle with his cassock flapping in the wind.' That priest, or rather 'her uncle who was a priest in the Congo', who had left for the heart of Africa in 1923 to bring souls to Jesus, made her decide to travel to present-day Zaire in his footsteps. Her literary guides are V.S. Naipaul and especially the Polish author Ryszard Kapusinski with his lesson: 'Never judge immediately what you see, try to understand why it is like that.' Lieve Joris therefore listens impassively to the stories of her Africa-bound fellow passengers on the *Fabiolaville* and tries to understand why they talk about blacks in such a denigratory fashion. Or she observes all those old fathers and sisters in Zaire, the last idealistic relics of a colonial past. But she is relatively quick to leave these friends of her uncle-priest, certainly after she

Lieve Joris (1953-)
(Photo by Chris van Houts).

realizes during a visit to Yongapompe, where he lived for a while, that she is raising high expectations among the people there: they think she has come to continue his work. Shame and a feeling of unease come over her, and from then on she decides to leave her uncle the priest to the past and to observe and understand Zaire as far as possible through the eyes of the Zairians themselves. She therefore throws herself into the *cités,* the black neighborhoods, and talks to their young, frustrated, enthusiastic and intellectual inhabitants. She therefore visits, in all of that vast country, eighty times the size of Belgium, the little village of Gdadolite, where president Mobutu had built a megalomaniac, hugely expensive palace in a dirt poor environment. She therefore makes the fascinating boat journey from Kinshasa to Kisangani, where whole courts are in session on deck, and where people live and die. She is also quick to discover what 'article 15' stands for, the corruption trick that is the only means by which many Zairians are able to provide for themselves. And she realizes that Belgium has left its former colony in a most lamentable condition, with no senior administrators and with a population subjected to mistreatment. 'We should've fought a real war of independence, like the Algerians,' she quotes Lukusa, the Zairian intellectual, 'we should've killed lots more Belgians, then you'd respect us now.' At the end of her journey she spends a brief spell in jail, but not before she has found a safe haven for her notes, which is good news for the reader, because in this way *Back to the Congo* could grow into what it has become: a compelling, moving, and detailed portrait of a country struggling with both its colonial past and a present ruled in the same dictatorial manner.

RUDI WESTER
Translated by André Lefevere.

Lieve Joris, *Back to the Congo* (Tr. Stacey Knecht). Macmillan, London, 1992; 231 pp.

Keeping Up J. Bernlef's *Driftwood House*

No successful poet, any more than a successful literary movement, can afford to stand still. This is certainly true of J. Bernlef's role in the development of Dutch Modernism. When he began writing, it was in reaction to the preceding generation of modernist pioneers known as the *Vijftigers.* For them poetry was a matter of the personal verbal gesture. In contrast to the inauthentic 'ordering of chaos' from without of traditional writers, their organization began within the verbal chaos of the text.

For Bernlef (1937-) and his generation this approach seemed as authoritarian as what it replaced. They questioned the place of personality and therefore the need for its intervention in the work of art. Instead, they opted for a variety of Neo-Dadaist gestures, emphasising chance as the organising factor, as it is in 'real life'. This was the stance taken by *Barbarber,* the magazine with which Bernlef was associated between 1958 and 1971. Later in the 1970s Bernlef was appearing in the radically experimental *Raster* alongside the *Vijftiger* Gerrit Kouwenaar. What brought together the former protagonists was a common interest in the text as a phenomenon, a parallel reality.

Subjective description of outside reality etiolates its subject. Kouwenaar therefore began by attempting to give to the text its own material solidity. Discovering, however, that the use of language for its own sake was equally subjective, he turned to analysing this phenomenon and striving for greater impersonality. Bernlef had also found that the reality of things was resistant to the text. His strategy now was to explore how far any relationship was possible.

Bernlef seems to have been particularly impressed by the parallel explorations of two elder writers. One of these was the American Marianne Moore, who is the subject of one of his essays and whose poetry he has translated. Her line about 'creating imaginary gardens with real toads in them' has become one of Bernlef's yardsticks. The reader must always be reminded that a text is no more than an arrangement of words, but that they have their own reality: a suggestiveness and polyvalence that gives fresh significance to their referents.

The other writer, whom Bernlef has also translated, is the Frenchman Francis Ponge. He too attempted to catch the solid reality of things in his texts, but in his case it was the abstracting nature of the language that had to be overcome. Ponge's strategy is the ingenious creation of personal textual surfaces, while maintaining an impersonal approach. As with Marianne Moore, subjects are swathed in linguistic textures which are in turn shaped by them. That is to say they are not arbitrarily made symbols but make of the text the sign of themselves.

Like Ponge, Bernlef tends to demonstrate his concerns through everyday things and examples drawn from popular culture. In 'Bobby Sadler', which appears in the recently published *Driftwood House* (the first English-language selection of Bernlef's poems in book form), the illusion the text creates is compared to a juggling act. Its magic reality creates a sense of wonder – of liberation, even; but, Bernlef comments ironically, this is because 'it reminds (us) of nothing'. He looks at the process from another angle in 'Sonny Rollins in London'. The flux of the jazzman's progress from tune to tune is like the mind's wandering over incidentals, never centring directly. In imitating this, the poem introduces the reader to his true 'self' just as Rollins' medley ends in *The True Is You.*

Reality outside of the mind remains impenetrable, given the mind's superficial and subjective operation. Many of Bernlef's poems resemble would-be meditations, failed attempts to centre on and render a true sense of their subjects. These subjects are incidental, since the real aim is to demonstrate how the failure comes about. Two reflections on this occur in connection with 'The Dead Lizard'. Since writing kills its subject by making static what is essentially a living flux, the only proper subject would therefore seem to be what is already dead. Even then the poet is liable to project himself into and thus falsify what is uniquely itself. Writer and subject remain alienated. Both themes come powerfully together in the final lines:

The ticking of my watch almost
penetrates the motionless surface mirror.

Dead things do indeed figure quite largely in Bernlef's work in one way or another. 'Acanthus' and 'Detective' are two other examples. Elsewhere the presence of death gives rise to mordant commentaries on the artistic product. According to 'That's What Art Does', it is a substitute for engaging with real life. But life-likeness is an illusion, according to 'Uncle Carl: A Home Movie'. By substituting the act of dying for 'real life' in these poems, the ridiculousness of art's pretensions are exposed.

What, then, should be the subject of the poem, apart from itself and its creation, too long a contemplation of which would degenerate into so much picking of fluff from one's navel? Writing is a parallel reality; our own life is another. Intimate realisation of the uniqueness of everything outside ourselves only comes rarely, and with a shock of recognition. Such epiphanies occur in 'Golden Delicious', 'On Systems', 'Score' and, most memorably, 'Winter Routes'. The last of these deals with tracks left in the snow by the many other beings that share our space with us. Winter, the freezing of the organic which art brings about, makes us aware of their presence but, hopefully,

When the winter routes melt
the assumption remains there's a map
under our feet.

All the themes we have been considering come together in Bernlef's beautiful prose poem, 'Still Life', the only example in *Driftwood House* of his exemplary use of this form. The ideal of creation, Bernlef says here, is not what the French call *'nature morte'* but the more positive sounding 'still life'. Even if it falls short of the living reality, the spectator is given a sense of the preciousness, the unique nature, of what has inspired the artist's vision. So long as the artist – any creator – strives, against all the odds, to give as true a sense of it as he can, so long as he does not stand still but runs to keep up with it, his work too will never be moribund.

J. Bernlef (1937-)
(Photo by Klaas Koppe).

YANN LOVELOCK

J. Bernlef, *Driftwood House* (Tr. Scott Rollins). Typographeum, Francestown, 1992; 36 pp.

Willem Elsschot *Villa des Roses*

The inclusion in the Penguin Twentieth-Century Classics series of the novel *Villa des Roses* by the Flemish author Willem Elsschot (1882-1960) is an important event. The more so, as this is an inexpensive series; price was after all the main problem when Elsschot was first launched in English in the splendid series *Bibliotheca Neerlandica*, the twelfth volume of which, published in 1965, contained the novels *Soft Soap* (Lijmen, 1924) *The Leg* (Het been, 1938) and *Will-o'-the Wisp* (Het dwaallicht, 1946). This publication failed to reach a wide readership, though it did serve as an eye-opener for receptive critics. It made possible a proper discussion of Elsschot, for example in Martin Seymour-Smith's *Guide to Modern World Literature* (1973), in which he was described as 'an unsensational, sophisticated, parodic, tender realist of genius' (p. 374).

His inclusion in the Penguin series will considerably raise the profile of this author, who is representative of both Flanders and the Netherlands. *Villa des Roses,* his first novel, was written in 1910 in Rotterdam, where the Fleming Elsschot was working at the time. When the book appeared in 1913 it did so through a Dutch publisher, as did the rest of Elsschot's compact oeuvre. He received support from Dutch critics when the majority of Flemings were not ready for his work, which was not idyllic enough for their taste. Not only was his work not appreciated in Flanders, it was also boycotted with the aid of the large resources available to the Catholic library and school network in the inter-war period. And the antipathy continued even after the War; right up to the 1960s *Villa des Roses,* which was unjustly labelled 'cynical' because it contains a description of an abortion, reached young readers only in homeopathic doses in school books. Luckily, this also gave Elsschot the aura of 'the forbidden', so that his work was often read clandestinely with heightened enjoyment ...

Daringly modern as the subject-matter of *Villa des Roses* was in Flemish eyes, this tragi-comic 'novel of manners' was completely traditional in style and structure, showing no links with the modernist movement. 1913 was also the year, for example, in which *Alcools* (Apollinaire), *Sons and Lovers* (D.H. Lawrence) and *Die Ermordung einer Butterblume* (Döblin) all appeared, as well as being the year in which *Le Sacre du Printemps* was created. Even at the time of Elsschot's spell in Paris in 1907, which inspired him to write *Villa des Roses,* Gertrude Stein had been experimenting with language in the same city for four years, and the first cubist painting, Picasso's *Les Demoiselles d'Avignon,* had just been completed. Elsschot, however, apparently had no time for this avant-garde movement. He continued the realist tradition: his portrayal of the ups and downs of daily life in a small Paris boarding house displays the solidity of specification in which, according to Henry James, Balzac excelled, adding perhaps just a touch of parody.

And yet an individual voice does come through, even in the English translation. It is a voice with a laconic overtone and an emotional, melancholy undertone, a voice which still retains its direct appeal. More ambitious works from 1913, such as Thomas Mann's *Der Tod in Venedig,* sometimes display more purple passages that have faded considerably. Naturally, some things are also lacking in Elsschot's work, such as the great vision of such giants as Lawrence and Mann. But Elsschot cherished no titanic ambitions, and what he undertook came close to perfection in its own right.

In addition to producing a splendid translation, Paul Vincent also provides the reader with a comprehensive introduction, with only two minor flaws. First, the term 'naturalistic' cannot be applied easily to Elsschot's realism, because of the deterministic tendency which the former implies, particularly in terms of heredity. Second the confusion in the use of 'Dutch', 'Flemish', etc.; but this is unavoidable as long as the Dutch Language Union fails to provide a clear lead by taking systematic action with regard to lexicons which spread misunderstanding in millions of copies. Anyone reading *Collins Dictionary,* for example, may well think that when speaking of 'Dutch readers' (p. 1.), Vincent is referring only to 'the citizens of the Netherlands', whereas the term in fact also includes the Flemings.

Vincent nicely differentiates between Elsschot, who aimed at a regional clarity, and champions of the Flemish variant of the Dutch language such as Felix Timmermans (p. 6); it is unfortunate that on the rear cover, Elsschot is situated in 'the Netherlands' (though this may have more to do with the publisher than with the editor). Elsschot's 'Flemishness', however, is no less authentic than that of Timmermans, even though he used dialect only in speech and was not a Catholic.

Elsschot's robust Flemishness is apparent, for example, in a poem written, in defiance of attitudes at the time, to honour the old radical leader August Borms, a cripple, who was executed in 1946. Here, although Elsschot hated the far right, he was against taking the life of someone who had trodden the wrong path more out of foolishness than calculation and whose folly had therefore not made him rich, while economic collaborators were spared. In the same way that he was now kicking Belgian shins, he had reacted against Dutch opportunism as early as 1934 in a poem about Marinus van der Lubbe, the Dutchman executed as an accomplice in the burning of the Reichstag: in order to avoid harming trade with the Nazis, this underdog was treated as expendable. In it, Elsschot furiously called for Russian revenge on the Nazis, but this did not prevent the intellectual establishment from rejecting him as untouchable for a while in 1947. Fortunately, Vincent does not suppress this fact. In 1992 right and left once again exchanged polemics over the origins of the Borms poem, demonstrating yet again that the effects of the War were greater and longer-lasting in Flanders than in the Netherlands.

The attempt by the left to whitewash Elsschot in the context of a scramble for political correctness is superfluous; as a man of emotion he had a right to his fury, quite apart from his left-wing standpoint, and it is quite possible that he was not manipulated at that time by right-wing intriguers. It is rather perverse, however, that the poem should *now* be misused again and again by rabble-rousers whose understanding of Elsschot's work is totally inadequate, since otherwise they would realise how intensely this master of understatement would despise their delusions of grandeur and their hollow rhetoric. And above all, he would hate their xenophobia, a theme which he treated with such unrivalled subtlety in *Will-o'-the Wisp,* his last and best book. 'Here Elsschot, in a novel of wide application, achieves a tenuous, sad sense of human brotherhood, of broken dreams, of sweetness.' (Seymour-Smith, p. 375).

Is it a pipe dream to wish for the slender masterpiece *Will-o'-the Wisp* a place in a handbook used by millions, such as the *Norton Anthology of World Masterpieces?* Van Gogh's selfportrait adorns the second volume, which is dedicated to the modern period, yet the book's 2,165 pages contain not a single reference to Dutch literature.

JORIS DUYTSCHAEVER
Translated by Julian Ross.

Willem Elsschot, *Villa des Roses* (Translated with an introduction and notes by Paul Vincent). Penguin Books, London, 1992; 140 pp.

Court and Culture

Court and Culture: Dutch literature, 1350-1450, an elegantly produced book, is the translation of Professor Van Oostrom's best known work to date. *Het woord van eer. Literatuur aan het Hollandse hof omstreeks 1400* (Amsterdam, 1987) rather burst upon the scene of medieval Dutch studies: the culmination, to date, of a lightning academic career by one of the most dynamic and original personalities of the present generation of medievalists in the Netherlands and Belgium.

F.P. van Oostrom's study was a landmark and an achievement of no small magnitude. It was received both with praise and also with some unease. Scholarly mores in the Netherlands are more Germanic than Anglo-Saxon. 'Publish and be damned' is not a statement that translates easily into Dutch. Where elegant, and speculative, synthesizing studies are generally welcomed by Anglo-Saxon scholars, Dutch scholars have a habit of falling upon each tittle and iota for which hard evidence seems to be lacking.

However, Van Oostrom's achievement does not lie only in the fact that this is, in many respects, an Anglo-Saxon rather than a Germanic *tour de force.* It is a panoramic book which focuses on very particular detail. This, it must be said, is more apparent in the title of the Dutch original than in that of the English translation. Those who expect the literary history of a century may be somewhat disappointed: those who take into account the specification 'literature at the Dutch court around 1400' will find a veritable treasure trove.

Cover illustration.

In effect, Van Oostrom constructs his hypotheses with the aid of a relatively small corpus of writings: the moralistic and didactic poetry of the itinerant poet Master William of Hildegaersberch; the courtly lovesongs of the Hague Song Manuscript and the Leiden fragments; chivalric ideology and knowledge as laid down in the chronicles of Bavaria Herald; the learned religious instruction of the *'summa theologica' Table of the Christian Faith* (Tafel vanden kersten ghelove) by the monk and doctor in theology Dirk van Delft; sophisticated and independent worldly wisdom *vis-à-vis* love and marriage as embodied in *The Course of Love* (Der minnen loep), the *Flower of Virtue* (Blome der doechden) and *Mellibeus* by the courtier Dirk Potter.

The study of this corpus is flanked by a concise and instructive cultural-historical chapter about the Bavarian Counts who ruled the provinces of Holland, Zeeland and Hainault between 1358 and circa 1417 and a final chapter surveying the significance of that rule for literary culture at the court in The Hague.

This relatively small body of writing produced in a fairly short period for a specific audience presents us nevertheless with the means of addressing a number of surprisingly diverse issues and aspects.

What makes this work so interesting both for the specialist of medieval Dutch literature and culture and for other medievalists, is the constant interaction between the detailed study of a particular situation and the background of concerns which were central to Western European culture. This comes particularly to the fore in the discussion of the work of Bavaria Herald. Chivalry and its values, particularly the concept of honour, were central to the court at The Hague as to many other European courts. Van Oostrom shows how these general values are reflected in the wars waged by the Bavarian Dukes, particularly the campaigns against the Frisians, and the military exploits they thought it necessary, or honourable, to involve themselves in, such as the Prussian campaigns. His discussion of the rise and fall of chivalric values, the way in which Bavaria Herald seems to have outlived what he saw as the only possible honourable mode of living, is the most intricate and innovative in a book that shuns neither complexity nor enriching speculation.

Another aspect of the culture at the Hague court which is of value for our understanding of the Netherlands as a society in which the bourgeoisie played an early and lastingly important part, can be found in the chapter on the life and the work of Dirk Potter, the courtier with a criminal past and of no particularly noble line, who makes and consolidates a position at court whilst voicing independent views in literary matters. Here again is a genre that is truly European, the ethics and morals in and of human relationships, particularly love and marriage, but with what the author calls 'incipient individualism'; an individualism still bound to a court culture, but in which one can discern values which will become part and parcel of a bourgeois culture in which the concept of honour no longer means the honour of chivalry.

In many ways this is a tantalizing book, in the sense that much is discussed in general because research in detail has not yet been carried out. Van Oostrom is his own fiercest and most thoughtful critic in this respect, and fortunately both he and his pupils are actively engaged in such further research. His brief development of the cultural-anthropological concept of shame cultures and guilt cultures, applied here to the Hague court culture, make one wish for more, and more detailed, research in this respect.

Finally, a word about the English translation. Van Oostrom writes a scholarly Dutch in the best tradition, varied, lively, witty. He states in his preface that his work is also intended for a wider public, but makes no concessions to any 'popularizing' style. The translator did not have an easy task, but he acquitted himself of it with honour. Both author and translator ought to be included in Master William's exhortation that:

Waer vrou Eren vrienden hoven,
Daer siet men dichters conste loven
Ende ander constenaers daer by;
Dat doet-het is een melodi
Die den goeden toebehoert.

(Where Lady Honour's friends hold court, there one sees the art of poets and other artists praised; that is as it should be; it is a melody which should accompany those of rank.)

ELSA STRIETMAN

Frits Pieter van Oostrom, *Court and Culture: Dutch Literature, 1350-1450* (Tr. Arnold J. Pomerans, with a foreword by James H. Marrow). University of California Press, Berkeley / Los Angeles / Oxford, 1992; 373 pp.

A Crown for Christine D'haen

On Wednesday 28 October 1992 the Dutch Queen Beatrix presented the Prize for Dutch Literature *(Prijs der Nederlandse Letteren)* to the Flemish poet Christine D'haen (1923-), thereby rewarding one of the most remarkable oeuvres in Dutch-language literature. That the most prestigious prize in the Low Countries went to this particular writer is surprising, yet at the same time certainly not undeserved.

The award came as a surprise even to insiders. The Prize is conferred just once every three years either on a Dutch or a Flemish writer and is regarded as the definitive consecration of an oeuvre. Stijn Streuvels, Herman Teirlinck and Hugo Claus are among the Flemings who have received the prize. In 1992 it was the turn of a Fleming again. If likely winners were tipped, then they were authors like Ivo Michiels, Paul de Wispelaere and Anton van Wilderode. And if one of those names had won the Prize, then perhaps fewer questions would have been asked by some literary journalists than was actually the case. The amazement of the general public is understandable because Christine D'haen's work is for many still *terra incognita.*

There are various reasons for this. The first is the poet's aversion to ostentation: she has seldom or never been seen at literary receptions, poetry evenings or other festive functions. A second reason for her relative obscurity is the limited promotion given to her work, which has been handled by various publishers – some of whom have since disappeared from the scene – with the result that it is almost unknown, particularly in the North. A third reason is the nature of her poetry, which is consciously anti-fashionable and complex. In a culture such as ours which favours easy reading, it would seem to appeal only to connoisseurs.

A remarkable choice, then, but also a totally justifiable one. A prize such as this can really only be awarded to an author whose work conjures up a large-scale world all of its own. That is only rarely the case among poets, many of whom spend the whole of their lives writing variations on the same theme. But with Christine D'haen, we are offered a truly impressive wealth of material and vision. She strives for the fullness of an all-embracing poetry. We find in her work not only personal poems about love, family and death, but also epic images and persona poems about mythological figures; existential propositions about birth, life as a woman and death, alongside archetypal explorations of phenomena such as celestial bodies, animals, plants, time and art. It is typical of her world view, which excludes nothing and integrates everything, that in one and the same collection (*Mirages,* 1989) she devotes one poem to mythological cosmologies and another to scientific views about the origins of the earth. It is no exaggeration to say that this poet has extended the field of what can be expressed in post-war Dutch poetry as far as – or perhaps further than – her modernistic male counterparts. Only critics who swear by a narrow 'I' lyric can fail to understand the miracle that has been performed in Dutch literature.

We encounter the same trend towards transcending borders in her style, which is so elusive that it has been

Christine D'haen (l.) and Queen Beatrix of the Netherlands (r.) at the presentation of the Prize for Dutch Literature in October 1992 (Photo by Vincent Menzel).

characterised in turn as classical, baroque, mannerist, modernist and even postmodernist. It is precisely this undefinability which proves just how unusual D'haen's use of the language is. If, for example, she permits archaisms in her spelling and vocabulary, it is not out of nostalgia for the past, but as a fundamental choice, opting for as wide an instrumentation as possible. In her search for the boundaries of the 'sayable', she transcends with ease syntactic and prosodic rules. So superior is the art of Christine D'haen, who has been crowned the queen of Dutch poetry by the Queen of the Netherlands.

PAUL CLAES
Translated by Alison Mouthaan.

Prize for Dutch Literature:
1956: Herman Teirlinck (1879-1967)
1959: A. Roland Holst (1888-1976)
1962: Stijn Streuvels (1871-1969)
1965: J.C. Bloem (1887-1966)
1968: Gerard Walschap (1898-1989)
1971: Simon Vestdijk (1898-1971)
1974: Marnix Gijsen (1899-1984)
1977: W.F. Hermans (1921-)
1980: Maurice Gilliams (1900-1982)
1983: Lucebert (1924-)
1986: Hugo Claus (1929-)
1989: Gerrit Kouwenaar (1923-)
1992: Christine D'haen (1923-)

A Love Affair

I wanted to write a coolly objective piece about Amsterdam, but how can you be cool and objective when you are in love? And on my last visit I fell in love with Amsterdam, head over heels.

I had accepted an invitation to stay in the Translators' House and expected the usual institutional accommodation. What greeted me instead was style, warmth, large rooms, purpose-built furniture, the latest computer equipment, a splendid hi-fi set and a whole armoury of writers' perquisites. To top it all, my hosts – the Foundation for the Production and Translation of Dutch Literature *(Nederlands Literair Produktie- en Vertalingenfonds)* – proved to be charming, kind, helpful, sympathetic and generous to a fault.

And as if that were not enough, I found myself sharing the place with Gheorghe Nicolaescu, a delightful Romanian colleague whose wife was so beautiful that I kept feasting my eyes on her when I should have been hard at work on my translations. In short, my visit started with a whole range of pleasant surprises. Moreover, having a Romanian to talk Dutch to removed all my inhibitions about a language I could read like a native but had not had nearly enough chances to speak. The upshot was that when I rang one of my Dutch publishers, he greeted me with *'Goedemiddag, Professor Alexandrescu'.*

I arrived just after the Bijlmer disaster (a large housing complex was destroyed by a plane crash). Friends kept ringing me from London with solicitous enquiries. And as the days went by and I kept seeing remarkable displays of human solidarity and interracial harmony in the streets and on the television, my heart went out to this grieving nation. While skinheads were running riot in other parts of Europe, the Dutch had obviously lost none of their proverbial humanity and neighbourly love, and I felt privileged to share their sorrow. And when I saw a visibly moved and shaken Queen Beatrix at the scene of the crash, I warmed to her and felt like waving the Orange banner. (My friend Paul Hogarth, incidentally, once told me that the caption to his illustration of a Belfast Orangeman for the German edition of the *Irish Sketchbook* had been rendered *'ein Belfaster Apfelsinenverkäufer'* by the translator.)

A few days later I was asked to meet several distinguished Dutch colleagues at Mulliner's Wine Bar and the experience proved unforgettable. Everybody was jovial, welcoming, full of sound advice and common sense – not a scrap of professional jealousy. Equally memorable were my brief encounters with writers, artists and publishers in *De Kring,* in *Arti,* in *Café de Zwart* and in *Bodega Keyzer.* For the first time in my life I began to be pleased about my profession.

And talking of notable places, who could improve on Berlage's South? So much space, so much water, so much greenery, so much air, and such blessed peace! Old ladies stop you in the park and talk about the autumn foliage, suggest snapshots of even better views, hope to see you again and bid you a pleasant day. When I closed my eyes for a moment I was back in Stellenbosch as it used to be fifty years ago, though the Amsterdam inflection was of course rather more *beschaafd.* If that is what they call *'het groene graf',* let me be buried there!

Dutch television. If you pass over those silly and pathetic parlour games which seem to go on forever, and turn to AT5 or the Art Channel *(Kunstkanaal),* you can look forward to seeing displays of honesty, maturity and soul-searching of a kind that other countries would do well to emulate. An interview with author and entertainer Annie M.G. Schmidt was a revelation, a truly mind-boggling event. And the good sense Dutch politicians show when arguing about, say, economic problems might be an object lesson to British Members of Parliament. If only Mieke van der Wey's face did not prevent one from concentrating on the subject matter.

I could go on like this and doubtless try your patience beyond endurance. Instead, I shall end this personal account on a personal note. Outside Amsterdam Central Station I watched a tramp go through a line of rubbish bins and fill a large bag with the pickings. Poor fellow, I thought. But when he started to fling his filthy rejects into the street and the river, my instinct was to take direct action and, God knows, I might easily have done just that if he hadn't been several inches taller and brawnier than I am. How could that lout do that to Amsterdam, to *my* Amsterdam! I knew then that I was at home.

ARNOLD J. POMERANS

Music

Gaudeamus

Contemporary music is flourishing all over the Netherlands, with dozens of ensembles and soloists specializing in the modern repertoire, with well-attended performances of this kind of music and interesting composers of it. Probably none of this would have happened without the *Gaudeamus* foundation. That foundation was started right after the war by the German textile engineer Walter Maas (1909-1992), who had fled to the Netherlands during the war and wanted to repay the hospitality that had been extended to him.

Maas lived in Bilthoven, a small village in the heart of the Netherlands, in a house shaped like a grand piano. The house, called *Gaudeamus,* was commissioned by the little known Dutch composer Julius Röntgen. It contains a beautiful semicircular music room.

Immediately after the war, Maas renewed an old tradition. In the music room of the *Gaudeamus* house he organized concerts in which musicians, most of them young, were given the opportunity to show what they could do. On 4 November 1946, Julius Röntgen's sons were the first to do so. But Maas's ambitions went beyond organizing concerts. He wanted to provide young musicians, and especially young composers, with moral and financial support. Maas became a Maecenas for the music of the younger generation trying to establish a foothold against strong opposition.

The *Gaudeamus* foundation is Walter Maas's brainchild. It was designed to attract members of the international musical avant garde. It was not only Dutch composers like Peter Schat and Ton de Leeuw who became Maas's house guests. Stockhausen had his *Gesang der Jünglinge* performed in Maas's house, Ligeti tried to explain his composition techniques there, using a primitive blackboard, and Cage invited the audience to listen to silence. The personal contacts between musicians and composers had a stimulating effect on the development of modern music.

In 1989 the then 80-year-old Maas received the Jan van Gilse prize for all he had done for Dutch musical life. The jury's report called his activities invaluable for the post-war boom in the composition of new music in the Netherlands: 'The prestige of the *Gaudeamus* foundation and its international and national appeal are to a great extent the work of Walter Maas. Dutch musical life and Dutch composers therefore owe him the greatest possible gratitude.'

In the meantime *Gaudeamus* has developed into a big official organization. Its activities, originally financed entirely out of Maas's private fortune, are now paid for with subsidies given by the Dutch government. Most important among those activities is the International Music Week, first organized in 1949-50. Composers from the Netherlands and abroad are invited to submit work for the Music Week, which is now organized on a yearly basis. A jury of international experts decides which music is worth performing. Many of the composers first heard at *Gaudeamus* become widely known afterwards; others disappear

The *Gaudeamus* house in Bilthoven.

into anonymity. This makes the *Gaudeamus* Music Week a good touchstone for the quality of composition, which was precisely what Walter Maas wanted it to be. He conceived of the composers' competition as a workshop for composers to which the audience is invited.

That audience is always treated to a varied programme. It was able to enjoy music by composers like Louis Andriessen, Luciano Berio, Karlheinz Stockhausen and Iannis Xenakis, whose reputation is now established. It was also treated to music by the French composer Francis Miroglio, his Belgian colleague Jacqueline Fontijn, the Swedish composer Maurice Karkoff and his Italian counterpart Vittorio Fellegara. English composers also regularly have their music performed at *Gaudeamus.* Brian Ferneyhough and Michael Finnissey are now probably the best known among them. Parneygough, who was awarded a third prize for his violin quartet sonatas in the sixties, failed to build up a similar reputation.

Since 1963 the Music Week has been expanded to include the *Gaudeamus* competition for young interpreters of contemporary music, from the Netherlands and abroad, an eminently sensible development, since modern composers would be effectively condemned to silence without the help of musicians interested in the contemporary repertoire.

PAUL LUTTIKHUIS
Translated by André Lefevere.

Address:
Gaudeamus Foundation
Swammerdamstraat 38 / 1091 RV Amsterdam
The Netherlands / tel. +31 (0) 20 694 73 49

Philosophy and Science

Leo Apostel In the Tradition of the Enlightenment

Leo Apostel (1925-)
(Photo by Filip Claus).

The Flemish philosopher Leo Apostel (1925-) is a typical representative of an intellectual culture open to enrichment by international influences. The young Apostel attended a secondary school in Antwerp where he had Jewish classmates, later becoming a student at the Free University in Brussels *(ULB; Université libre de Bruxelles),* where he adopted French, Belgium's second national language, as his intellectual language. As a result, much of his early philosophical work was published in French. Although during his student years he explored European – particularly German and French – philosophy and literature with eager curiosity and an unprecedented intellectual hunger, the more mature Leo Apostel increasingly turned his attention to the way in which thinkers in the Anglo-Saxon world approached philosophical problems and attempted to find solutions to them. The thought disciplines which interested him were logic, the study of the laws of thought, and epistemology, the critical study of the validity of knowledge. Apostel sought to refine these two disciplines, logic and theory of knowledge, in order to arrive at the most adequate description of reality. His ultimate aim was to know what *is* – a knowledge referred to in philosophy as ontology. And it was in the Anglo-Saxon world, in the United Kingdom and the United States, that specialists from every corner of the world had gathered to apply themselves to the possibilities of this philosophical discipline using the most accurate means, namely mathematics and scientific method. In 1951 Leo Apostel, by then a member of the academic staff at the Free University in Brussels, moved to Chicago where he studied under the renowned Rudolf Carnap, a man for whose work he retains a tremendous admiration to this day. Apostel spent a year in America, during which time he also visited other university towns such as New Haven (Yale) and New York.

Back in Brussels, he completed his dissertation *Law and Causes* (La loi et les causes) and was accepted as a member of the National Fund for Scientific Research. He published regularly, became an active member of the Flemish humanist movement, took part in conferences and, in the period 1955-6, was part of the research team of the eminent Swiss philosopher-psychologist Jean Piaget. His professorial career began in the second half of the 1950s. As a Fleming and a Dutch-speaker he obtained a post at the newly-founded Dutch-language Free University of Brussels *(VUB; Vrije Universiteit Brussel)* in 1956, and a year later he was also awarded the chair in logic at the University of Ghent, the scene of his main activities from then on. Apostel, born in Antwerp and a student in Brussels, thus finally settled in Ghent, where he still lives and works and where he can still be seen in (preferably quiet) cafés and restaurants, involved in discussions or even reading and writing.

Before becoming increasingly involved in Flemish cultural and philosophical life, Apostel returned for a second time to the United States, where he taught at Pennsylvania State University for two semesters (1958-9), an opportunity which he grasped mainly for its promise of fruitful intellectual contacts with a number of brilliant figures from the world of mathematics.

From the 1960s to the present day, Leo Apostel has not allowed personal, university or health problems to deter him from, as he himself once said, striving with the stubbornness of a mule, the innocence of a dove and the cunning of a snake to create a contemporary form for the ideals of the Enlightenment; from striving to create an emancipated, independent human being who is constantly in search of insights into himself, his history and his cosmos. In this perspective, he founded a moral philosophy department together with several colleagues in the 1960s. He encourages his outstanding students to adopt an interdisciplinary approach and, so as not to lock himself away in a single specialism, seeks out those with a different philosophy of life in order, jointly with them, to give concrete shape to ideological and religious tolerance. He uses his talents as a thinker to try and make those in liberal, humanistic and masonic circles aware that they too are not immune from intellectual renewal. Most recently, he has been devoting all his energies to the organisation of study projects aimed at providing guidance in the search for a world image suited to the 21st century – hence his project *Worldviews.*

JACQUES DE VISSCHER
Translated by Julian Ross.

The best impression of Leo Apostel's oeuvre can be gained from the three-volume work *The Philosophy of Leo Apostel* by F. Vandamme & R. Pinxten (Ghent, 1989). With respect to his Enlightenment ideal, see also Apostel's *Freemasonry, a Philosophical Essay* (Brussels, 1990).

Ad Peperzak (1929-)
(Photo by Ron Moes).

Ad Peperzak Philosophy as Dialogue and Quest.

When in December 1992 the Dutch philosopher Ad Peperzak (1929-) dealt with the subject of Eros in his farewell lecture, given in the great hall of the Catholic University of Nijmegen before a select group not just of Dutch and Flemish colleagues, but also of friends and former students, everybody knew they were present at the valedictory address of a philosopher who had no intention of resting on his laurels. Not primarily because in the previous year he had already been appointed Arthur J. Schmitt Professor at Chicago's Loyola University, with the specific task of teaching continental thinking, but mainly because Peperzak has always revealed himself as an almost tireless, or in any case very busy author, lecturer, editor, driving force behind all kinds of discussion groups, teacher, dissertation supervisor and participant in all kinds of congresses and conferences. A man like that may say farewell to one university – he spent thirty years at Nijmegen, performing various teaching tasks – but not to sit back and relax. On the contrary: he goes to another university. Peperzak also taught at Amsterdam, Utrecht, and Delft, and was a frequent guest professor at German, Flemish, French, Italian, Indonesian and American universities.

Ad Peperzak established his world-wide reputation with his study of the work of the German philosopher Hegel on whom he wrote his doctoral dissertation for Paul Ricoeur in Paris in 1960. He introduced his Paris teacher, whom he called the best teacher of philosophy he ever met, into the world of Dutch philosophy by translating Ricoeur's essays himself, or having them translated, and providing them with an instructive introduction and explanatory notes. Because Ricoeur's reputation was established in the Anglo-Saxon world relatively early on, Peperzak did not have to introduce him there. The Dutch philosopher did, however, introduce into that world the work of another French colleague, Emmanuel Levinas, author of many profound studies of the metaphysics of the ethical relationship to the Other. Peperzak boosted Levinas not only in the Netherlands, but also in the United States, Germany, and Italy.

Ad Peperzak certainly allowed himself to be influenced by the great figures of Western thought, from Plato to Levinas, but this does not mean he limited his work to interpreting these great examples. He did pay homage to those from whom he was allowed to learn so much, but he also traced a philosophical path of his own. No philosopher can shy away from that task. For Peperzak this meant his own search for meaning in dialogue and friendship with others. His search is by no means a self-willed one: he knows he owes a great debt to history and tradition, but that very debt means that he has been entrusted with a task for the future, one he has to perform in a creative manner, in a dialogue with his time and his contemporaries. His Christian background is by no means omitted in this, on the contrary. It is inconceivable for him that his quest for meaning should be able to do without the inspiring and fertilizing sources of European civilization. Meaning is transcendent and presupposes a rising above the immediate, above the loss of self in the purely material where no distinction is made between good and evil, sacred and profane. The quest is an exploration of the self, of one's time and of history. This implies a systematic interrogation for which philosophy, which seeks to achieve much more than knowledge for knowledge's sake, is the traditional way. For that reason Ad Peperzak has always cultivated in his thinking the relationship between philosophy and a Christianity critical of itself, as has his master Paul Ricoeur. His other master, Emmanuel Levinas, also remains a shining example to him, since this religious Jew never abandoned the reading of the Talmud and the Bible. Hegel remains Peperzak's inspiring model in the study of the historicity of the quest for meaning.

All of this leaves us with the question whether this is merely an empty search. That is impossible. We only have to look at the hundreds of publications and lectures (in at least seven languages) by the Dutch philosopher to discover highly concrete topics that testify to a care for man's well-being: war and peace, education, practical ethics, education, suffering, life and death – in short, the philosophy of everyday life.

JACQUES DE VISSCHER
Translated by André Lefevere.

Most noteworthy in Peperzak's voluminous oeuvre are: *System and History in Philosophy* (Albany, 1986); *Philosophy and Politics, A Commentary on the Preface of Hegel's Philosophy of Right* (Dordrecht / Boston, 1987). A *Liber Amicorum* was presented to him on the occasion of his retirement from the University of Nijmegen. Edited by P.J.M. van Tongeren a.o., it is entitled *Eros and Eris* (Dordrecht / Boston, 1992) and contains contributions by, among others, E. Levinas, P. Ricoeur, L. Dupré, W.J. Richardson, O. Pöggeler, J.L. Marion, C. Verhoeven, S. IJsseling, J. Sallis and R. Bernasconi.

Research at the Free University of Brussels

A Breakthrough in Assisted Fertilization

Infertility is a problem which confronts 10 - 12% of all couples. It used to be thought – erroneously – that the cause must lie with the woman. Contemporary research knows better. In one couple out of three the problem is with the man. He may be unable to produce sperm at all, or not enough sperm, or the sperm may be of inferior quality and therefore unable to unite with the woman's ova. In the past, such couples could only rely on sperm from a donor. This situation has recently changed, enabling men whose sperm is of inferior quality to have children biologically their own. A few years ago the technique of 'subzonal insemination' was developed. A very fine micropipette is used to insert a few sperm, activated in the laboratory, between the outer layer and membrane of the ovum. This is a technological wonder of assisted reproduction. Yet it appears that even chemically treated and activated sperm are not always able to fertilize an egg.

Researchers at the Free University of Brussels *(VUB; Vrije Universiteit Brussel)* recently succeeded in developing an even more refined procedure. Professors Devroey and Van Steirteghem of the *VUB* Centre for Reproductive Medicine succeeded in fertilizing an ovum using a single activated sperm cell. They used a pipette so fine as to be nearly invisible to introduce one sperm cell directly into the centre of the ovum. It has been established that 80% of sperm survive this kind of 'injection'. Provided the ovum remains intact, the first cell division will occur within twenty-four hours; fertilization has then occurred. After a further twenty-four hours a few more cell divisions will have taken place. It is then possible to implant the embryo into the uterine wall via the vagina. Once the embryo has embedded itself in the uterine wall the pregnancy develops like any normal pregnancy.

This new procedure was called ICSI, or 'Intracytoplasmatic Sperm Injection'. It represents an important step forward in assisted fertilization: ICSI helps out where nature fails. This procedure cannot be applied inside the woman's body. It is therefore necessary to surgically remove a few egg cells from the ovaries by means of a small operative procedure known as 'laparoscopy'. This needs to be done when the egg is fertile, and this is induced by means of hormonal stimulation. The ova are transferred to a small container and their outer layer is removed in the laboratory. They are kept in the incubator under the conditions of temperature and humidity normally obtaining in the mother's body. Meanwhile, the man produces a quantity of sperm. The most mobile of these are chemically activated. The ova and the sperm cells can then be united under the microscope. This procedure requires precision of the highest order: the pipette used has a diameter of hardly one thousandth of a millimetre. Several ova are fertilized in this way, which means that several embryos are produced. To avoid pregnancies resulting in multiple births, only two embryos are implanted. The others are kept frozen in liquid nitrogen in case a second attempt at implantation becomes necessary. To date, ten pregnancies have been induced by means of this new procedure, and all have produced normal babies.

Since the fifties, a significant decrease in male fertility has been observed in the West. It is suspected that factors connected to work, lifestyle, and environment may be responsible for this. The ICSI procedure will not be able to change these to any significant extent because it can only be used on a limited number of couples, those who will do anything to have a baby of their own; while millions of couples spend a significant part of their lives trying to avoid pregnancy at all costs ...

PIET DE VALKENEER
Translated by André Lefevere.

Elsevier and Reed A Marriage of Giants

For some years now Pierre Vinken, Chairman of Elsevier, has been saying that the world market in publishing necessitates an increase in the scale of operations. By about the year 2000, according to Vinken, the industry will consist of only a few very large companies. Elsevier has been the world's largest scientific publisher for several years now, but in such conditions that will not be enough. Consequently, to ensure itself a place among the world's ten largest information concerns Elsevier had been looking for a major merger possibility since the mid-eighties.

In 1987 Elsevier tried to absorb Kluwer, one of its largest competitors in Dutch publishing, by means of a sudden hostile takeover bid. The main strength of the Kluwer group lay in the publishing of specialist, often loose-leaf, information for professional groups such as lawyers and tax experts. Kluwer succeeded in fighting off this unwanted takeover through a strong defensive move: a rapid merger with Wolters, a company active in the same field, resulted in the creation of a second large Dutch publishing concern, Wolters Kluwer. In the same year, Elsevier began to court Britain's Reed International. However, while discussions with Reed continued behind the scenes, for some considerable time it seemed that Elsevier had a better chance of a successful merger with the Pearson group. Negotiations with Pearson came unstuck, however, as did the off-and-on talks with Wolters Kluwer, which in Vinken's view was still the ideal candidate for a merger. In the spring of 1992 Elsevier announced that detailed discussions with a possible partner were taking place, and in September the plans to merge with Reed were made public. Although the sharply falling pound sterling made it necessary to adjust the merger conditions at the last moment, two months later the shareholders of the two companies approved the merger as per the 1st January 1993.

A giant new company was born of this marriage. The merger resulted in the setting up of a new holding company, Reed Elsevier, controlling all the operating companies of the two organisations. Their respective financial companies were placed under the control of a second holding company: Elsevier Reed. Both companies, Elsevier and Reed, continue to have separate legal status and each has a fifty percent share in the new holding company. To compensate for the higher price of its shares, Reed also received a minority holding in Elsevier. The combined Board of the holding company consists of six senior directors from Reed and five from Elsevier. Pierre Vinken is currently Chairman of the Board, but when he retires in 1995 he will be succeeded by Reed director Peter Davis, the present Vice-Chairman.

The combination of Elsevier and Reed brings together a number of disparate elements. Elsevier is by far the largest scientific publisher in the world, specializing in high-quality material at the top of the information market. In particular, Elsevier Science Publishers (scientific journals) and Excerpta Medica (medical research publications) are among the most respected and most profitable publishing divisions in the world. Back in 1991, after the failure of its negotiations with Pearson, Elsevier had sold the holding it had acquired in the British company. The proceeds of this sale enabled it to buy the prestigious and highly profitable Pergamon Press, Oxford, from the bankrupt estate of the media tycoon Robert Maxwell. The Pergamon acquisition meant that Elsevier had surged ahead of all its scientific competition; at the same time it highlighted the company's strongest point: maximization of profits.

As a result of a shrewd policy of well-targeted takeovers, reorganization, and the dismantling of all those divisions which did not fit in with the company's core business strategy, Elsevier became, in the space of a decade, one of the world's most profitable publishing companies. The market capitalization of the company has increased thirty-three times since the beginning of the eighties. In the first half of 1992, Elsevier made a profit of some 282 million guilders on a turnover of 1.22 billion guilders. A large proportion (44%) of these results derives from sales of subscriptions to scientific journals, which produce high returns.

Reed is a completely different kind of company. In 1985 the then paper and packaging manufacturer decided to concentrate exclusively on publishing. It quickly divested itself of the low-profit-producing parts of the company and, instead, invested in magazines, tv guides, travel books and computerized information technology. However, the company is strongest in its trade journal and legal publications division. Reed is also involved in publishing free distribution newspapers ('freebies') and books in general.

Through its association with Reed, Elsevier has become more exposed to market forces than it used to be because a higher proportion of its total turnover is dependent on (uncertain) advertising revenue, while a relatively smaller part comes from (prepaid and consequently very reliable) sales of subscriptions. Conversely, the merger means that matching divisions of the two companies – such as the medical publications and financial departments – can be amalgamated. The combined turnover of Elsevier Reed is 8 billion guilders, achieved with a total workforce of 25,000. In all probability the new company will for the time being continue to rid itself of its comparatively low-profit activities, including Reed's publishing subsidiaries such as Secker and Warburg, Heinemann and Methuen. And then? We can certainly expect further investment in CD-ROM and other electronic information transfer applications. And, doubtless, in the longer term, a further increase in market share, whether through mergers and takeovers or otherwise.

ED VAN EEDEN
Translated by Alison Mouthaan.

Flanders has played an important role in both my personal and my professional life. This has been true of French, Belgian and Dutch Flanders.

Since my boyhood I have spent various periods living in different parts of the great Flemish plain stretching from North-West France through Belgium to the Netherlands. As always, it is the region's geographical position and distinctive geographical features which are the source of its character. The dominant feature of Flanders is its smooth, highly fertile expanse of earth, which lies sandwiched between Germany, France and the sea. Where occasionally there are hills these provide unparallelled views, while the flat landscape is also a setting for skies and for a light that have a unique quality, and which have inspired writers and painters over the centuries.

Less happily, Flanders has also comprised an area that has proved ideal for military campaigning. Ever since the War of Independence of the United Provinces, armies have marched to and fro across the Flemish landscape in one cause or another. After the Spanish troops of the Duke of Alva, it was the turn of the French soldiers of Louis XIV to wrest a portion of the territory for France from William of Orange. And it was the misfortune of the region that part of the Front in the First World War ran through Belgium, so that names like Ypres and Passendaele became household words in my country. The Flemish fields of poppies are recalled to this day when, at the time of the annual Remembrance Day ceremonies each November, a poppy is worn by virtually every Briton in the land.

I spent a large part of my boyhood in French Flanders. I have recently written about that experience in a book published in 1992, *A House in Flanders* which has also now been translated into Dutch. As a boy, I well remember that when the villagers spoke among themselves, it was not in French, but in a Flemish patois which was so local as to be difficult not only for a Frenchman, but for even a Dutchman or a Belgian to understand. However the Flemish names, the big churches, and the red brick farms gave a strongly individual character to a region which had as much in common with Belgium or with southern Holland as it did with France. Many of the customs were also Flemish rather than French: I recall the Easter Parade of plaster giants who were carried through our village and were known as *Papa* and *Maman Reus*; the relics you were invited to kiss when you filed past the coffin at a funeral, the men on one side, the women on the other; and the beer which flowed on every social occasion in preference to wine.

My next encounter with Flanders (the Dutch-speaking part of Belgium) was towards the middle of my diplomatic career when I found myself working for ten years in Brussels in the European Commission. This was in the 1970s and 80s. I came to know Brussels extremely well; indeed my children grew up there and for them the city will forever be associated with their childhood. Brussels is of course a fascinating town. It is dominated by Flemish culture but there is a large population of French-speaking citizens who have themselves helped to form its social and cultural structure. Personally, I could never understand why Walloons and Flemings have been unable to get along better with each other. Their shared history as two peoples living side by side in a part of Europe which has experienced so many triumphs and tragedies ought to bind them together. If it has not done so, it is true that they are not the only communities who live as close neighbours but cannot get on with each other. But the examples of Yugoslavia and Ireland should provide a terrible warning of the need for such communities to do all they can to overcome what are often tribal rather than national barriers.

I came back to the Low Countries for a third time in 1988 when I was appointed British Ambassador to the Netherlands. In this role I have been able to witness at first hand the many qualities which the Dutch people have passed on to their Flemish cousins: plain speaking, a sturdy self-confidence, and a capacity for hard work, to name but three. There is also the Dutch love of the arts, and notably of painting, which finds its expression in the magnificent picture collections that you can visit in every part of the country. But along with shared values there is also diversity among the peoples of the Low Countries. The more austere Dutch would be the first to say that they attach less importance to some of the more sybaritic pleasures of life than do their southern Flemish neighbours. You will not find in the Netherlands the great restaurants or the luxurious shops which are such a feature of Brussels; indeed sometimes one wonders whether the phrase 'consumer society' has any meaning at all in the Netherlands! On the other hand this country skilfully combines a strong attachment to traditional values with a great talent for experiment and modernism. Amsterdam was famous in the sixties for new and sometimes way-out artistic and social trends, a reputation it retains to this day, but at the same time it contains more bookshops than London does.

Flanders has much to teach Europe as a result of its long and rich experience. It has been the source of great wealth, of the creation of an overseas Empire, and of several schools of painting which were the dominant influence on the European continent for various periods between the fourteenth and eighteenth centuries. But it has also suffered repeatedly from the predatory instincts of its neighbours. Flanders was too attractive, prosperous and important a region to be left in peace to dream its way through the centuries. Its history, therefore, has been the history of our times and it is surely no accident that the Netherlands and Belgium have been at the forefront of the post-war drive for greater political and economic integration in Western Europe. The search for unity, while maintaining diversity, has been a task which this people have set themselves over many hundreds of years, and it is a task which now confronts Europe as a whole.

SIR MICHAEL JENKINS

In November 1992, the Dutch feminist monthly publication *Opzij* (whose title means both *aside* and *about her*) celebrated its twentieth anniversary. *Opzij* was started in November 1972 by two out-and-out Dutch feminists: Hedy d'Ancona (today the Dutch Minister of Culture) and the journalist Wim Hora Adema. It was the time when feminism was gaining in popularity in the Netherlands: the years of blunt injustice, when everyone was still sexist and antifeminist. As a small, radical feminist journal, in those early days *Opzij* was more of a club paper for a small group of women. Yet from the outset the magazine was able to count on the unpaid collaboration of a large number of feminists of some stature. There were no financial resources, nor as yet advertisers.

After one year *Opzij* was taken over by a large, Dutch publishing company (De Weekbladpersgroep). It received professional treatment, though still with very limited resources and much amateurish improvisation. Advertising was canvassed, and later the design was changed, the sales strategy tightened up and there were advertisements. In 1976 the number of subscribers went up from 1,100 to 4,000, and reached 10,000 in 1981. Only then was there money for paid staff: at that point, Ciska Dresselhuys, who had been involved with *Opzij* since its second year, became its chief editor and a part-time journalist was taken on. Three years later the *Opzij* formula was broadened and the journal became more than just a radical action paper. The result was more female readers: a trend which has continued ever since. *Opzij* had become a power to be reckoned with in the Netherlands.

As part of the management's drive to achieve higher sales in Flanders, a Flemish supplement was launched in May 1986, with four pages of women's news and a detailed calendar of women's activities in Dutch-speaking Belgium. The editorial staff was made up of several women from the defunct Flemish feminist magazine *Lilith*. From then on *Opzij* was found everywhere, including at all sorts of women's events. *Opzij* sales in Flanders, which until then had totalled no more than 200 copies, rose by 75-100% a year.

The jubilee issue of *Opzij*.

In 1987 *Opzij* celebrated its fifteenth anniversary. With a circulation of 40,000 copies, the journal had secured a place for itself in the Dutch magazine market. Despite that status, some advertisers were prejudiced against it and the number of advertisements in *Opzij* continued to be very low. No advertisements for makeup or household products in *Opzij*, and none for cigarettes or associated products, because of an editorial ban. To mark its fifteenth anniversary *Opzij* published its own survey on 'Feminism and Desire', thereby devoting more attention to the pleasant sides of life. And for the first time in 15 years a man appeared on the cover, with the title 'Man as an Object of Desire'. During the same period, *Opzij* also organised a series of lectures which have become an institution in the Netherlands. And every year *Opzij* awards an emancipation prize: the Harriët Freezerring. On the journal's twentieth anniversary, this prize went to its founders: Hedy d'Ancona and Wim Hora Adema. *Opzij* has now been in existence for 20 years. Over the years the tone has changed, the militant content has gradually been recast to give it more colour, while the content in general has shifted from exclusively pioneering articles about the women's movement to a broader range covering every possible subject, though it is still true to say that politics is one of the main ingredients. The cover has also seen great changes and improvements during the course of the years. The circulation has now reached 78,000 copies in the Netherlands of which 40,000 go to subscribers, and 3,000 in Flanders.

No other journal in the Netherlands or Flanders writes in the same way about feminism and the women's movement. Expressed per head of the (Dutch) population, *Opzij* can even claim to be the largest feminist magazine in the world. The reasons for the differing success in the Netherlands and Belgium lie in the different traditions of these two countries. Unlike Flanders, the Netherlands has a tradition of progressive and quality publications. Moreover, the Dutch read more, both books and magazines. However, the main reason is that there is a far larger feminist movement and tradition in the North where feminism became structured much earlier on, with civil servants for equal opportunities, official publications and studies; in Flanders people had to wait until 1986 for a Minister for Equal Opportunities.

The evolution of the women's movement in Flanders is mirrored in the history of the feminist magazines. Despite all the efforts of volunteers, in the eighties Flanders lost all its small feminist magazines, including those which had links with organisations and local journals. A professional magazine such as *Opzij* has never existed, and would in any case never have been able to make a profit.

As well as its regular articles on cultural, literary and all kinds of social topics, *Opzij* has for some time also included an interesting section devoted specifically to culture. And every year *Opzij* publishes a women's diary with quotations and contributions from well-known feminists on a particular theme such as jealousy ('92) and daydreams ('93). The diary has a total circulation of 55,000 in the Netherlands and 2,500 in Flanders.

What is the average *Opzij* reader like? She is 35, single, has a job in education or the social sector, earns a good salary, is very interested in politics and the environment, votes for a woman in elections, buys and reads numerous literary books, newspapers and magazines, has a car, goes on holiday regularly, does not watch much television but regularly goes to the cinema and often keeps cats. And twenty-five percent of *Opzij*'s readers are men!

JET VLOEMANS
Translated by Alison Mouthaan.

Dutch Catholics on Women and the Priesthood

Since the decision in November 1992 by the Church of England to allow women to be ordained into the priesthood, the question of 'women in the ministry' has also become a live issue in the Netherlands. The majority of the many protestant churches and communities have little difficulty in welcoming the Anglican Church's decision; after all, female ministers are already to be found in the Netherlands, although in terms of ecclesiastical law, and also in terms of their function, their office is not entirely comparable with the Catholic priesthood.

It is precisely among the Catholics that a debate has now arisen on this issue. And for the first time a Catholic bishop, Monseigneur Ernst of the diocese of Breda, has said that the possibility cannot be ruled out that *one day* there will be women priests in the Roman Catholic Church. However carefully Mgr. Ernst chose his words, his statement stands in direct contradiction to the view of the Dutch Cardinal and Archbishop Simonis of Utrecht and other Dutch bishops who regard the present exclusively male priesthood as being enshrined for ever. Rome holds firmly to the view that there is a fundamental spiritual difference between men and women, which is laid down in the order of creation. As evidence, supporters of this view remind us that Jesus assumed the form of a man and that the Bible refers to God mainly in 'masculine terms'. The conclusion which then follows is that during the Mass (the Eucharist) only a man can represent God.

It is no surprise that there is great opposition among feminist Dutch Catholics to the views promulgated in Rome. The theologian Dr Tine Halkes of the University of Nijmegen, for example, has expressed the view that the leaders of the Roman Catholic Church harbour the idea that the sacrosanctity of the priesthood would be desecrated if it were conjoined with the sexual idea of which, according to the Vatican, woman is the symbol. The Christian dogmatist Dr A. van de Beek put it in more simple terms. In answer to the question of whether the Messiah could have been a woman, he told a group of theology students: 'Yes, why not? If God chooses to reveal Himself on earth in human form, it makes no difference whether that person is a man or a woman. The important thing is the fact that it is a human being.'

The 'Eighth of May Movement', a collection of more than a hundred progressive Catholic organisations, through its (female) chairperson, does set a condition for the ordaining of women into the priesthood: 'The hierarchical element must first disappear from the Catholic Church. If women simply become part of the existing hierarchical establishment, you haven't really achieved anything. You then simply have authoritarian women in place of men.'

The debate on 'women in the ministry' cannot be seen as totally unconnected with the shortage of priests in the Catholic Church in the Netherlands: the number of priests has fallen by 65 % over the last thirty years. One fifth of the 1,700 parishes have no priest of their own. Already hundreds of priests have to serve three or more parishes (per *man*). However, when last autumn Rotterdam's Bishop Bär suggested admitting 'more mature' married men into the priesthood, this idea was forcefully rejected by Cardinal Simonis.

JAN VERDONCK
Translated by Julian Ross.

Half a Century of *Trouw*

In January 1993 the Dutch newspaper *Trouw* celebrated its fiftieth anniversary. If this does not seem a particularly long history, the year in which the newspaper was born is all the more noteworthy: 1943, for Holland the third year of the Second World War, the year of Germany's first major defeat at Stalingrad. As the defeat of the German occupiers loomed nearer, their regime became even harsher. The Dutch resistance, at first carried on by a few individuals, became more and more structured. And within this organised resistance movement, the question began to be raised: How will we organise the Netherlands, politically and socially, when the War is over? It is helpful to be aware here that the Netherlands was not completely liberated until May 1945, and that in the months between the Allied invasion of Normandy on 6 June 1944 and the Liberation, the behaviour of the German occupiers became increasingly ruthless. One only has to think, for example, of the extermination of 100,000 Dutch Jews, or of the 'Hunger Winter'.

In talking about plans formulated during the War, it is useful to bear in mind that, until 1940, the Netherlands was still a strongly 'pillarized' society, a society vertically divided along ideological lines, with the Catholics (1/3), the Protestants (1/3) and the socialists (1/3) each having their own, autonomous institutions, with their own newspapers, social organisations, political parties, youth organisations, etc. During the

War, the Catholics in particular (for whom the process of social emancipation had been speeded up, due largely to the radical opposition of Mgr. (later Cardinal) Jan de Jong, Archbishop of Utrecht) were inspired by the so-called 'breakthrough ideal'; the socialists, for their part, were in favour of breaking the links with the anti-confessional movement. The reformist element of Dutch society embraced two movements: one seeking to break out of its own isolation, and a small but well-organised group which wanted to continue its tight-knit structure after the War. Those supporting this latter movement were known as the 'Orthodox Reformed' (*Gereformeerden*). They belonged to a church community which in 1834 had set its face against the liberal ideas of the Enlightenment as these had manifested themselves in the large (and more or less national) Dutch Reformed Church (*Hervormde Kerk*). They called themselves – with a reference to the French Revolution – the 'Anti-Revolutionaries'. They were a tightly organised group of intensely practising Christians, highly active politically and socially. In 1880, using their own resources, they set up a university, giving their own community the support of a highly-developed intellectual foundation.

Immediately after the occupation by the Germans in May 1940, protestant Holland decided to publish an underground paper: *Vrij Nederland* (Free Netherlands). January 1943 saw the first conflict among its editors, with one group wishing to 'de-pillarize' Dutch society after the War and the other, smaller group wanting just the opposite: '*In isolation lies our strength*' was the slogan of this latter group. The specific cause of this internal conflict was the fact that a majority of the editors supported radical resistance, including for example the derailing of a train containing Germans going on leave. The smaller, Anti-Revolutionary group of editors felt that such action was motivated too much by a desire for revenge, was unevangelical and therefore un-Christian, and was also at odds with the provisions of international law. (It is interesting to note in this context that the Dutch Resistance termed itself the '*Illegaliteit*' (Illegality), a term which says something about the strong need in the Netherlands to take the law, the *'leges'*, seriously).

In January 1943 a small Anti-Revolutionary group decided to start publishing their *own* resistance newspaper. The initial masthead, *Oranje-bode* (Orange Messenger), later became *Trouw*, 'Loyal' – loyal to the familiar trinity in those circles of God-Netherlands-Orange. In general it can be said that the underground ('illegal') press enjoyed a wide circulation among the avid readers of the Netherlands. The paper was of course produced by volunteers: small editorial teams (because of the underground nature of the publication) who were able to purloin paper from the occupiers; printers who were prepared to do the typesetting, and so on. Ultimately the circulation reached around 500,000 copies. In order to spread the risk, printing was carried out at several locations. The typematter and printed newspapers were distributed mainly by young girls and older women. The paper was funded by voluntary donations to these distributors. The 'illegal' press attracted a mercilessly harsh response from the German occupiers, ultimately leading to 200 deaths by firing squad, including 80 female *Trouw* workers.

After the War – in May 1945 – a number of the underground newspapers became 'legal'; one of these was *Trouw*. Where most of the formerly 'illegal' papers were sympathetic towards the 'breakthrough ideal', *Trouw* was a notable exception. The paper became the exclusive mouthpiece of the Anti-Revolutionary party and the Orthodox Reformed Churches. This position also had other consequences: no film reviews, no reports on Sunday sports events, letters to the editor in which readers argued from the basis of Bible texts. The paper acquired the image of being 'dull' and of little social relevance. Beyond its own closed circle of readers, the paper was hardly read, and little by little the number of subscribers melted away.

The cultural revolution which took place in the turbulent sixties brought a change in this situation; strict observance of the Gospel with regard to society and one's fellow men radicalised the editorial board. In the mid-seventies a new editor in chief was appointed, whose formative years had been shaped by the ecumenical and progressive IKON, the media institute for the reformist churches. The result was that a group of orthodox readers abandoned the paper and a new confessional paper was launched: *Het Reformatorische Dagblad* (The Reformist Daily). *Trouw* changed from an Anti-Revolutionary newspaper into the self-aware daily it is today. It is produced by a staff of 130 (including a strikingly large number of women) and has a circulation of 120,000 to subscribers with a further 9,000 being sold separately. *Trouw* characterises itself as implicitly (rather than explicitly) Christian, in the ecumenical sense of the word (15% of its readers are Roman Catholics). It is the only national daily newspaper in the Netherlands which consciously sets aside a page every day for information on Spiritual Life. 'There is no country where religion plays such an important background role in the thought and actions of the nation, as it does in the Netherlands', says editor in chief Greven. The solid Podium page also bears daily witness to an intellectual interchange of social, political and theological views.

In an ecclesiastical sense, *Trouw* is a remarkable newspaper, not least because many other 'ideological' newspapers have disappeared (e.g. the socialist *Vrije Volk* (Liberated People) and many Roman Catholic newspapers). *Trouw* is praised in political circles for its sharp analysis, the way it follows developments at a distance, unaffected by the fashions of the day, its professional journalistic approach, its tight composition (using sans serif type). It is a quality newspaper which makes no attempt to deny its roots. It is no coincidence that its staff have been among the prizes on several occasions.

Trouw is a newspaper with an individual and widely respected voice among the Dutch media; the echo of a principled resistance was and is still there between the lines, however 'law-abiding' the paper may be.

KEES MIDDELHOFF
Translated by Julian Ross.

Radio Netherlands World Service

In about 1925 a cartoon of a radio mast appeared in an English magazine. High up in the mast was a broom, in the hands of a 'Flying Dutchman' who was 'sweeping the ether clean'. This was a reference to the four seventeenth-century Anglo-Dutch wars, in which the Dutch fleet swept the sea of enemy ships. Thanks to Philips, the Netherlands was the first country to use shortwave radio to reach those Dutch who were overseas; Edward Startz and his 'Happy Station' soon became a household name for the lucky few in possession of a shortwave receiver. The transmitter, located near the Hilversum radio centre, could be turned to within the nearest centimeter to broadcast to any part of the world. It was not surprising that the Nazis wanted to commandeer this valuable instrument when they invaded the Netherlands on 10 May 1940. Neither was it surprising that the Dutch themselves blew up the showpiece on the same day.

Not long afterwards, the BBC also discovered the uses of shortwave radio. The Dutch government, exiled in London from 1939 to 1945, made use of the 'overseas service' to support the Dutch resistance movement.

Almost immediately after the liberation of the Netherlands on 5 May 1945, the shortwave tradition was revived; the significance of shortwave had become only too clear during the war. In 1946 the Radio Netherlands World Service (RNWO; *Radio Nederland Wereldomroep*) was created. As a corporation independent of Government and the domestic broadcasting network, the RNWO's task was to transmit the Dutch character and outlook to the world.

Originally intended to maintain a link with the many Dutch people scattered around the world, the RNWO soon began to follow in the footsteps of the BBC by broadcasting in other languages, respectively:

- Bahasa Indonesia, in order to serve the native population of the Dutch East Indies.
- English and Arabic, in order to convince Asia and the Orient of the Netherlands' good intentions regarding the decolonization process in Asia.
- Spanish (and later also Portuguese), geared towards South America when the independence of Indonesia obliged the Netherlands to search for new markets.

Other languages were also used, albeit much later. French, for example, was used in order to convince the African population of the Netherlands' interest in the Third World. This was soon followed by the use of so-called 'transcript programmes', designed to increase audiences and to perfect reception. These programmes were produced in Hilversum and sent to radio stations throughout the world, where they were broadcast on FM transmitters.

This export service became extremely important in the transmission of Dutch culture outside the Netherlands. For example: Pieter Geyl, lecturer at University College London from 1919 to 1936, compiled a spoken history of the Low Countries (including Flanders); Garmt Stuiveling, man of letters, devised a series on Dutch literature. In 1992 some 180,000 programmes were sent out, destined for 1,500 radio stations in some 100 countries.

350 American stations purchase, as broadcast in the Netherlands, performances of the Royal Concert Hall Orchestra in Amsterdam and the Rotterdam Philharmonic Orchestra. In addition, special programmes of Dutch music are recorded and distributed. The music can be anything from Jan Pieterszoon Sweelinck (1562-1622) to Hendrik Andriessen (1892-1981), who was commemorated in 1992. Recordings are also made of events of European importance in the Netherlands, such as the Festival of Old Music in Utrecht, and of jazz performances and interpretations of Latin American music, where the link between the Netherlands and the Antilles is an important factor.

As far as literature is concerned, distinguished American actors and actresses have recorded readings of 26 short stories (translated into English) by Dutch authors. RNWO is working with BRT-N (Belgian Radio and Television) on a similar series for the *Frankfurter Buchmesse,* and Flemish writers will also participate. 'Arts Monthly' gives a survey of cultural events in the Netherlands such as the Holland Festival, North Sea Jazz Festival, etc. The programme 'European Culture' reports on a number of similar events from Salzburg to Oxford.

All these programmes are offered free of charge to sister organizations. They are especially popular with public stations. The RNWO also makes television programmes along similar lines, albeit on a small scale, which may be broadcast free of charge. The RNWO's yearly budget is 75 million guilders (approx. 28.8 million pounds) which is taken out of Dutch radio license fee revenue. Since 1969 RNWO has had an associated training centre for (advanced) programme makers from the Third World. RNWO is also a leading member of the EBU (European Broadcasting Union) and the ABU (Asian Broadcasting Union).

The RNWO is a remarkable station, particulary when compared to similar stations in other small European countries. The quality of its programmes has earned it a good reputation in the international media world. Remarkable? Perhaps not: in the sixteenth and seventeenth centuries it was possible, in the Netherlands, to print and publish material that could not be printed or

The RNWO-studio near Hilversum.

published anywhere else in Europe. The RWNO is simply upholding an ancient tradition, using the most modern mass-media.

KEES MIDDELHOFF
Translated by Yvette Mead.

Radio Netherlands World Service
P.O. Box 222 / 1200 JG Hilversum / The Netherlands
tel. +31 (0)35 72 42 11 / fax +31 (0)35 72 43 52

Publishing in the Low Countries

The Netherlands and Flanders are neighbours who share the same language and, through the Dutch Language Union, are working towards a common language and literature policy. Yet, despite this, there is no uniform Dutch-language book market. In this article, we will highlight some of the major differences in publishing, book retailing, readership and government initiatives.

The market for general books in the Netherlands has become much more concentrated over the past decade. As a result three concerns, namely Wolters Kluwer, Meulenhoff / Malherbe and the Weekbladpersgroep, now control more than half the literary market. Meulenhoff / Malherbe alone is responsible for a quarter of the turnover in general books in the Netherlands. Since Meulenhoff took over Malherbe in 1991, more attention has been paid to non-fiction.

The educational publishing house J.B. Wolters grew out of the Wolters bookshop in Groningen. In 1987 Wolters-Samsom merged with the printing and publishing concern Kluwer. Wolters Kluwer publishes mainly loose-leaf legal, fiscal and technical publications. Through acquisitions, the Wolters Kluwer group has expanded its interest in the scientific information sector in all West European countries and in America. In 1990 the Wolters Kluwer group bought the American medical publishing house Lippincott, and is also active in the literary market, through its imprints Contact, Atlas and Veen.

There has been specialization as well as concentration, especially by Elsevier and VNU (Verenigde Nederlandse Uitgeversbedrijven; Associated Dutch Publishing Companies), the two largest publishing groups in the Netherlands. Elsevier, formerly renowned for publishing general books and encyclopaedic works, aims expressly at the scientific (journal) market. On 1 January 1993, Elsevier merged with Reed International. Reed Elsevier now has 25,000 employees worldwide.

VNU concentrates on broad-interest newspapers and magazines and also has interests in other media. It is involved in commercial television (RTL4 in the Netherlands and VTM in Flanders), and a variety of new media such as cable television and teletext.

There have been hardly any such structural developments in Flanders. Yet the aforementioned Dutch publishing companies are prominent in the Flemish book market. They have a large share (45%!) in the Flemish market through subsidiary companies, some of them based on Flemish concerns acquired by Dutch parent companies. One example of this policy is the Weekbladpersgroep, which operates in the Flemish market through the literary publishing house Dedalus.

Dutch publishers also shape the character of the Flemish book trade through exports. Dutch publications account for approximately 56% of the Flemish market. They dominate the market for general books (65% Dutch import) and the scientific market (55% Dutch import). The markets for comics and educational books are, however, firmly in the hands of Flemish publishers.

Flemish exports to the Netherlands are weak (the exception being comics and books for children and young people). This is partly due to the small size of Flemish publishing houses. If a Flemish publisher wants to launch a book on the Dutch market, he will invariably opt for co-production with a Dutch concern. The Dutch publishing groups also offer advantages in administration, promotion and distribution. Flemish publishers, however, supported by graphics companies with high quality equipment (Brepols, Proost, Lannoo), have a strong presence in the art, humanities and cartoon comic markets.

It also often happens that a Flemish author, having made a successful debut, rapidly switches to a Dutch publisher for his / her next book. A number of renowned Flemish authors are comfortably settled with Dutch publishers. Hugo Claus, for example, is with De Bezige Bij.

The more difficult position of Flemish publishing is also reflected in the number of titles published: half that produced by Dutch publishers. In the Dutch language-area a new title appears every 44 minutes. However, Flanders produces only 37 titles per 100,000 inhabitants, while the corresponding figure for the Netherlands is 65. By European standards, Flanders produces comparatively few new titles each year, while the Netherlands is in line with the European average. As far as translations are concerned, these tend to be imported into, rather than exported from, Flanders and the Netherlands.

Titles published in the Netherlands and Flanders:

	The Netherlands			Flanders			Nl + Fl
	total	of which new	recognized publishers	total	of which new	recognized publishers	total
1983	11,880	69%	555	2,654	?	75	14,534
1985	12,649	73%	566	2,714	77%	80	15,363
1990	13,691	71%	555	3,027	?	101	16,718
90: new per 1000 inhabs.			= 65		= 37		= 56
90: new & reprint			= 91		= 47		= 78

By comparison: New & reprint per 100,000 inhabitants		
	Great Britain = 112	Spain = 97
	France = 69	Sweden = 132
	Italy = 59	Denmark = 211
	Germany = 100	Switzerland = 150

New Dutch titles are mainly in the category 'Science and Technology'. In Flanders, the genre with the most new titles is children's literature. Comics play an important part here, and are a rare Flemish (or more generally, Belgian) trump-card on the international book market. Comic heroes such as Lucky Luke and the Smurfs have even found fame in American cartoon films.

Title production by category is as follows:

	Flanders	The Netherlands
general	2%	1%
science & technology	27%	41%
language & literature	16%	22%
children's literature*	30%	11%
religion	5%	4%
art	2%	3%
educational	17%	16%
sport & leisure	1%	2%
	100%	100%
TOTAL	(= 3,027 titles, new & reprint)	(= 13,691 titles, new & reprint)
* including comics		

In the Netherlands, too, book retailing is handled more professionally. There are about 6 times as many specialized bookshops (those whose main activity is bookselling) in the Netherlands as in Flanders; on 1 January 1991, 1,564 out of a total of 3,344 bookselling outlets, as against 272 out of 2,700. The Flemish reader is often obliged to buy his books from a non-specialist outlet, or to order direct from the publisher. The most important chains in Flanders are Standaard Boekhandel, CLUB and the French FNAC chain. The ECI Book Club (Bertelsmann) has 17% of the market in the Netherlands, and an estimated 18% in Flanders.

Booksellers, like publishers, recognize the importance of systematic co-operation. A large proportion of Dutch bookshops belong to one of a number of chains, such as the Boekhandelsgroep Nederland and the department-store chains De Bijenkorf and Vroom & Dreesmann, and co-operatives like Libris and Parnassus. There is also an extensive chain of smaller bookshops and kiosks.

It is not only in publishing and selling that Flemish and Dutch attitudes differ. Research has shown that the Flemish readership is smaller than the Dutch. In the Netherlands the growing group of non-readers represents 23% of the population; in Flanders 37% on average. The Flemish also spend less time reading books, magazines and newspapers than the Dutch.

The library situation shows that this difference has more to do with attitude than with the supply of reading matter. Although there are more lending outlets in Flanders than in the Netherlands (1 per 9,100 inhabitants against 1 in 12,500), the Dutch make considerably more use of their libraries. While 20% of Flemings are members of a public library, borrowing on average 30 books per year, in the Netherlands 30% of the population use the libraries and borrow on average 40 books per year.

Finally, there is the question of government support for the book trade. The policy in both countries is mostly one of direct subsidies and promotional support for increased usage of public libraries.

In the Netherlands subsidies are granted to authors, translators and publishers of both fiction and non-fiction. For authors these subsidies take the form of grants, for translators a supplementary fee. Publishers can rely on the government for direct project subsidies. In addition, literary journals receive direct subsidies, which have become a *sine qua non* for such publications.

Flemish subsidies are mostly granted to authors of fiction. This excludes other 'participants' in the book trade. Moreover, a number of protective government measures in the Netherlands would not be legal for the book trade in Flanders: payment for the reproduction of textbooks and academic works, lending rights for authors and publishers, retail price maintenance for books, and active support for training and research projects in the book industry. At the 1992 Flemish Book Fair in Antwerp the Flemish Minister of Culture did promise to tackle the issues of lending rights and fixed retail prices. On that occasion he also talked of an increase in subsidies to authors.

There is a clear European dimension to the issue of retail price maintenance. The European Commission has already stated that the establishment of a fixed price across the frontiers is not possible. However, the European Floor Price system is under consideration. In this system the price is based on the price at which a book is sold in the country of publication. Although this would not lead to a binding fixed price, it would nevertheless prevent price differences between EC member states, since a book could not be sold anywhere at a lower price than this Floor Price.

The European Floor Price could offer a pragmatic solution to the fixed-price problem. Nevertheless, some members of the European Parliament have been calling for a 'real' fixed price. This became evident when the Parliament accepted a resolution to this effect on 22 January 1993.

It is clear that the mainly structural differences between the Dutch and Flemish book industry have resulted in a Dutch-dominated book market in the Low Countries. Nevertheless, the survival of Flemish as well as Dutch publishers, booksellers, authors, translators, etc. depends in the last resort on the buying public. As long as publishers supply books with which the buyer can identify, he will continue to spend time and money on books. A well-organized bookseller will have to be constantly aware of the reader's need for information, entertainment, instruction, and general culture. Through Flemish, Dutch, or universal books ...

CARLO VAN BAELEN
Translated by Yvette Mead.

Visual Arts

Peter van Straaten Drawn from Life

In 1984 the cartoonist Peter van Straaten (1935-) published *Scandal* (Aanstoot), a book containing 52 indecent drawings, so indecent indeed that Her Majesty's Customs have forbidden the entry of copies of it into the United Kingdom. All the drawings show the sexual act literally brought into the open, in a public setting, so that there is an outrageous collision between intimacy and provocation coupled with the kick of a dual voyeurism, that of the spectators in the drawing and of the 'reader'. *Playboy* has compared Van Straaten to Rembrandt. And rightly so, for his cartoons display an immense technical mastery; they give us the impression that he can tell *every* story, express *every* emotion with his pen.

The cartoons do indeed tell stories. A good example is one from the collection *I'm Not Happy, Ma* (Moeder ik ben niet gelukkig) which shows a lonely man eating a croquette from a slot machine and thinking, as the caption reads, 'I think I'll make an early night of it'. In this case word and image are engaged in a conflict in which the drawing speaks the truth while the text lies or, to say the least, draws a veil over the truth. The depiction of the locale conveys how a human being has been plunged into a squalid and desolate situation. Language must make it bearable or gild the pill in a bitterly ironic fashion. 'Everything hot', the legend over the slot machines, is in stark contrast with the bleakness of the locale.

The conflict between word and image is even more poignant when the subject is physical love. Here the body tells the truth, here too the words deny the truth. This is the underlying theme of a book like *Am I Doing OK?* (Doe ik het goed?) Failures are shrouded in words, but the cartoon shows the averted faces of the bewildered lovers and the expression in their eyes which silently tells of failure and disappointment while their mouths find words of comfort like 'Doesn't matter, better next time.' The humorous effect of the combination of word and picture is derived from the recognizably hopeless battle waged by language against the humiliations of reality.

Whether the cartoons are with or without words, when brought together in book form they owe their coherence to two central themes: the inadequacy of human endeavour and the frequent failure of human relations. These are melancholy subjects, as titles like *Not My Idea of Fun* (Leuk is anders) and *There's Always Something* (Het blijft tobben) indicate. Each book concentrates on a particular aspect of these subjects: relations between the sexes, literary life, the world of business and, in a long series of Brétécher-like cartoon strips, relations between father and son.

Later, Van Straaten the cartoonist entirely separated words and pictures, and the writer Van Straaten was born. Alongside his cartoons and cartoon strips, some

'Doesn't matter, better next time.'

with no words at all, others with a usually melancholy one-liner, since 1970 he has also turned his talents to column-writing. Short sketches from daily life have appeared in daily and weekly newspapers and later in book form. Genre scenes, one might say, springing from an old Dutch pictorial tradition: the interiors, domestic scenes, streets and courtyards of Vermeer, De Hooch, Steen, Troost. Like these painters Van Straaten records what is within arm's reach, the reality of the here and now, recognizable, indeed almost verifiable.

These fictional sketches all revolve around a young woman called Agnes, who, divorced with one son, leads a somewhat irregular life, drinking, sitting around in cafés, having affairs with serious and less serious lovers. The strength of the *Agnes* stories lies not so much in their psychological insight as in their cultural authenticity: the language is up-to-date, even trendy; what is in, what is out, the situations, the venues, cafés, holiday resorts, work places, manners, food and drinks, they all ring true. To read *Agnes* is to take a walk through Amsterdam.

The number of books containing these sketches is growing steadily. Written in an unpretentious style, minimalist it could be called, the Agnes series holds up a mirror to contemporary mores; to some readers it is a revelation, others recognize their own stamping ground, while to very many it is simply a rich source of enjoyment.

AART VAN ZOEST
Translated by Elizabeth Mollison.

Translations of Peter van Straaten's work have been published by Fourth Estate, London.

Rudi Fuchs Grabs his Chance

The change in the curatorship of the Stedelijk Museum in Amsterdam passed off smoothly and uneventfully at the end of 1992. Rudi Fuchs (1942-), who lost the less than edifying battle for the position to Wim Beeren (1928-) in 1985, was this time invited to take up this much-discussed post, an offer which he naturally accepted. In accepting the post, Fuchs has also accepted the challenge of leading the most renowned museum of modern art in the Netherlands towards the next century – a not inconsiderable task, particularly in view of the fact that the approach of the 21st century is likely to force us to develop different criteria for assessing what is now considered to be modern art. Fuchs has already indicated in several interviews that the Stedelijk Museum will become more than simply a podium for contemporary art; he wants to concentrate to a much greater extent on exhibiting high points in the existing museum collection. In a change from the policy pursued to date, masters of modern art will acquire a more permanent place in the exhibition rooms, a move which will be made possible by the new extension to be built at the rear of the museum during Fuchs' curatorship.

Rudi Fuchs is probably the best known and most controversial museum director in the Netherlands. His idiosyncratic exhibition policy has always been a source of great controversy, a fact exacerbated by the way in which he has defended that policy both verbally and in writing. Fuchs' career is marked by his curatorship of two major Dutch museums, the Van Abbemuseum in Eindhoven from 1975 to 1987, and the Gemeentemuseum in The Hague from 1987 to the beginning of 1993. His off-beat exhibition policy also quickly drew international attention, and led among other things to Fuchs being invited to organise the seventh *Documenta* in Kassel in 1982, an exhibition which enjoyed and continues to enjoy great prestige and which shapes many developments in the art world. Fuchs' main concern during this *Documenta* was to show that contemporary art is dominated by a central core of major figures surrounded by a larger group of mostly younger artists. 'I see art as a genealogy,' says Fuchs, 'as a sort of branched family tree. Relationships crisscross each other, illegitimate children are born, incest takes place.' Opponents of Fuchs' policy claim that, since then, he has advanced no further than a continual rehashing of this 'family tree', of which diverse artists such as Dibbets, Kounellis, Judd and Baselitz can count themselves members. The fact is that every product he delivers bears a recognisable Fuchs stamp. He appears to be imbued with a clear vision of the hows, the whys and the wherefores of pictorial art. The refusal of this vision to brook any contradiction is an inherent part of its severity.

Fuchs has also made his mark elsewhere. Shortly after taking the reins at the Gemeentemuseum in The Hague in 1987, for example, he completely remodelled the museum and arranged for a start to be made on compiling an inventory of the extremely large collection – an operation which showed that the museum was almost bursting at the seams. In order to improve the manageability of museum collections, discussions regularly take place, particularly in the countries surrounding the Netherlands, on the clearing out of items held in store. In addition, it is not unusual for museums, in the United States and Switzerland for example, to sell off certain works of art in order to raise money for new acquisitions. Against this background Rudi Fuchs put forward a proposal in 1989 that an acquisition fund should be set up, to be funded by the sale of a number of the most important works in the Gemeentemuseum. The proposal led to a storm of protest, in which every interested faction became involved in the debate conducted in the Dutch press. The main question asked was whether the Dutch cultural heritage is still safe in museums if curators have the power to dispose of works from the collections as they see fit. Whatever the feelings about these plans, it cannot be denied that Fuchs is once again the man who has placed this thorny issue on the table. As a result, there is a possibility that the Dutch government will decide to pass a law protecting museum collections and individual works of art.

At the end of his curatorship in The Hague, Fuchs laid out the museum's new annexe in accordance with his own ideas; the former working palace of Princess Juliana, on the Lange Voorhout in the centre of The Hague, was transformed into a Fuchsian museum. Walking over the parquet floor designed by Donald Judd, through rooms in which each of the walls is a different colour, the visitor comes across many well-known names. Pictures by Flanagan, Lüpertz and Visser have been given a place among much older works of art, such as paintings by Goltzius, a classicist statue by Canova and a Chinese Buddha from the time of the Ming dynasty. It seems an unexpected parting gift to the city of The Hague.

From 1993 on, Fuchs will be able to throw himself to his heart's content into Amsterdam's collection of nineteenth and twentieth-century art. After the carefully thought out, if rather dull, exhibition policy of Wim Beeren, this will certainly liven things up somewhat. With great interest and measured distrust, we await what he has to offer us.

INGEBORG WALINGA
Translated by Julian Ross.

Rudi Fuchs (l.), together with Wim Beeren (former curator of the Stedelijk Museum, m.) and E. Bakker (Alderman of the City of Amsterdam, r.) at the presentation of the design of the extension of the Stedelijk Museum (4 February, 1993). This design is by the American architect Robert Venturi.

The Ninth *Documenta* and its Director, Jan Hoet

The large international exhibition *Documenta*, which was held in Kassel (Germany) for the ninth time in 1992, was in many ways remarkable. The eighth exhibition in 1987 had proved problematic right from the outset because the *Documenta* Board had difficulty agreeing upon the appointment of an artistic director (it was eventually the German Manfred Schneckenburger), and it seems that the exhibition also left behind it a rather unsatisfactory impression. With a deficit of 910,000 DM, the question was finally raised as to whether this reputable enterprise still had a future.

However, contrary to all expectations, there was a ninth event in 1992, and Jan Hoet (1935-), the Flemish Director of the Museum of Contemporary Art in Ghent, was appointed its artistic director. Jan Hoet was already known internationally on account of the much talked-about exhibitions he had organised in Ghent, and his *Chambres d'Amis* in particular. The *Chambres d'Amis* was an exhibition of contemporary art which invited Belgian and foreign artists to produce works of art in about thirty private homes. After his appointment to *Documenta*, this flamboyant and charismatic figure became known internationally as an art promoter who went to work in a distinctly idiosyncratic way. He organised the so-called 'art marathons' for the media in Ghent and Weimar, surprising the press and art enthusiasts by showing hundreds of slides of works of art which he had seen during his many exploratory trips all over the world and from which he was to draw up a shortlist. In actual fact, he disclosed nothing of his concept and that aroused considerable annoyance, especially in Germany where they were already suspicious of Hoet because he was not a German. Anyway, the form this particular *Documenta* would take remained a publicly open question right up until the day of the opening in June 1992. It soon became clear, however, that Jan Hoet had not gone to work in an impromptu fashion, as had been feared. His ideas created confusion, but behind them lay a sound concept, and while that concept may have been very subjective, it was exciting nonetheless. He broke new ground by selecting ten artists from his own country, and it proved a successful choice. In addition, he had looked for participants in countries belonging to the former Eastern Bloc and he had looked beyond Europe to places like Cuba, Brazil, Chile, Australia, Argentina, the Philippines, Senegal and Korea, countries from which we had seen little in the way of contemporary art until then. In the United States he went for artists who were not in the mainstream, like the Cherokee Jimmie Durham, who was received as a revelation. Of course, well-established artists were not ignored, but Hoet's greatest merit was that he carried out long and personal preparatory work with all these participants so that they executed new works *in situ* and often surpassed themselves.

All these factors contributed to the overwhelming success of *Documenta IX*. Typical art enthusiasts were frequently heard to comment that they had seen exciting art again, while the critiques in the international press – with some exceptions – were positive. The practical results could also be evaluated: during the one hundred days the exhibition was open, there were 609,235 paying visitors, 27% more than on the previous occasion. Despite the fact that the outgoings had never been so high and the exhibition area was larger than ever, this time no financial loss was incurred.

All in all, the outcome was favourable both artistically and financially, and signified a further triumph for Jan Hoet, whose *Documenta* proved that great achievements can also come from a small country.

LUDO BEKKERS
Translated by Alison Mouthaan.

Jonathan Borofsky (USA), *Man Walking to the Sky.* 1992. Fiberglass, aluminium, painted steel, 24 m and 198 x 141 x 550 cm. Friedrichsplatz, Kassel (Photo by Dirk Bleicker).

Jan Hoet (1935-).

Paleis Lange Voorhout

Paleis Lange Voorhout, Princess Juliana's former winter residence in The Hague, has been turned into an annex to the Gemeentemuseum. Rudi Fuchs (1942-), the museum's former director, has made the palace a house of memories. It has become 'an interior'.

Fuchs, appointed director of the Stedelijk Museum in Amsterdam at the beginning of 1993, faced a shortage of space in The Hague. Paleis Lange Voorhout offered new possibilities. The eighteenth-century palace, designed by the court architect Pieter de Swart for Anthony Patras, was built to house the representative of the province of Friesland in the States-General. In 1811 it was owned by the banking tycoon Archibald Hope – the *hôtel de Hope* – who made it available to Napoleon during his visit to the city.

From 1901 to 1934 the Queen Mother Emma lived in the palace. Until 1984 the golden coach in which each year the Queen rides to Parliament to give her Speech from the Throne always started its journey from here. The history of such a house cannot simply be forgotten. 'With this exhibition Paleis Lange Voorhout begins a new phase in its history,' says Fuchs. 'But the idea is that this change of function should be a gentle one.'

It is a historic building, a town palace in the heart of The Hague. Until 1984 it was used by Queen Beatrix as a place to work in. Hardly anything is left of the royal furniture except for Ger van Elk's portrait of the Queen, left in tribute. The Court took everything else.

A few years ago Princess Juliana sold her winter residence to the city council for the very low price of four and a half million guilders on the condition that it should be used for a cultural purpose. At the Princess's express request it may not be used as a museum exclusively for contemporary art: not just Baselitz or Dibbets or Gilbert & George, but also Mannerist silver, Asiatic sculpture or Turkish ceramics.

Fuchs is a great believer in intimate relations with art. A museum is not a zoo. 'It's only apes that twelve of you can stand and stare at together.' Some works of art you must see on your own, and more than once – in the salon as it were.

'The great fascination of the Gemeentemuseum in The Hague is the building,' said Fuchs when he was appointed director. There are odd alcoves, large rooms, small rooms, dark rooms and others with plenty of light. There is a courtyard, a garden and a pavilion. 'The interesting thing is that modern museum developments have bypassed The Hague.' In Fuchs' view the Gemeentemuseum had the advantage of lagging behind: that was why the building was exciting. And that was the exciting thing about Paleis Lange Voorhout.

Fuchs does not like spotless white. Most museums are too concerned with the walls; they are far too neutral. When he was made artistic director of the *Documenta* exhibition in Kassel in 1982, he referred explicitly to the architectural history of the Orangerie and the Fridericianum. 'A museum building is not neutral.' A few years ago he converted the Castello di Rivoli near Turin, a baroque palace with dozens of very different rooms. Paleis Lange Voorhout is also a highly varied museum, with painted ceilings, fine panelling and, above all, a great deal of colour. It is built in Louis XVI style with a rococo interior; the front is austerely classical, while the balcony is richly decorated. New parquet flooring has been laid on the ground floor and the first floor.

Paleis Lange Voorhout is very much a Fuchs museum, a building with odd corridors and intimate cabinets. The opening exhibition *The Interior* was concerned with the past residents and guests: who came to dinner, who was seen there, who talked to whom. The palace has remained a house, one with rooms, mantelpieces, doors, alcoves, stairs, panels, windows, mirrors, corners, irregular light and shadows.

The curling mirrors and the undulating mantelpieces, even the gilding on the ceiling, remind us of 'all the time that I was in this house' – so said Fuchs, who transformed the palace into a house of memories. He saw the exhibition *The Interior* as the history of the house, Juliana's former palace. 'The richly coloured and sometimes melancholy interior of Paleis Lange Voorhout shows traces everywhere of having been long in use; we wanted to leave that past as a presence.'

The Room, the Window, the Mirror and the Garden – a working title because in the end it became *The Interior* – refers to Mario Praz's autobiography, a book to which Fuchs says he is 'greatly attached'. In *The House of Life* Praz describes his life through the objects and art treasures he has assembled in his house,

Paleis Lange Voorhout,
The Hague.

the Palazzo Ricci in Rome. Each object has a story to go with it. To Praz everything he has ever collected is a memory; all the works of art and books are 'journeys into the past, to people he has known about whom he writes sometimes movingly and sometimes maliciously'.

At the entrance stands *The Chamberlain* by Rodin. The sturdy figure reminds the visitor of a closed door – the key to Fuchs' house. It is an attractive, welcoming museum, with parquet by Donald Judd and walls in red, green, orange and lemon. Everything has its own place: the etchings by Piranesi, the sculptures by Lüpertz (*The Burghers of Florence*) and Zadkine, the set designs for *The Magic Flute*, the birds by Carel Visser.

An important part of the exhibition on the first floor (and in the garden) was devoted to sculpture. On the second floor Fuchs had drawings by Penck and graphic work by Judd. 'Their beauty in the decorated house is certainly appropriate, but where exactly they should stand or sit – that is the theme of this first exhibition, which is why it bears the simple title *The Interior*,' wrote Fuchs.

Fuchs suggested that the visitor should follow the works discreetly 'to see how they converse with each other'. In his view works of art are just like people: they know each other by sight and now try to start a conversation. 'For it is that conversation which makes possible the intimacy of this house; in that conversation the works of art come to life while at the same time they again fill the house with life.'

PAUL DEPONDT
Translated by John Rudge.

Panamarenko 30 Years of Thinking about Space

'Stand up, you crippled andive! Stand up and show thy beauty!'
General Geronimo, *Letters from the Front*

In the story of Flemish art in the second half of the twentieth century, Panamarenko (1940-) is quite possibly the most spectacular figure. The work of this Antwerp artist falls completely outside the normal categories within which the majority of artists are active, and his artistic career accordingly has an extremely international orientation. One characteristic he does share with many of his fellow-countrymen, however, is the stubborn, almost obsessive working out of a number of fundamental ideas, regardless of prevailing fashions. In Panamarenko's case, this expresses itself in a mixture of poetry, fantasy, humour and light-hearted theory, a mix of which there are also other examples in twentieth-century Flemish art – particularly in the work of the painters James Ensor and René Magritte.

The recent publication of a major book in three languages (English, French and Dutch) provides an overview of Panamarenko's complete work at a time when a major retrospective of his work is touring a number of Japanese museums. It is a weighty, voluminous tome which covers Panamarenko's work from 1963 to 1992. Every aspect of his work is discussed: reliefs, pictures, machines, contraptions, happenings, drawings and graphic art. The author, the young art historian Hans Theys, has created a combination of *catalogue raisonné*, monograph and essay collection; in doing so, he has employed the device of contributions from fictitious collaborators such as *Dr. J.S. Stroop* (J.S. Jam, PhD). The book is impressively illustrated, and is a fine example of the quality work produced by Flemish printers: in addition to the hundreds of colour illustrations spread throughout the text, there are also 21 double-page reproductions which, thanks to the dimensions of the book, are standard poster-size.

The sixties in Antwerp

Panamarenko made his debut in Antwerp in 1963, with a series of ten reliefs entitled *Copper Plates with Bullet-holes*, which in essence were very traditional. Following a few further productions which fitted into the Pop-Art tradition, he began to concentrate on 'happenings', though little of this aspect of his work remains. One of his most striking early works, *Crocodiles* (1967) – which is now in the collection of the Museum of Contemporary Art in Ghent – is a good example of the way in which the artist drew the boundary between showing, demonstrating and withholding. This work, which consists of three crocodiles (actually plastic sacks) in an empty (!) aquarium, also recalls the lizards of the artist Maurits Escher, who was receiving a great deal of attention at the time; however, Hans Theys does not go into this aspect. In the same year Panamarenko designed *The Aeroplanes*, a very large work (16 meters long) which was to herald his international breakthrough. Aircraft, and all kinds of machinery related to flying, remain a constant feature of Panamarenko's work. His imagination knows no bounds in this area, and his best works often have a light, airy, fleeting feel, whether they be small works or monumental in scale. In 1988, thanks to the mediation of

Swiss Bike, a collage by Panamarenko (1965).

Joseph Beuys, he was able to exhibit *The Aeroplanes* in the *Staatliche Kunstakademie* in Düsseldorf; this exhibition was so successful that within a short time Panamarenko became the best-known Flemish artist internationally. Thereafter he produced further spectacular works, such as *The Aeromodeller* (1969-1971), a now-legendary work more than 27 metres long which was bought by Jan Hoet for the Museum of Contemporary Art in Ghent.

Flying on paper

While Panamarenko may have attracted a great deal of media attention with his spectacular objects and happenings, this does not necessarily mean that it is in these works that the great strength of his art lies. Hans Theys' book also presents a complete overview of Panamarenko's drawings, a less well-known and less popular aspect of his work, but a discovery for all that. Panamarenko – as one would expect – makes a large number of design drawings for his intriguing machines. In addition, he occasionally produces drawings, with a care and refinement which one would not immediately expect from such an exuberant artist, of elegant flying objects, surrounded by a gracious interplay of lines. Poetry triumphs over theory in these works – and this comes as a relief, for there is still room for the dreams of the viewer. One day, when we have forgotten all the experiments which were made in the wake of the sixties, we will still be talking rapturously about Panamarenko the draughtsman.

Hans Theys clearly sees things differently, tending rather to place the emphasis on the objects and the associated 'Closed System Theory' which the artist had developed. The style of the book probably fits well with his temperamental argumentational style, something which is illustrated by a fragment from the final chapter of the book: 'Panamarenko? Sheer irresponsibility. Amusement. Sheer amusement. None of these preoccupations with the deeper sense of the concept of experience or the dilemmas of Form, at least not when he is working or playing – which is the same –, only when he is made to think about the horror world of art, which, by the way, I wouldn't recommend to anybody (to think about art, I mean). Amusement! New amusement! And whether there is any weight, one has to *feel* for oneself. And those who don't feel it: get lost!'

JOOST DE GEEST
Translated by Julian Ross.

Panamarenko. A book by Hans Theys. Exhibitions International, Tervuren, 1992; 288 pp.

Flemish Art Symbolism to Expressionism

The outbreak of the First World War drove several Belgian painters to the United Kingdom, where they found a safe haven thanks to the mediation of the art-loving British government minister David Lloyd George. The artists George Minne, Gustave van de Woestijne and Valerius de Saedeleer ended up at various places in Wales (Llanidloes in the Cambrian Mountains and the seaside resort of Aberystwyth, Rhyd-Y-Gelyn in Cardiganshire, Llandinam), while Emiel Claus, Jules de Bruycker, Leon de Smet, Baertsoen, Daeye, Opsomer and many others settled in London. Constant Permeke, called to arms and seriously injured in the siege of Antwerp, was also evacuated to England (via London he arrived at Stanton Saint Bernard in Wiltshire, and from 1916 onwards he lived in Chardstock in hilly Devon). Over a period of four to five years, these places together saw the development of an important slice of Flemish art, whose history has yet to be studied with any degree of thoroughness. A great deal of research remains to be done even on the individual artists themselves.

In the meantime, other Flemish artists had fled to neutral Holland. The most important of these – Gustave de Smet and Frits van den Berghe – found shelter there (first in Amsterdam, later in the heathland village of Blaricum in the Het Gooi area) and did not return to Belgium until the end of 1921.

The majority of the artists named above – all of whom, with one or two exceptions, were born in Ghent – had lived and worked between 1898 and 1913 in a small village on the River Leie near Ghent, Sint-Martens-Latem – which since then has rightly gained fame as an artists' village, comparable with Barbizon in France, Bergen in the Netherlands or Worpswede in Germany.

Several other important artists lived in Sint-Martens-Latem, who had not fled from the violence of war; among them artists such as Albijn van den Abeele and Albert Servaes.

These 'Latem' artists, as they later became widely known, came to the village in two groups, one following the other. In the first 'core' group were – to name only the most important of them – the sculptor / drawer George Minne and the painters Van de Woestijne and De Saedeleer. The poet Karel van de Woestijne also belonged to this first group, who can be categorized as 'symbolists'. The second, younger group consisted of Permeke, Gustave de Smet and Van den Berghe. Albert Servaes, who was a contemporary of the last three (all were born between 1877 and 1886), but had not enjoyed an academic education, remained somewhere between these two groups.

The entire, fascinating history of artistic life in this quiet, still (at that time) rural artists' village between around 1900 and 1930 has recently been written by the Dutch art historian Piet Boyens. Or, rather, *rewritten*. For there were already a number of older studies about 'Sint-Martens-Latem, village of artists' in existence (Paul Haesaerts, 1940, 1945 and 1965; André de Ridder, 1945-46). These authors, who were contemporaries and friends of the second core group, presented a certain picture of Sint-Martens-Latem, one which, from an art-historical perspective, had gained almost universal currency during the previous half century. And this picture, at least in part, was incorrect, as is now apparent.

Dr Boyens, with the unprejudiced gaze of someone examining the subject again from a distance (both in time and space), has made important corrections and added significant nuances to that 'Latem-image' which had gradually become accepted as fact.

Let us look at the two most important ways in which Boyens has 'retouched' this picture: on the one hand there is the 'regrouping' of the two core groups (Minne – Van de Woestijne – De Saedeleer / Gustave de Smet – Permeke – Van den Berghe), and on the other hand the exploding of the myth that 'Flemish Expressionism' was originally a (purely?) Latem phenomenon. Using clear arguments, Dr Boyens asserts that the true expressionists among these artists developed their expressionism *after* and *outside* Latem: Permeke virtually under his own steam and without any direct influence from elsewhere during his banishment in England, and the other two, Gustave de Smet and Van den Berghe, through their international contacts in the Netherlands (with the influence of Le Fauconnier and the Dutch artists Jan Sluyters, Leo Gestel and Piet Mondrian, as well as their acquaintance with German expressionism, which had a distinctly urban character). During their 'Latem period' (before World War I), Permeke, Van den Berghe and Gustave de Smet were all disciples of the impressionist master from the nearby village of Astene, Emiel Claus. In fact Leon de Smet, Gustave's brother, remained an impressionist all his life; in London he was a very successful portraitist, his subjects including George Bernard Shaw, John

Gustave van de Woestijne, *The Bad Sower.* 1908. Panel, 56 x 46 cm. Private Collection.

Galsworthy, Thomas Hardy, Joseph Conrad and the rest of England's high society. Only Albert Servaes appears to have arrived at a sort of idiosyncratic pre-expressionism – for totally different reasons – around 1909.

For this corrective re-telling of the artistic history of Latem Dr Boyens possessed a number of important trump cards: an unprejudiced distance in his approach, the completeness of the factual material he had collected and, finally, the scientific meticulousness with which he pursued the analysis of the works of art themselves – virtually year by year and artist by artist; it was on this foundation that he based his conclusions and brought them together in a thorough synthesis. The result is a new, re-new-ing Latem-book. It is also a very attractive, not to say luxurious edition, with a beautiful, balanced layout, and an exquisite choice of illustrative material (180 selected works of art reproduced in colour), which provides evidential support for the written text. An exhaustive bibliography with no gaps and a catalogue section (1870-1970) reproduced in miniature, complete this masterful study by Dr Boyens. The book deserves to receive a lot of attention, and its author is worthy of a plaudit. This Dutchman has done Flemish art (history) a splendid service.

PAUL HUYS
Translated by Julian Ross.

Piet Boyens, *Flemish Art: Symbolism to Expressionism.* Lannoo / Art Book Company, Tielt, 1992; 640 pp.

Old Masters from the Low Countries in American Collections

In 1889 James E. Scripps, who was born in England and whose family started the first US newspaper chain, donated seventy paintings of Old Masters to the Detroit Institute of Arts. He must have thought something like 'Why should not Detroit aspire to the honour of becoming the Florence or Munich of this continent?' The history of American museums is unthinkable without these benefactors. The owners of sometimes phenomenal collections which perpetuated their names found it easy to find homes for donations beyond European curators' wildest dreams. The amazing story is told by Walter Liedtke in the 560-page catalogue edited by Ben Broos for the exhibition *Great Dutch Paintings from America* held in 1990-1991, first in the Mauritshuis in The Hague, and later in the San Francisco Fine Arts Museum. In 'The Battle Against the Dollar' in the same volume Edwin Buysen tells the other side of the story: the opposition in the Netherlands to American 'raids', an attempt to keep the heritage of Dutch art at home. That opposition was rarely blessed with success and the Netherlands even lost experts into the bargain. The American predilection for old Dutch Masters is a matter of taste and therefore also of the education that helps define that taste. Susan Donahue Kuretsky analyzes the phenomenon, which reminds readers in the Low Countries of their own eighteenth-century Art Academies with their collections which were to prove the cradles of many museums. The pedagogical concept behind both is similar: education demands examples. The first US museums were founded on university campuses in 1785 and 1811; the great public museums were founded later, from 1870 onwards. American patronage proved astute at all times. In the Spring of 1933 the Nazis had decimated Jewish civil servants in Germany. In 1937 Harvard 'acquired' Jacob Rosenberg from the print cabinet of the Berlin Kaiser Friedrich Museum. Peter C. Sutton tells the story of recent acquisitions in the US. The 1986 tax laws strongly influenced art collecting. Prices skyrocketed and not everyone is able to do what the J. Paul Getty Museum in Malibu did. Attention is therefore focused on less well-known work, partly influenced by monographs like the one devoted to Uytewael. These four essays make up about a quarter of the catalogue. The rest, from p. 128 to p. 560, describes seventy-three items to perfection, concentrating on the sometimes stormy pedigree of some paintings, and supplying an abundance of illustrations.

At about the same time as the Mauritshuis published this catalogue, the Antwerp Mercatorfonds published *Flemish Paintings in America.* The Antwerp book harks back to the grandeur of Plantin which is the hallmark of all art books published by the Mercatorfonds. This monumental volume represents the other side of a diptych devoted to the art of painting in the Low Countries. Once again the reader encounters Walter Liedtke as the author of the introductory essay explaining why US museums possess so many old Flemish paintings, a story of inexhaustible patronage in a gigantic country in which state subsidies are the very-rare-exception. The book appears to be the catalogue for an ideal exhibition (which never happened), containing some five hundred paintings, of which one hundred and two have been singled out for preferential treatment. The others have been relegated to the summary deposit list at the end of the book. The one hundred and two paintings selected are each the subject of a commentary written by one of a team of nineteen specialists, and each is presented to the reader in the form of a full page reproduction. Let me give one example: Baltimore possesses the most important painting by Anthony van Dyck in the USA: *Rinaldo and Armida* (1629), taken from Tasso's *Gerusalemme Liberata*. This adventure epic of the crusades was a great success at the English Court, in Edward Fairfax's translation published in 1600. Charles I paid £ 78 for the work, including his adviser's commission. He recognized in it Titian's Venetian court style which he liked so much, and which the court painter from Antwerp had made his own; witness his Italian sketchbook now in the British Museum. The royal collection was put up for auction on 27 October 1649. The Van Dyck painting went to Colonel William Webb for £ 80. Prices were stable in those days. It later became part of the collection of the Dukes of Newcastle, was acquired by a London dealer in 1913, and then departed: destination USA.

Anthony van Dyck, *Rinaldo and Armida*. 1629. Canvas, 236,5 x 224 cm. Baltimore Museum of Art (The Jacob Epstein Collection).

Anyone who wants to know about the image of Old Masters from the Low Countries in the USA cannot do without these two volumes. They replace a whole library.

GABY GYSELEN
Translated by André Lefevere.

Great Dutch Paintings from America. Catalogue by Ben Broos. With contributions by Edwin Buysen, Susan Donahue Kuretsky, Walter Liedtke, Lynn Federle Orr, Juliette Roding and Peter C. Sutton. Final editing by Rieke van Leeuwen. Waanders, Zwolle, 1990, for the Mauritshuis, The Hague.
Flemish Paintings in America, a volume in the *Flandria extra muros* series. Selected by Guy C. Bauman and Walter Liedtke. With an introduction by Walter A. Liedtke. Mercatorfonds, Antwerp, 1992.

Jan Dibbets In the Tradition of the Dutch Light

Dutch pictorial art has a strong tradition, which rests on two fundaments: a concentration on the changeable light in the sky above the flat countryside, and an openness to artistic expression in surrounding countries. In the Netherlands, as elsewhere, trends in modern art follow one another in rapid succession: shortly after the liberation of the Netherlands in 1945 CoBrA, an international collaborative venture involving artists from Copenhagen, Brussels and Amsterdam, placed free, emotional spontaneity at the forefront. The next development brought a reaction to this, precedence being given to the expressive power of the material over the personal experience of the individual work of art. At the start of the 1970s the accent shifted once again, with interest now focusing primarily on the ideas which can be brought out through the medium of visual art. The emphasis was not on the emotions of the artist, nor on the work of art itself, but on the study of the ideas which are utilised by pictorial art. How does the process of observation and distancing from reality develop?

Jan Dibbets (1941-) is a representative of this latter school. He is interested in the conceptual value in pictorial art and in related disciplines such as land art and minimal art. At the same time, Dibbets is a Dutch artist who continues the tradition of concentrating on the changeability of light in space. It is these two aspects which give his works their specific identity.

Dibbets studied at the St Martin's School of Art in London, where he became acquainted with the work of Anthony Caro and Richard Long. He shares with these artists an interest in nature and the way in which natural phenomena are observed and can be recorded in an image. In his studies Dibbets makes use of the camera, which records precisely the changes in form brought about by changes in lighting.

In 1969 Dibbets made his first perspective correction: he photographed a square drawn on the wall of his studio and adjusted the drawing to create an equal-sided form within the perspective illusion. He then repeated this operation on grass. By moving the camera, or by taking a series of pictures in conditions of increasing or decreasing light intensity, or by shortening or lengthening the exposure time, the changes in the perception of the object resulting from the differences in light intensity become clear. The area of the concrete, square form becomes mingled in a series of constantly changing nuances with the photographic-spatial illusion. A first series of mounted photographs, first in black-and-white, later in colour, was created, which reflected Dibbet's rational experiences with natural light. They form the beginning of a monumental book containing 132 reproductions, which illustrate the way in which Jan Dibbets, with an ever-increasing input of his personal vision, records and transforms nature.

The author Rudi Fuchs, director of the Stedelijk Museum in Amsterdam and long a close friend of the artist, holds Dibbets in high esteem as a newcomer in the Dutch tradition of the still-life, a tradition stretching from the seventeenth-century painter Saenredam to the modern artist Mondrian. In the words of Fuchs, space is approached atmospherically in their work, and it is this which distinguishes it from the frontal approach of an artist such as Cézanne.

Saenredam, Mondrian and Dibbets work with transparent spaces, concentrating on light changes in the depths of the interior. Dibbets is undoubtedly aware of these characteristics and remains faithful to his concept.

The changes which he effects on different shapes and in different spaces are developed in series. They are supported in the book by art-historical quotations relating to art in general or to Dutch pictorial art in particular. Dibbets' work also fits in with these historical views. As a result, *Interior Light* is more than a book about Dibbets: it also gives an insight into pictorial art and offers a perspective on Dutch painting from the viewpoint of Dibbets and his ilk.

Jan Dibbets' approach is conceptual, individual and universal. The geometrical square on the concrete wall is gradually replaced by the window, the skylight and later the circular shape of church windows. Earthly light is now tending towards Godly light. At the same time, the individual presence increases: after the correction of the perspective in space and after the recording of the exposure time, the light colour is now also changed, and once again Dibbets uses an optical form distortion by tilting the window within an outline drawn on the coloured surface. The methodical continuity guarantees the natural order. A tension is created which is at the same time logical and alienating. The opposition between the artist who creates and who is thus in competition with the Heavenly creation, becomes tangible while remaining mysterious.

In this way, too, Dibbets' work is related to Dutch landscape, still-life and architectural painting. And this is no one-sided relationship. The later window pictures offer a prospect both of Heaven and of earthly nature, just as the early squares were drawn on the shadowy wall or on the grass. In this way the analyses gain a

higher level of intuition. The treatment of colour, light and space moves smoothly away from the cool abstraction of Saenredam and approaches the warmth of his contemporary Vermeer, who instils more emotion into his work. This intuitive quality also makes Dibbets' painting receptive to the tonalities of, for example, Mediterranean light. In another chapter Gloria Moure illustrates this rapprochement in Dibbets' distinctive work. His Barcelona windows form the majestic conclusion to a book which records Dibbets' work, his exhibitions and his bibliography in accordance with the views of his artistry, a view which is characterised by a constant striving for perfection.

ERIK SLAGTER
Translated by Julian Ross.

Rudi Fuchs & Gloria Moure, *Jan Dibbets. Interior Light – Works on Architecture 1969-1990.* Benjamin & Partners, Groningen / Barcelona, 1991.

Splendours of Flanders Flemish Art in Cambridge

In the summer of 1993 a major exhibition of late medieval Flemish art was held in the famous Fitzwilliam Museum in Cambridge. The exhibition, made up of works from local collections, was the brainchild of a Flemish researcher, Dr Alain Arnould, who for several years was attached to the university library as a manuscript expert. In the course of his researches he tracked down large numbers of Flemish manuscripts, many of which had never before been described in detail or published. His interest in Flemish art from the fifteenth and sixteenth centuries was shared by Dr Jean-Michel Massing, a Fellow of King's College. In 1990, the two men worked out a plan for an exhibition of these manuscripts, supplemented by a few paintings on wood, a number of sculptures and a tapestry. Their proposal was well-received by the then curator of the Fitzwilliam Museum, Dr Jaffé, and was put into effect by his successor, Dr Simon Jervis. The exhibition was financially supported by both the Flemish Government and Gemeentekrediet.

There was no lack of Flemish art in Cambridge. Works of art were being imported directly from Flanders as early as the fifteenth century, including altarpieces, manuscripts and stained glass windows (at least half of the splendid stained glass windows in the chapel of King's College, for example, were made by Flemish or Dutch craftsmen). Two of the top works, panels by the Master of St Goedele, which are housed at Queen's College, were probably sent to England as soon as they were completed. Jean-Michel Massing used these panels as the basis for the reconstruction of the original altarpiece. Other paintings came into the hands of the museum only in later centuries, mainly through gifts. In fact the museum itself owes its existence to Dutch capital; it was founded in 1816 by Richard, seventh Viscount Fitzwilliam of Merrion, who had inherited a very large collection from his Dutch grandfather, a banker. The interesting, early sixteenth-century *Annunciation* is taken from his collection. Another masterpiece, the fine – and still anonymous – portrait of Filip Hinckaert, once *maitre d'hôtel* to Philip the Good, is a reminder of the extraordinary splendour of the court of Burgundy in Brabant. This work has remained virtually unseen since the now legendary exhibition of Flemish Primitives in Bruges in 1902.

The love of splendour of those who commissioned these works, with their backgrounds in the princely courts and in the Church, was even more evident in the many illuminated manuscripts which formed the main body of the exhibition. It is a striking fact that, as early as the fifteenth century, there was an export trade geared specifically to England, involving books whose content was totally adapted to an English readership and the English calendar of Saints. One notable title among the first printed books is the *Recuyell of the Histories of Troy:* this was the first book to be printed in English, and was produced by William Caxton, probably in Bruges (1473-4). The exhibition also displayed the only known fragments of the first printed version of *Reynard the Fox* (Van den Vos Reynaerde) (Gerard Leeu, Antwerp 1487-90). These are just two examples from an impressive collection, which is also extensively illustrated and described in the catalogue, jointly published by Cambridge University Press and Gemeentekrediet.

Flemish School, *The Annunciation.* Early 16th century. Panel, 68 x 54 cm. Fitzwilliam Museum, Cambridge.

JOOST DE GEEST
Translated by Julian Ross.

Alain Arnould & Jean-Michel Massing, *Splendours of Flanders. Late Medieval Art in Cambridge.* Cambridge University Press, Cambridge and Gemeentekrediet, Brussels, 1993; 275 pp.

Benoît's Smile A Minimal Registration of the Nonsensical

The young Flemish cartoonist Benoît van Innis (1960-) saw his talent recognized by the international press after the publication of *Scrabbling in Autumn* (Scrabbelen in de herfst, 1989) and *The Forbidden Museum* (Het verboden museum, 1990). Editors in chief of Flemish (*De Morgen*, *Panorama*), Dutch (*Vrij Nederland*, *De Volkskrant*) and French (*Le Magazine Littéraire, Lire*) newspapers and magazines invited him almost immediately to become a regular contributor to their publications. Even American interest was not lacking: British editor Tina Brown, who is the current editor in chief of the leading magazine *The New Yorker*, accepted Benoît as a member of that magazine's very select circle of in-house cartoonists. He has already designed several covers for the *New Yorker*, and has also contributed to *Travel and Leisure* and to *Esquire*. And yet reading Benoît's oeuvre is no simple matter. The imaginary(?) world in which his characters evolve is bathed in an absurd and somewhat disconcerting banality. Whether his extremely proper ladies and gentlemen strike arrogant or flashy poses, they always turn out to be ridiculous. They move with amazing ease in literary and artistic circles, love nature and good conversation, open themselves to every form of modernity, but are not seldom left behind in a state of utter confusion when the unexpected punctures their petrified thought patterns. Most of the time they are hardly, or even not at all aware of the absurdity of a situation, or else, by way of concession, they adopt an attitude whose frenetic artificiality they do not seem to realize.

These well-groomed people succeed in facing the most painful situations in a dignified manner. In nature they reveal themselves as respectable representatives of culture: the writer who launches himself on the water with a certain grandeur and loses none of the respect he is owed by doing so.

The settings in which this distinguished company thrives mirror in the most perfect manner their tendentious, eclectic thoughts and their ambitious intentions. They all like to be different, once in a while, in their lifestyles and in their attitudes, but they do it in such a clumsy way that they invariably elicit a smile of pity from the reader. When Benoît introduces artists in his cartoons he criticizes their often tragicomical seriousness, the exaggerated impact of their grandiose actions, and their extravagant performances. With great subtlety and a certain generosity of spirit he registers the funny madness, the nonsensical spectacle of a world that seems imaginary, but is ours after all.

Sometimes a cartoon is accompanied by a caption that reveals a fraction of the conversation, a minuscule aspect of what is happening, but the viewer often has to rely on his own intuition, his own insight, to 'get' the tableau. Interdisciplinary reminiscences (literature and the arts), intertextuality, childhood memories, literary doodles, they all engender the strange windings of Benoît's mind. A solid advance knowledge of the matter in hand seems to be indicated, and yet Benoît's refined humour appears to have appealed to a wide audience ever since he, when still a student, used his teacher, the painter Dan van Severen, as the subject of his first cartoons.

The main reason for this popularity may well be that Benoît's cartoons link up with both the French and the Anglo-Saxon traditions. The social engagement we find in Sempé, Bosc's sarcasm, Baxter's understatement, Searle's 'gag', the sublime observation with which Bateman, himself influenced by the French artist Caran d'Ache, registered in particular the behaviour of characters in closed spaces, these are only a few of the building blocks that constitute the world of Benoît van Innis's thought. The 'setting' of his topics always remains unmistakably French, but the phlegm of his characters is British to the core. But more remains to be said: Benoît's jokes cannot be catalogued. He satirizes the senseless actions of his characters in a very subtle way. In spite of their noble motivations and their almost natural dignity, whatever they attempt degenerates into a grotesque spectacle. The situation's potential for universal recognition is often great, and precisely this 'irritating' little feature turns Benoît's cartoons into so many small, but real masterpieces.

KAREL PUYPE
Translated by André Lefevere.

Bibliography

of Dutch Publications translated into English (1991 and 1992)

Anschütz, Marieke.
'But who made God?': a parent's guide to religion in the home. [S.l.]: Floris, 1991. [128] p.
Translation of: Over religieuze opvoeding. 1988.

Augustijn, Cornelis.
Erasmus: his life, works, and influence / Cornelis Augustijn; transl. [from the Dutch] by J.C. Grayson. Toronto [etc.]: University of Toronto Press, 1991. x, 239 p.: ill.; 24 cm. (Erasmus studies; 10).
Includes bibliographical references and index.
Translation of: Erasmus. 1986.

Bernlef, J.
Public secret / J. Bernlef; transl. [from the Dutch] by Adrienne Dixon. London [etc.]: Faber and Faber, 1992. 229 p.; 23 cm.
Translation of: Publiek geheim. 1987.

Blei, Karel.
On being the church across frontiers: a vision of Europe

today / Karel Blei; [transl. from the Dutch by Ann F. Mackie]. Geneva: publ. for the World Alliance of Reformed Churches by WCC publications, cop. 1992, 81 p.; 22 cm.
Translation of: Kerk-zijn over grenzen heen. 1992

Blok, M.J.C.
The Epistle to the Galatians, seven outlines / by M.J.C. Blok. Rev. ed. London, Ont.: Inter-League Publication Board, 1991. 47 p.; 23 cm.
First edition: 1977.
Includes bibliography.
Translation of: De Brief aan de Galaten: 7 schetsen. 1959.

Bruggen, J. van.
Annotations to the Heidelberg Catechism / by J. Van Bruggen; transl. [from the Dutch] by A.H. Oosterhoff. Neerlandia, Alberta, Canada: Inheritance Publications, cop. 1991. 299 p.; 22 cm.
Translation of: Aantekeningen bij de Heidelbergse Catechismus. 1951.

Bruna, Dick.
Miffy / Dick Bruna. London: Methuen Children's, 1991. [26] p. ill.; 21 cm.
Drawings originally published in: Nijntje. 1955.

Corbijn, Anton.
Allegro / Anton Corbijn; with a text by Els Barents; [transl. from the Dutch by Els Barents]. London: Schirmer's Visual Library, [1991]. 111 p.: foto's; 20 cm. (Schirmer's visual library; 6).

Cortel, Tine.
How to use mixed materials: creativity and technique / [research and text Tine Cortel and Theo Stevens]; [editor Carla van Splunteren]. Newton Abbot: David & Charles, 1991. [116] p.: ill.; 26 cm. (The fine arts series).
Originally published in Dutch.

Couperus, Louis.
The hidden force / Louis Couperus; transl. from the Dutch A.T. De Mattos. New ed. [S.l.]: Quartet Bks., 1992. [258] p.; 21 cm. (Quartet Encounters Series).
Translation of: De stille kracht. 1887.

Danneels, Godfried.
Christ or Aquarius?: [exploring the New Age movement] / Godfried Cardinal Danneels; transl. by Elena French. Dublin: Veritas, 1992. 45 p.; 18 cm.
Translation of: Christus of de waterman? 1990.

Dantzig, Rudi van.
For a lost soldier / Rudi van Dantzig; transl. from the Dutch by Arnold J. Pomerans. London: The Bodley Head, 1991. 261 p.; 23 cm.
Translation of: Voor een verloren soldaat. 1986.

Deddens, K.
Response to your baptism: a word to ponder for all those who are going to celebrate the Lord's Supper / K. Deddens; [transl. by Elizabeth Englefield; ed. by Debbie Lod[d]er Marian Meinen. [1st ed.], 3rd pr. [1992]. London, Ont.: ILPB, cop. 1985, 94 p.; 23 cm.
Translation of: Antwoord op je doop: een woord ter overdenking aan allen die Heilig Avondmaal gaan vieren. 1979.

Deursen, Arie Theodurus van.
Plain lives in a golden age: popular culture, religion, and society in seventeenth-century Holland / A.T. Van Deursen; transl. by Maarten Ultee. Cambridge [England]; New York: Cambridge University Press, 1991. 408 p.: ill.; 25 cm.
Includes bibliographical references.
Translation of: Het kopergeld van de Gouden Eeuw. 1978-1990. 4 dln.

Dros, Imme.
Annelie in the depths of the night / by Imme Dros; with drawings by Margriet Heymans; transl. [from the Dutch] by Arnold and Erica Pomerans. London [etc.]: Faber and Faber, cop. 1991. 114 p.: ill.; 21 cm.
Translation of: Annetje Lie in het holst van de nacht. 1987.

Duijker, Hubrecht.
The wine atlas of Spain and traveller's guide to the vineyards / by Hubrecht Duijker. London: Mitchell Beazley, 1992. 240 p.; 30 cm.
Includes bibliographical references and index.
Translation of: Wijn- en reisatlas van Spanje: een toeristische gids voor de wijnliefhebber: met wegenkaarten, wijnroutes, reisinformatie. 1992.

Duijker, Hubrecht.
The wine atlas of Spain and traveller's guide to the vineyards / by Hubrecht Duijker. New York: Simon and Schuster, 1992. 240 p.; 30 cm.
Includes bibliographical references and index.
Translation of: Wijn- en reisatlas van Spanje: een toeristische gids voor de wijnliefhebber: met wegenkaarten, wijnroutes, reisinformatie. 1992.

Dunning, A.J.
Extremes: reflections on human behaviour / A.J. Dunning; transl. from the Dutch by Johan Theron. New York: Harcourt Brace Janovich, 1992. (A Helen and Kurt Wolff book).
Includes bibliographical references.
Translation of: Uitersten: beschouwingen over menselijk gedrag. 1990.

Elsschot, Willem.
Villa des roses / Willem Elsschot; transl. with an introd. and notes by Paul Vincent. London [etc.]: Penguin Books, 1992. 140 p.; 20 cm. (Penguin twentieth-century classics).
Translation of: Villa des roses. 1913.

Francke, Joh.
Justified by faith / Joh. Francke. London, Ont.: Inter-League Publication Board, 1991. 267 p.; 22 cm.
Includes bibliographical references.
Translation of: Gerechtigheid uit het geloof: schetsenbundel over de brief aan de christenen te Rome. 1974.

Gelderen, D.M. van.
Rhododendron portraits / by D.M. van Gelderen and J.R.P. van Hoey Smith; transl. from the Dutch language by Nancy Handgraaf and Ton Handgraaf. Portland, Or: Timber Press, 1992.
Includes bibliographical references and index.
Translation of: De rhododendron atlas.

Hamaker-Zondag, Karen M.
The twelfth house / Karen Hamaker-Zondag. York Beach, Me: S. Weiser, 1991. 162 p.; 21 cm.
Includes bibliography.
Translation of: Het twaalfde huis: verbeelding en werkelijkheid: de verborgen kracht in onze horoscoop. 1990.

Heijden-Biemans, Trude v.d.
Withof lace / Trude van der Heijden-Biemans, Yvonne Scheele-Kerkhof, Puck Smelter-Hoekstra. London: Batsford, 1991. 160 p.: ill.; 26 cm.
Translation of: Withof Duchesse. 1989.

Herwig, Rob.
Growing beautiful houseplants / Rob Herwig. New York: Facts on File, 1992. [384] p.: ill.; 28 cm.
Translation of: Het volkomen kamerplantenboek. 1987.

Hoedeman, Paul.
Hitler or Hippocrates: medical experiments and euthanasia in the Third Reich / Paul Hoedeman; forew. by E. A. Cohen; transl. from the Dutch by Ralph de Rijke. Lewes: Book Guild, 1991. 260 p.: ill.; 23 cm.

Hofman, Wim.
A good hiding and other stories / written and ill. by Wim Hofman; transl. from the Dutch by Lance Salway. Stroud, Glos [etc.]: Turton & Chambers, 1991. 132 p.: ill.; 20 cm.
Translation of: Straf en andere verhalen. 1985.

Jong, Trude de.
Lola the Bear / Trude de Jong; ill. by G. Overwater; transl. from the Dutch: P. Campton. London: Faber, 1992. [96] p.: ill.; 20 cm.
Translation of: Lola, de beer. 1987.

Jonge, Marinus de.
Jesus, the Servant-Messiah / Marinus de Jonge. New Haven [etc.]: Yale University Press, cop. 1991. VIII, 115 p.; 22 cm.
Based on: Shaffer lectures delivered at the Yale Divinity School in February 1989.
Includes bibliographical references and index.
Translation of: Jezus als Messias: hoe Hij zijn zending zag. 1990.

Joris, Lieve.
Back to the Congo / Lieve Joris; transl. from the Dutch S. Knecht. London: Macmillan, 1992. [266] p.; 22 cm.
Translation of: Terug naar Kongo. 1987.
Parts originally published in Avenue, Haagse post, Intermagazine, Nieuw wereldtijdschrift en NRC-Handelsblad.

Kuitenbrouwer, M.
The Netherlands and the rise of modern imperialism: colonies and foreign policy, 1870-1902 / Maarten Kuitenbrouwer; transl. from the Dutch by Hugh Beyer. New York; Oxford: Berg, 1991. VII, 407 p.; 22 cm.
Includes bibliography and index.
Translation of: Nederland en de opkomst van het moderne imperialisme: koloniën en buitenlandse politiek: 1870-1902. 1985. Thesis.

Kuyper, Abraham (1837-1920).
The problem of poverty / Abraham Kuyper; ed. by James W. Skillen. Washington DC: Center for Public Justice; Grand Rapids, Mich: Baker Book House, cop. 1991. 94 p.; 20 cm.
Includes bibliography p. 81-94.
Translation of: Het sociale vraagstuk en de christelijke religie: rede bij de opening van het sociaal congres op 9 November 1891 gehouden. 1891.

Lievegoed, Bernard.
Developing communities / Bernard Lievegoed. [S.l.]: Hawthorn, 1991. 216 p.; 22 cm. (Social ecology series).
Translation of: Organisationen im Wandel: die praktische Führung sozialer Systeme in der Zukunft. 1976.
Originally published as: Organisaties in ontwikkeling: zicht op de toekomst. 1969.

Lievegoed, Bernard.
Managing the developing organisation: tapping the spirit of Europe / Bernard Lievegoed; with a forew. by Ronnie Lessem. Oxford [etc.]: Blackwell, cop. 1991. XXI, 176 p.: fig.; 24 cm. (Developmental management). First English edition: 1973.
Translation of: Organisaties in ontwikkeling. 1969.

Limburg, Astrid.
Women giving birth / Astrid Limburg and Beatrijs Smulders; photographs by Saskia van Rees. Berkeley, Calif: Celestial Arts, cop. 1992.
Includes bibliographical references.
Translations of: Baren: verticale baring, eerste contact, invloed van water, complicaties. 1984.

Lindwer, Willy.
The last seven months of Anne Frank / Willy Lindwer; transl. from Dutch by Alison Meersschaert. New York: Pantheon, 1991. 204 p.: ill.; 24 cm.
Translation of: De laatste zeven maanden: vrouwen in het spoor van Anne Frank. 1988.

Loon, Paul van.
The deserted island / Paul van Loon. London: Bodley Head, 1991. [26] p.
Translation of: Alleen op een eiland. 1991.

Marlee, Paul.
Guinea-pig / by Paul Marlee. London: Karnak, 1990. 106 p.; 23 cm.
Translation of: Proefkonijn. 1985.

Mees, Rudolf.
Money for a better world / Rudolf Mees; transl. by John Weed. Stroud: Hawthorn, 1991. [64] p.; 22 cm. (Social ecology series).
Translation of: Een andere kijk op geld. 1986.

Minco, Marga.
Bitter herbs: a little chronicle / Marga Minco; transl. from the Dutch by Roy Edwards. New ed. London [etc.]: Penguin Books, 1991. 115 p.: ill.; 20 cm. (Penguin international writers).
Translation of: Het bittere kruid. 1957.

Mooij, Antoine.
Psychoanalysis and the concept of a rule: an essay in the philosophy of psychoanalysis / Antoine Mooij; [transl. by S. Firth and J.H. Scheffer]. Berlin [etc.]: Springer-Verlag, 1991. 99 p.; 24 cm.
Includes bibliography p. 88-94.
Translation of: Psychoanalyse en regels: werkwijze en grondslagen van de psychoanalyse. 1982.

Moolenburgh, H.C.
A handbook of angels / H.C. Moolenburgh; translated from the Dutch by Amina Marix-Evans. Reprinted 1991. Saffron Walden: C.W. Daniel, [1985]. 254, [2] p.: ill.; 21 cm.
Includes bibliography.
Translation of: Engelen: als beschermers en als helpers der mensheid. Deventer 1983.

Nederveen Pieterse, Jan.
White on black: images of Africa and Blacks in Western popular culture / Jan Nederveen Pieterse. New Haven: Yale University Press, 1992. 260 p.: ill.; 25 cm.
Translation of: Wit over zwart: beelden van Afrika en zwarten in de Westerse populaire cultuur. 1990.

Nooteboom, Cees.
In the Dutch mountains / Cees Nooteboom; transl. from the Dutch by Adrienne Dixon. Harmondsworth [etc.]: Penguin, 1991. [7], 128 p.; 20 cm.
Translation of: In Nederland. 1984.

Nouwen, Henri J.M.
Thomas Merton, contemplative critic / Henri J.M. Nouwen. New York, NY: Triumph books, 1991. 158 p.; 21 cm.
Includes bibliographical references.
Originally published as: Pray to live: Thomas Merton: a contemplative critic. 1972.
Translation of: Bidden om het leven: het contemplatief engagement van Thomas Merton. 1970.

Okhuijsen, Gijs.
Celebrating life through liturgy; liturgical services with mentally handicapped people / Gijs Okhuijsen and Cees van Opzeeland; transl. by G.P.A. van Daelen; forew. by Henri J.M. Nouwen. Collegeville, Minn: Liturgical Press, cop. 1992.
Translation of: In de hemel onweert het niet: liturgie vieren met zwakzinnigen: een inspirerend avontuur. 1988.

Olst, E.H. van.
The Bible and liturgy / E.H. van Olst; transl. by John Vriend. Grand Rapids,

Mich: Eerdmans, cop. 1991. 159 p.; 22 cm.
Translation of: Bijbel en liturgie: een pleidooi voor het vieren. 1983.

Palmen, Connie.
The laws / Connie Palmen. [S.l.]: Secker & Warburg, 1992. 240 p.; 20 cm.
Translation of: De wetten: roman. 1991.

Palmen, Connie.
The laws / Connie Palmen; transl. from the Dutch by Richard Huijing. London: Minerva, 1992. 196 p.; 20 cm.
Translation of: De wetten: roman. 1991.

Presser, Jacques.
The night of the Girondists / Jacques Presser; with a foreword by Primo Levi; transl. from the Dutch by Barrow Mussey. London: Harvill, 1992. XII, 79 p.; 22 cm.
Translation of: De nacht der Girondijnen. 1957.

Reest, Rudolf van.
Israel's hope and expectation / Rudolf van Reest. Neerlandia, Alta: Inheritance Publications, 1991.
Translation of: De grote verwachting: historische roman uit de volheid des tijds. 1953.

Schmidt, Annie M.G.
Minnie / Annie M.G. Schmidt; ill. by P. Vos; transl. from the Dutch L. Salway. Woodchester, Stroud, Glos: Turnton & Chambers, 1992. [160] p.: 55 ill.; 22 cm.
Translation of: Minoes. 1970.

Schmidt, Annie M.G.
Pink lemonade: poems / by Annie M.G. Schmidt; transl. by Henrietta ten Harmsel; ill. by Timothy Foley. Michigan: Wim. B. Eerdmans Publ. Co., 1992. 63 p.: ill.

Schulte Nordholt, Jan Willem.
Woodrow Wilson: a life for world peace / Jan Willem Schulte Nordholt; transl. by Herbert H. Rowen. Berkeley [etc.]: University of California Press, cop. 1991. VII, 495 p., [16] p. of plates.; 24 cm.
Includes bibliographical references and index.
Translation of: Woodrow Wilson: een leven voor de wereldvrede. 1990.

Stikker, Allerd.
The transformation factor: towards an ecological consciousness / Allerd Stikker. Rockport, MA: Element Books, 1991. XI, 138 p.; 23 cm.
Includes bibliographical references.
Translation of: Tao, Teilhard en westers denken. 1986.

Velthuijs, Max.
Frog and the birdsong / Max Velthuijs. London: Andersen, 1991. [24] p.; 24 cm.
Simultaneously published in Dutch as: Kikker en het vogeltje. 1991.

Velthuijs, Max.
Frog and the birdsong / by Max Velthuijs. New York: Farrar, Straus and Giroux, 1991.
Simultaneously published in Dutch as: Kikker en het vogeltje. 1991.

Vestdijk, Simon.
The garden where the brass band played / S. Vestdijk; [transl. from the Dutch by A. Brotherton]. New ed. London: Quartet Books Ltd, 1992. 320 p.; 21 cm.
Translation of: De koperen tuin. 1950.

Vondel, Joost van den.
Gijsbrecht van Amstel / Joost van den Vondel; transl. and with introd. and notes by Kristiaan P. Aercke. Ottawa: Dovehouse Editions, 1991. 127 p.; 23 cm. (Carleton Renaissance plays in translation; 24).
Translation of: Gijsbreght van Aemstel, d'ondergang van zijn stad en zijn ballingschap: treurspel. 1637.

Vos, Ida.
Hide and seek / Ida Vos; [transl.: Terese Edelstein and Inez Smidt]. Boston: Houghton Mifflin Co., 1991. 132 p.; 22 cm.
Translation of: Wie niet weg is wordt gezien. 1981.

Waal, C. van der.
Hal Lindsey and biblical prophecy / C. Vanderwaal. Neerlandia, Alta.: Inheritance Publications, 1991.
Originally published: 1978.
Translation of: En het zal geschieden in de laatste dagen ...: is de Openbaring een politieke Enkhuizer almanak of een boek van het Verbond?: naar aanleiding van: Hal Lindsey, 'De planeet die aarde heette ...'. 1977.

Werumeus Buning, J.W.F.
Mária Lécina: a song in hundred verses / J.W.F. Werumeus Buning; (transl. from the Dutch by Hendrik Fayat); with a forew by the Vice-Chancellor of the Vrije Universiteit Brussel. Brussels: VUB, 1991. 27 bl.: ill.; 21 cm.
English translation together with the original Dutch text.
Translation of: Mária Lécina: een lied in honderd verzen met een zangwijs. 1932.

Wijnen, Gaston.
Discovering Paris bistros / Gaston Wijnen; transl. from the original Dutch by the author. New York: Interlink Books, 1991.
First American edition.
Translation of: De kleine restaurantgids van Parijs. 1985.

Wit, Han de.
Contemplative psychology / by Han F. de Wit; transl. by Marie Louise Baird. Pittsburgh, Pa: Duquesne University Press, cop. 1991. XIII, 248 p.; 24 cm.
Includes bibliographical references and index.
Translation of: Contemplatieve psychologie. 1987.

Zoeteman, Kees.
Gaia-Sophia: a framework for ecology / Kees Zoeteman. Edinburgh: Floris, 1991. 374 p.: ill., krt.; 21 cm.
Includes bibliographical references and index.
Translation of: Gaiasofie: anders kijken naar evolutie, ruimtelijke ordening en milieubeheer. 1989.

Zoeteman, Kees.
Gaiasophy: the wisdom of the living earth: an approach to ecology / Kees Zoeteman. Hudson, NY: Lindisfarne Press, 1991. 374 p.; 21 cm.
Includes bibliographical references and index.
Translation of: Gaiasofie: anders kijken naar evolutie, ruimtelijke ordening en milieubeheer. 1989.

Editor:
Dutch Books in Translation
Koninklijke Bibliotheek,
The Hague
The Netherlands

Contributors

Svetlana Alpers (1936-)
Professor of the History of Art
Dept. of the History of Art, 405 Doe Library, University of California, Berkeley, CA 94720, USA

Saskia Bak (1964-)
Staff member of the Fries Museum, Leeuwarden
Oude Kijk in 't Jatstraat 42, 9712 EL Groningen, The Netherlands

E.M. Beekman (1939-)
Multatuli Professor of Dutch Literature, Language and Culture (University of Massachusetts)
15 Franklin Street, Northampton, MA 01060, USA

Geert Bekaert (1928-)
Chief editor *Archis*
Koepoortbrug 4, 2000 Antwerp, Belgium

Ludo Bekkers (1924-)
Art critic
Tentoonstellingslaan 6, 2020 Antwerp, Belgium

Marten Jan Bok (1958-)
Research worker
Dept. of the History of Art, University of Utrecht, Kromme Nieuwegracht 29, 3512 HD Utrecht, The Netherlands

Ignace Bossuyt (1947-)
Professor of Musicology (Catholic University of Leuven)
Lostraat 40, 3212 Pellenberg, Belgium

Hugo Brems (1944-)
Professor of Modern Dutch Literature (Catholic Universities of Leuven and Brussels)
Huttelaan 263, 3001 Heverlee, Belgium

Christopher Brown (1948-)
Chief curator
National Gallery, Trafalgar Square, London WC2N 5DN, United Kingdom

H. Brugmans (1906-)
Rector Emeritus of the European College, Bruges
Langestraat 167, 8000 Bruges, Belgium

Paul Claes (1943-)
Writer / Translator / Lecturer in Literary Translation
P. Daensstraat 12, 3010 Kessel-Lo, Belgium

Anton Claessens (1936-)
Teacher / Member of the editorial board *Ons Erfdeel*
Honkersven 29, 2440 Geel, Belgium

Piet Couttenier (1947-)
Director of the Centre for the Study of Guido Gezelle
D. Mellaertsstraat 78, 3010 Kessel-Lo, Belgium

Wim Daems (1948-)
Editor / Journalist
EOS Magazine
J. Cardijnlaan 87, 1860 Meise, Belgium

Joost de Geest (1942-)
Cultural attaché
Gemeentekrediet
Erf de Keyzer 23, 1652 Alsemberg, Belgium

Jozef Deleu (1937-)
Chief editor / Managing director 'Stichting Ons Erfdeel'
Murissonstraat 260, 8931 Rekkem, Belgium

Paul Depondt (1953-)
Journalist *De Volkskrant*
Korenmarkt 25, 9000 Ghent, Belgium

Wim de Poorter (1939-)
Teacher / Film critic
Koningin Astridlaan 23/9, 8200 Bruges, Belgium

Frans de Rover (1946-)
Professor of Dutch (Free University of Berlin)
Nassauische Strasse 16A, 1 Berlin 31, Germany

Piet de Valkeneer (1935-)
Journalist
Dekenhof-Dorpsplein 14, 3071 Erps-Kwerps, Belgium

Jacques de Visscher (1943-)
Lecturer in Philosophy (St. Lucas Institute, Ghent)
Gustaaf Callierlaan 175, 9000 Ghent, Belgium

Erik Duverger (1932-)
Research leader for the National Fund for Scientific Research
Coupure 385, 9000 Ghent, Belgium

Joris Duytschaever (1944-)
Professor of English Literature (University Institute Antwerp)
E. Casteleinstraat 28, 2020 Antwerp, Belgium

Charles Gehring (1939-)
Director of the New Netherland Project
New York State Library, Albany, NY 12230, USA

Walter Goddijn (1921-)
Professor of the Sociology of Church and Religion
St. Jozefstraat 11, 5087 VD Diessen, The Netherlands

Jaap Goedegebuure (1947-)
Professor of Literary Theory and Literary History (Catholic University of Brabant)
Antoniusstraat 5, 2382 BD Zoeterwoude-Rijndijk, The Netherlands

Myriam Guns (1959-)
Staff member of the Certificate of Dutch as a Foreign Language
Loonbeekstraat 3, 3040 Huldenberg, Belgium

Gaby Gyselen (1923-)
Art critic
Kan. Van Hoonackerstraat 37, 8000 Bruges, Belgium

Paul Hadermann (1931-)
Professor of Dutch Literature (*ULB;* Free University of Brussels)
2 Drève des Chataîgniers, Domaine de la Motte, 1470 Bousval, Belgium

Theo Hermans (1948-)
Reader in Dutch / Head of the Dutch Dept. (University College, London)
2 Moorland Road, Boxmoor, Hemel Hempstead HP1 1NQ, United Kingdom

Paul Huys (1933-)
Cultural advisor for the Provincial Council of East Flanders
Drongenstationstraat 90, 9031 Ghent, Belgium

Hans Ibelings (1963-)
Staff member of the Netherlands Architecture Institute, Rotterdam
Curierestraat 50, 1013 CH Amsterdam, The Netherlands

Sir Michael Jenkins (1936-)
HM Ambassador at The Hague
British Embassy, Lange Voorhout 10, 2514 ED The Hague, The Netherlands

Roland Jooris (1936-)
Poet / Art critic
Scheestraat 44, 9270 Kalken, Belgium

Janica Kleiman (1965-)
Co-ordinator at the Schiedam Art Library
Oldambt 23, 3524 BD Utrecht, The Netherlands

Ariejan Korteweg (1955-)
Editor / Journalist
De Volkskrant
'Drie Gebroeders', Amstel t.o. 316, 1011 PX Amsterdam, The Netherlands

E.H. Kossmann (1922-)
Professor of History
Thorbeckestraat 180, 9722 NJ Groningen, The Netherlands

André Lefevere (1945-)
Professor of Dutch (University of Texas, Austin)
1706 Coturnix Drive, Austin, TX 78758-6120, USA

Pieter Leroy (1954-)
Professor at the Faculty of Political Science, section 'Environment, Nature and Landscape' (University of Nijmegen)
Weezenhof 68-13, 6536 BL Nijmegen, The Netherlands

Gerdin Linthorst (1946-)
Film critic / Chief editor *De Filmkrant*
Admiraal de Ruyterweg 274, 1055 MR Amsterdam, The Netherlands

Yann Lovelock (1939-)
Writer / Translator
80 Doris Road, Birmingham, W. Mids B11 4NF, United Kingdom

Paul Luttikhuis (1959-)
Musicologist / Journalist *NRC Handelsblad*
Vossegatselaan 39bis a, 3583 RP Utrecht, The Netherlands

Filip Matthijs (1966-)
Editorial secretary *The Low Countries*
Murissonstraat 260, 8931 Rekkem, Belgium

Kees Middelhoff (1917-)
Radio commentator / Journalist
Sterrelaan 13, 1217 PP Hilversum, The Netherlands

Martin Mooij (1930-)
Director *Poetry International Rotterdam*
Operalaan 39, 2907 KA Capelle aan den IJssel, The Netherlands

Anne Marie Musschoot (1944-)
Professor of Dutch Literature (University of Ghent)
Nieuwkolegemlaan 44, 9030 Ghent, Belgium

Jos Nijhof (1952-)
Teacher / Theatre critic
Berkenkade 14, 2351 NB Leiderdorp, The Netherlands

Arnold J. Pomerans (1920-)
Translator
Battle House, Polstead Heath, Colchester CO6 5BD, United Kingdom

Karel Porteman (1938-)
Professor of Dutch Renaissance Literature (Catholic University of Leuven)
Predikherenberg 59, 3010 Kessel-Lo, Belgium

Karel Puype (1964-)
Writer
Stationstraat 130/1, 8020 Oostkamp, Belgium

Manu Ruys (1924-)
Journalist / Former chief editor *De Standaard*
Londenstraat 2 (Zeedijk), 8380 Zeebrugge, Belgium

Gary Schwartz (1940-)
Research worker for the Dutch Organisation for Scientific Research
P.O. Box 162, 3600 AD Maarssen, The Netherlands

Erik Slagter (1939-)
Art critic
Eemwijkstraat 1, 2271 RC Voorburg, The Netherlands

Bianca Stigter (1964-)
Journalist
Jan van Galenstraat 89/1, 1056 BJ Amsterdam, The Netherlands

Elsa Strietman (1947-)
Lecturer in Dutch (University of Cambridge)
New Hall, Cambridge CB3 0DF, United Kingdom

A. Teeuw (1921-)
Professor of Malay and Indonesian Language and Literature
Thorbeckestraat 14, 2313 HE Leiden, The Netherlands

E.M. Uhlenbeck (1917-)
Professor of Javanese Language and General Linguistics
Dr. Kuyperlaan 11, 2215 NE Voorhout, The Netherlands

Donald Unger (1945-)
Journalist
Pieter Aertszstraat 46/1, 1073 SP Amsterdam, The Netherlands

Hans Vanacker (1960-)
Editorial secretary *Septentrion*
Murissonstraat 260, 8931 Rekkem, Belgium

Dirk van Assche (1955-)
Editorial secretary *Ons Erfdeel*
Murissonstraat 260, 8931 Rekkem, Belgium

Carlo van Baelen (1948-)
General director Kluwer Belgium
Oosterlinckhoflaan 41, 2180 Ekeren, Belgium

K. van Berkel (1953-)
Professor of the History of Natural Sciences (University of Groningen)
Fonteinkruid 8, 9801 LE Zuidhorn, The Netherlands

Paul van der Plank (1952-)
Theatre critic
De Sitterlaan 94, 2313 TS Leiden, The Netherlands

Ed van Eeden (1957-)
Journalist / Translator
Amsterdamsestraatweg 489, 3553 ED Utrecht, The Netherlands

Pieter van Hees (1937-)
Staff member of the Dept. of Political History (University of Utrecht)
Prof. Ritzema Boslaan 95, 3571 CP Utrecht, The Netherlands

Jan van Hove (1953-)
Journalist *De Standaard*
Dambruggestraat 6, 2060 Antwerp, Belgium

Paul van Velthoven (1947-)
Journalist *Het Binnenhof*
Geestbrugweg 68, 2281 CP Rijswijk, The Netherlands

Marjan van Zijtveld (1963-)
Art critic
Jan van Scorelstraat 148, 3583 CV Utrecht, The Netherlands

Aart van Zoest (1930-)
Writer
Broekerwaard 154, 1824 EW Alkmaar, The Netherlands

Jan Verdonck (1919-)
Journalist
Laanhorn 7, 1181 BD Amstelveen, The Netherlands

Jet Vloemans (1949-)
Publicity agent *Opzij*
Grote Hondstraat 99, 2018 Antwerp, Belgium

Jeroen Vullings (1962-)
Teacher / Reviewer
Madelievenstraat 25, 1015 NV Amsterdam, The Netherlands

Ingeborg Walinga (1965-)
Journalist
Snikkevaardersgang 4, 9711 RW Groningen, The Netherlands

Rudi Wester (1943-)
Deputy director of the Foundation for the Production and Translation of Dutch Literature
Frederiksplein 14, 1017 XM Amsterdam, The Netherlands

Ad Zuiderent (1944-)
Lecturer in Modern Dutch Literature (Free University of Amsterdam)
Zacharias Jansestraat 52hs, 1097 CN Amsterdam, The Netherlands

Translators

James Brockway, The Hague, The Netherlands

Paul Brown, London, United Kingdom

Paul Claes, Kessel-Lo, Belgium

Christine D'haen, Bruges, Belgium

Jane Fenoulhet, London, United Kingdom

Lesley Gilbert, London, United Kingdom

Annie Goddaer, Vichte, Belgium

Tanis Guest, London, United Kingdom

James S Holmes (†)

Steve Judd, Haacht, Belgium

Greta Kilburn, Amsterdam, The Netherlands

Peter King, Cottingham, United Kingdom

André Lefevere, Austin, Texas, USA

Ria Leigh-Loohuizen, Norwich, United Kingdom

Yvette Mead, Chestfield, United Kingdom

Elizabeth Mollison, Amsterdam, The Netherlands

Alison Mouthaan, Antwerp, Belgium

Peter Nijmeijer, Rosmalen, The Netherlands

Scott Rollins, Amsterdam, The Netherlands

Julian Ross, London, United Kingdom

John Rudge, Amsterdam, The Netherlands

Michael Shaw, Haslemere, United Kingdom

Hidde van Ameyden van Duym, Roundup, Montana, USA

Rachel van der Wilden, Rijswijk, The Netherlands

Paul Vincent, London, United Kingdom

ADVISOR ON ENGLISH USAGE

Tanis Guest, London, United Kingdom

As well as the yearbook *The Low Countries,* the Flemish-Netherlands foundation 'Stichting Ons Erfdeel' publishes the following booklets covering various aspects of the culture of the Netherlands and Flanders:

O. Vandeputte / P. Vincent / T. Hermans
Dutch. The Language of Twenty Million Dutch and Flemish People.
Illustrated; 64 pp.

J.A. Kossmann-Putto & E.H. Kossmann
The Low Countries. History of the Northern and Southern Netherlands.
Illustrated; 64 pp.

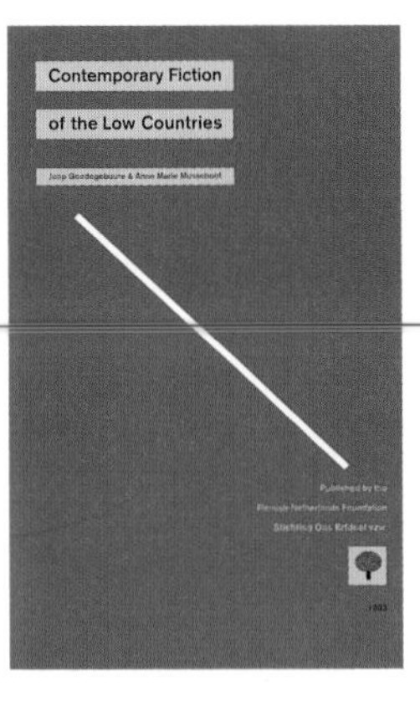

Jaap Goedegebuure & Anne Marie Musschoot
Contemporary Fiction of the Low Countries.
Illustrated and with translated extracts from 15 novels; 128 pp.

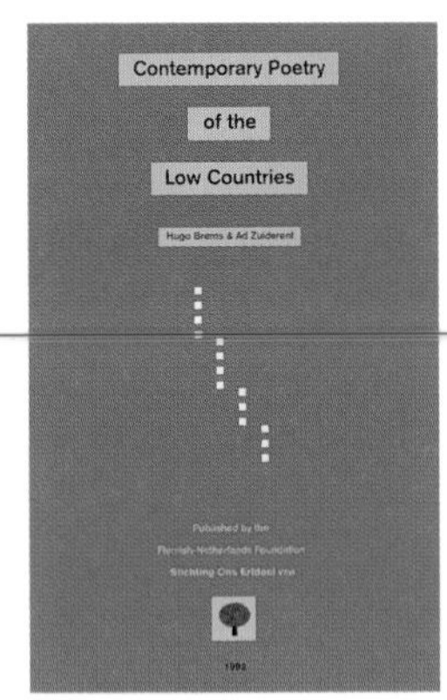

Hugo Brems & Ad Zuiderent
Contemporary Poetry of the Low Countries.
With 52 translated poems; 112 pp.